B D
S

me
and

WILEY COMPUTER PUBLISHING

JOHN WILEY & SONS, INC.
New York • Chichester • Brisbane • Toronto • Singapore

£45.00

D1765511

Publisher: Katherine Schowalter

Editor: Tim Ryan

Managing Editor: Angela Murphy

Electronic Products, Associate Editor: Mike Green

Text Design & Composition: Pronto Design & Production Inc.

Library of Congress Cataloging-in-Publication Data:

White, Josh.
    Designing 3D graphics : how to create real-time 3D models for games and virtual reality / Josh White.
       p. cm.
    Includes bibliographical references.
    ISBN 0-471-14926-8 (paper/CD-ROM : alk. paper)
    1. Computer graphics. 2. Three-dimensional display systesm.
   3. Real-time data processing. I. Title.
    T385.W538 1996
    006.6—dc20   96-18355
Printed in the United States of America

10 9 8 7 6 5 4 3 2 1

Contents

Introduction vii

Chapter 1 Development teams in commercial projects 1
    Prologue 2
    Typical Professional RT3D Development Teams. 2
    Interactions 6
    The Peer Issue. 9
    Basic RT3D Game Development Scenario 10
    Problems Unique to VR Development 11

Chapter 2 The Basics of 3D Computer Graphics 13
    The Basics 14
    Real Time 3D Graphics Terms and Concepts 19
    Basic Frame Rate/LOD Paradigms 25

Chapter 3 Getting Our Feet Wet 31
    Creating a Streetlight 32

Chapter 4 Exploring 3D Studio as a Real-time Modeler 43
    Available Building Methods. 44
    3D Editing. 48

Chapter 5 Advanced Tool Studies 65
    Prologue 66
    Backing Up While Working 66
    Visualization 66
    Visualizing Entities We Didn't Build 69
    Exploring a Single Object in Detail 82
    Display Geometry Menu Tree. 89
    Understanding Edges. 93
    2D versus 3D Editing Commands 99

Chapter 6 Mapping 103
    Prologue 104
    The Many Meanings of Mapping 104
    Why Is Mapping So Difficult? 104
    Simple Mapping Example 105
    Intro to UV Anomalies 107
    Exploring 3D Studio's Mapping Tools. 110
    Messier Mapping Issues. 114

Chapter 7 Creating Textures 127
    Prologue 128
    General Editing Tips. 128
    Choosing the Right Size of Texture. 129
    How Textures are Scaled in RT3D 132
    Understanding Flickering 134
    Paletted Color 137
    Using the Histogram 138
    Generating Textures from 3D Models. 142
    Chapter 8 RT3D Modeling Step-by-Step 143
    Summary of Steps for Building RT3D Models 144
    Details for Each Step for Building RT3D Models. 145
    Example: Basic Chair. 164

Chapter 9 Modeling Specific Types of Objects 165
    Prologue 166
    Modeling Vehicles 166
    Open Environments (Landscapes) 231
    Unnatural Open Environments 233
    Closed Environments 244
    Human Figure 257
    Texturing Robots in Descent 266

Chapter 10 273
    Prologue 274
    Common Problems (and Solutions)
    Related to Converting a Model to RT3D 283

Chapter 11 Animation 295
    Prologue 296
    Basic Types of Animation. 296
    Animation Modeling Techniques. 300
    Motion Capture. 304

Chapter 12 All About Graphics Engines 307
    Prologue: Why Read This? 308
    The Pipeline 308
    Graphics Engine Variations 315
    Specific Real-Time 3D Platforms 321

Chapter 13 VRML 331
    Required Knowledge 333
    How Does VRML Work? 334
    Comparing VRML to "Normal" RT3D 335
    Guided Tour of VRML v1.0 336
    What can VRML Do? 340
    Building for VRML 342
    VRML Browsers 344
    Modeling Tools 351

Chapter 14 RT3D Environment Design 359
    Prologue 360
    World Design Theory 360
    Story-Telling in RTSD 364
    Field of View (FOV) 365
    How to Create a Feeling in a 3D World 366
    Special Effects: What Works (and what Doesn't) 369
    Getting into the Artistic Vision 370
    The End 371
    . . . is Just the Beginning 371

Index 373

Acknowledgments

Greg Hammond deserves thanks for his substantial contributions to the animation section of this book, as does Adam Pletcher; David Nadeau, for the use of the VRML Repository web site. A world of thanks go to Gjon Camaj, Adam Pletcher, Matt Toschlog, Mike Kulas, Steve Seitz, and Ben Discoe, for their support, technical and otherwise, during the writing.

I am very grateful to Charis Baz (especially), Gjon Camaj, Jordi Davis, Mike Kulas, Jeff Lander, Ned Lerner, Carlos Newcombe, Christie Gable, Wendy Stein, Dan Brooks, and Sloan Venables, for their timely, salient manuscript technical-accuracy reviews, and all the members of the VRML Modeling and RT3D Modeling mailing lists for their answers and support.

Special thanks go to Jordi Davis, who shouldered much responsibility for our company, Vector Graphics, during the writing of this book. Julie Coburn, Aimee Centivany, and Kim Hahn, as well as my extended family, also are deserving of gratitude fore their donations of food, understanding, and general kindness during my book-writing heritage.

In the unrepayable-debt category are Alan Murphy and Ned Lerner, who gave me my first opportunity to get involved in this industry; and my father Lee White for being totally supportive, loving, and encouraging from Day One onward.

This book is dedicated to my grandmother Ann Leon White, who was the first writer in the family, infected all her offspring with writing, and hasn't stopped writing since.

INTRODUCTION

Welcome to a whole new field within computer graphics: real-time three-dimensional (RT3D) graphics. With this book, you can learn how to make real-time 3D art that works.

This introduction tells you what the book is about (and what it's not), whom it's written for, what you'll need to use it, and what you'll get out of it.

What's the Big Deal?

Why do you need an entire book to explain real-time 3D modeling, especially if you already know about 3D modeling? Real-time 3D modeling is a small but very different branch of the 3D modeling family tree. It can be quickly divided from the rest of the tree like this:

- We (real-time 3D modelers) deliver 3D objects.
- They ("normal" 3D modelers) deliver 2D pictures.

When we deliver our work, we hand off 3D files (FINAL.3DS or FINAL.ASC). Most 3D modelers hand off 2D animations (FINAL.AVI or FINAL.TGA). This distinction obviously separates the two groups, but there's something even more fundamentally different.

Real-time 3D is fundamentally close to the hardware. It's not all drifting out into the ether of pure artistic expression; it's performance-envelope-pushing, technically oriented art. Because of this, creating excellent real-time 3D artwork is a hard balancing act. It requires one foot in the exploding, shifting stacks of technological advance, the other in the vague, fickle cloud of artistic beauty. It pays off, though, when we give our audience the freedom to explore a world never before possible, not just stare wistfully at an unchanging animation.

It's a new medium, really, and it's very different from "normal" 3D modeling.

Virtual Reality and Real-Time Artwork

If you haven't heard that VR is the future, you're a very unusual person. Over the last couple years, that concept has been pitched to the public in movies, magazines, and most other forms of mass media.

Whatever VR is, it always seems to involve real-time 3D graphics that represent some kind of virtual world. Who's going to build that world? Real-time 3D artists, whether they wear a different job title or not.

The field of virtual world creation is young still, and although we must face some difficulties (immature modeling tools, for example), the reward is ample opportunity to explore untrodden ground. Not many people have the knowledge in these pages (yet!), so welcome to the edge.

Overview (What's Covered?)

This book is organized somewhat linearly. Most chapters can stand alone, but some assume the reader has read the previous chapters. Here's a basic summary of the contents.

Basics

After the introduction, Chapters 1 and 2 establish context for the rest of the book, as described below. With this background, Chapter 3 takes us through a quick and easy exercise in building a real-time 3D model, just to get our feet wet.

Learning Our Tools

Next, we delve into understanding our modeling tools. Since 3D Studio is the editor of choice among real-time 3D modelers. It is covered in two chapters: Chapter 4 explains the commonly used commands, while Chapter 5 addresses problems we encounter when using 3D Studio for our own purposes.

Mapping and Texturing

Texture mapping may be the most troublesome part of real-time 3D modeling. Chapter 6 attacks the nasty problem of mapping real-time objects. In Chapter 7, we explore the technical issues in the 2D world of real-time texture creation.

The Master Plan

From there, we arrive at a key point in the book. In Chapter 8, "RT3D Modeling Step-by-Step," we discuss each step in creating a real-time 3D model. It serves as a general plan for building any kind of model and is especially handy for difficult assignments.

Applying the Plan

We then use this plan in Chapter 9 to discuss approaches to several common types of modeling: landscapes, vehicles, humans, and so on. This chapter includes a very detailed exercise for building a sports car, start to finish, as well as some discussions of other types of modeling.

Advanced Knowledge

Chapter 10 addresses a task we all face at some point: taking an existing model and reducing its face count (and making other edits) so it will work in a real-time environment. In Chapter 11, we examine "graphics engines" — the code that makes real-time 3D possible. First, we take a look at how a graphics engine works, then we examine some common graphics engines. In Chapter 12, we discuss real-time animation, then look at issues involved when building VRML worlds in Chapter 13. Chapter 14 concludes the book with some "world design" ideas. It suggests ways to evoke certain feelings or ideas with real-time 3D models.

What's on the CD-ROM?

The companion CD-ROM to this book contains a treasure trove of useful tools. There is a collection of shareware and freeware 3D modeling tools and graphics engines. This is a handy way to take a look at some of the tools now available.

There are also sample models and textures, including each 3D model that appears in the images in this book. This can be handy if you're working through a exercise and don't understand what the next step should look like. Also included are ready-to-use textured models: a racetrack, some buildings, a Formula One race car, and detail objects like light poles, billboards, and so on.

There's a lot of VRML-related stuff on there, including demonstration VRML browsers. Finally, there are some resources, in electronic form such as a text file with useful URLs, so you don't have to type them in, that are hard to track down.

To find out exactly what's on the CD-ROM, open the README.TXT in the root directory.

This Book Has a Web Site!

This book has a companion web site at http://www.vectorg.com/book. It has resources, including the ones mentioned in this book, as well as lists of modeling software with reviews, shareware utilities with reviews, example textures, and other useful things. If you are interested in interacting with the author, you can email him from there, as well as read any updated information about the book that may be available.

What This Book Isn't

Sometimes it helps to define something by saying what it isn't. Here is what this book is not.

This Isn't a Book for Hype-Lovers

In case you haven't guessed yet, let's just state it clearly here: This book is technical and in-depth, providing professional knowledge that requires effort to learn and use, but pays off in the quality of the resulting artwork.

All books claim to be for "professionals," but this book is straight from the top RT3D modelers in the industry, many of whom had to be pried away from their top-secret real-time 3D projects to scribble down their contributions. That, sadly enough, is unusual; many books aren't written by people who do what they're writing about.

Specifically, the author has worked on early RT3D games like FZZ, a flight simulator for the Sega Genesis, and Ultima Underworld, A RT3D adventure game for the PC. More recently, the number of products has included Descent,

Locus, Legoland Island, Zone Raiders, and many more. If you're curious to see a complete list, visit http://www.vectorg.com.

Other contributors include lead artists for games from Interplay, Virgin, Mindscape, and other professional freelance RT3D artists and VRML world builders.

There is some discussion of the applications and implications of all this knowledge, but this book teaches practical technique. It's not about glorifying the future potential of this exciting new medium—though great fun to write about, that perspective is well covered in countless other sources.

This Book Doesn't Teach Creativity or Design Concepts

We're all creative people, in one way or another, and it's assumed that anyone reading this book has enough creative designs to keep them busy their whole life, if only they had the tools, time, and money to express them all. Of course, this book can't help with the time or money aspect, and we aren't going to try to capture artistic creativity on paper. Instead, it will provide a very thorough grounding in the knowledge we artists need to make real-time 3D artwork.

We won't talk much about how to make a realistic walk cycle, or create Disney-esque cuteness. This book is primarily about providing the tools and practical knowledge in a real-world way.

This Isn't a Book for Programmers

You won't find instruction on 3D graphics engine programming (or any real programming) here, though you'll find pointers for more information on programming where appropriate. For example, writing your own 3D Studio plug-ins will not be covered. This book is for the artists, modelers, and anyone else who has to create 3D artwork.

This Isn't a "How to Draw with 3D Studio" Book

Though this book refers extensively to 3D Studio, you won't find basic or generalized "how to use 3D Studio" lessons here. Plenty of other books cover that topic (and don't forget the manuals!). On the other hand, some areas of 3D Studio aren't very well documented and are very important to RT3D modeling. These are explained as they are encountered.

This Isn't a Total Beginner's Book

Though all material is presented from the ground up, this book assumes you already know something about computer graphics.

Who Should Use This Book?

Answer: Computer artists who want to make real-time 3D art. Here are some examples:

- Virtual Reality world (including VRML) designers
- Computer game artists
- Computer-based architects

This book was written for people who are learning as they read; it's expected that you will use this book next to your computer, building as you go.

To the Ones Sitting Way in the Back

You may be reading this book even if you don't have the background that you'll need to get everything out of it. Maybe you're just curious about this new field and want to learn what it's about.

Computer game producers, programmers, and designers who want to know how artists think about 3D modeling, as well as hobbyists who can't afford the equipment and software but want what knowledge they can get all can benefit from this book.

What Equipment Do I Need to Have?

You don't need $60,000 hardware to make real-time 3D artwork. All you need is the following:

- A computer capable of running 3D Studio ($2000 or less)
- A 3D modeling tool—the good option (if you can afford it) option is 3D Studio version 3 or newer ($3000 new or less)
- A paint program — Photoshopis a great option ($300 or less)
- This book

Also recommended (but not critical) is the 3D Studio Optimize plug-in.

Should I Buy Superhot Hardware?

Because real-time models are very simple, the computer doesn't have to be fancy: A 486DX with 8 MB of RAM, any basic video card with 1 MB RAM, and a 300 MB hard disk will work fine. Of course, a better system is always nicer. If you can, get a better video card (2 or 4 MB ram), a really nice monitor (19", 1280×1024), a faster CPU (586/120 works great), and 16 MB memory. If you still have any money left, blow it on a huge hard disk (sky's the limit) and even more memory (32 MB is great).

I Don't Have Photoshop!

If you don't have Photoshop, but have some similar bitmap editing software, it should be no problem to use it instead and still make sense out of this book. Here are some examples of programs that fit this description:

- Picture Publisher by Micrografx
- Painter by Fractal Designs

- Corel PhotoPaint by Corel
- Animator Studio by Autodesk

I Don't Have 3D Studio!

If you plan to use a modeling software tool other than 3D Studio to create your real-time 3D models, you can benefit from this book, but you'll need to make sure your modeling software works in a similar way. For example, a spline-based modeling package like Alias isn't going to work, but you could probably stumble through using something like Truspace. Make sure you know how to deal with nitty-gritty stuff like vertex editing and mapping.

As mentioned before, this book is not a 3D Studio tutorial. If you're new to 3D Studio, you might find it helpful to read a "how to use 3D Studio" book and learn 3D Studio's terms and concepts. This is recommended even if you don't plan to use 3D Studio, simply because 3D Studio nicely bridges the artist's view of 3D modeling and the way it works in real-time environments.

To make full use of the 3D Studio tips in this book, you should be familiar with the following sections of the 3D Studio manual:

- Exercise 1: A Quick Look (basic overview of 3D Studio)
- Exercise 2: Creating a 3D Scene

You should also complete the following exercises, if at all possible:

- Exercise 8: The 3D Editor: Geometry
- Exercise 11: The 3D Editor: Mapping Coordinates
- Exercises 3 and 4: 2D Shaper and 3D Lofter

If you've completed all the 3D Studio exercises, great! You have more than enough knowledge to use this book, and if you really understand all that, you know 3D Studio quite well.

There are other ways to get 3D Studio besides buying it at full cost from a dealer. Used copies, especially version 3 or 4, are quite cheap (definitely less than $1,000) if you can find them. If you're a student, you can buy educational versions for under $1,000 as well.

What About All the IPAS Plug-ins for 3D Studio?

As useful as IPAS plug-ins are, we don't really *need* any of them. The majority of IPAS plug-ins are written for 2D effects and fancy render-time tricks that are rarely useful to real-time modelers since we're producing 3D objects, not renderings.

That said, one IPAS plug-in is nice to have: Optimize, by the Yost Group, allows us to reduce the face count in any object simply and quickly. It's great for reducing a 1,000-face object to 500 faces, but it has some limitations. See the section on Optimize in Chapter 10. Again, it's not required, but it is handy.

This Book's Design Philosophy

Now I just want to say a few words about how I put this book together and why.

Less Theory, More Facts

This book assumes that you have plenty of talent and design ability and don't need a book to tell you how to make good artwork, but, most computer artists haven't had a chance to gain the concrete, detailed knowledge necessary to build artwork for a real-time environment.

That's why this book concentrates on technical issues, always emphasizing super-efficient use of all the resources we can lay our hands on, with the assumption that you will take this knowledge and run with it.

Mistakes This Author Won't Make

As an avid self-teacher, I've noticed there are some problems when learning from "how-to" books.

Idealized Examples

One common problem encountered with "how-to" books is theory versus real-life problem solving. "Yeah, that technique works on simple cubes, but what about when I've got a textured hand model?" In this book, examples are as real-world as possible so that actual problems that you encounter are addressed. In part, that's also why the book refers to specific software: 3D Studio is so widely used that it's pretty safe to assume you'll be using it to build real-time models.

Undefined General Terms

Another problem I've encountered, especially for advanced topics in a new field, is an assumption that the reader knows certain vague yet common terms. For example, how many different meanings does the term "image" have? I wrote the short "Basics" chapter (Chapter 2) even though the concepts are familiar to most readers. It could work as a refresher for those who need it, but it also serves to define common ground, linguistically.

Terse Descriptions of Subtle Concepts

Last, and most important, there's what I call the "auto mechanic repair book" problem. This occurs when the book simply lists steps dryly ("Remove the alternator from the engine") without imparting any of the knowledge you really need to solve the problem ("You'll need to wedge a block of wood in the cooling fins to prevent it from spinning, and don't hammer with a steel hammer on the wimpy aluminum case; it'll shatter"). There are lots of reasons so many books don't include the small stuff: It takes a lot of time to capture this kind of detail; the authors may not know themselves; the specifics may change (especially in computers); and it's really hard to express this kind of knowledge in words.

This book will lay on the detail for the really hard problems. For example, an entire chapter is devoted to mapping, simply because it is so problematic in real-time modeling.

Designing 3D Graphics

Game Industry Bias Warning

Though this book attempts to be useful for every industry that uses real-time 3D graphics, my background as a professional RT3D artist includes many years in the computer game development industry, and this experience inevitably shines through in the content. For example, there is much discussion of problems relating to graphics engines that don't use Z-buffering, which is common in the game industry, but rare in other industries where the target platforms are more powerful.

The Really Weird Part: Intuition for RT3D

Detailed information is very important, but it's not everything. There's more to having a full understanding of a topic than simply executing lots of detailed steps. This book will attempt to help you gain a sense of intuition for real-time 3D modeling. "Intuition" doesn't easily translate to words on paper, but it's very important to develop if you want to know how real-time 3D works behind the scenes. If you have this intuition, you'll be able to make good guesses about the source of, and solutions to, most problems you encounter in this field.

Intuition transcends basic, step-by-step procedures, and though it is based on a broad knowledge base of facts, it is far different from large-scale application of logic. It is essentially a feeling of deep, intuitive understanding, a sympathy almost, for a problem. If you've ever seen a car mechanic open the hood and listen to the engine running roughly, looking a little spaced out, then give a diagnosis, or if you know someone who can come over to a broken computer and guess the problem before gathering enough information to prove conclusively that this was, in fact, the problem, you've seen that intuition in action.

Once you have that, solutions come easily.

How Will This Be Accomplished?

We'll start seeding intuition in Chapter 2, "The Basics of 3D Computer Graphics." Many of the horrible problems we face are directly rooted in compromises made years ago, and these roots frequently poke up and crack the foundations of the paradigm we now work in. It's definitely a good point to start developing intuition.

Chapter 1, which describes how development teams work, will also contribute by providing a real-life context, a proposed working environment, for the modeling work we will learn. This background will be especially useful if you're planning to work in such an environment.

Then, throughout the course of the book, we'll answer such questions as, "Why do we care about this?" as we encounter the really hairy technical details that may seem irrelevant. With some effort on your part, these methods will provide the subtle understanding that we're seeking.

Feedback

I'd be interested to know what you think of this approach. Write me at josh@vectorg.com.

DEVELOPMENT TEAMS IN COMMERCIAL PROJECTS

This chapter covers the structure of a typical RT3D development environment, the relationship of the 3D modeler within the development teams, and some aspects of the interactions between team members.

 Prologue

In this book, we'll discuss teamwork issues when we, the artists, must interact with the rest of the development team. We'll talk about this as we encounter it, but we must first know who this "development team" is: Are they artists? Some crew of genius hackers in Africa? Clueless Dilbert-manager types? That's what this chapter will explore.

Now, let's look more closely at why we need to talk so much about our working environment.

Why Is This Important?

No matter what our job is, the situation we work in always affects the way we work—doing a good job means pleasing our customer. To do that, we must know who our customer is and what they want. We'll get into what customers want later; for now, let's figure out who they are.

For professional RT3D modelers, the working environment is so important that it cannot be separated from the work itself. To make excellent RT3D artwork, we depend on our team. We can't just create artwork out of the blue and expect it to be smoothly integrated into the application. Our artwork has to fit within very important limitations, and we learn to work with (and around) those limitations through our team members.

These limitations sound like nitpicky details, perhaps some final translation steps, but they are very important. They are the laws by which we create our model, and the better we understand them, the closer to the performance edge we will be. We'll work through the common limitations in detail later in the book.

 Typical Professional RT3D Development Teams

We artists all have our own unique working environment—some of us don't work with anyone else, while others work as members of a huge art department. As we describe below, discussion of the working environment is important, but which environment type should be discussed?

This Scene May Not Be Yours

As usual, there is a trade-off between specific, detailed knowledge and broad applicability of that knowledge. This chapter, like the rest of the book, chooses to be spe-

cific at the expense of alienating readers who don't fit the specifics mentioned.

The following largely applies to commercial real-time 3D development environments such as game or VR project development. It's unlikely that this information will be helpful if you're in a different kind of working situation, like an architectural firm's real-time walkthrough, a hobbyist's private project, or a VRML virtual museum project.

The "Core" Development Team

The core development team's structure varies widely, but there are two basic groups of jobs. First, several critical roles must be filled. Each role may not be handled by a single individual, but for most projects, they are. Unless stated otherwise, assume that the core development team consists of the following people:

- One or more programmers, who understand the technical issues and write the code that constitutes the application we are developing. The programmer is usually the only one on the team who knows the technical information we artists so often need.

- The manager, who is responsible for keeping the team on schedule and resolving large-scale product design issues and conflicts. Some managers have risen through the ranks and have an area of technical knowledge and experience (often they are ex-programmers), while others are managers who understand projects and teamwork, but who lack comprehensive technical knowledge.

- One or more real-time 3D artists. They are responsible for creating the 3D objects within the virtual environment. This position is what this book is all about, and though 3D artists can be involved in other places (such as hired by the publisher), we'll assume that we are a member of the core team, hired by the developer.

The core team must perform other functions as well. Sometimes these functions are filled by existing core team members, and sometimes they are separate, full-time positions. This variability depends on the nature of the project—some projects don't need a level designer, while others need several.

- Designers are responsible for the creative structure of the whole application we are developing—plot, AI behavior, artistic "look," and sometimes the shape and design of each piece of artwork in the game.

A few notes about the role of the game designer vs. artist: Designers' primary activity usually occurs early in the project, sketching characters, scenes, and devising plots. When there is a full-time designer, the 3D artists are often uninvolved with the design aspect; instead, the artists build the resulting designs. This relationship mimics that of a real-life architect and general contractor—they are approximate peers, but creative control is primarily with one party.

- 2D artists are responsible for creating backdrops, font design, intro animations, and "overlays", such as dashboards for racing games.
- Level designers (for games) create the large-scale shape of the player's virtual environment, using pieces that the 3D artist builds.

Level designers are experts at game strategy, and they understand how to create a fun sequence of events—challenging, but not impossible—that the player will enjoy. If the project doesn't need a full-time level designer, the game designer and/or 3D artist will often do this work. Level designers usually work closely with the 3D artists, providing feedback on the shapes being created and making requests for new shapes.

- Sound designers create an aural environment, which covers music as well as sound effects, for the application.
- For projects that use specialized hardware (such as customized graphics accelerators, motion sensing equipment, head-mounted displays, 3D sound processors, and 3D input devices), a hardware engineer is required to make all this equipment work in harmony.

The Secondary Team

Many people besides the "core team" are involved in producing a major interactive 3D project. These people are not the core team (we'll call them the "secondary team"), and they are often employed by the publisher.

- Testers work through the application once it is done, looking for problems and ensuring that it works as expected.
- The manual writers' job is obvious: to create the written instructions and other documentation that goes with the application.
- Advertising/PR content creators market the application.
- Dedicated support staff—office managers, secretaries, and so on—help coordinate and process all the work.
- The core team, except the manager, can also be present in the secondary team. It's quite common for 3D artists to be hired as part of the secondary team, not the core team.

Core Team versus Secondary Team

Distinguishing a secondary team member from a core team member is sometimes difficult. One way is to imagine the person in question quitting their job during the project. If a core team member quits, the project would be drastically delayed and possibly in danger of collapse. On the other hand, if a secondary team member quits, it's possible to replace them without damaging the project very much. Other ways to distinguish between core and secondary team members are where they work (on-site vs. off-site), how often they talk with a core team member (hourly, daily, or weekly), and if they are working on the project full-time.

Who pays for the team member is another big indicator—if the publisher is paying the salary, he or she is not a core team member.

That's not to say the secondary team isn't important—they are! They're simply different—think of them as an "outer loop" around the core team.

Relationships between the core team and the secondary team are messy and unpredictable. This can cause problems, as we'll discuss once we bring in the last big piece of the picture: the publisher.

The Publisher

For products funded by a software publishing company, such as most commercial computer games, the publisher usually plays a large part in the development of the product. When we discuss publishers, we'll use the term "developer" to refer to the core development team and any secondary team members who are paid by the core team.

The producer is the person employed by the publishing company who is responsible for the project being developed. The producer is the publisher's main contact for the developer; they are the person to whom issues are presented, and usually they make the crucial decisions about the project on the publishing company's behalf. (Note: when the "publisher" is referred to as a person, we are usually referring to the producer.) If the developer is analogous to a book's author, the producer is analogous to the editor.

What is the publisher's role? From the product's point of view, the publishing company's overall function is to make copies of the game, advertise it, and get it on all the software sellers' shelves; however, the publisher often does much more than that.

To the development team dependent on the publisher for money, the publisher is essentially their primary customer—if the development team wants to get the money, they must please the publisher. This is especially accurate for standard commercial game development situations.

If the Publisher Is Bad...

If the publisher is bad, we'll get symptoms similar to those of a bad office boss: Because the publisher controls the purse strings of the project, the publisher has ultimate veto power over any part of the project they don't like. They will win any design conflicts they care to enter simply because they are the boss; thus, we may find ourselves building a product that we don't think is any good simply because the publishers insist on it. In a worse situation, the publisher may suddenly decide that the project is not worth funding, even in the middle of a project, and leave the developers weeping in the gutter.

If the Publisher Is Good...

In this scenario, the publisher acts as a rich, organized, somewhat silent business partner to the developer. A good publisher avoids strife by starting out on the

right foot, establishing a positive environment from the start. They examine the prospective development teams carefully and don't fund groups they don't believe in.

When they do find a development group they believe in, they not only provide money, but offer many other forms of valuable support: additional workers, plenty of good computer hardware, beautiful, high-quality testing environments, and so on.

The good publisher may have to push the developer to keep the project on schedule, but they don't micro-manage the development process; instead, they trust the development team to do the job better than any outside force could dictate.

In the best case, the developer produces a truly amazing product, thanks to the funding and support of the publisher, on time and under budget. The publisher does a great promotional job, and together they achieve a huge success. Afterwards, the two parties are on the best of terms and continue working together, building a great line of products based on the solid foundation of a successful working relationship.

Interactions

As a member of the core team, we artists need to know how our customers interact with their customers, simply because we are often involved in that interaction. Here is a description of how these situations can work.

Interactions of the Publishers and the Developers

Publishers and developers can have a sharing relationship, but they are always aware that they are not peers and do not pretend to be. This simple point is usually clear between the producer and the core team manager, but often it's less clear for the other people involved in the project.

It can get really messy, team-interaction-wise, when the publisher is an active member of a development team. Here's an extreme example: The producer assigns an employee of the publishing company to work on-site with the core developer, performing secondary team functions (like designing level layouts). Is this employee a core team member, a secondary team member, or a representative of the publisher? Who should the employee answer to—the manager or the producer? These questions are hard to answer even in a clean-cut example, and they become very sticky when we add in factors like personality differences and political maneuverings.

Ideally, the questions are answered from the start. The publisher would have started by asking the core team manager what kind of help the team wants. If the publisher does provide its employees to the developers, the producer should clearly indicate what the employee's role and purpose are to both the employee and the developers.

Interactions of the Core and Secondary Teams

Core team members, sometimes excepting the manager, are almost always peers to each other: sharing information, opinions, suggestions, and helping each other out whenever possible. They work as a tight team, communicating almost constantly, and though theoretically it's not necessary, they are often physically in the same office. Creativity is encouraged and welcomed, sometimes even at the expense of making deadlines.

In many ways, the "secondary team" works with the core developers in a less tight but similar method: They, too, offer opinions, help each other out, and work together toward a common goal. However, there is a very important difference. Secondary team members are not peers to the core team members. Their opinions do not weigh as heavily, and core team members are apt to have less patience for wild, creative suggestions from them. Though it may sound like it, the unequal relationship between core and secondary team members is not a bad thing. It simply reflects the reality of the working environment.

Why Are The Secondary Team Members Not Peers?

Here are some common reasons: compared to the core team members, the secondary team members may be less experienced in the industry, are newer to the project, or are paid by the publisher, not the developer. They may also be part-time employees or temporary subcontractors instead of full-time employees or partners, which may cause a feeling of isolation because they constantly miss out on communication by being gone part of the day.

An important difference between the two teams is that secondary team members are often not in the same office physically as the core team and do not communicate with the core team very often. (If an off-site secondary team member talks to a core team member twice a day, that's a lot.)

Design versus Execution

Creative work on real-time projects is often divided between design and execution. This concept is rooted in the field of hand-drawn cartooning: A senior design staff sketches characters and key frames, providing a consistent, professional look, and implementers fill in the detail and specifics.

This division works well when the designers are experienced in implementation and the implementation is a known, standardized procedure, allowing the design work to be split cleanly from execution. However, unlike hand-drawn animation, creating a real-time computer application is a very complex task that requires wildly varying abilities. It's unreasonable to expect the designers to be amazing character artists, experts at real-time 3D modeling, top-notch game coders, Photoshop masters, and ace level designers. Inevitably the designers will create ideas that they don't know how to implement. This is a source for problems; some approaches to avoiding disaster are discussed in Chapter 7.

Also, in our line of work, much of the design occurs during implementation. Designs must constantly flex and adapt to reflect our changing working environment, which means the design work has to happen during execution, not before. Also, the executor is often the only one who really understands the changes, so it makes sense for them to do some design revisions. This becomes a problem when the executor doesn't have the right to change the design. Fortunately, this rarely occurs.

Project Concept Design

When someone created the basic concept that got the project funded, they became the concept designer, charged with developing the basic game structure. This is frequently the manager described previously. They almost always share more specific creative control with the other team members, and they may hand off large parts (like interface design) to others, but the basic concept is usually theirs alone.

However, some project concepts are not created by the development team. One example of this situation occurs when a publisher or client creates a concept and pays the development team to have it implemented. Obviously, the core design is not the developers' responsibility in this case, but much of the design occurs during implementation. This means the developers still have a large influence on how the project appears, and careful, clear communication must occur for the project to go smoothly.

Artwork Designer

On a more relevant level, a similar split sometimes occurs between design and execution in artwork. For example, the game's logo artwork, the buttons on the user interface, and the final boss character all must be designed and implemented. Sometimes the design and construction are separate tasks. Often one person in the development team is assigned the "lead artist" or the equivalent role; that person dictates the appearance of the game to the others.

Other projects are more cooperative and peer-driven, where each artist designs and builds their own version of the basic assignment, and the responsibility for creating a unified artistic look is shared.

Communication with Designers

Communicating with designers can be really tough, even aside from the technical issues. Sometimes artists may feel frustrated at implementing someone else's designs, but we should remember that the designers may be just as frustrated at handing off their precious creative ideas to someone else. In a sense, they're trusting us to have their baby, to create their design without the complete understanding that only the creator has. It's an emotionally delicate situation, which makes communication even more difficult.

As we communicate, we'll gain trust and respect if we stay human—admit mistakes, express confidence, and doubt, acknowledge areas we don't know well, ask for input, and generally interact without pretense or posing.

Designing 3D Graphics

This "human" approach is opposed to having a "professional image" or persona. For example, take the enigmatic "total expert—I know all" persona, who doesn't say much and acts as if he or she is so smart that he or she understands the whole design without asking any questions. Another common persona is the "no problem" attitude: all agreement, totally optimistic, nothing's ever a problem, I can build anything! Again, no questions are asked, and no doubt is expressed; instead, uncontrolled buoyant enthusiasm covers over any real issues that should be discussed. This persona tends to leave the designer happy after the first meeting, and often disappointed when the model is completed.

Personas are a problem when the goal is to empathize with the designer's view, to get in their head and really understand the needs and priorities. The shell of behavior that a persona requires interferes with really understanding the designer's vision.

Why do we want this close connection to the designer? Why not just work from blueprints and blame the designer if the blueprints aren't totally complete? The closer we get to seeing the design from the designer's perspective, the less disagreement (and thus revisions) we'll have once we complete the model.

We should be aware of the danger of over-communicating. If we drag the designer into every tiny decision we make, we are wasting their time and ours. As we gain experience, we'll need to call on the designer's input less. For the beginning, ask if in doubt, but gauge the designer's attitude and feeling when handling your requests.

The Peer Issue

Most people working on a game are intelligent and open-minded, and they tend to assume that everyone—core team member, secondary team member, or publisher—is a peer. This is encouraged by the casual, friendly nature of the whole industry, and especially fostered during the "romance" of the game publishing deal—when the publisher and the developer befriend each other and agree to work together.

As nice as it sounds to say "we're all working on this together," it just isn't accurate in most cases, and it usually causes some real problems. The problems arise when the true nature of the relations is forced to appear—for example, if a publisher withholds payment because a milestone is incomplete, the developer may feel betrayed. The developer may feel that the goodwill and laughter they remembered at the beginning of the project meant that the publisher was their friend, willing to bend the rules. When it turns out not to be true, they may harbor anger toward the publisher. If these issues are not straightened out, it's no exaggeration to say they could destroy the entire project.

Why Worry About It?

Unfortunately, it is a disaster if the developer and publisher develop an antagonistic relationship. The basic issue is trust—if either party doesn't trust the other,

they're both in trouble. The foundation of trust is predictability and understanding of the other party, which is, in turn, affected by clear communication.

Specifically, each party should know its basic responsibility and range of power clearly. If these are clear, there is much less chance for the kind of major misunderstandings that can destroy projects.

As a core team member, we artists do have influence. We provide a lot of input into the people who are involved in a specific project; in fact, we are involved ourselves. We even lose our jobs if this kind of problem were to stop the project!

● Basic RT3D Game Development Scenario

As employees or subcontractors, we artists are rarely shown the commercial development model, and who's paying whom can be fuzzy. Though not strictly necessary for us to do our job, it's helpful to understand this basic process, especially when we try to understand how the teams interact with the publisher. Here's a summary of one common model for real-time 3D game development:

1. A development team assembles itself, puts together a viable game idea, and shows it to a publisher.

2. The publisher decides to give the development team "advances": money to pay their salary and expenses while they develop the game.

3. The development team develops the game (over a 6–12 month period), sometimes with help from the publisher.

4. The publisher tests, packages, promotes, and distributes the game to resellers.

5. The publisher collects all of the money from sales of the game. A percentage of that money is used to repay the advances and to pay the developer the royalty, and the publisher keeps the rest. It is used first to repay the costs incurred for the project (for example, production, distribution, advertising, and in-house salaries); and the rest is profit.

Here's a simple example of this process with some optimistic but somewhat realistic numbers:

1. Tracy Manager, drawing on years of experience in the industry, decides to make a game. She starts MicroGames Inc., names herself as president, and hires Joe Programmer and you, the 3D artist. With her own money she pays two months of salaries for you and Joe to develop a simple prototype. She shows this prototype to Tina Producer at MegaPublisher. Thus, MicroGames is the core developer.

2. Tina likes the prototype and decides it is worth funding. She and Tracy

agree on this deal: MegaPublisher gives MicroGames $100,000 in advance money, paid out in ten $10,000 milestone payments during a ten-month period. This advance will be repaid from 7 percent of Mega-Publisher's sales of the game; once the advance is paid, that 7 percent will be for MicroGames.

3. MicroGames hires a part-time game designer and makes the product, paying Tracy, you, Joe, and the designer as well as covering office expenses and computer equipment from the advance moneys. All goes well, and MicroGames delivers all milestones and "alpha" (incomplete prototype) versions as promised. At the end of nine months, a "beta" (first draft—functional but rough) product is delivered. The last month is spent QA'ing (QA means Quality Assurance—fixing problems that the testers at MegaPublisher find) and generally making a polished, finished product.

4. During the last few months of development, MegaPublisher has begun promoting the game, getting early copies in reviewers' hands, sending out press releases, and generally starting to get excited about it. MegaPub-lisher also creates packaging and manuals with their in-house artists and handles reproduction, distribution, etc. Once the game is done, they release a sales campaign as the game is distributed to the retail software stores.

5. During the first six months, the game sells 100,000 copies—it's a good-selling game. The publisher gets $20 of each copy's selling price, which means the game's sales is $2 million. MicroGames' 7 percent share is $140,000. After the $100,000 advance is repaid, MegaPublisher pays MicroGames the remaining $40,000 and 7 percent of any sales thereafter.

In the end, MicroGames spent all of the advance money on salaries and expenses, and it made $40,000 in profit over a ten-month period. MegaPub-lisher's situation will vary widely, but let's guess that it spent $500,000 on adver-tising and promotion, paid $100,000 in salaries for the producer, testers, and in-house artists, and spent $500,000 on production and distribution. That leaves it with a profit of $750,000 from its $1,860,000 gross income.

In addition to this basic model, many other situations work out—the share-ware model, the "in-house" development scenario (in which everyone is an employee of the publisher), and countless others.

● Problems Unique to VR Development

When working in VR, we artists are in a tricky position. Because lots of people organizing VR development are visionaries with innovative, unusual approaches to everything, the team designs are not very consistent. That's good, in general,

because it fosters exciting, unique working environments that, in the best case, can produce unusually good results.

However, VR projects consistently identify the modeler as the "virtual architect." Of course, this designation is compared to a real-life architect, and that's where we can easily be assigned too much responsibility. We end up being the place where the rubber meets the road, bridging the gap between fantasy and reality, between theory and application.

Here's an example scenario: Imagine rich venture capitalists, high on hype, putting together a team of experts to build the Virtual Vegas of their dreams. You get picked as the virtual architect, are given a high salary, and are told to go to town: to design and build a virtual environment. Ideal situation, right?

Well, maybe. It's quite likely that you will encounter some problems that are outside the skill set and knowledge of an artist. For example, conflicts between what they want and what the computer can handle may arise, and the "virtual architect" will be expected to solve them.

It may seem odd that the artist would be expected to deal with this, so think of it this way: The VR environment (hardware and software) has the potential to show a virtual world within certain known limits (for example, perhaps it can render 2,000 textured triangles in 320 × 200 pixels 30 times per second). Now, what does this mean to the investors, our customer? Almost nothing.

This describes the weave of the canvas to an art patron; it's not art. It's not even clear how it's related to the art. What they want is good art, and in VR, the virtual architect (that's us) promises to provide it. Thus, if the "canvas" isn't good enough (or the customer's expectations are high), we can end up being responsible. When issues arise, they usually result from a lack of realism, and an inexperienced patron could blame the "virtual architect."

The solution is to be really clear on what our role is. Being a "virtual architect" involves much more than just design skills. It's a lot closer to the role of the manager, with some designer thrown in, in a game development environment.

We artists should be sure we can do what we're asked to do (perhaps "virtual construction worker" is a more appropriate analogy for the managers to understand). We should not take on more than our knowledge allows us to do well. Of course, we could expand our skills and abilities and then rightfully assume the role of "virtual architect." That's fine, but that requires a different set of skills—that is not what this book is about.

THE BASICS
OF 3D COMPUTER
GRAPHICS

This chapter introduces computer graphics, covers the definition of the basic terms and concepts used in real-time 3D modeling, and discusses how 3D models are handled in real-time environments and 3D Studio alike.

For people who grew up with personal computer graphics as a second language, this chapter is obvious; these people should simply skim the definitions to make sure we agree on the terms used in this book.

This chapter is written for those of you who haven't been playing with bitmaps since childhood. It is here that we not only lay the foundation for understanding real-time 3D modeling, but also try to communicate the real knowledge behind the definition.

In the definitions we firm up the linguistic soup of which computer graphics are usually composed. As with all new fields, the terms are not always clear or well-defined, but for this book, specific terms are used with a particular meaning.

 The Basics

Starting from ground zero, let's define "computer graphics":

Computer graphics: Graphic images displayed on a computer.

"Computer graphics" — this is the most basic, broad term around. In fact, it's so general that it may seem totally meaningless, but it does have meaning. To illustrate, here's what it doesn't cover.

"Computer graphics" doesn't mean that the graphics were created by a computer; in fact, the term can include traditional hand-created drawings and paintings that are simply scanned in a computer. The term indicates only that we are not talking about plain text data, sound clips, or programming algorithms, and we're not talking about traditional art—real-world oil painting or sculpture.

In this book, we'll be dealing with a subset of computer graphics: real-time 3D graphics. How are RT3D graphics different from the rest of computer graphics? Glad you asked! Let's answer that by taking a look at the family tree of computer graphics.

2D versus 3D

The difference between 2D and 3D computer graphics is the most fundamental division—the first branch on its family tree. The difference between the two is usually assumed to be obvious, but several differences are usually grouped together under "2D vs. 3D." These are all very important and need to be recognized as basic paradigm shifts.

Raster versus Vector

In computer graphics, there's a big split between two main methods of showing an image: vector and raster.

Vector Using mathematical lines to represent an image. It's based on high-school-geometry Cartesian coordinates. For example, CAD drawings are vector-based. Adobe Illustrator is a vector-based graphics tool.

Raster Using colored dots (pixels) to represent an image. Bitmaps are raster-based. Photoshop is a raster-based graphics tool.

Most 3D graphics are assumed to be vector-based, and many 2D graphics are raster-based.

Vector-based Graphics

There are no strict rules about what standard entities are in a vector-based image, but some of the common ones are points, lines, arcs, filled regions, triangular surfaces, and spline-based surfaces.

The advantages to vector-based graphics are numerous. Easy scalability, hardware independence, and (sometimes) compact file size are features of a vector-based file.

Of course, there are also disadvantages to vector-based graphics. These problems come from the abstract mathematical foundation combined with finite computing power. As you can imagine, it's nearly impossible to portray realistic detail like dirty, peeling paint using crisp, solid-filled lines and arcs. Each piece of detail that is added to a vector-based image has to be calculated by the computer (unlike a bitmap, which takes the same amount of computing power whether it is a complicated image or empty white).

Vector-based graphics are commonly used when precision and clarity are more important than realism. Some examples of vector-based file formats are the following:

- EPS—encapsulated PostScript, 2D vector-based
- DXF—drafting interchange standard
- IGES—drafting interchange standard
- TTF—vector-based font
- 3DS, ASC, PRJ—3D Studio file formats
- WRL—VRML 3D file format

Common applications that are based on vectors include AutoCAD, 3D Studio, Adobe Illustrator, Micrografx Designer, CorelDRAW!, and all 3D modeling software.

Raster-based Graphics

Raster-based graphic images, also known as bitmaps, are the most common and fundamental form of graphics on computers because that's how any computer image is finally shown to the user. The monitor works by simply showing a grid of colored dots at various intensities, which is exactly what a bitmap is.

The simplest raster-based graphics are arrays (grids) of bits; each bit in the array represents a black or white dot in the image. For full-color images, three bytes are stored for each point. Each byte contains an integer from 0 to 255;

together these three integers store the level of red, green, and blue that define the point's color.

Almost all animation files are raster-based, even if they were generated by a vector-based program like 3D Studio; conceptually, they are simply a series of bitmaps combined into one file. Examples include .AVI, .FLI, and .MPEG files.

There are many file formats for raster bitmaps. Here's a few of the common ones:

- GIF—Copyrighted bitmap format; can store only 256-color images, any size
- PCX—General bitmap format; any size and most color depths supported
- TGA ("Targa")—General bitmap format; any size and most color depths supported
- TIF—General bitmap format; any size and most color depths supported
- PICT—Macintosh's format for bitmaps
- JPG—"Lossy," highly compressed bitmap format; any size supported, but only high-color and gray-scale supported (no 256-color support)

Common applications based on raster graphics include Photoshop, Deluxe Paint, Paintbrush, Painter, CorelPAINT, and video/animation editing software.

The advantages to raster-based graphics are plentiful: Bitmaps are easy to manage, fast to display, and give predictable results when translated to other computers or mediums.

When raster graphics are compared to vector graphics, there are some disadvantages. First, using raster graphics to portray 3D is very impractical (for this decade, though it is possible using a concept called "voxels"). In the restricted realm of 2D graphics, many images can be displayed more quickly and stored in smaller files using vectors. Fonts are an excellent example: Compare a TrueType font to its raster-based ancestors, and you will see more flexibility and superior quality with a drastically smaller file size.

Vector Plus Raster

Ideally, we would have the power of vector-based graphics plus the realism of raster graphics. For this reason, many 3D applications, including 3D Studio, use both vector- and raster-based graphics in combination. Because these two forms are fundamentally different, there are plenty of technical issues (yes, that's doublespeak for "irritating problems") to be dealt when we combine them.

What Is Real-Time 3D Modeling?

Now that we've established the most basic terms, let's take a look at the branch of computer graphics most relevant to us: real-time 3D Modeling.

What Is 3D Modeling?

We all use the term, but it can mean many things, depending on context. In this book, 3D modeling means creating a representation of a three-dimensional object and storing it as data in a computer. It doesn't say anything about the way

it's stored (straight-edged faces vs. splines) or what it's used for (pre-rendered vs. real-time). For those distinctions, we need some modifiers.

What Does Real-Time Mean?

"Real-Time" originally meant that the computer works in sync with "real-world" data; that is, it's taking input from the real world, thinking about it quickly, then producing a result that is immediately used by the "real world." Real-time is the opposite of batch processing, in which a computer takes a pile of data and says "I'll get back to you when this is done."

The term has acquired another meaning as well. In the context of computer graphics, it means that the images on the screen are generated while you watch, often under your control. This is opposed to "pre-rendered" graphics in which the image you are viewing was generated some time in the past.

The term "interactive 3D game" is sometimes used to mean "real-time 3D game," but the two terms are not the same thing. For example, Myst is interactive, but the graphics are all pre-rendered; therefore, it's not a real-time 3D game. We can tell that the graphics are pre-rendered because very little changes in each picture; we can't wander around freely and peek under the chairs.

What Are Real-Time 3D Graphics Like?

Real-time 3D graphics are composed of points in space connected by simple surfaces. The surfaces are always flat with straight edges (though they can appear curved if we use a lot of small ones).

These surfaces are called polygons (means "many sides"). The points are called "vertices," or "verts" for short. Raster images called "textures" are combined with the polygons to portray realistic detail.

Two types of polygons have special names: three-sided polygons are called "tris," obviously short for triangles, and four-sided polys are called "quads."

Hollow and One-Sided

A very astute observer would take these definitions and realize that the world of real-time 3D is composed of infinitely thin faces, like a paper shell, instead of solid objects. Also, these thin faces are like one-way mirrors: they're invisible from one side.

This is not how humans intuitively think of 3D objects, but it's not as weird as it sounds. Most 3D artists can think of their thin, one-sided faces that enclose a volume as solid, and it's a reasonable assumption to make. If you're used to 3D Studio, you're already there—that's how it works. Its faces are one-sided, thin shells, and everything in 3D Studio is made out of faces.

As with most strange behaviors in real-time 3D graphics, the reason we build with one-sided and hollow concepts is because it's easiest for the computer to draw. Because the major limitation is the computer's speed of drawing, we have to cater to its whims. We use some tricks to prevent the user from ever discovering the one-sided, hollow truth, but it's something we artists have to understand.

What's the Story About Frame Rate?

Now we'll take a look at the essential challenge of modeling for real-time 3D applications. This boils down to building beautiful 3D shapes that can be rendered in a small fraction of a second.

If you've been building "normal" 3D Studio models, rendering scenes and animations (that is, your final product has been a 2D flic or still image), then follow along this analogy:

Imagine you're a clay sculptor creating excellent sculptures—real works of art. When these sculptures are shown to the world, the response is, "Nice form, but it doesn't move. Make it dance, nice, smooth waltzing or something." To meet this demand, the sculptor would make massive changes, not only in the model itself, but in the way they think about sculpture. Likewise, the 3D modeler will think differently when shifting from pre-rendered to real-time artwork.

Like the sculptor trying to add motion, we are now asked to use a whole new criteria for our artwork: frame rate.

What Is Frame Rate?

Frame rate: The rate at which the computer renders each frame of a RT3D application. It's usually measured in Hertz, which is a unit borrowed from physics, meaning cycles (rendered frames) per second.

What's an acceptable frame rate to portray smooth motion? This really varies. Human eyes see about 60 frames per second, though for commercial real-time computer graphics, 30 frames per second is considered quite good and smooth. Anything less than 10 frames per second is noticeably unsmooth, and it's difficult to perceive motion at all if the frame rate is below 2 frames per second—the images start to look unrelated, like a slide show.

The minimum frame rate is a very important number to consider during development of a real-time application, and it's a hard decision to make. In cold reality, computer games usually start shooting for 15–20 frames per second on their target hardware (that is, the computer that the buyer is likely to have), and settle for 8–15 by the time the game ships. VR applications usually do better because they can depend on better hardware.

Frame Rate as a Value Judgment

In the context of artistic value, frame rate means more than statistics. The speed at which our model is rendered is a new basis for judgment, along with the old factors of beauty and the time it took us to build it.

In other words, if our real-time model can be rendered twice as fast as a similar model, it's a better model, even if it looks slightly worse. And if an incredibly detailed model looks great but kills the frame rate, it's a bad real-time model.

To summarize, our goal is to achieve high frame rates while preserving, as much as possible, the beauty of our designed shapes. Obviously, the two parts of this goal are in conflict—this is where we bring our awesome problem-solving human brains into the picture.

An Analogy of RT3D versus "Normal" 3D Modeling

There is a misconception among 3D artists that making real-time 3D models is really easy. Just build a normal 3D Studio model, but keep it simple and maybe run the Optimize plug-in. No problem, right? Well, not really. Here's a comparison of two jobs to help explain this.

First, think of the person who has the job of creating a one-off show car, custom machined and hand manufactured at great expense and labor. They are unconcerned with practical technical issues (for example, how can we make this double-compound, curved glass window on a normal factory floor?).

Now, consider the person who takes this show car and redesigns it with standardized sheet metal stampings and off-the-shelf components, creating a design for a mass-produced car to be purchased by anyone with an average income.

In this analogy, "normal" 3D artists build models that are complicated, beautiful, and so huge that it takes the computer several minutes to render a single frame. The job of the real-time 3D modeler is to redesign and custom-build the model for a specific rendering environment, losing as little of its beauty as possible, getting it in a form that can be rendered by an ordinary computer ten times every second.

This skill is not generally recognized as a great talent or ability, but it is what makes mass production possible. The person who can design with minimal expense and difficulty is (arguably) the key creative person in the whole process of mass production.

● Real-Time 3D Graphics Terms and Concepts

This section will first define some basic, general terms we use, and then introduce the entities on which real-time 3D graphics are based. Once we have this foundation, we'll go for some additional concepts like pseudo-entities, common units and coordinate systems, and a concept called LOD.

RT3D: Acronym for "real-time three-dimensional."

Application: The shipping product in which the 3D models will be used (for example, the game or real-time VR demo we're developing). Also called "real-time application."

Despite the computer game emphasis in this book, "application" generally refers to any thing that uses RT3D graphics. Examples of applications include games that use RT3D, flight simulators, VRML, immersive architectural walkthroughs, most types of Virtual Reality programs, driving simulators, immersive 3D art projects, and 3D military training simulators. Note that, in this book, "application" doesn't mean the programs we artists use, like 3D Studio or Photoshop—they are called "tools" here.

Graphics engine: The part of the code in the application that takes the RT3D artwork and renders it onscreen in real-time. Also called "graphics pipeline," "3D graphics engine," "3D engine," "rendering engine," or sometimes simply "engine."

The graphics engine's function is analogous to the "render" command in 3D Studio, except that it happens continuously as the application runs. The term doesn't refer to other parts of the application, such as code for the user interface, the high-score screen, or the joystick calibration section.

Run time: The time when the real-time application is running. This is opposed to when the application is being created or compiled.

The term "run time" can be confusing; here are some examples. When the player is using our completed application on their own computer, that's run time. When we use the application to test the new model we just built, that's run time. But when we're building the world in 3D Studio, that's not run time—the application isn't being used; nothing is being rendered in real-time.

Units

In the interests of avoiding annoying foot-inch conversion problems, we'll use the metric system and usually use the simple ratio of 1 3D Studio unit = 1 meter.

Coordinate System

Let's take a quick look at the basic coordinate system we'll be using throughout this book. To do this, we'll need to agree on some terms:

Coordinate system (CS): A special triad that forms a foundation for describing locations in space.

3D Studio uses a standard coordinate system that we'll call the "world coordinate system" on those rare occasions when we must refer to it. It's possible (and, alas, sometimes necessary) to change it, but it's really confusing because any models created in a different CS will be disoriented when loaded with the new CS.

Origin: The intersection point of the X, Y, and Z axes of the world coordinate system. The origin's coordinates are (0,0,0).

In the basic coordinate system that is standard with 3D Studio, "Up" refers to the positive direction of the Y axis, "right" refers to the positive X axis, and the positive Z axis must point toward us. The usual "ground" surface is the XZ plane (that is, the plane that the X and Z axes both lie on), as shown in Figure 2.1.

Entities

Entity: A single face, vertex, or object in a scene; when used ambiguously, it

Designing 3D Graphics

FIGURE 2.1 Triad in 3D Studio's basic orientation.

usually refers to objects but also has a vaguer meaning: "something in 3D space, in general."

This is the vaguest term we have to refer to something in our 3D world.

Point: Three numbers X, Y, and Z (coordinates) that define single location in space.

Vertex: A specialized kind of point. It is a point with additional "mapping" data for locating texture maps. Also called "vert." Plural is vertices, or "verts."

Vertices appear in 3D Studio as dots or small crosses, but the user can't ever see them in the real-time application (or when 3D Studio renders, as I'm sure you've noticed). Verts act like tent stakes: They act as a place to attach other things (faces, actually), but are not much use by themselves.

Polygon: A bounded surface defined by a closed chain of straight lines connecting verts. Polygons usually have some additional data, like the name of the material they use and the visibility of their edges, that goes with their basic shape definition.

Face: A triangular polygon (also known as a "tri"). Faces have only three edges.

Quad: A four-sided polygon.

If verts are tent stakes, polygons are tents. Without the verts, they don't define anything. They rely on the verts for their location in space, but they are the big, obvious surfaces that define the object.

The only kind of polygon that 3D Studio supports is faces. Some graphics engines support only faces (especially hardware-accelerated ones); others support faces or quads, and still others support almost any kind of polygon.

In 3D Studio and most graphics engines, two or more faces can, and often do, share verts. Sharing a vert is like using the same stake for two different tents. See the definition of element, below, for more on this.

Like a tent stake, if you move a vert, faces that use it will move also. This is a very important concept in real-time 3D modeling. Other modeling environments, such as AutoCAD, don't work this way.

Tri-mesh: Faces that "mesh" together; that is, their corners are all matched so they form a continuous but arbitrary surface like a bumpy fishnet. Tri-meshes can be thought of as surfaces.

Object: 3D Studio's term for a bunch of faces and vertices, along with some other miscellaneous data.

A 3D Studio object usually defines a single conceptual thing, like a brick, a car, or a phone booth (though there is nothing to prevent you from making objects from unrelated, randomly selected faces and vertices throughout your model).

Scene: A collection of objects that form the entire virtual environment that the user sees during the real-time simulation.

The term *scene* is not fully established; some call the scene the *world* or *virtual world*. It isn't a 3D Studio term; it usually refers to the objects assembled in the real-time application, not in 3D Studio. An entire scene can be stored in a single .3DS file (as a collection of objects), but usually each object is saved and compiled separately, then dynamically combined into a single scene at run time.

For example, let's say our project is a virtual museum. We'll build chairs, desks, picture frames, lighting fixtures, and the building itself. We build each one in 3D Studio, and save it under its own name (BUILDING.3DS, CHAIR01.3DS, etc.). Taken together, this artwork composes a "scene," but each piece by itself is only an object.

Pseudo-Entities

Edges and elements are not really entities—they don't show up in saved .ASC files like a face, object, or vertex. They are an abstraction, a conceptual convenience.

The trick is, these abstract concepts sometimes behave like real entities. If you look on the 3D Studio menu, you'll see "Modify/Edge/Divide" and a host of other editing commands that imply that edges are similar to faces. Don't be fooled! Because they aren't "real," these pseudo-entities can be confusing to work with— they can appear and disappear, change, and generally behave unpredictably.

On the other hand, these conceptual abstractions can be incredibly useful once we realize how to use them, so let's take time to understand their construction.

Edges

Edges are the lines that are drawn to represent a wire-frame face in 3D Studio. Edges connect the verts on a face. As we might expect, faces have three edges; however, things start to get strange when verts are shared. If two faces connect to the same two verts, there is still only one edge.

A shared edge is a common situation; in fact, most edges are shared in a typical model. Because of this, some of the Modify/Edge/… editing commands are designed to work with shared edges only. Modify/Edge/Turn, for example, works only when you click on an edge shared by two faces.

Because there is no actual "edge" entity, Modify/Edge/Delete doesn't delete the edge itself—it's really a shortcut for deleting any face that uses that edge.

There are two types of edges—visible and invisible. There is no functional difference between them other than appearance, but this alone can be very handy—using Display/Geometry/Edges Only, we can hide certain edges. Occasionally, this proves useful.

Elements

Elements are less intuitive, but they are more important to understand.

Element: A group of faces that share vertices.

Elements sometimes are treated like objects, and they are often confused. An element can seem to be what an object "should" be: a collection of faces that all touch each other. This similarity is superficial—elements are very different from objects.

The most important difference is that an element is not "real": it does not appear in an ASC file. Thus, creating or removing elements is a very subtle, vague operation, unlike the straightforward ways we deal with creating and deleting objects.

Many other differences come from the way elements are defined. For example, verts are included in elements only if the faces in that element refer to them. An isolated, unused vert can never be part of an element.

Like objects (and unlike many other modelers' way of grouping), a face can be in only one element at a time. Here's how that works: To join a face to another element X, we must make the face share a vert with another face in X. Then they're all sharing verts, so they all become the same big element. This is how we "delete" elements. The official Modify/Element/Delete command is really a shortcut to deleting all the verts and faces that make up the element.

To create an element, we take a group of faces and make sure they don't share verts with any other group. We can use Create/Element/Detach to do this, among other ways. This means that any isolated face is a element all by itself.

3D Studio allows us to assign mapping (UV coordinates) to elements. This is a big deal, and it is discussed in Chapter 7.

Aspect

Aspect: Comparison of one dimension to another; the proportions (length vs. width vs. height) of an object. For bitmaps, aspect is also known as "aspect ratio." To calculate the aspect of a bitmap, divide its width by its height. For example, a 320 × 200 bitmap has an aspect ratio of 1.6.

In this book, we use the concept of aspect for a 3D object or a bitmap.

Orthogonal: An orthogonal line is parallel to the X, Y, or Z axis. An orthogonal plane is parallel to the XY, XZ, or YZ plane.

Degrees of freedom (DOF): A way of describing the available range of motions that the graphics engine is capable of. There are six possible degrees of freedom for a single object: movement along the X,Y, and Z axes, and rotation around any one of these axes. The rotation around the X axis of our coordinate system is called pitch. Around the Y is yaw, and around the Z is roll.

Triad: A set of three mutually perpendicular intersecting lines in 3D space. Each line, called an "axis," is named X, Y, or Z.

See Figure 2.1 for an example of a triad.

Latitude and longitude: Lines of latitude and longitude are curved lines on the surface of a sphere. Lines of latitude never touch, like croquet ball stripes, and are usually horizontal. By contrast, longitudinal lines connect one pole to the other, usually vertically.

Normal: A line that penetrates a plane and forms a 90-degree angle with the plane is normal to that plane. For example, in Figure 2.1, the Y axis is normal to the XZ plane. In 3D graphics, "normal" can be either an adjective or a noun.

"Normal" is an unusual concept to most people, but it's really useful in 3D graphics because it defines a plane's orientation. For example, think of a paper spindle (the metal spike that people stick bills onto). The spindle's spike is nor-

Designing 3D Graphics

mal to its base. If we know which way the spike points, we also know which way the base is oriented. This is handy for computers because the math for lines is simpler than the math for planes.

The term has a more specific meaning as well. In reference to a face, the "normal" is a vector that is normal to the face, but because it's a vector, it also means a certain direction. Imagine building a face using Create/Face/Build. If we pick the verts in a clockwise direction, the normal will point away from us. "But hold on," you say, " 'clockwise' is relative to my viewpoint!" This is true, so we must realize that our viewing direction matters in this situation.

LOD: Level of Detail

Most graphics engines support a concept called Level of Detail, or LOD.

> *Level of Detail (LOD):* A group of models, each one simpler than the last, that all portray the same object. The complicated models are shown when the user is near the object, and the simpler models are shown when the object is far away from the user.

The term is sometimes used to refer to simpler versions of the original model. For example, we could say, "That model has a lot of faces, but the LOD uses only a few faces." It can also refer to the whole concept of levels of detail; for example, "This engine does not support LOD."

The benefits of using LODs in an open environment are very strong for objects like trees, telephone poles, streetlights, cars, or any other commonly repeated, identical objects.

Using LODs doesn't always make sense, however. The simpler model takes up the same space on the screen, so there are usually the same number of pixels to calculate; if this is the bottleneck in your 3D application, you won't see much improvement by using LODs. On the other hand, if your 3D application is spending most of its time doing math on the verts, LODs could help a lot.

The main drawback to implementing LODs is the increase in modeling time. It takes a lot more time to make different versions of each model, and doesn't always gain enough in frame rate to justify the artist's time.

● Basic Frame Rate/LOD Paradigms

We wily humans have figured out only two main ways to get a decent compromise between frame rate and detail in real-time 3D graphics. We know of other methods, but they have problems that prevent us from using them.

Below, we look briefly at polygonal modeling, then at 3D Sprites, and finally at some of the stranger forms of RT3D modeling.

Polygons

Understanding how polygonal modeling works is crucial to building good models. Let's start by defining some terms we'll need, then exploring the simplest geometry we can: a solid-color tetrahedron.

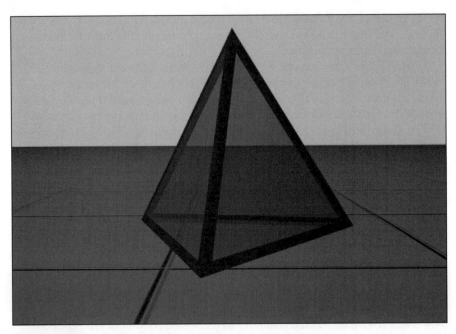

FIGURE 2.2 Tetrahedron.

Create a simple tetrahedron, save it to disk, then play with the numeric data that defines it.

1. Start 3D Studio. In the 3D Editor, choose Create/GSphere/Values, and set the slider to 4, the smallest number possible.

2. Choose the Faceted menu option and type 0 <Enter> 0 <Enter> 0 <Enter>. This sets the center of the tetrahedron at 0,0,0.

3. Type 1 <Enter> to set the radius to 1.

4. Type 0 <Enter> to set the rotation angle to 0. Accept the default object name.

You should now see a tetrahedron on your screen line the one shown in Figure 2.2.

5. Save the file to disk, in ASC format (press Control-S, choose the *.ASC button, and enter a temporary filename).

6. Choose F11 to invoke the built-in text editor and press Control-L, then open the file you just created. It should look something like this:

```
1. Ambient light color: Red=0.039216 Green=0.039216 Blue=0.039216
2.
3. Named object: "Object01"
4. Tri-mesh, Vertices: 4    Faces: 4
5. Vertex list:
```

```
 6. Vertex 0: X: 0    Y: 0    Z: 1
 7. Vertex 1: X: -0.471404   Y: -0.816497   Z: -0.333333
 8. Vertex 2: X: 0.942809   Y: -0    Z: -0.333333
 9. Vertex 3: X: -0.471404   Y: 0.816496   Z: -0.333333
10. Face list:
11. Face 0:   A:0 B:1 C:2 AB:1 BC:1 CA:1
12. Face 1:   A:0 B:2 C:3 AB:1 BC:1 CA:1
13. Face 2:   A:0 B:3 C:1 AB:1 BC:1 CA:1
14. Face 3:   A:1 B:3 C:2 AB:1 BC:1 CA:1
```

ASC files are a great way to understand how polygonal geometry is structured. Let's take a look at each line of this file.

Line 3 starts off the part of the file that defines the tetrahedron.

Line 4 is a description of the object that follows. 3D Studio's objects are all labeled "tri-mesh," so it's a bit redundant to have the name spelled out for every object; however, ASC files are designed for clarity not efficiency, so it's appropriate here.

Line 5 "Vertex list:" is the header for the first half the tetrahedron's definition. This is where the corners of the faces are defined.

Lines 6 though 9 define the vertices. Each vertex starts with a unique ID number and is followed by three real numbers that are the X, Y, and Z coordinates of the point in space.

Line 10 is the header for the second half of the definition of our tetrahedron: the face list.

Line 11 defines the first face. First, the face is given a unique number. Next, the three corners of the face are assigned to verts by listing the ID number of the vertex to which it connects.

There is some additional data on Line 11 that determines if the edges of the face are "visible." This, along with the next line, is covered later; for now, it's irrelevant.

Now, we mess with the file and observe the result:

7. Double the X value of the first vertex: On line 6, erase the number following X: and type -1. Be sure there's at least one space before and after the number.

8. Save the file (^S <Enter>), and go back to the 3D Editor (<Esc>). Load the ASC file.

   Looking in the top view, we see one corner of the tetrahedron stretched out along the X axis. Cool, huh?

9. In DOS, delete the ASC file (unless you want to save it for some reason).

Problems with ASC Files

ASC files are a convenient way to see how 3D Studio works fundamentally, but they do have some problems. These problems are pretty technical; we'll get into

those later, but for now, we can say that there are some good reasons not to use ASC files commonly.

ASC File Structure

Let's look at the reasons for the structure. Something that will stand out to people familiar with AutoCAD's DXF files is the separation of the XYZ coordinates from the faces. It may seem simpler to have the XYZ coordinates next to each face, but there are some good reasons to keep them separate.

Why are the vertices listed separately from the faces? Most importantly, for efficiency. In our example, each vertex is used by three different faces. By referring to the vertex instead of storing the XYZ coordinates three times, we save disk space and computing time, and if we save computing time, we're improving the frame rate.

Also, when we're animating, all the computer has to do is change the vertices—no need to look at the faces. From our point of view, this isn't a big deal in 3D Studio, where we can easily move either faces or vertices, but it matters inside the real-time graphics engine.

3D Sprites

3D Sprites are another conceptual method for portraying 3D graphics in real-time. Their lineage is firmly raster; originally, the term "sprite" meant a small, usually animated, bitmap with transparent edges. This kind of sprite is how almost all 2D games (for example, Pacman, Sonic, Mario) are made.

3D sprites are related in that they are also small, sometimes animated, bitmaps with transparent edges, but there is a big difference. 3D sprites represent a three-dimensional object and thus can be bumped into, seen from behind, and generally interacted with, as if they were solid.

How do you show a 3D object with 2D bitmaps? The concept is to pre-render every conceivable view of the 3D sprite so that no matter what angle the player looks at the object, there is a pre-rendered view of the object from that angle; all the computer has to do is grab the correct bitmap from its files and then show the object. In practice, there are some severe limitations, mainly due to the huge amount of memory that all these bitmaps consume.

For example, Doom's enemy characters are 3D Sprites. The player can walk behind them and see a different view of the character then from the front side.

This book does not cover 3D Sprites. For more information on them, you can read a basic article on it, accessible from the book's Web site (http://www.vectorg.com/book), or see the more detailed, illustrated December 1995 *Game Developer* magazine article on the topic. Contact the author if you are unable to find that article.

Other Methods

Other methods of portraying 3D objects in real-time are interesting, but usually they are not too useful. Let's start with a look at one of those "looming-on-the-horizon" concepts: voxels.

Voxels

Voxel: A 3D analogy to a pixel. In the same way a bitmap is a two-dimensional array of pixels, a 3D object can be defined as a three-dimensional array of tiny colored cubes. These cubes are voxels.

The concept of voxels is interesting because in a sense, it combines the power of vector-based imagery with the realism of raster images. It promises to define volumes instead of shells, and to work toward a more fundamentally accurate method of displaying an object than the "vertex/face" concept. It's much closer to a clay analogy than other methods of 3D modeling because the voxels function something like a big sticky pile of particles, in that there is something at every point in the object. Imagine working with an object that had vertices covering every bit of it—it'd be much easier to edit than a typical model.

The reason that voxels have not been used traditionally is processing power. In the worst case, storing a voxel image would use a bitmap for every "slice" of the object. For example, a 256-color, 512-voxel cube would require $512 \times 512 \times 512$ bytes, which is 134 MB. Not only must we store this, but we must manipulate it in real-time! In reality, the situation isn't that bad, and it's possible to do some cool tricks and get a reasonable voxel-based model without resorting to storing every point. Some interesting developments are in progress now; with any luck, these will turn out well, and we'll be seeing voxel-based RT3D graphics widely available soon.

Sphere-Based RT3D Modeling

On the practical-but-specialized side of the spectrum, we have something that is quite rare but very interesting. The idea is to use only spheres—no faces or anything else—to build the model.

Why spheres? Spheres have some special properties that allow a real-time graphics engine to deal with them quickly. These special properties are as follows:

- No rotation issues—Spheres look the same no matter which way we spin them; thus, our graphics engine only has to move them to the right location.

- Simplified sorting—One of the harder problems that RT3D graphics engines face is "sorting," figuring out which objects block the other ones, and intersections, when one object penetrates another. Colliding spheres are much easier to figure than other objects because all we have to do is add the radii and compare that sum to the distance from one center to the other.

- Simplified rendering—Because there are only spheres, and because they always look the same, rendering can be optimized quite a bit. It could even be hacked to simply scaling a circular, radially symmetric bitmap.

Other advantages include the simple fact that the roundness of spheres really looks refreshing, compared to the normal straight-edged RT3D world.

On the down side, not all objects in the world can be reasonably represented, or even roughly approximated, with spheres, and only radially symmetric textures can be used on the spheres.

GETTING OUR
FEET WET

Okay, Chapters 1 and 2 have given you enough background information. Let's build something already! This short chapter will walk you through the basic procedure of creating a simple real-time 3D object. You will get your hands dirty and the chapter may raise some issues that aren't fully explained. These issues will be addressed in later chapters.

● Creating a Streetlight

We start by acquiring source art—that is, we need pictures or sketches of what we're building. That's what Figure 3.1 is. Normally, we'd ask a bunch of nosy questions so we could figure out exactly what kind of model we're building, but

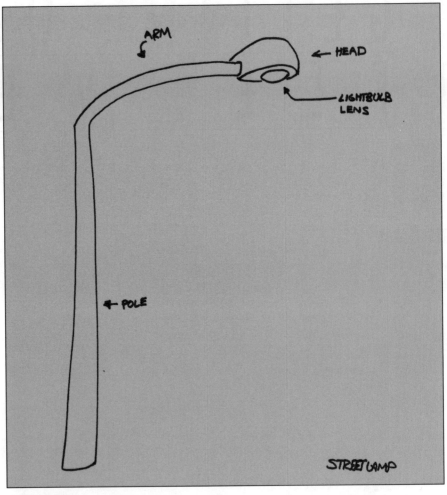

FIGURE 3.1 Sketch of the streetlight, with arm, head, and pole labeled.

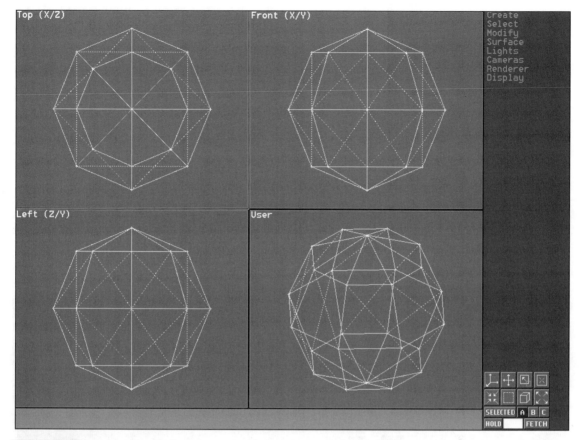

FIGURE 3.2   Creating the streetlamp (beginning).

let's assume that we just want a basic streetlamp, reasonably detailed but simple enough that we can have several in each scene. It won't use any textures, but it will have a different material for the lightbulb part.

The first modeling decision is to choose the correct starting geometry. Our streetlight has a ellipsoid head, an arm, and a simple round pole. The most complicated part of the object is the curved head, so we'll start with it.

Explore the creation of a streetlight by modifying 3D objects:

1. In 3D Studio's 3D Editor, choose Create/LSphere/Values. Set the slider to 8.

    Click in the top view and choose Create/LSphere/Smoothed. Type in
    0<Enter> 0<Enter> 0<Enter> for the center, 1.5 for the radius, and 0 for
    the rotation angle. Enter the name "SLHead" for the object's name.
    Zoom all viewports to the extents (right-click on the zoom extents icon,
    the cube). Your viewport should now look like Figure 3.2.

2. 2D Scale the object 50 percent along the Y axis. To do this, choose Modify/Object/2D Scale in the Left viewport. Change the cursor to indicate

up/down (along the Y axis) by pressing Tab. Click, then move the mouse until the percentage at the top of the screen reads 50%.

3. 2D Scale the object 70 percent along the X axis.

4. In the Left view, select bottom row of faces and assign material WHITE LIGHT to them. These faces represent the lightbulb.

5. Invert the selection (Select/Invert) and assign material GREY PLSTC to them. Invert the selection again.

6. Move the selected faces .48 meters +Y.

The purpose of this edit should make the bottom surface nearly flat, except for the lightbulb poking down a little. See Figure 3.3 for an idea of what it should look like.

7. In Top view, move the faces .28 meters -Z, making the lamp portion offset toward one end.

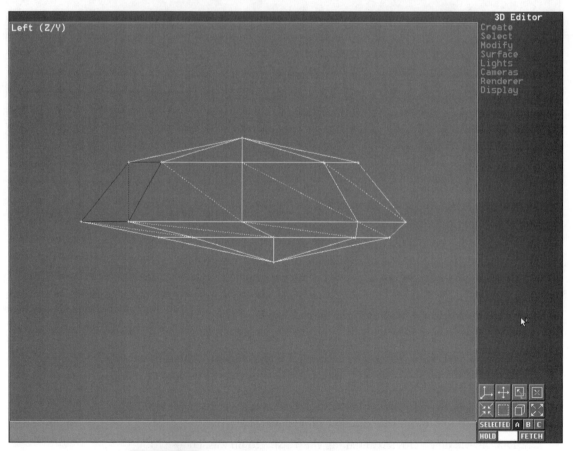

 FIGURE 3.3 Creating the streetlamp.

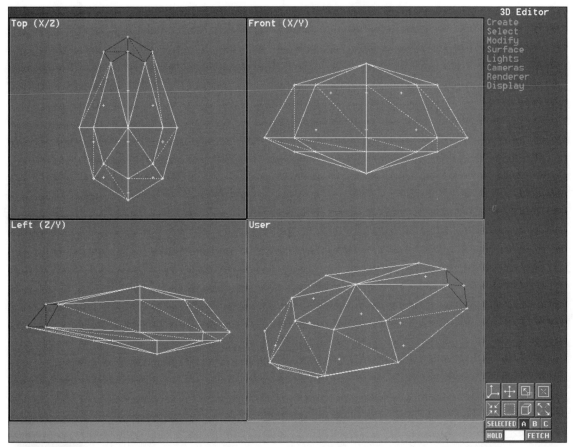

3D Editor
Create
Select
Modify
Surface
Lights
Cameras
Renderer
Display

Top (X/Z)   Front (X/Y)

Left (Z/Y)   User

SELECTED A B C
HOLD   FETCH

FIGURE 3.4   Streetlamp head, isometric view, with four faces selected.

8. Clear the selection set (Alt-N). In the Left view, choose Select/Face/ Quad/Window and draw a window around the faces marked in Figure 3.4. These are on the other end from the lightbulb; they'll be where the arm attaches to this object.

9. Turn on the local axis (click the X button) and choose Modify/Face/3D Scale. Scale the selected faces by 70 percent.

10. Move the selected faces 0.5 meters in +Z.

   Choose user view and hold down arrow keys to visualize the shape we have so far. It should look like Figure 3.5. The next step is to smash the selected faces (let's call them the cap faces) flat, which will form a smooth, flat connection point for the arm/head connection.

11. Choose Modify/Face/2D Scale. Click in the Top view, and change the icon to point up and down (in the Z-axis direction). Make sure you are

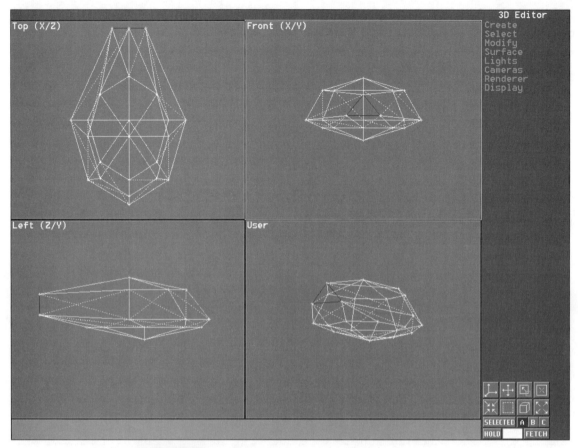

FIGURE 3.5   Streetlamp head with a single cap face.

using local coordinates (the X icon should be red) and 2D Scale the selected faces by 1 percent, three times.

Now, we're going to combine these four faces into one because we don't really need four faces for this joint. The easiest way to do this is to weld the undesired faces' verts together. This will collapse the faces, and 3D Studio then deletes these collapsed faces automatically.

12. In the front view (or user view, if it's easier), weld the top left vert to the top center vert. Weld the top right vert to the top center vert. Weld the bottom center vert to the bottom right vert.

There are three remaining verts surrounding the single selected cap face, as shown in Figure 3.5. Now, we'll make the cap face closer to an equilateral triangle.

13. 2D Scale the face in the Front view 60% along the X axis (left/right).

14. Choose Modify/Edge/Autoedge, select the object, choose 1 degree. This shows a solid edge between any two faces that are bent more than 1

degree out of plane from each other, helping you see where there are holes or bent geometry. Our object should now look like Figure 3.6.

15. In the top view, choose Create/Face/Extrude, push the space bar to use the selected cap face, and click in the top view to start the extrusion. Drag the line 10 meters and click, then choose the out extrusion direction.

When using Create/Face/Extrude, it isn't important that the extrusion line is exactly along the Z axis because 3D Studio is using only the length, not the direction, we're providing. The direction is figured out from the average of the extruded faces' normals (that is, the direction they face).

3D STUDIO HINT

PROBLEM: When we want to operate on selected faces, we turn on the "selected" button by clicking it or pressing the spacebar, then clicking in the active viewport. It's easy when you're working quickly to forget to press the spacebar, and if you click on geometry, you may modify an entity instead of a selected group. SOLUTION: Click out in space, away from any geometry, when operating on selected groups of entities. You'll get an error message if you forgot to choose "selected" first, instead of accidentally moving a single entity.

WHY USE EXTRUDE TO CREATE NEW FACES?

In these circumstances, extruding is the easiest way to generate new geometry while adding the fewest new verts. Compare what we just did to the obvious alternative: building the arm out of a new box object. If we had created a box for this connection bar, it wouldn't align perfectly with the head, so we'd have to do some editing to get it to match correctly, then we'd have to collapse the top edge of the box, weld all the connecting verts to the lamp, then delete the fully enclosed faces.

Admittedly, we have spent a little time getting the cap face all set up, but it's still faster and produces cleaner models than the alternatives. Also, there are some other small advantages; for example, the existing faces' material is automatically assigned to the new faces.

Build the pole:

1. Zoom all views to extents. In the Left view, move the cap face 3 meters down (-Y).

2. Zoom in the Top view until it mostly shows the cap face. Create a six-sided, one-segment smoothed cylinder in the top view. Click to place the center in the middle vert of the cap face. Set the radius to 0.6 meters, which should make a single side as wide as the cap face. Be sure the

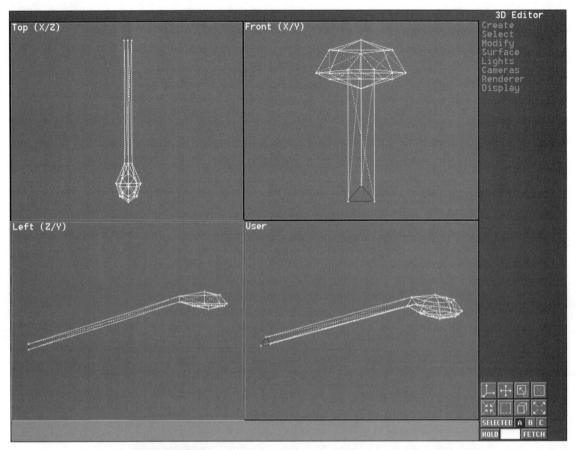

FIGURE 3.6 Head and arm, with cap face selected.

angle, shown at the top of the screen, is 0. Type 20 to set the pole's length to 20 meters. Choose the name Streetlamp01.

3. Assign material GREY PLSTC to the pole.

4. In the Left view, move the head/arm object up (+Y) so the end of the arm is slightly above the top of the pole. In the Top view, move the arm along the Z axis so it just touches the pole. Zoom the user view in to the intersection.

Our database should now look like Figure 3.7.

Now we'll attach the arm to the pole, and we'll make the arm taper a little, too. To do this, we will weld the verts on the pole and the arm together, which means we will have to make these two objects into one.

5. Choose Create/Object/Attach and click on the head/arm object, then click on the pole.

6. Weld the bottom two verts of the cap face to the nearest corresponding

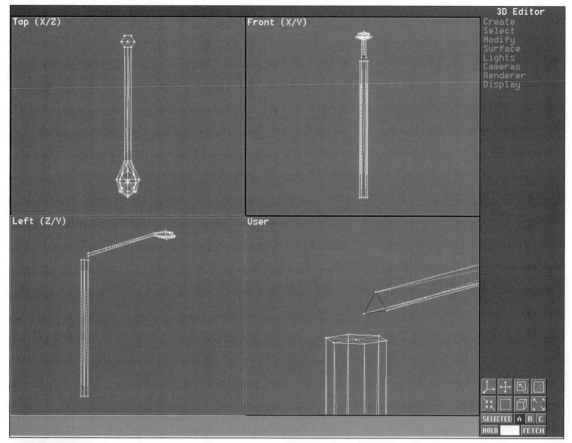

3D Editor
Create
Select
Modify
Surface
Lights
Cameras
Renderer
Display

Top (X/Z)

Front (X/Y)

Left (Z/Y)

User

SELECTED A B C
HOLD   FETCH

FIGURE 3.7   Pole and head, with intersection shown in
user view.

verts on the pole. Be sure to pick the verts in the cap face first, since we
want these to move.

7. Weld the vert at the center of the pole end (pick this one first) to the top
vert of the cap face.

Now, the cap face is completely inside the arm, so we should delete it.

8. Choose Modify/Face/Delete and delete the selected faces (after first looking to be sure only the cap face is selected).

There's also another face, using the same verts as the cap face, that used
to be part of the end of the pole, but now is completely inside. We'll
delete that one, too.

9. Redraw all the viewports. Choose Select/Face/Quad/Window and, in the
Left view, draw a window around the place where the cap face was. There

CHAPTER 3 • **Getting Our Feet Wet**   **39**

should be a face selected, in the same place as the cap face was. Be sure only that face is selected, then delete it.

10. 3D Scale the verts at the bottom of the pole by 120 percent.

11. Select everything (Alt-A) and choose Surface/Smoothing/Object/Clear All. Click on the streetlight. Choose Assign, and click on the streetlight again.

The previous step is necessary because 3D Studio automatically sets up some smoothing groups for its prefab objects like cylinders which have sharp creased edges around the ends. Because we don't want creased edges anywhere on our streetlamp, we had to remove the object from all but one smoothing group.

12. Delete the vert in the center of the bottom of the pole.

Deleting a vert also deletes all the faces that connect to it. This is danger-

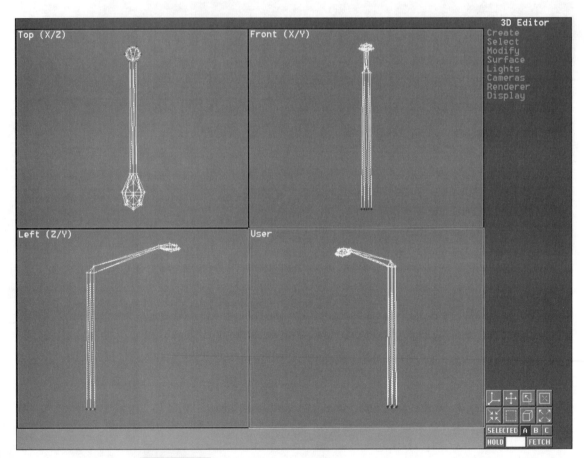

FIGURE 3.8 Finished streetlamp.

Designing 3D Graphics

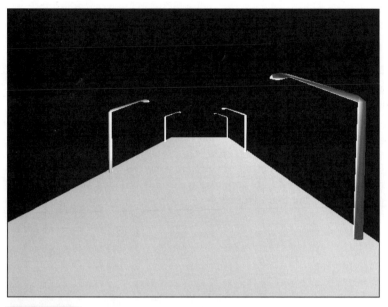

FIGURE 3.9   Rendered streetlamp scene.

ous, but useful for quickly erasing related groups of faces. In the step above, deleting the verts in the center of the cylinder neatly deletes the lid faces, leaving only the side walls. That's what we want since these faces would point toward the ground and would never be seen.

13. Zoom all viewports to extents, clear the selection set, and see that the model looks like Figure 3.8. Save the project.

Our lamp is now ready to be imported into the real-time application. Now let's build a little scene with it.

Build a scene for the real-time application:

1. Create a box from -200,-5,-30 to 200,5,30 and name it ground. Assign the BLACK PLSTC material to it.

2. Delete the verts on the bottom half of the ground, leaving only two faces.

3. In the Left view, move the streetlamp to the edge of the ground, as if it were near the curb of a street.

4. In the Top view, make a copy of the streetlamp by holding down Shift while moving it near the edge of the ground—about 150 meters +X. Make another copy on the other side (150 along -X).

5. Turn off the local axis and make a copy by rotating the original streetlight 180 degrees. This should put the new copy on the other side of the street.

6. Move this new streetlight 75 along +X, then copy it 150 meters in -X.

A Top view of this arrangement should look like a staggered array of streetlights along a short street.

7. Create a camera that looks down the street. Change the User view to the Camera view (click in it and type C).

8. Create a dim (L=100) omni light for each streetlight, placed just below each one's lightbulb.

9. Render the view, using Gouraud shading, and all rendering options turned off.

We're using this limited rendering to simulate what our scene will really look like when we load it into the RT3D application. A rendered view from the cameras should show something like Figure 3.9.

EXPLORING
3D STUDIO AS
A REAL-TIME
MODELER

In this chapter we will gain depth of knowledge about our modeling software. In it, we'll first look at different basic modeling methods we can choose to build RT3D models. Then we'll look at each of three categories of commonly used editing commands (changing, adding, and deleting) and discuss how they're used when building real-time 3D models. As promised, the specifics in this chapter all concentrate on 3D Studio, and the concepts are more generally applicable to any kind of real-time 3D modeling.

Available Building Methods

When we sit down to build an entirely new object using 3D Studio, our available methods are lofting, Boolean construction, and modifying simpler objects.

Lofting/Extrusion

Lofting means taking a 2D outline and converting it into a 3D object. There are many ways to loft in 3D Studio: extrusion, lathing, path-following, and shape-fitting. These methods are all related, and they are all limited in the type of shape they can handle. Below, we'll briefly describe each method, then talk about the limitations and common uses of lofting.

Extrusion is the simplest and most intuitive method of lofting. With *extrusion*, we simply take a 2D outline (like a star), drawn in the XZ plane, and copy it along the Y axis. The actual construction of the 3D object from these two outlines consists of building the side walls and the end caps. The side walls are created by connecting the matched vertices in each of the two outlines with faces. The end caps are made by filling in the outlines with faces.

Lathing can be thought of as extruding a short distance and rotating the outline, many times. We start with a 2D outline in the XZ plane and then rotate it around the Z axis, leaving copies every few degrees. Then we connect each copy to the next with faces, leaving us with a revolved/lathed object. For example, lathing an outline of the letter O would give us a macaroni-shaped object.

Path-following is an advanced form of extrusion in which the original outline is copied in 3D space (not necessarily along the Y axis) and scaled, rotated, or otherwise modified. The construction is done much the same as lathing: Each outline is connected to the next by faces. This is a versatile but time-consuming lofting process.

Shape-fitting is somewhat different from the other methods of lofting. With *shape-fitting* in 3D Studio, you must have three outlines that describe the top, front, and side views of the object you want to create, like a mechanical blueprint. These outlines must meet fairly strict criteria (which we'll go into later). 3D Studio will then use these outlines to create something that fits within them all—probably not the shape you need, but it can be quite close to what you want.

Inside 3D Studio, shape-fitting is really an automated form of path-following. One view (for example, the top view) is used as the 2D outline, and it lies in the XZ plane. The other two lie in the YZ and XY planes; together, they form a

Designing 3D Graphics

sort of extents "cage" that the 2D outline is scaled to fit in as it is copied up the Y axis. Once these 2D outlines exist, they are connected with faces as with the other techniques.

Limitations of Lofting

Lofting is powerful, but there are some constraints on the geometry:

- 2D outlines must be closed.
- 2D outlines cannot self-intersect.

Shape-fitting has some additional constraints:

- The Fit Shapes must be concave.
- The Fit Shapes must have a single vertex at the top and bottom.

It's worth noting that the lofting process in 3D Studio is fairly cumbersome and long. Also, though it's possible to avoid, lofting usually generates a lot of faces, not always where they are most useful.

Additionally, the results of a lofted object need editing. You will almost always spend some time cleaning up the lofted 3D object—removing extra faces, scaling and locating, and applying materials and remapping. This is often a substantial amount of time.

In general, lofting sounds like a better tool than it is; however, for some shapes, especially complicated organic forms that aren't on a very tight polygon budget, there is no better tool than lofting.

Boolean Construction

Boolean construction is based on the concept of CSG (Constructive Solid Geometry), in which mathematical cubes, spheres, and other simple geometrical solid shapes are added together or subtracted from each other until the desired shape is reached.

Boolean construction is available in 3D Studio (under Create/Object/ Boolean), and in some ways, it is greatly extended because it allows us to combine *any* kind of object, not just simple cubes and such.

The problems come because Boolean operations reliably work only with solid geometry, not hollow objects made out of faces. Every object in 3D Studio is made from faces only, which form thin-walled structures; there's nothing solid inside. What 3D Studio does when we ask it to "Boolean" objects is to attempt to simulate solid objects. This works surprisingly well, but it's far from perfect.

Boolean operations have other problems for real-time modelers. Face count can quickly increase because the Boolean construction must make new faces. Also, some rendering engines can't deal with the very long, thin faces that Boolean constructions often have.

Problems notwithstanding, Boolean operations in 3D Studio are tremendously powerful and time-saving for certain situations. They allow us to compose objects from either simple geometry, like cubes, or any two airtight objects.

How to Make Objects that Boolean Well

The secret to successful Boolean operation is the concept of "air-tight". If both objects are air-tight, Boolean operations generally work well.

Air-tight: An object whose faces form a single surface, uninterrupted by holes or breaks. This usually means that all the faces' edges are shared with only one other face, and faces share vertices with all their neighbors. Imagine that the object must be able to hold air like a balloon, and it can't have walls inside this volume (as clumps of soap bubbles do).

Not only do air-tight objects do well with Boolean operations, but they also sort well (a complicated issue that is more fully covered later), and generally, they avoid a lot of strange rendering problems that can arise.

How Do We Make an Object Air-Tight?

Unfortunately, keeping geometry air-tight is not easy. It means we can't use any intersections that aren't fully welded and sealed. Thin, one-sided protrusions like a one-face airplane wing are generally confusing to 3D Studio, because they don't define any volume.

Using extrusions to create new geometry goes a long way to helping keep our objects air-tight because, generally, it's hard to join two different objects manually and keep the resulting combination air-tight. For an example of how to do this correctly, see the streetlamp exercise in Chapter 3. When the cylinder pole is attached to the arm, it is welded all the way around, then the internal faces are deleted, leaving an air-tight seal where once there were two objects.

If possible, building models with Boolean operations in mind is a good practice. This way we can first build air-tight models, then do the Boolean operation, then add on the areas that are likely to be a problem.

Many of the models that are created in this book are air-tight, including the streetlamp model in Chapter 3.

When Should Boolean Construction Be Used?

For example, imagine you have made a complex volume like a space ship's hull without modeling the inside, only to find out that you'll have to show the inside after all. To create a concave surface that parallels the outer hull is very difficult with standard modeling methods; however, if you can make your model survive a Boolean operation (that is, if you have made it air-tight), you can simply copy it, scale it down, and use the Boolean subtract operation to carve out an interior.

Using Boolean Operations to Find Intersections

Booleans allow us to find intersections between objects. This is very useful for making one face rest in the middle of another face perfectly.

For example, imagine we're modeling a WWII fighter plane like a Zero, and we have a compound-curve airplane wing that intersects the fuselage (the main body of the plane). We want the wing to meet the airplane's fuselage perfectly—not penetrating, and with no gaps.

If our objects were air-tight, we could probably just Boolean-union the two, but imagine we can't use Boolean because our fuselage isn't anywhere near air-tight. When we tried using Boolean construction, the resulting object was a horrible mess (luckily, we had a backup!). Here's how we do this:

1. Create copies of the two objects.

2. Do a Boolean intersection from these copies, with the usual horribly messy results.

3. Delete almost everything from this new object, saving only the verts that define the intersection points we want. These points probably should correspond to the verts on the wing that we are going to move.

4. Align the original verts on the wing to these construction points. We do this using the Modify/Origin/Align/Vertex command to move the axis to the construction point. Then we use Modify/Vertex/3D Scale with the local axis turned off to move the wing's vertex to the construction point.

5. We repeat this for each vertex (yeah, it could definitely take a while!) and then we can clean up—perhaps delete any of the wing's faces that are fully inside the fuselage, weld the verts along the fuselage if we want to avoid T-intersections.

Modifying 3D Objects

This method of modeling consists of starting with simple objects such as spheres and using edit commands to mold them until they form the shape we want. This method of building is the least dependent on converting 2D shapes into 3D—it's all native 3D objects and edits. It's the most time-intensive method of modeling, and it requires a deep understanding of the modeling tools, but it allows us the most low-level control.

The streetlight exercise in Chapter 3 is a simple example of this method.

Using this method feels something like a cross between working with clay and building objects out of cardboard (except the interface is much less intuitive!). With a little creativity we can make just about anything from simple objects like spheres and cubes. The final object rarely resembles the source object, of course.

This is the basic method that many professional real-time 3D modelers use when building in 3D Studio, and it's the one we'll concentrate on in this book.

Problems

Most problems with this method of construction have to do with the large amount of time it takes to build geometry "by hand" and with keeping in touch with your model—really, truly understanding exactly what you are doing.

The first problem doesn't require much explanation: It just takes a lot of time to click your way through 3D Studio menus, make edits, save your intermediate models, and generally do all the steps you need to do. The speed of the computer isn't usually the problem either. The solution, once we learn our modeling tools thoroughly, is provide (loud!) feedback to the tool makers so they improve them in ways that matter to us.

The second problem is easy to describe and hard to achieve: mastery of your modeling tools. This can be divided into knowing what each editing command does (and doesn't do) and visualizing—having a full understanding of what you are seeing when working in 3D Studio's wireframe.

We'll work on both of these areas, beginning with the editing commands.

 # 3D Editing

Now we'll explore the editing commands that are most commonly used when modeling for RT3D in 3D Studio. The purpose here is partially to explain syntax and basic usage for the commands, but mainly we will learn how these very important commands are used in day-to-day life when building real-time 3D models.

The commands under the Modify menu in the 3D Editor are the most commonly used options in normal 3D Studio modeling. Though these commands are designed to change existing geometry, we frequently use them to create new objects (by holding down the Shift key during editing), making them more versatile than the menu title suggests.

Basic Issues for All Modify/... Commands

The following issues are factors, sometimes hidden, for almost all of the editing commands in the Modify/... menu tree.

Modify/Vertex/... versus Modify/Element/...

Anyone who's poked through the Modify menu in 3D Studio probably noticed the repetition of many editing commands under the Vertex, Element, Face, and Object submenus. Why is 3D Studio organized this way?

The reason is convenience. If we move all the verts in an object or move the object itself, the result is the same, but choosing an object with one click is more convenient than having to carefully select all the verts in that object.

There are some exceptions, but usually the Modify editing commands work the same whether you're operating on faces, verts, or objects. Because all entities ultimately depend on vertices' XYZ coordinates, we can think of the other menu trees as convenient ways to select the vertices we wish to change. Thus, in the discussions that follow, we'll refer to editing commands affecting vertices, but they usually apply to the other entities as well.

Elements and edges are "virtual" objects; they're not stored in the database and 3D Studio handles them fairly differently, despite the fact that they look like peers to faces and objects, judging by the menu structure. There's more about this important difference in Chapter 3.

Local versus Global Origin

Almost every editing command gives very different results depending on whether we've got the origin set at local or global. When the origin is set to

Designing 3D Graphics

local (that is, when the X icon in the lower right is turned on), the editing command uses a point near the center of the verts.

Note "near the center" in the sentence above. We expect the local axis to be at the true center of the object—an average of all the vertices in the object. This is not what we get! The following exercise demonstrates this problem, then shows how to work around it.

Demonstrate the local origin point's location:

1. In 3D Studio's 3D Editor, choose Create/Cylinder/Values. Choose minimum values—three sides, one segment.

2. Choose Faceted and type 1<Enter> 6<Enter> 7<Enter> to place the cylinder base at an arbitrary point in space. Enter a radius of 10, angle of 0, and a length of 10. Use the default name.

3. Zoom all views to extents by right-clicking on the zoom extents icon. Choose Display/Geometry/All Lines. Choose Display/Geometry/Backface. Your view should now look like Figure 4.1.

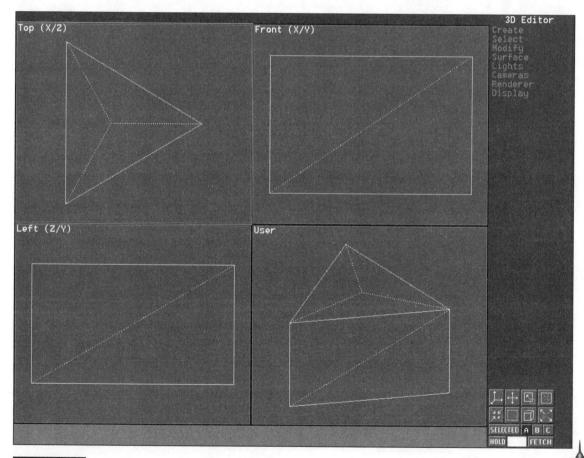

FIGURE 4.1 Basic three-sided cylinder.

The true center of the cylinder is clearly visible in the top view—it's where all the dotted lines connect.

4. Turn on the local coordinate button, if it's not already on.

5. Choose Modify/Object/Rotate. In the Top view, hold down the Shift key and click on the cylinder, then rotate the maximum distance (180 degrees) clockwise. Your screen should now look like Figure 4.2.

Notice that the center point of the new cylinder does not meet the center of the old. That's because 3D Studio did not average the XYZ coordinates of the object's verts to find the local coordinate center point; instead, it used the cruder method of finding the center point of the rectilinear box that the verts fit in.

For rectangular objects this method works perfectly, but for almost any other type of object, it does not find the true center of the object. Not only

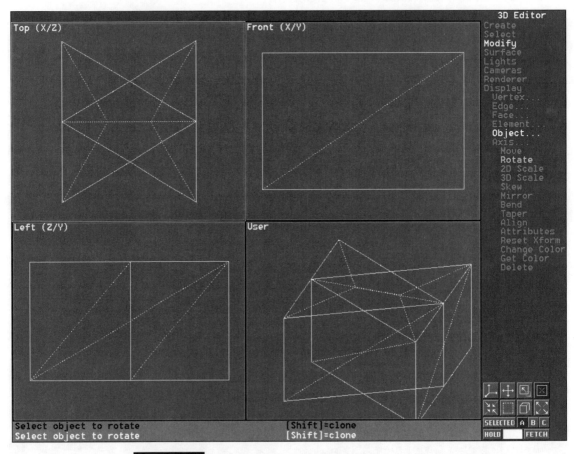

 FIGURE 4.2   Cylinder's local axis is not at true center.

Designing 3D Graphics

does the resulting "center" point miss the true center of the object, but it doesn't always find the same spot! Because the bounding box, and thus our "center" point, is calculated when we click to start the rotation, our "center" point depends on the orientation of the object in the active view. If either the view or the object has moved, we get a different "center" point.

Next, we'll explore the workaround. To get the object to rotate around its true center, we'll have to find the true center, move the global origin there, and rotate around that.

Finding the true center is the hardest part. There is no handy command in 3D Studio that allows you to do this. If it's critical, we can write the object out in .ASC and actually average the X, Y, and Z coordinates to obtain the center point, but this is usually far too much trouble. Usually, we get by with simply guesstimating a point, but luckily we have an existing vertex at the center of our cylinder. (This happy accident frequently occurs when modeling.)

6. Choose Display/Hide/Object and click on the second, newer cylinder. Type ~ to redraw all viewports.

7. Choose Modify/Axis/Align/Vertex, then choose the vertex at the true center.

8. Turn off local coordinates.

9. Choose Modify/Object/Rotate, hold down Shift and click on the cylinder. Rotate it 180 degrees.

10. Zoom all viewports to extents. Your screen should now look like Figure 4.3.

Breakdown of Common Editing Commands

Now we'll explore the commonly used editing commands in 3D Studio.

Bending

Bending (Modify/.../Bend) is a fun, easy, intuitive, and useful command that distorts a group of vertices in a manner like a tree bending in the wind. Note that bending is non-reversible: If we bend an object 15 degrees left, then bend it back 15 degrees right, it will not be the same. Bending an object back and forth can be a useful way to add bulges to it.

Scaling

Scaling (Modify/.../3D Scale) operates exactly as we'd expect: It uniformly changes the size of the entity we're editing without changing any of the proportions. This is different from 2D Scaling. Because it's a true 3D command, it doesn't matter what viewport we're working in when we do it (unlike almost every other editing command in 3D Studio).

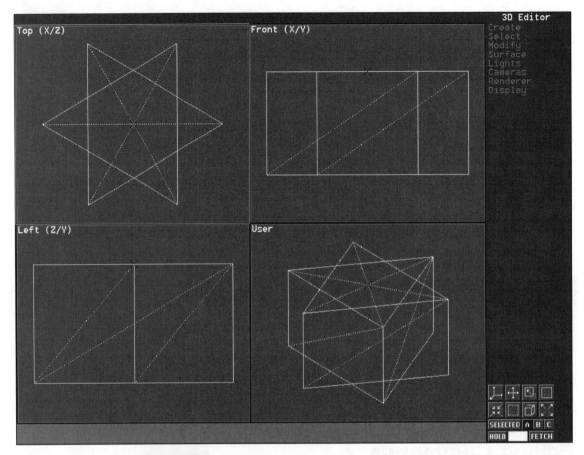

FIGURE 4.3   Cylinders rotated around true center.

Distorting (2D Scaling)

The command Modify/.../2D Scale is very powerful but is badly misnamed in 3D Studio: It has almost nothing to do with what most people think of as "scaling." 2D Scale is really a distorting command—it allows us to stretch our verts along one or two axes.

It's important to understand that 2D Scale will always change the proportions (aspect) of the 3D object, unlike 3D Scale. It can change only two of the three axes, which means one axis, at least, does not change when we're 2D scaling.

Once we realize what 2D Scale really does, we can go on to explore its power. It can be used for a variety of purposes, including some tricky but very useful ones. Let's take a look at some examples.

A basic use of the 2D Scale command would be to lengthen a pipe or stretch a boat's hull to be a little longer. To do this, we select the object and choose Modify/Object/2D Scale, with "selected" on. Then we click in the appropriate viewport and use Tab to select only the direction in which we want to change our object. Once we click, the square bounding box appears and we can stretch it interactively.

52   Designing 3D Graphics

One of the less obvious but most useful techniques is aligning two objects that must meet along a plane. This is a solution to a common problem in 3D Studio—frequently we have a building that must precisely meet the sidewalk, or a pipe that should end exactly at a spigot, and there is no easy way to make the two objects connect exactly.

Align a set of vertices to a plane:

1. In the Front view, create two cylinders, and then in the Top view, move them so their ends don't line up evenly.

   Our goal is to align the ends of these two cylinders.

2. Select the verts that constitute the ends that we wish to align, as shown in Figure 4.4.

3. Choose Modify/Vertex/2D Scale and click on the local axis button (if it's not already on).

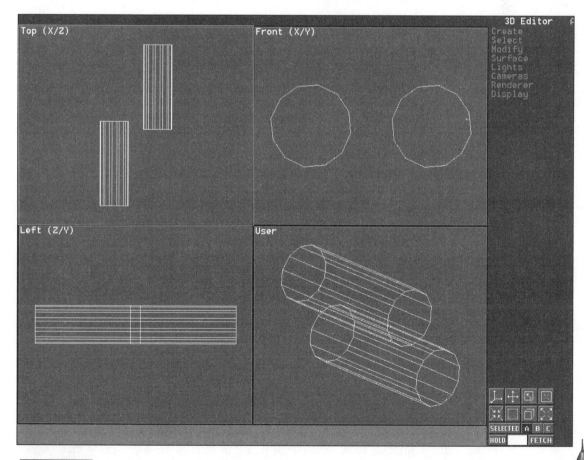

FIGURE 4.4   Unaligned cylinders.

4. Press Tab to rotate the cursor's icon to point parallel with the cylinders, choose Selected, and click. Move the mouse until the box containing the verts collapses. The header bar should say "Selected Scale 1%," which is the smallest we can make it.

5. Make the Top view fill the screen and zoom in until part of both cylinders is on the screen. Press Alt-W to get a crosshair cursor and use it to measure the gap between the two ends of the cylinder.

Notice that because we scaled the distance to 1 percent, we did not fully get rid of the difference; we just made it very small (100 times smaller than it was, to be precise). We must repeat this step until the difference becomes so tiny that it is lost altogether—usually this takes at least three rounds of scaling.

6. Right-click to cancel the Alt-W selection. Repeat the 2D Scale command until the gap disappears.

That's it—the two objects are now aligned. This technique can be made more versatile by placing the local axis on the plane on which we wish to have the objects converge. If the plane is not orthogonal, we can use this technique in the User view, but not for every case.

Which cases won't work? Because the Y axis is always vertical in the User view, we can do this only if we can arrange our geometry. Note that our trick requires that the direction to compress is horizontal or vertical (so we can use the Tab key to reduce the edit to one axis), and because the Y axis is kind of fixed, we may not be able to arrange our geometry correctly. Still, most situations can be handled well.

Edge Turning

The Modify/Edge/Turn command in 3D Studio allows us to make a very specific edit that is surprisingly useful. It's also extremely easy to damage our model with this command. This command works only with shared edges; we will get an error message if we try to turn an unshared edge. If you don't understand edges thoroughly, be sure to read the section in Chapter 3 and work through 3D Studio's information about them.

Imagine four verts in the square pattern. We create two faces that form the square surface and these faces share a diagonal edge. Now imagine that we want to change the diagonal so it runs the other way. How do we do it? With Modify/Edge/Turn, of course!

Modify/Edge/Turn is one of the few edit commands that is insensitive to the active viewpoint—it doesn't matter which viewpoint we click in when we turn the edge; the edge turns the same in any case. It's a strange edit command; when we click, we just point at a certain edge, and 3D Studio does the rest.

Why on earth would we care which way the diagonal runs? Modify/Edge/Turn is actually a powerful edit command; there are lots of time we want to be able to do this. To understand the power of turning the edge, let's work though a short demonstration.

We will erase all the faces of a sphere except for a single slice, modify the slice using Edge/Turn, and then use the Array command to re-create the sphere from the single slice. Though it might be faster to perform the Edge/Turn modification to each side of the original sphere, it is easy to make mistakes and difficult to see what we're doing; this way, we can clearly see the modification we have done.

Quickly create unusual shapes from simple geometry, without adding any faces:

1. In 3D Studio, Choose Create/LSphere/Values. Set the slider to 8. Choose Create/LSphere/Faceted and type 0<Enter> 0<Enter> 0<Enter> for the center, set the radius to 10, and set the angle to 0. Give the object a memorable name, like "Sphere." Zoom all views to extents.

2. Choose Modify/Face. Type Alt-W, and in the top view, drag a box around the faces that compose the slice of the sphere at 2 o'clock. This will select the faces, along with some from the neighboring slice. Remove these by holding down Alt as we drag a box around them. The result should look like Figure 4.5.

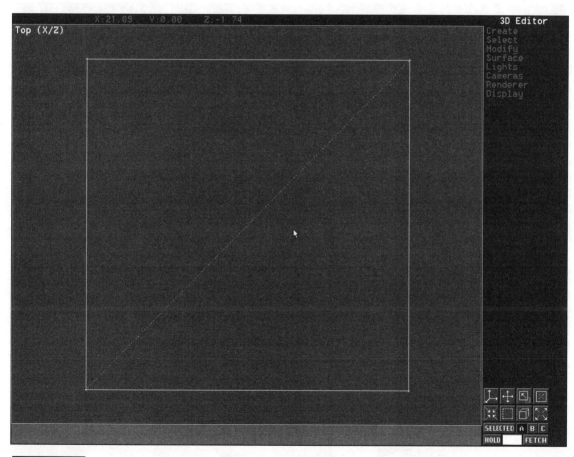

FIGURE 4.5   All but slice selected.

3. Choose Select/Invert, then choose Modify/Face/Delete, press the space bar to choose the selected faces, and click. Answer "yes" to the question about deleting isolated verts. Type Alt-N to clear the selection set.

We're now left with a single slice of the sphere. The screen looks like Figure 4.6.

It's important to understand the geometry we have so far, though it's not too complicated or subtle. Take a minute to examine it carefully if it's not obvious how it works. Click in the User view and hold down the arrow keys to animate it. We should agree that we have a slice of "skin" of a sphere, like the peel from a slice of orange. There are three lines of latitude, the center one being what we'll call the equator.

4. Choose Modify/Edge/Turn. In the Left view, click on the equator. It will become a long diagonal line.

Take this opportunity to examine the new geometry carefully by rotating the

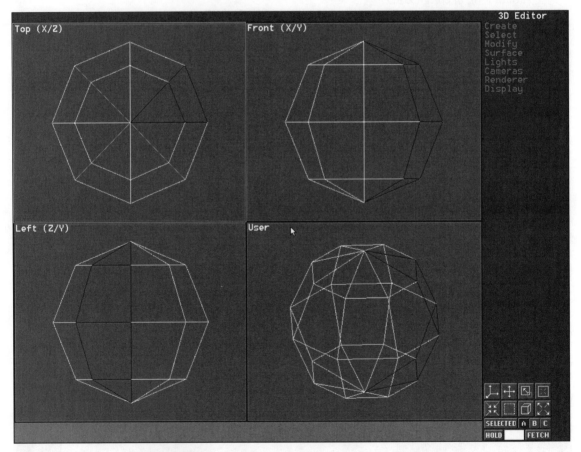

 FIGURE 4.6   One slice of sphere.

User view with the arrow keys again. A diagonal cut into the surface of the sphere, like a canyon, has been formed.

This is a very important point: We've changed the actual shape of the surface just by turning an edge.

5. Click in the Top view and choose Create/Array/Radial. Pick the object.

6. In the resulting Radial Array dialog, set the following values: total number in array: 8, Arc Length: 360. Select the Arc Length button. Make sure Rotate Objects is selected. Click OK.

The Array command creates a bunch of separate objects, which, in turn, create lots of unnecessary verts. Our final step is to join all the faces into a single object and weld the coincident verts.

7. Type Alt-A to select all faces, then choose Create/Face/Detach. Choose the selected faces, and assign a name, like "NewSphere."

8. Type Alt-A to select everything again. Choose Modify/Vertex/Weld, choose the selected verts, and click OK on the warning dialog.

That's it! Admire your handiwork (shown in Figure 4.7) by spinning the User view. Notice that the surface of the sphere is quite different from that of a normal sphere, all from that single edge swap.

Face Addition Operations

These commands deal with methods of creating new faces. Many of these commands can be used to build new objects as well as add on to existing ones. In general, adding faces to an existing object is usually a difficult thing to do because there must be vertices before there can be faces, and adding vertices means messing up mapping and is often difficult and laborious. Therefore, if we're trying to hand-build a fairly complicated new piece onto an existing object, it might be easier to redo the existing object entirely than to try to tack on new faces one by one.

Extrusion

Extrusion (Create/Face/Extrude) is the process of using an existing group of faces as a kind of "die," a silhouette-type outline of holes. Though it sounds (and conceptually it is) similar to the 2D Lofter, this command is quite different in practice. See the streetlight exercise in Chapter 3 for an example of how to use extrusion to create entirely new geometry.

Edge Dividing

Edge division is a simple, easy-to-understand method of adding verts and faces to an existing object. To create new faces with Modify/Edge/Divide, simply click on an existing edge. It is immediately split in half: A new vert is added in the middle, and the faces that shared the old edge are replaced with faces that con-

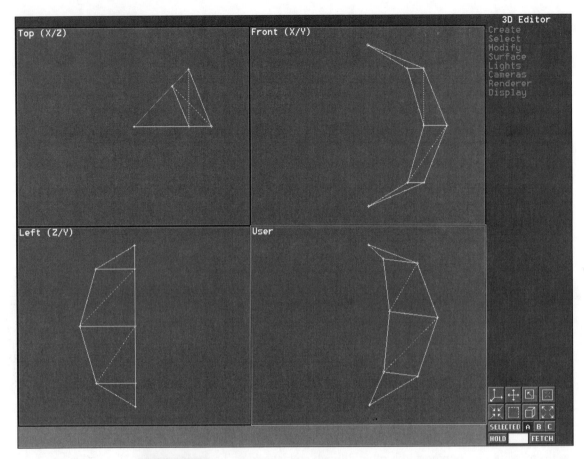

3D Editor
Create
Select
Modify
Surface
Lights
Cameras
Renderer
Display

Top (X/Z)

Front (X/Y)

Left (Z/Y)

User

SELECTED A B C
HOLD   FETCH

FIGURE 4.7   Modified sphere.

nect to the new vert. This means that new faces have been added because there are more verts to be connected now. This technique is described specifically in the chair exercise in Chapter 8, but it's used in most exercises in the book.

Any edge—shared or unshared—can be divided. If we divide an unshared edge, only one new face is generated. We can use edge division as a crude debugging tool: If an edge appears to be shared but only one new face is generated when we divide the edge, then we know that the edge was *not* shared, which might indicate a problem in the model. (Of course, it's a good idea to save before using this destructive method of testing, so we can restore the undivided model once we figure out the problem.)

Tessellation

What is tessellation? This beautiful word means subdividing a face. Here's exactly what it does: It takes a face, puts a vert in the middle, and replaces the face with three new ones, all of which connect to two of the original face's verts as well as the new middle vert.

Tessellation versus Edge Division

Tessellation and edge division are very similar conceptually, but there are some differences that are well worth understanding.

Dividing edges gives us one or two new faces for every new vert, which is less than the three new faces for each new vert that tessellation gives. In most cases, to add new faces and verts in roughly the same numbers, we should use edge division. This is not always true, though.

Figure 4.8 shows a comparison of tessellation to edge division. The circle on the left is the original, unmodified object with 13 verts and 12 faces. The circle to its right has had a single face tessellated, which added two faces and one vert. Below it, the circle has had all its faces tessellated, yielding 25 verts and 36 faces. Compare this to the circle to its right, which had all its shared edges divided. It has the same count: 25 verts, 36 faces. Above it is the original with only one edge divided.

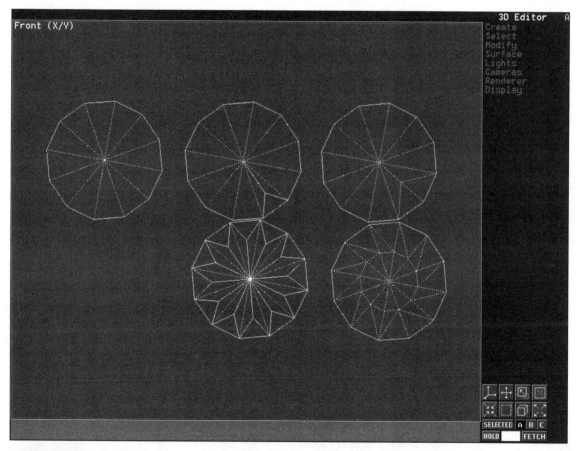

FIGURE 4.8   Tessellation compared to edge division.

There are more edges than faces in any 3D model; by dividing edges, we have more flexibility as to where the division occurs. This is important because we can't dictate where the new vert is placed on the edge or face—it's always placed in the middle. Of course, we can always move the vert, but we often want to keep the vert on the plane of the existing geometry, and it's inconvenient to move a vert while doing that. (To do it, we align the User view with the plane, then move the vert only in the User view).

The most important difference between edge division and tessellation is the isolation of the changed geometry. When we divide an edge, the faces that share the edge are split in half; in this way, edge division impacts the surrounding geometry. Tessellation, by contrast, affects only a single face; no surrounding face is disturbed. This is somewhat apparent in Figure 4.8, but it's much more obvious when we use it in day-to-day work.

Tessellation may seem be the preferred tool because it disturbs less, but we often *want* to affect the surrounding geometry, so edge division usually is more useful. Both are good tools, however, and are useful for their own purposes.

Boolean Operations

Boolean operations are really separate category of edits, but technically they are a way to add to an existing object, so they are mentioned here for completeness. Boolean operations can be quite powerful and useful for adding to an object, if the object is of the right type. See the section earlier in this chapter for more information on Boolean operations.

Manual Construction

The "last resort" for creating new geometry is the most obvious and most labor-intensive: manual construction. This means creating new verts, usually one by one, and then using Create/Face/Build and clicking on three verts at a time. Both steps are tedious and error-prone, and mapping and materials must always be applied to the new faces.

If we find ourselves in a situation requiring lots of manual construction of faces, it's a sign of trouble—we'll consider rebuilding with a different approach if at all possible. On the other hand, at times using Create/Face/Build is the only way to do what we must do, and it is the right tool. Several exercises in this book use manual construction, but only in limited amounts.

Fortunately, we rarely need to do this—as we've seen, other methods of adding faces are plentiful.

Face Reduction Operations

Face reduction is a very basic step in real-time 3D modeling. These operations remove faces from an existing model in a variety of ways, but there are two broad classes of operations.

The first kind is pretty savage—it simply leaves a hole where the faces used to exist. This is usually not desirable (so much for air-tight!), but sometimes it's

just the right tool. Specifically, all the Delete menu items (Modify/.../Delete) are this type.

The second class stretches the surrounding geometry to close up the hole. Though this can cause a distortion or inaccuracy in the model (depending on the shape of the deleted faces), it's usually better than leaving a hole. Modify/Vertex/Weld is this type, as is Modify/Face/Collapse.

Welding

Deleting verts by welding is the easiest, most intuitive method. Figure 4.9 shows an example of this.

When one vertex (vert A) is welded to another (vert B), the user simply clicks on vert A, then drags it to vert B. Vert A is then deleted, leaving vert B. But what happens to all the faces that were connected to vert A?

All faces that refer to vert A are transferred to vert B. If a face happens to refer to both A and B (as well as one other vert), the weld operation described

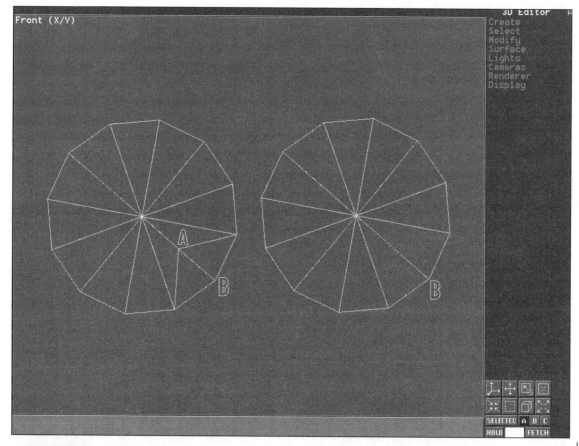

previously would cause it to become a line, so 3D Studio deletes this invalid face automatically. That's what happened to the two faces that shared edge AB.

Welding has one potential problem: the mapping coordinates. If two verts have different coordinates, then one set is lost when the verts are welded together, and all the faces will now have a new set of mapping coordinates (in the illustration, vert B will supply the changed faces with their mapping coordinates because vert A is gone). Though it doesn't always happen, this can easily result in mapping problems, so it's important to do welding *before* mapping if at all possible.

Another problem with welding is a 3D Studio UI problem. We must click precisely on the second vert, which is annoying enough. On top of that, our cursor disappears! All we have is the face's edges, which disappear at the end when they overdraw each other. Welding a large hole can take a lot of time, and unfortunately sometimes it's our only way of solving a problem.

An only slightly related use of Modify/Vertex/Weld is for combining verts at the same XYZ point (or within a certain tolerance distance).

"Tolerancing": welding all nearby verts:

1. Decide the tolerance distance. How far away should the two verts be? Usually this amount is one-half of the closest two verts in the model, but it can be any amount. In fact, by setting this number large, it can be used as a crude alternative to the Optimize command—it will collapse anything small. To envision how this works, picture a sphere, with the tolerance as its diameter, around each vert. Any other vert within the sphere will get welded.

2. Set the tolerance in the Weld Threshold box in the System Options dialog (from the Info menu at the top of the screen).

3. Once this is set, we select the verts to check (use Alt-A to select them all).

4. Choose Modify/Vertex/Weld and click with Selected on. Click OK to the mapping warning dialog.

After a second, the deed is done. Like the other use of welding, this one can really damage mapping coordinates; it is best used *before* mapping, if possible.

Mass-Deleting Faces

Now let's look at our options for deleting large numbers of faces.

Face Collapsing

Modify/Face/Collapse removes a single face and the three verts it connects to, adds a new vert at the old face's center, and stretches any surrounding geometry to connect to this new vert, thus filling in the hole.

Because face collapsing removes three verts and affects all faces that connect to those verts, this command really changes things fast. It's a sledge hammer—used rarely, and with caution—but it can really clean up a complicated mesh, fast!

Modify/Vertex/Delete

This command deletes a single vertex along with any face that refers to it, leaving holes. It's simple to use and good for quickly but precisely making holes in existing objects or for purging large areas by hand. When used with selected groups of verts, it can quickly delete vast quantities of faces.

This method is superior to deleting the faces themselves because it doesn't leave the unused verts behind. On the other hand, it doesn't work for deleting a single face. Use Modify/Face/Delete for that.

Modify/Element/Delete

As Chapter 2 covered, elements and edges are really different from verts, faces, and objects. Deleting an element is just a shortcut to deleting all the verts that constitute the element, and though it's a useful command on occasion, using Select/Element, then Modify/Vertex/Delete is usually safer because you can see what you're about to delete with that method.

Modify/Edge/Delete

Deleting an edge causes the face(s) that use it to be deleted, leaving a hole. No verts are affected. This command can be handy because edges are easier to select than faces, and it can be quite speedy to use. The downside is that edges must be picked one by one; there is no way to select a group of edges. Thus, this method is not usually used to delete vast areas of geometry.

ADVANCED TOOL STUDIES

This chapter covers some strangely behaving areas that we have to maneuver around when real-time 3D modeling. We'll examine several different areas that need to be explored and understood: visualizing wireframe objects in 3D Studio, using backups as editing tools, understanding edges, and comparing 2D editing commands to 3D ones.

 # Prologue

It is true that 3D Studio was not designed to be used for building real-time models, and that explains why these problems exist. Even very expensive tools that are custom-built for real-time 3D models have some of the problems listed here. A lot of the difficulty is inherent.

 # Backing Up While Working

Backing up is usually seen as an annoying chore that really is worth the time, but few people are actually doing it. Long-time computer users all accidentally lose valuable data sooner or later, and that's when they realize the power of backups.

However, in 3D Studio, backups are more than just accident prevention. Because 3D Studio V4 and earlier doesn't have undo capability, we can use regular backups as a part of the modeling process.

Basic Backups

The basic backup principal is like checkmating with two castles: Each time we make a change, we have at least one copy of the previous version to revert to. This frees us to try dangerous operations (like massive Boolean merges) with the assurance that we can simply throw out the changes if we make errors.

More Than One Backup = Multiple Undo

Going beyond that, we can save into a *different* file for each backup. We're fortunate that we can do this because our files consume so little disk space. Many 3DS users building pre-rendered objects would quickly fill up their disk with backups.

When we build a house, for example, each time we make a major change, we save a new project file. At the end we have 15 files: HOUSE01.PRJ— HOUSE 15.PRJ. Now, let's say the client comes back later and needs major revisions done. Because we have all these backups, we're able to go back to any of 15 points in the construction process and resume modeling with a minimal amount of wasted effort.

● Visualization

One of the hardest things about using 3D Studio is understanding what's on the screen when the geometry gets complicated. This section will describe some ways to better understand what we're seeing when we have four viewports of wireframe to comprehend.

Visualization Exercise 1

Our goal with this exercise is to gain a basic understanding of the wireframe views by experimenting with simple objects.

Build two simple objects:

1. Create a cube from 0,0,0 to 1,1,1.

2. Create a second cube from .5, .5, .5 to 1.5, 1.5, 1.5.

3. Change the second cube's color to yellow (Modify/Object/Change Color, choose #17).

The screen should now look like Figure 5.1.

We can see that the two cubes apparently cross, but there is no way to know if they truly intersect by looking at only one viewpoint.

For example, if we look at the top viewport only, we see two squares overlapping. How do we know where they are along the Y axis, which isn't shown in that view? The squares could be miles apart from each other in only the Y axis, and we would not be able to tell. Let's prove it.

Press Hold and move the second cube 100 units along Y and redraw all viewports.

Notice that that top view did not change at all. That's why we need more than one viewport: When we look at the top view and the side view together, we can see movement on any of the three axes.

Theoretically, that's all we need to understand all the geometry we build, but in reality, it's extremely confusing and difficult to visualize with only two orthographic viewports. Three is tolerable, and 3D Studio's default setup, top/front/side, plus a User view, is pretty good for most circumstances.

Isometric versus Perspective

Now we'll take a closer look at the User view. It's obviously different from the others. It shows an isometric projection; this means that it's not a top, front, or side view, but it's not a true perspective view either.

Every view has a "blind" direction like this: for the Left view, it's the X axis; for the Front view, the Z axis is not visible. It's not a coincidence that this "blind" axis is the one that is perpendicular to the view's defining surface (that is, normal to the plane).

Why can we have this limitation? It's the nature of our display device. It can show only two axes at once—length and height. The different viewports let us

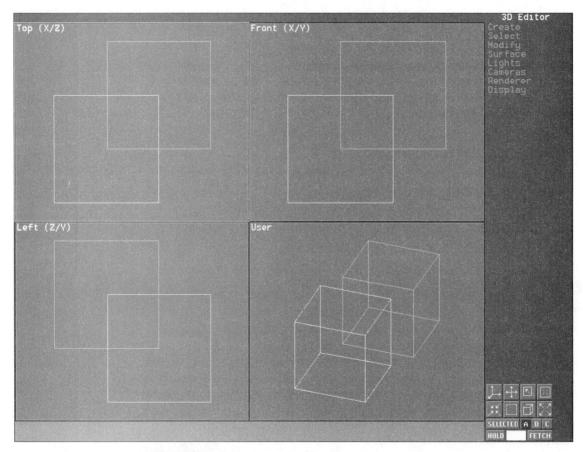

FIGURE 5.1 Two cubes.

WHAT IS "ISOMETRIC"?

The difference between a User view and a true perspective view is that the User view is defined by a plane in space; there is no single camera point. The main result of this is that objects that are far away don't get smaller, as they do for cameras (and our eyes). Thus, we can't judge distance along the line normal to the User view's plane.

Let's expand on that last sentence a little. All views except camera views in 3D Studio are represented by a plane in space (and a zoom factor, but we can ignore that for now). For the top view, the plane is parallel to the XZ plane. As we explored earlier, that means that the Y axis is not represented at all; any changes that happen along the Y axis aren't visible in the top view.

assign the length and height to various 3D axes, but it's up to us viewers to assimilate that collection of 2D views into a 3D object in our heads.

So what is the normal (the "blind direction") for the User view? It doesn't usually align neatly with any of the origin's planes as the other viewports do, so that makes it difficult to figure. The User view does have a normal, though, and as the other viewports, it points away from its plane.

See the normal in User view:

1. Create a medium-sized box (Create/Object/Box) in the User view using mouse clicks. Use any size and name.

   Take a look at the box we just made in the other viewports. Its orientation is the same as the current User view, and its thickness is impossible to see in the User view. Thus, the direction of the thickness is the User view's normal.

2. Press Fetch to restore the intersecting cubes.

   Take a look at the cubes again, and think about the blind direction. Looking at only the User view, can you imagine the cubes being far away from each other, just as we did for the Top view at the beginning of this exercise?

3. Rotate the User view with the left arrow key while holding down the Shift key. Watch the cubes move relative to each other as the model rotates.

Notice how it becomes clear that the cubes definitely intersect as the viewports spin. Why does spinning the viewport help us understand the placement geometry so clearly when the still view doesn't? Doesn't the User view still have a blind direction? Spinning the User view works because we see several views from different angles, and we're able to mentally compare each frame to the last and correlate the movement. It works similarly to using the Top and Right views together to pin a point in space, but it's more intuitive and natural to see because it's similar to spinning a real-world object with our hand.

Summary

Every viewport except camera has a normal (a blind axis that can't be seen or edited). The User view's normal depends on its orientation. Spinning the User view helps us see around that problem, allowing us to visualize a 3D object quickly and easily.

Visualizing Entities We Didn't Build

It is not uncommon to receive a 3D model from someone else and be asked to clean it up—patch holes, reduce face count, erase duplicate and unnecessary verts and faces, and eliminate T-intersections.

The hardest part of this is really understanding the original model—not only the shape of the object, but exactly how it is constructed. There are many ways to build the same model, and if we are going to make edits, we need to understand how the model is built, not just its basic shape and how it looks. Often, we may plan to edit or convert the model to something that is appropriate for a real-time application, so we'll be looking for modeling methods that could cause problems for us.

Common Techniques

When we first look at a really complicated object, we may not be able to figure out how to start understanding it. There are several methods and techniques we can use to explore. This list shows the most commonly used ones:

- "Connect-the-dots"—Start with understandable geometry and examine each object that connects to it, one by one. This procedure is appropriate when the scene has a complicated section that we must understand. We start by identifying the first object whose meaning we can guess, then selecting the nearest object that connects to it, hiding the rest of the objects if necessary. We then examine how these two parts fit together. Once we understand their relationship, we unhide the next object that connects, hiding the original object if necessary, until we have examined all the objects in the area.

- "Select by Name"—For a quick overview of the organization, use "Select by Name" to see the objects, one by one. Using the Select command simply turns the objects red, which makes them stand out against their neighbors. By using Alt-N to clear selections, followed by ^N, the "select by name" shortcut, we can quickly, easily, and comprehensively view each object in the scene. This is a good way to begin when the objects are not named clearly and not obviously organized. If we plan to work with the object again in the future, it may be worthwhile to change its name to something meaningful (Choose Modify/Object/Attributes, then pick the selected object) and even recolor it (Modify/Object/Recolor).

- Hide objects that overlap other geometry (Display/Object/Hide). This simple method is a very common way to view objects that are intertwined with or cover each other.

- Use different geometry settings. If the object is very complicated, and the Display/Geometry/All lines are set, we can see fewer lines by selecting Display/Geometry/Edges Only. Similarly, we can reduce clutter by changing the verts to dots rather than crosses (Display/Geometry/Vert Dots), and so on. If the model is so simple that we can't understand how it is made, we will choose the opposite settings to view all the detail.

- Render the object within 3D Studio. We have to be a little careful when we depend on a rendered image to understand the shape of an object. Modeling problems can occur that rendering doesn't show. For example, any objects that are hidden inside other objects aren't visible in a rendering. Rendering is powerful and very useful, but it should be used in conjunction with working through the wireframe, not instead of it.

What Problems Are We Looking For?

When we explore our model, we must keep a sharp eye out for strange areas that don't make sense. What exactly are we looking for? The answer depends on what our real-time environment can handle. We're looking for situations that violate those limits.

Though we can't know precisely what problems we're looking for without knowing what our real-time environment can handle, here are some common problems we often are looking for: intersecting faces, intersecting objects, extra verts, holes in geometry, faces that depend on two-sided rendering, T-intersections, high-aspect faces, unwelded objects, and unsupported material attributes. For a complete description of these problems and how to fix them, see Chapter 9.

Now, we will work through getting a basic understanding of a complicated model we did not build.

Visualization Exercise

1. Load the file ENGINEANI.3DS that comes with 3D Studio. This file is also included on the CD-ROM.

2. Click in the User view and type Alt-E to turn off the Video Safe Frame lines (the yellow and green lines surrounding the viewport).

3. Type Alt-L to hide the lights.

4. Zoom all viewports to extents (right-click on the Zoom Extents icon).

5. Click in the lower right viewport and type U, then click without moving the mouse. This changes the Camera view into a User viewport with approximately the same view.

6. Choose Display/Geometry/Vert Dots.

The screen should now look like Figure 5.2.

Probably the first thing we notice is that the redraw times for this model are not instant (unless you've got a really fast computer!). That is our first clue about the nature of this model: It's got lots of detail.

Perhaps the second thing we notice is the colored objects. This is a feature of 3D Studio version 4 designed for visualization convenience; for models like this, where there are lots of overlapping objects, it's very handy.

Next we do what everyone does when first loading a new model: just take a look at what's on the screen. The shape is pretty complicated (as shown in Figure 5.3). All we can really tell at first glance is that there's a four-bladed propeller connected to a complicated object.

If you've ever seen a model airplane engine, you will recognize this, and this exercise will probably be quite easy. This is true in general; knowing the objects we are modeling is an advantage. However, there will inevitably be times when

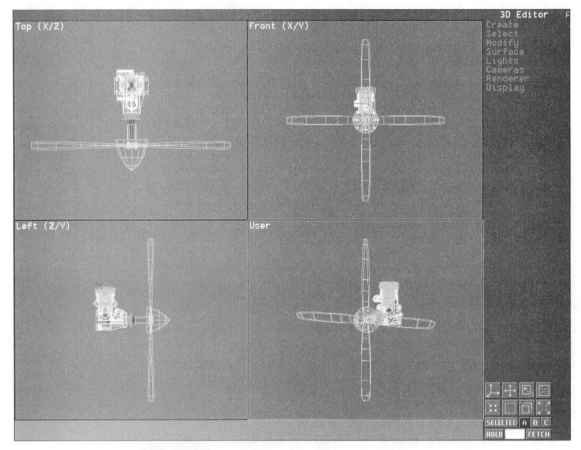

Create
Select
Modify
Surface
Lights
Cameras
Renderer
Display

Top (X/Z)

Front (X/Y)

Left (Z/Y)

User

SELECTED A B C
HOLD FETCH

FIGURE 5.2   Object to visualize.

we don't know the object we're exploring, so if you do know what this is, try to imagine you don't.

Let's look at the model more closely. Start by looking at the parts we understand. In this case, we'll look at the propeller first. It's composed of four blades that go to a pointed cap. We can see that the blades go to the cap, but we can't immediately see if the faces intersect.

1. Click in the User view and type W to make it fill the screen. Zoom in until the propeller hub and some of the blades are visible, as indicated below:

As we can now see, the propeller blades do indeed intersect the hub (marked "A" in Figure 5.3). Not only that, but they intersect each other at the center (marked "B").

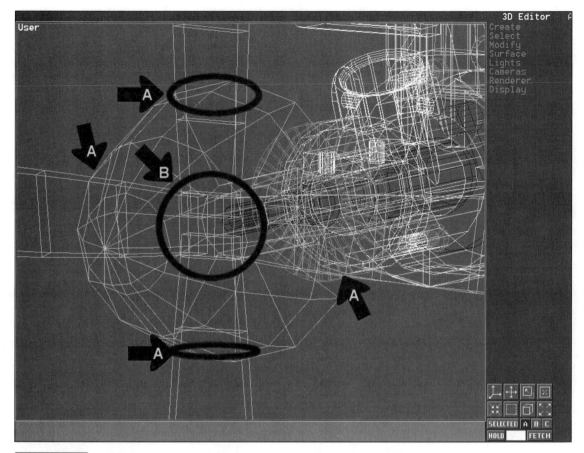

FIGURE 5.3   "A" is intersection of blades and hub, "B" is blades' self-intersection.

Let's explore the model by the "connect-the-dots" method. We'll start by looking at the hub object itself, then we'll examine each object that touches it.

2. Choose Modify/Object/Attributes and click on the hub object. Note the name of the object (NOSE CONE) and press Esc to clear the dialog. Hold down the Control key and click on the hub object again. Choose Select/Invert to select everything but the hub, and then choose Display/Hide/Objects and hide the selected objects by pressing the spacebar, then clicking in the viewport.

The screen should now look like Figure 5.4.

We can now see, moderately clearly, that the hub object contains the intersecting pieces of the propeller blade.

3. Press the left square bracket ([) to save the User view's current posi-

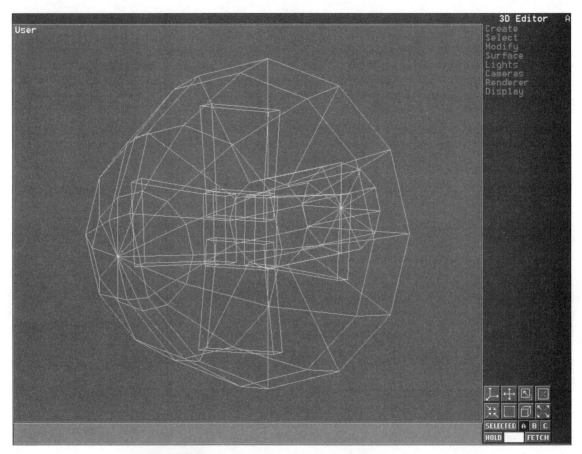

FIGURE 5.4   Most stuff hidden.

tion. Spin the viewport using the arrow keys and try to visualize the position of the propeller blade pieces relative to the rest of the hub object. Are they fully inside the object, or could they be seen from certain angles?

What should be apparent is that the propeller pieces form a cross that is fully enclosed by the conic hub. Unless the hub is transparent, has holes, or is otherwise unusual, these faces are fully enclosed and were probably not intended to exist. Let's take a second to find out if they share any verts with the rest of the hub object.

4. Choose Select/Element and click on each of the four propeller pieces, being careful not to click on the hub object itself. (If you do accidentally click on the hub object, simply click on it again to unselect it).

Selecting the elements verifies that we do not have any shared verts between the hub shell and the propeller pieces. This step, combined with our visualization, lets us see that these pieces are unnecessary.

Though it isn't strictly part of our current task, we real-time modelers feel instinctive urges to erase unnecessary faces like these. It's like being a mechanic who notices a loose hose and fixes it while it's convenient. We will delete the unnecessary faces, but only after we are sure we can get back the original model. Deleting these faces without having the original is a bad idea because we still aren't sure how this model will be used. Of course, we have the original model, so we don't need to do anything special.

5. Choose Modify/Vertex/Delete and pick the selected verts. Spin the model again to verify that we didn't accidentally delete anything.

As we spin the model, we'll notice how much more clear the object is without those other objects in the way (that's how we'll justify ourselves if anyone asks why we were deleting faces when we're only supposed to be visualizing the model). It's just a simple hemisphere with a little stem.

6. Choose Display/Unhide/All.

Now let's take a look at the objects that connect to the hub. The easiest objects are the propeller blades, so let's start with them.

7. Type Alt-N to clear all selections, then Choose Select/Object/Single. Click on the propeller blades and the hub. Hide the rest of the objects using the method described earlier. Invert the selection, then hide the selected objects.

8. Type Control-Z to zoom to extents and examine the two parts by spinning the viewport with the arrow keys. Once we have the picture, press the left squiggly bracket ({) to restore the zoomed-in view of the hub. Spin the viewport some more until the intersection of the propeller blades and the hub is clear.

As we spin the view, we can see that the propeller blades intersect the surface of the hub a little, but that the intersection points do not have verts at them. This could be a problem if this model was to be used in a real-time environment. Because it's not trivial to fix, we'll just make a note of it and move on for now.

9. Choose Modify/Object/Attributes and click on the propeller blade object. Note its name (PROP) for future reference. This step is very important when exploring an object, especially one like this whose objects cross each other and are difficult to select by clicking.

10. Select PROP (hold down Control and click on the object), then choose Display/Unhide/All.

Our next step is to explore the other objects that touch the hub. To do this, we need to select them. Unlike PROP, it's not immediately obvious which other

objects touch the hub. There appears to be a hollow inner shaft (marked in Figure 5.5 as A) that runs into the stem of the hub.

There may be other objects behind it that touch the hub as well, but let's start with the inner shaft first.

11. Choose Modify/Object/Attributes and select the inner shaft object. Note its name (SHAFT). Press Esc to clear the dialog, and hold down the Control key while clicking on SHAFT. Hide the remaining selected objects and zoom extents. Spend a minute looking at SHAFT by the usual method of spinning the viewport.

Though at first glance this new object doesn't look too complicated, as we examine it more closely we will see that there is a lot of detail in it! We'll fully explore this object in a separate exercise.

12. Unhide all objects, then hide the propeller and the shaft by choosing Display/Hide/Object/By Name, then clicking on PROP and SHAFT.

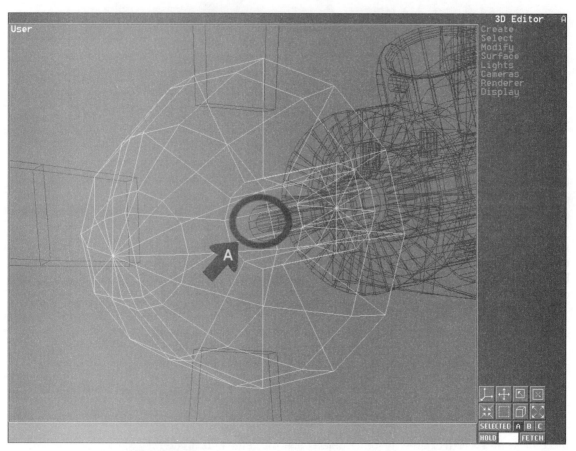

FIGURE 5.5   SHAFT object, with left end marked A.

13. Type W to return to the four views and zoom all views to extents.

We can now see clearly that no other objects touch the hub. Now that we've explored the hub, let's explore all the objects that it touched in the same way. PROP doesn't touch any other objects, so let's hide the hub and start on SHAFT.

14. Hide the hub object and zoom all windows to extents again. Type Alt-N to clear the selection set.

Now that we're familiar with SHAFT, we can see that it runs right down the middle of the whole object. We can guess that it's some kind of key central piece to which everything attaches. Working along all the objects that connect to it is not going to be as easy as the hub! Let's use another approach and look at the remaining objects in a different manner.

In general, it looks like the largest object is the white block with a bunch of fins visible in the Front view. Let's find out its name and take a look at it without all the other objects cluttering our view.

15. Choose Modify/Object/Attributes and click on any part of the white object (for example, the fins) in the Front view. Verify that the object's name is BODY.

16. Choose Display/Hide/All, then Display/Unhide/By Name, and choose BODY from the list.

17. Click in the User view and type W. Choose Display/Geometry/See Thru, Display/Geometry/Edges Only, and Display/Geometry/Vert Dots, then spin the model with the arrow keys.

We certainly picked a hard one here. This object is full of holes and complicated attached objects, but by spending a couple of minutes spinning it, we find that its basic construction is not too complicated. It's mainly formed by two large cylinders that intersect at a right angle. The SHAFT object runs down the axis of one cylinder, and that seems to act as a base.

The other big cylinder has the fins attached to it that we first saw in the Top view. There are a lot of other little attachments, and there are two other medium-sized ones: a third cylinder that attaches at a non-square angle to the base cylinder and an oval-shaped extrusion that attaches to the fins of the secondary object.

Let's take a look at how the shaft fits with this piece.

18. Choose Display/Unhide/By Name and choose SHAFT from the list.

19. Restore the view and return to the four viewports.

Our screen should now look like Figure 5.6.

We can see here that SHAFT runs through BODY, but we can't tell if the two objects touch. The hole in the main part of the shaft lines up with the slanted cylinder attachment, and the little arm is near, but not at, the center of the main finned cylinder.

That's enough of a look at this object for now—let's see what else we have.

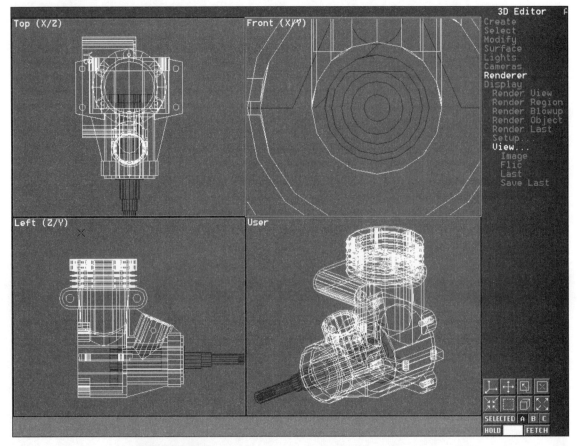

Top (X/Z)　　　　　　　　　Front (X/Y)

3D Editor
Create
Select
Modify
Surface
Lights
Cameras
Renderer
Display
　Render View
　Render Region
　Render Blowup
　Render Object
　Render Last
　Setup...
　View...
　　Image
　　Flic
　　Last
　　Save Last

Left (Z/Y)　　　　　　　　　User

SELECTED | A | B | C
HOLD | | FETCH

FIGURE 5.6　Shaft and prop nose shown.

20. Type W to see only the User view again. Unhide all objects, then hide BODY, PROP, and NOSE CONE. Spin the User view, then return to the four views.

In the left view, we can see that there are only two areas where objects connect to the shaft: a green circular thing near the propeller end, and a yellow bar with a red cylinder inside it at the shaft's little arm.

Besides these objects, there are three other groups. There's a yellow plate with four green bolts running through it, looking a lot like a simple cap on the end of the base cylinder of BODY, and there's a complicated yellow disc with fins on it that looks as if it fits on the top of the second, finned cylinder that forms BODY.

The third group is not clear, but it's contained in a cyan cylinder that runs inside the finned cylinder. Except for this unknown area, we now have a basic grasp of the structure of this object, so let's hide some of these other objects and try to figure out what's going on in that cyan cylinder.

21. Choose Display/Object/Hide and click on the shaft, the green thing, the yel-

low plate with the four green bolts, and the yellow finned disc. Zoom extents and spin the objects around a little, then return to the four viewports.

Three objects seem to be in there: the yellow arm that connected to SHAFT, the cyan outer cylinder that seems to be mostly hollow, and a green inner cylinder that fits within the cyan one. There's also a small red cylinder in the arm.

The cyan cylinder doesn't look too complicated, really. It's a basic hollow cylinder—what 3D Studio calls a tube—with some notches and holes cut in it and a lip on the top. The yellow arm is also a pretty straightforward construction, apparently. The red cylinder is simple, though its purpose is a little mysterious. The green cylinder's shape, on the other hand, is still not obvious.

22. Hide the cyan cylinder, the yellow arm, and the red cylinder.

23. Examine the remaining green cylinder by getting its name (CYLINDER), spinning the User view, then showing all four viewports.

Our screen should now look like Figure 5.7.

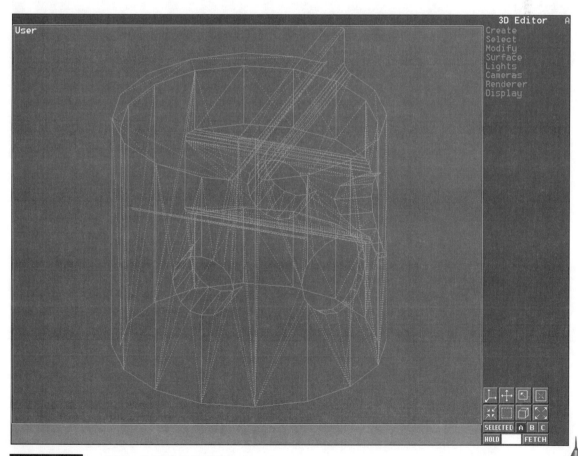

FIGURE 5.7 Object CYLINDER shown.

The Front view has a lot of information for us about this object. In it, we can see a fin sticking out of the top of the cylinder and two holes that fully penetrate the cylinder. One hole is a clean cut at the center of the viewport, and the other seems to penetrate at an angle.

If we are very observant, we can trace the edge of the cylinder and notice that there is another cylinder inside the first one. Let's try to look at this cylinder separately from the outside one.

24. Expand the Front view to fill the screen. Type Alt-N, then choose Select/Face/Quad/Window. Pick the two points indicated by triangles in Figure 5.8, so all the faces except the outer walls are included.

25. Choose Select/Invert, then hide the selected faces.

26. Choose Display/Geometry/Backface and show all four views again.

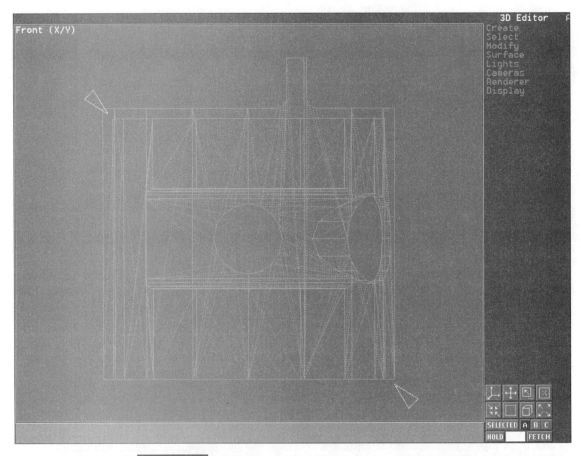

 FIGURE 5.8   Marks showing corners of a window to select the inner cylinder.

In the top view, we can see that we hid most of the outer ring of faces, but a few are still left, but that's not important. If we look carefully at the User view as we spin it, we'll notice that this "inner cylinder" is actually inward-facing. The whole green cylinder is mostly hollow, like an upside-down paint can with no lid.

Inside the can is another pair of features, similar to thick, shallow, flat shelves built into the inner wall where the central holes penetrate.

This object looks cleanly modeled; there are not obvious problems with it.

At this point we've gained a basic understanding of the whole object, and this exercise is over.

To summarize, we've explored the objects that comprise ENGINEANI.3DS. If our goal is to completely understand this model, the next step is to explore each of the objects in detail. The exercise later in this chapter will do this for one of the objects in ENGINEANI.

Why Did They Build the Model That Way?

If we need to really understand any model, we should be thinking not only about how it is shaped, but about how it was created and why it was created that way. In other words, we should be able to understand how the original modeler worked when they made the model.

The questions that occur to us are illustrated by the example of the hub and propeller's odd intersection in the discussion below.

Let's start with the questions:

- Why were the pieces of the propeller blades that we erased inside the hub?

- Why did they intersect each other?

- Why were they part of the hub object when they seemed to belong to the propeller object?

- Why aren't the hub/blade intersection points modeled? Why do the blades stick through the hub surface?

Most of these questions can be answered by imagining the method in which this model was created. Certainly the propeller blades and hub were modeled separately. Probably a single blade was built, then it was copied and rotated three times.

As to why the inner ends of the blades intersected each other, here's one theory: The modeler created the first blade model well within the hub to be sure there weren't any gaps between the blade and the hub. They then created the other three blades by rotating around the hub's center. When they did this, they either didn't notice or didn't care that the propeller blades started close enough to the center of the object that they crossed each other. It's possible that the modeler intended that intersection, but not likely. If the modeler had, they probably would have modeled it more cleanly, with the corners meeting and sharing verts, rather than intersecting.

We'll assume the blades intersected each other because it was simply not worth the modeler's time to clean up. Because this model was intended for still

rendering (where slight inefficiencies aren't significant), the modeler's decision is understandable.

The question about the intersecting pieces of the blades being part of the hub object is a little more mysterious. The most likely scenario is that the modeler accidentally combined the blades and the hub into a single object, and rather than separating them by selecting elements, they chose the faces in the hub with Select/Face/Quad/Window, then used Create/Face/Detach to recreate the hub object. During this process, they either didn't notice or didn't care that the inner parts of the blades were included in the hub object.

Another, more unlikely theory is that the modeler intended for those center pieces to be part of the hub object, since they were fully enclosed by the hub. This seems unlikely, unless there is a purpose for these faces that we haven't discussed. Once the faces were noticed, it would make more sense simply to delete them.

The last question is easy. 3D Studio handles intersections like these without problems; only certain other real-time graphics engines have problems with them. This does tell us that this model was probably not designed for a real-time environment, but we could have guessed that just from the face count.

Exploring a Single Object in Detail

If you worked through the exercise earlier in the chapter, you've taken a look at the entire engine object and how all its parts connect. Let's examine a single part of it in detail.

Explore the SHAFT object in ENGINEANI.PRJ:

1. Load the file ENGINEANI.3DS that comes with 3D Studio. This file is also included on the CD-ROM.

Make sure the following settings are set under Display/Geometry: Vert Dots, See Thru, Edges Only.

2. Choose Display/Hide/All, then Display/Unhide/Object/By Name, and choose SHAFT from the list of object names.

3. Click in the lower right viewport and type Alt-E to turn off the Video Safe Frame lines (the yellow and green lines surrounding the viewport). Type Alt-L to hide the lights.

4. Click in the lower right viewport and type U, then click without moving the mouse. This changes the Camera view into a User viewport with approximately the same view.

5. Zoom all viewports to extents (right-click on the Zoom Extents icon).

Now we can see our object fairly clearly, but it's still a little confusing because the circles along the shaft cross each other.

6. Press the right arrow key three times, then save this view by typing [.

The screen should now look like Figure 5.9, and now we're ready to work through this object. The object is a series of cylinders attached to each other, with an eccentric little arm at the top (as seen from the Top view).

7. Click in the User view and type W to cause it to fill the screen. Hold down the arrow keys to spin the object pressing, pressing Shift to slow down the spinning motion if necessary.

TIP

As a side note, we can also change the rate of spin by activating the Snap Angle, then changing the angle in the Drawing Aids dialog box (press Control-A to see it).

We'll start with the smallest end. We see that there is a hollow center, a sort of cylindrical indentation that goes into the end of the shaft, perhaps like a threaded hole where the bolt that holds the propeller to the shaft would go.

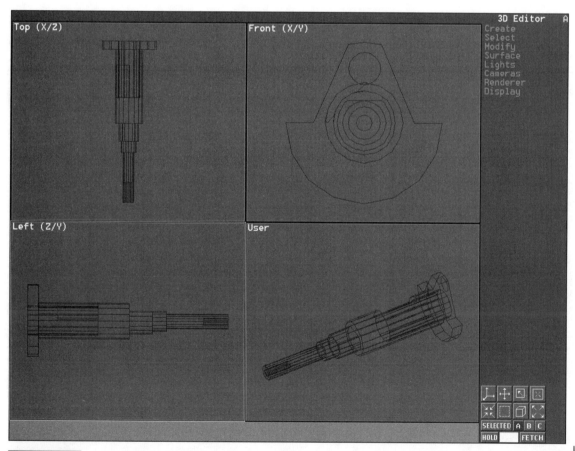

FIGURE 5.9   "SHAFT" object, ready to go.

We can see that each change in diameter has two concentric circles, as we might expect. The first diameter change is straightforward and short, but if we look closely at the outer circle of the second diameter change, we'll notice that there is a flat spot on the circle. This flat spot looks intentional, like a mechanical piece that fits over this part of the shaft, and the flat spot keeps it aligned with the shaft.

The next diameter change is a normal circle, but in the middle of this section of the shaft, there is an oddity whose shape and purpose are not immediately obvious. Our next mission is to understand this oddity.

8. Zoom to extents and spin the User view with the up arrow key. After letting it spin for a while, when the flat part of the mysterious area is near the top of the shaft, stop rotating. The view should look something like the User view in Figure 5.9A.

We can now see from the profile that this is apparently some kind of flattened area of the shaft, somewhat like the flattened area before. The other flat

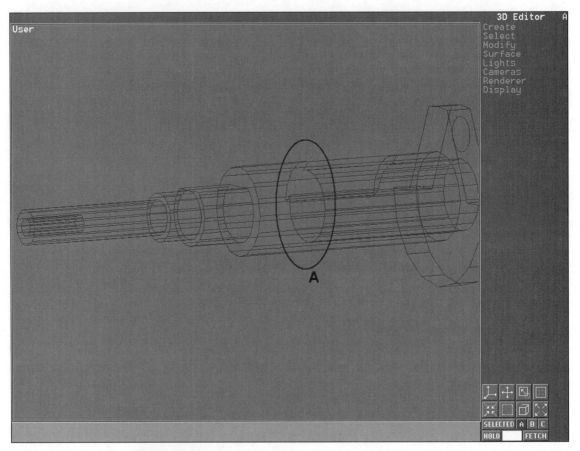

FIGURE 5.9A Flat area on shaft.

Designing 3D Graphics

area didn't have any verts around the circumference (marked as "A" in Figure 5.9A) as this one has. The more observant among us will have noticed that these verts (we'll call them MCP, for Mysterious Circumference Points) are not on the surface of the shaft; they are inside it.

Whenever we find verts inside an object we think is solid, we should be careful to understand them fully. They are frequently a sign of trouble of some type and alert us to a complicated area that deserves our full attention.

9. Type W to see all three viewports, and zoom the three viewports to their extents. The view should now look like Figure 5.9.

The Top and Side views show us similar views, so let's discuss the Top view first. We can see that from the MCPs upward, there are some additional lines inside the shaft. These are probably faces that connect to the MCPs, but we can't be sure.

The Front view shows the end of the shaft, which appears as a series of concentric circles. If we needed to, we could correlate each circle with a diameter change on the shaft, but it would be fairly tedious, so let's explore other methods before we do that.

10. Choose Display/Geometry/All Lines, Display/Geometry/Vert Ticks, and Display/Geometry/Backface.

11. Choose Select/Face/Quad and, in the Top view, draw a box surrounding the MCPs and toward the top of the shaft (before the large object at its end).

If we selected the window correctly, we see four vertical red lines that connect to the MCPs and end at another group of verts like the MCPs, but farther up the shaft. Let's take a closer look at these faces we found.

12. Click in the User view and type W to fill the screen with it. Rotate the view with the left arrow key.

There are several new things to notice now. First, we see that faces appear and disappear as we rotate. This is caused by Display/Geometry/Backface setting. Briefly, this setting hides faces that point away from our viewing direction (see elsewhere in this chapter for a complete explanation).

The other obvious point of interest is the group of faces we selected. As we spin, we can see a group of faces inside the shaft that connect the MCPs together in a disc, as well as a rectangular border around the flat spot. The disc is interesting because it is pointing toward the big end of the shaft, away from the hub, like a cap to the end of the shaft.

This clue may be enough for us to guess that this disk is the inside of a hollow section of the shaft. Looking at the disc's shape near the selected rectangular faces, we see that it notches outward to meet the outer surface of the shaft. It seems that this part of the disc, combined with the rectangular faces, forms the edges of a cut through the shaft, into the hollow section. Let's test our hypothesis by predicting what a rendered image of this view would look like, then rendering it and comparing the result to our prediction.

13. Type Alt-L to make the lights visible, W to see all the views, and then zoom all views to extents.

14. Delete the lower left omni light in the Top view. Move the upper right light to just above the top end of the shaft. In the Left view, move the light to just above the top end of the shaft.

15. Type Alt-L to hide the lights again, and type W to fill the screen with the User view.

16. Type L, then U, and click without moving the mouse.

The sequence described in the previous step resets the User view to the Left view's orientation.

17. Push the left and up arrow keys six times each. Save the view. The User view should now look like Figure 5.9B.

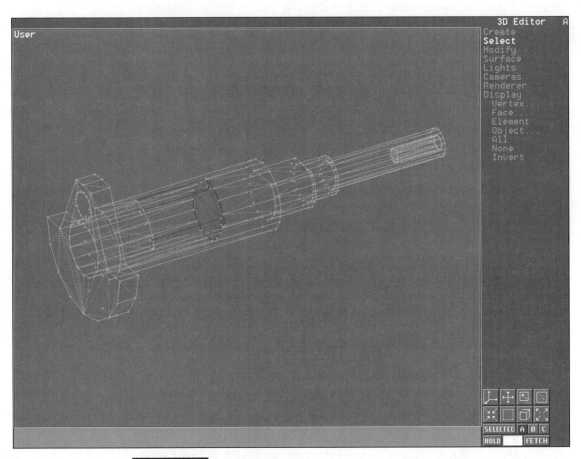

 FIGURE 5.9B Inner area.

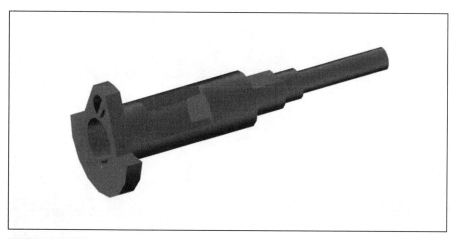

FIGURE 5.9C Rendered inner area.

Now that we know there is a light near our viewing position, we'd expect to see the outer shaft surface smoothly curving around, brightly lit near the center and getting darker as the surface turned away from the light. We'd expect to see the rectangular edges of the hole cut into the surface, and inside the hole, we'd see part of the disc and some inner walls of some kind.

18. Press Alt-R to bring up the render dialog. The following options should be set: Shading limit: Metal, all on/off options to Off. Choose OK to render. We should see a rendering like Figure 5.9C.

This rendering tells us a lot about the shape besides proving that we were right about the hole. We can also see that the hole apparently continues through the end of the shaft, and we can also see the shape of the object on the end of the shaft quite clearly. So, we can consider the mystery of the circumferential points solved.

It seems that there is a sharp-edged flat object stuck on the end of the shaft that has two holes in it. One hole correlates with the shaft hole we just discovered, and the other one is smaller, at the end of a little arm.

When we go back to our wireframe after looking at the rendering, the next step is to correlate the observations we made about the shape with the wireframe view.

If we look at the smaller hole discussed above as we spin our User view, we should notice that there is something strange about it. No faces line the inside of the hole, and only verts form the edge of the hole on one side of the little arm! Something strange is definitely going on here, so let's investigate using some new techniques of visualization.

19. Restore the view, then push the left arrow key six times. Zoom in on the suspect hole. Our screen should look like Figure 5.9D.

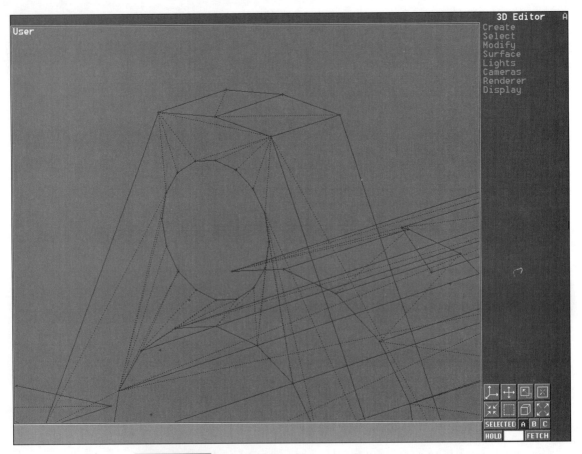

3D Editor A
Create
Select
Modify
Surface
Lights
Cameras
Renderer
Display

User

SELECTED A B C
HOLD   FETCH

FIGURE 5.9D Arm close-up.

Yes, there's definitely a modeling oddness here! The hole is not a "proper" hole; rather, it's simply a rip in the shell of faces that forms this shaft. We can see that there are no faces at all that connect inside the hole; the only faces that use the hole's verts connect to the outside.

If this is intended to be a normal-looking hole, it has a problem. At first, it seems possible that the inner lining faces were accidentally detached and are now part of a separate object. Unfortunately, we know this can't be true when we look at the other side of the little arm: There aren't even verts forming a hole there! The hole will not work correctly without verts around its perimeter on both sides of the arm. Even normal rendering in 3D Studio is likely to show up problems. If we rendered a view that showed this side, we'd see no hole at all.

It's still possible that this was not intentional. Perhaps the hole was not intended to go all the way through the arm. Perhaps it's supposed to be an indentation, not a hole, like the screwhole in the far end of the shaft.

Another possibility is that this wasn't intended to be a hole at all. Perhaps something was intended to protrude outward from this circle, like a pedal of a bicycle.

If so, we are still missing faces that form this indentation or protrusion. When we explore the other objects, we will look for the missing faces. In the meantime, this should be noted as a problem area.

Other than that, the geometry looks pretty clean and corresponds with what the rendering showed.

To wrap this up, we'll say that the object SHAFT from the ENGINEANI.3DS model is cleanly modeled, except for a strange half-hole in the end of the small arm.

● Display/Geometry Menu Tree

Let's explore the menu options that affect the wireframe view. Under the Display menu, choose the Geometry option and take a look at the list that appears. The available options are actually pairs of either/or choices. The currently active choice is shown with an asterisk, as shown in the figures.

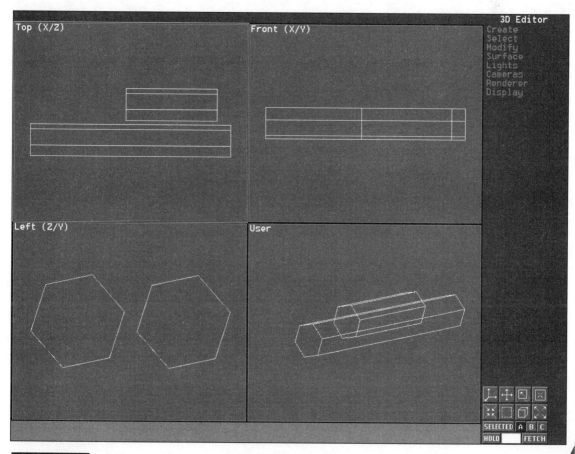

FIGURE 5.10 Display/Geometry/Backface.

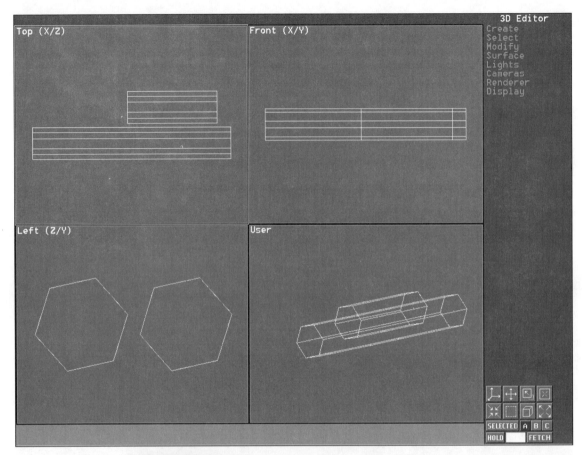

3D Editor
Create
Select
Modify
Surface
Lights
Cameras
Renderer
Display

FIGURE 5.11   Display/Geometry/See Thru.

See Thru vs. Backface

These two options (Figures 5.10 and 5.11) are handy because they simulate what other graphics packages call a "hidden-line" wireframe. That means that if a face is not pointing toward the viewpoint, it isn't shown in that viewpoint. This can be a little confusing because faces disappear and reappear as we rotate the User view, but it's really helpful for seeing what's going on. Note that these undrawn faces are not protected (unlike Display/Hide/Face); they are fully editable—for example, they can be selected in a Select/Face/Quad selection window, even if we couldn't see them when we drew the box.

When we have two overlapping objects in the User view, we'll see that Backface is a hack for a hidden-line view. Look at the backface version illustrations above—we can see the short cylinder right through the long one. It is no substitute for a "real" hidden-line visualization, such as the one we get when we render, but it's still useful.

Backface rejection is a concept used widely in real-time 3D, so you should become familiar with it and understand how it works and when it doesn't work. As we explore elsewhere in this chapter, backface rejection can be used to find holes in geometry; turning that idea around, if the model we build is going to work with one-sided rendering, it can't have any holes.

We can use Display/Geometry/Backface to test our objects for problems related to backface rejection (such as holes or normals pointing the wrong way). Because most rendering engines also use 1-sided rendering in the same way 3D Studio does, we can assume that if it works in 3D Studio, it'll work in the real-time environment.

All Lines vs. Edges Only

This option allows us to prevent 3D Studio from drawing what it calls "invisible edges." As we can see on the end faces of the cylinders in the illustrations in Figure 5.13, when Edges Only is active, we can't see all the faces that constitute an object (Figure 5.12). This is handy for large objects with lots of faces, but real-time modelers usually need to see every face. We usually want to have All Lines active, though occasionally we have a need for Edges Only.

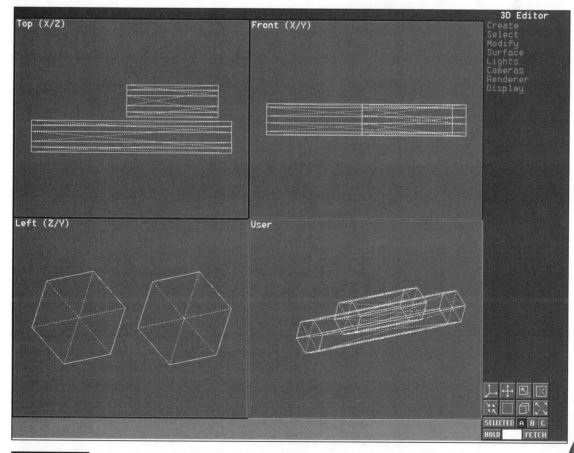

FIGURE 5.12   Display/Geometry/All Lines.

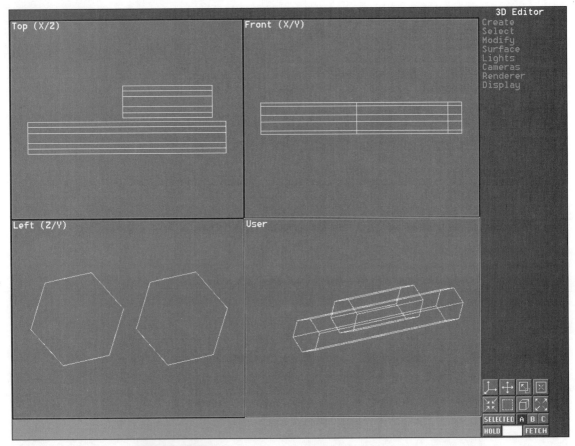

FIGURE 5.13   Display/Geometry/Edges Only.

Vert Dots vs. Vert Ticks

3D Studio draws verts as either tiny dots or more visible, but messier plus-sign marks, depending on which symbol we choose. For our models, we usually use Vert Ticks—the only reason to select Vert Dots is if there are so many verts on the screen, or the faces are so small, that we can't see the faces clearly.

Using Vert Ticks is very handy when selecting verts simply because it's hard to see if the single pixel used to show a Vert Dot on a 1024 × 768 screen is red or white. For an example, look at the vertex in the center of the ends of the cylinders in Figure 5.15, as compared to Figure 5.14.

Full Detail/Box

This option draws a bounding box around each object instead of drawing the object itself. This feature was designed for models with so many faces that redrawing the wireframe display is slow.

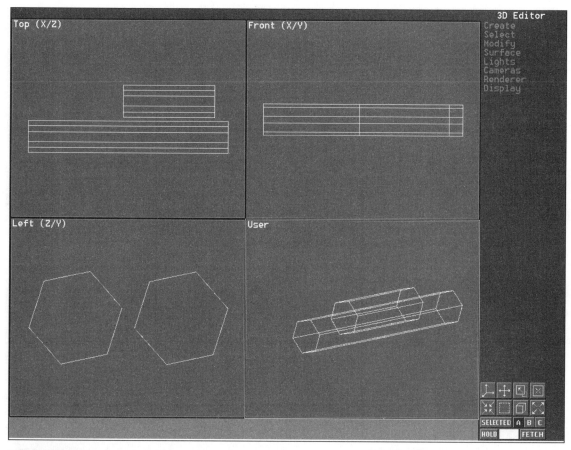

FIGURE 5.14   Display/Geometry/Vert Dots.

Because our models typically don't have many faces, it isn't often useful for real-time modeling, but if we need it, we can use the shortcut key Alt-B instead of going through the menu with the mouse.

⬤ Understanding Edges

Edges are one of the trickiest methods of editing that 3D Studio gives us. Unlike faces and verts, edges aren't entities unto themselves. They are simply concepts that go with faces, just as "inside" is a concept that goes with a house. Thus, we can't have edges without faces, and vice versa. For more discussion of this concept, see Chapter 2.

There are two kinds of edges: shared and unshared. A shared edge is formed when two (or more) faces share two verts.

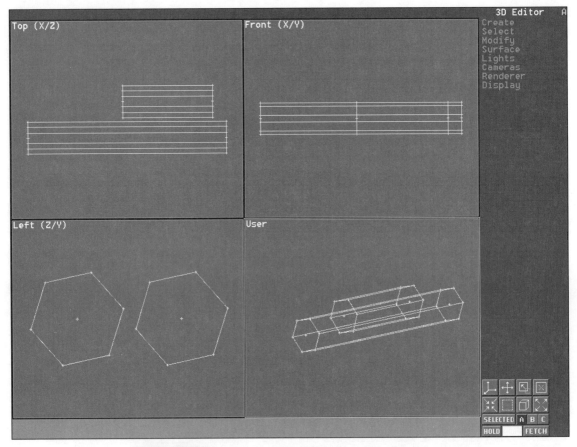

3D Editor   A
Create
Select
Modify
Surface
Lights
Cameras
Renderer
Display

Top (X/Z)

Front (X/Y)

Left (Z/Y)

User

SELECTED A B C
HOLD   FETCH

FIGURE 5.15   Display/Geometry/Vert Ticks.

The pair of faces on the left in Figure 5.16 share the diagonal edge between them. As is common in 3D Studio, the shared edge is invisible (drawn as a dotted pattern instead of solid). The middle pair of faces does not shares any verts; they cannot have a shared edge because of this. The rightmost pair of faces shares one vert, which isn't enough.

One of the easiest ways to start exploring edges is to try to find a hole in an element (as you may recall, elements are groups of faces that share verts).

Finding Holes

In this exercise, we'll demonstrate the basic problem with wireframe by erasing a face from a continuous surface, then exploring methods of finding the hole we made.

Erase a face and find the resulting hole:

1. Create a cylinder with 16 sides and 16 segments, smoothed. Place the origin

Designing 3D Graphics

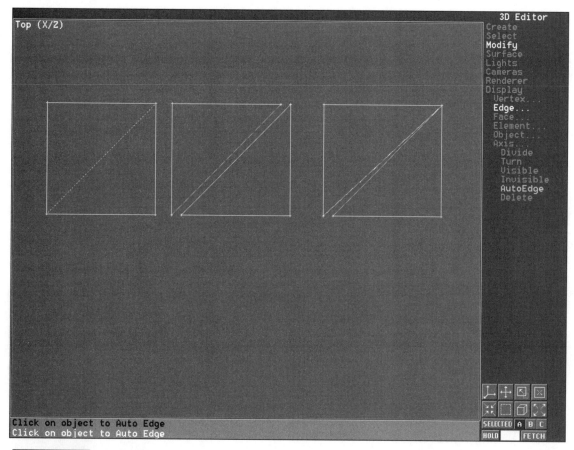

Click on object to Auto Edge
Click on object to Auto Edge

FIGURE 5.16 Edges.

at 0,0,0 and choose a radius of 50, angle of 0, and a height of 100. Use the default name.

2. Save this as an ASC file (CYLINDER.ASC).

3. Zoom all the views to the drawing extents (right-click on Zoom Extents icon). Go into the Display/Geometry menu and make sure the following options are on: See-thru, All Lines, and Vert Ticks.

Our screen should now look like Figure 5.17.

4. Type ? and verify that the model contains 82 verts and 160 faces.

5. Click in the User view, choose Select/Face/Single, and click on a vert near the center of the User view. Click again to select a face that connects to that vert.

We should now see the face as red in all four views.

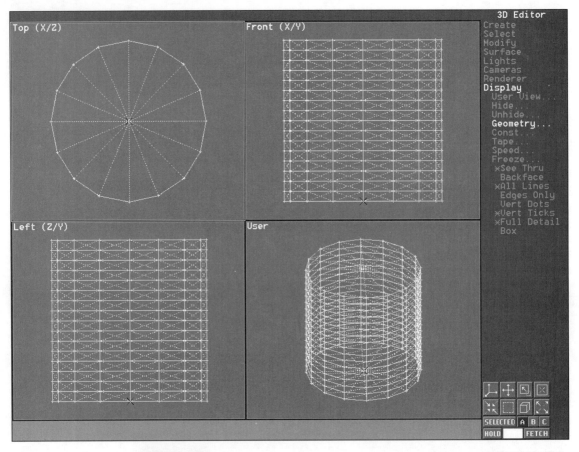

FIGURE 5.17 16-sided cylinder.

6. Choose Modify/Face/Delete and delete the selected face. Redraw all viewports by typing a tilde (~).

This is the interesting point. Notice that the mesh looks exactly the same. We didn't see anything change because 3D Studio shows the presence of a face only by drawing its edges. The face we deleted was surrounded by other faces, so when it was erased, 3D Studio still drew the edges it used to share.

Though it isn't literally true, it can be helpful to picture 3D Studio drawing shared edges twice—once for each face that uses the edge. So, if we delete one face, 3D Studio still draws that edge because another face still uses it. The result is that the edge doesn't look any different, even though it's no longer shared.

This behavior causes the problem: What if we have a hole in our mesh like the one we created, but we don't know where it is?

If we can't see it in the editor, the normal solution is to view the model where the triangles are filled in, not drawn in wireframe. We can do this if we render a still frame, use the keyframer preview, use the Gouraud-shaded viewing plug-in in 3D Studio V4, or even bring it into our real-time environment.

These options work but they're a little time-consuming and annoying and we have to remember where the hole was when we go to edit in the wireframe view. It would be helpful if we could find the hole right in the 3D editor. Now we'll take a look at some different ways we can do just that.

7. Choose Modify/Edge/Autoedge. Click on the cylinder, and type 80 degrees in the dialog box asking for an angle.

Modify/Edge/Autoedge is a very handy tool that changes the visibility of all the edges in an object. If a face shares an edge with another face, then this command measures the angle that the two faces form (Figure 5.18), and if the angle is more than the amount we entered, that edge is drawn as solid. If the angle is less, then the edge is made invisible.

We should see that most of the edges are now shown as dotted lines, which means they are invisible. However, the edges of our hole are not dotted. That's one of the side benefits of the Autoedge command: It changes all unshared edges to solid. Since our hole is composed of unshared edges, this command works nicely for us.

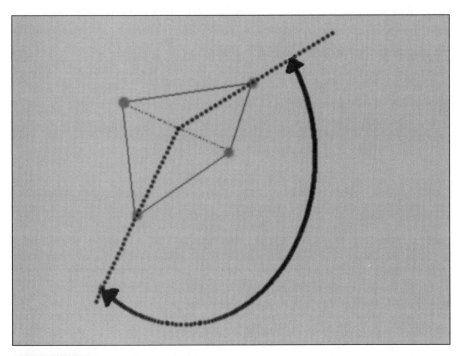

FIGURE 5.18 Angle between two faces.

Though this command is handy, it doesn't solve the hole-finding problem perfectly. With objects that have edges designed to be unshared, seeing which edges are intentionally unshared and which are the borders of a hole can be difficult.

Let's look at some other methods of finding a hole.

8. Choose Display/Face/Hide and select (Alt-W) a row of faces that border, but do not include, the hole. Hide these selected faces.

We should now see the hole because one of the faces that bordered it has been hidden. This method is simple, but it requires a lot of tedious guesswork if we have no idea where the hole is; we can also accidentally build duplicate faces if we fill in a "hole" that is simply a hidden face.

9. Choose Display/Geometry/Backface. Rotate the User view, using the arrow keys and the Shift key to slow it down, until the missing face is near the edge of the cylinder.

Note that as the faces rotate so they point away from the viewpoint, they are not drawn. As the hole gets to the edge, we will see the hole's edge disappear where the other faces' edges do not. This is similar to hiding the bordering faces, but it's quicker and requires less clicking. The bad side is that we can't control which faces disappear easily. For our cylinder it's easy, but for a complicated, mountainous terrain it would not be so handy.

That's the end of this exercise. As we can see, finding a missing face in a mesh isn't easy, but at least there are some quick alternatives to rendering.

Edges in the .ASC File

Let's take a look at how edges are stored in the .ASC file we created in the previous exercise. If you didn't complete the previous exercise, do steps 1 and 2 now to generate the following CYLINDER.ASC file:

```
1.     Ambient light color: Red=0.039216 Green=0.039216 Blue=0.039216
2.     Named object: "Object01"
3.     Tri-mesh, Vertices: 82      Faces: 160
4.     Vertex list:
5.     Vertex 0:  X: 50      Y: -0.000007    Z: -0.000001
6.     Vertex 1:  X: 46.193977    Y: 19.134167    Z: -0.000003
7.     Vertex 2:  X: 35.355339    Y: 35.355335    Z: -0.000006
8.     Vertex 3:  X: 19.134171    Y: 46.193966    Z: -0.000007
9.     Vertex 4:  X: -0.000002    Y: 49.999989    Z: -0.000008
10.    Vertex 5:  X: -19.134176    Y: 46.193962    Z: -0.000007
11.    Vertex 6:  X: -35.355339    Y: 35.355335    Z: -0.000006
12.    Vertex 7:  X: -46.193974    Y: 19.134169    Z: -0.000003
13.    Vertex 8:  X: -50    Y: 0     Z: -0.000001
14.    Vertex 9:  X: -46.193981    Y: -19.134167    Z: 0.000002
15.    Vertex 10:  X: -35.35535    Y: -35.355331    Z: 0.000004
16.
17.    [...]
18.
19.    Face list:
20.    Face 0:    A:0 B:1 C:17 AB:1 BC:1 CA:0
```

```
21.    Smoothing:  1
22.    Face 1:     A:0 B:17 C:16 AB:0 BC:1 CA:1
23.    Smoothing:  1
24.    Face 2:     A:1 B:2 C:18 AB:1 BC:1 CA:0
25.    Smoothing:  1
26.    Face 3:     A:1 B:18 C:17 AB:0 BC:1 CA:1
27.    Smoothing:  1
28.    Face 4:     A:2 B:3 C:19 AB:1 BC:1 CA:0
29.    Smoothing:  1
30.    Face 5:     A:2 B:19 C:18 AB:0 BC:1 CA:1
31.    Smoothing:  1
32.    Face 6:     A:3 B:4 C:20 AB:1 BC:1 CA:0
33.    Smoothing:  1
34.    Face 7:     A:3 B:20 C:19 AB:0 BC:1 CA:1
35.    Smoothing:  1
36.    Face 8:     A:4 B:5 C:21 AB:1 BC:1 CA:0
37.    Smoothing:  1
38.    Face 9:     A:4 B:21 C:20 AB:0 BC:1 CA:1
39.    Smoothing:  1
40.    Face 10:    A:5 B:6 C:22 AB:1 BC:1 CA:0
41.    Smoothing:  1
42.    Face 11:    A:5 B:22 C:21 AB:0 BC:1 CA:1
43.    Smoothing:  1
44.    Face 12:    A:6 B:7 C:23 AB:1 BC:1 CA:0
45.    Smoothing:  1
46.    Face 13:    A:6 B:23 C:22 AB:0 BC:1 CA:1
47.    Smoothing:  1
48.    Face 14:    A:7 B:8 C:24 AB:1 BC:1 CA:0
49.    Smoothing:  1
50.    Face 15:    A:7 B:24 C:23 AB:0 BC:1 CA:1
51.    Smoothing:  1
52.    Face 16:    A:8 B:9 C:25 AB:1 BC:1 CA:0
53.    Smoothing:  1
54.
55.    [...]
```

As we have discussed, faces are defined by a list of three vertex references (for example, face 16 is A:8 B:9 C:25). After that, there are three pairs of letters, followed by a 1 or a 0. The pairs of letters denote an edge of the face, and the number tells if it is visible.

For example, face 6 has two visible edges and one invisible edge. The invisible edge is the one connecting vertex 9 to vertex 25. This data is sometimes used by the real-time engine to mark faces that should be joined into quads, and possibly for other uses as well.

● 2D versus 3D Editing Commands

It may come as a surprise that almost all 3D editing commands affect only two of the three XYZ coordinates.

Why does this 2D editing limitation exist? The reason is simply the limitations of the 2D display and the 2D mouse. If 3DS allowed us to move an object along all three axes at once, how would we do it? We can indicate only two

axes' worth of movement with the mouse, and, in the worst case, we can see only two axes' worth of movement on the screen.

Improved input and display devices are on the market that can provide full three-axis information, but they are not yet readily available to 3D modelers. If this changes in the future, we can expect our modeling software to change along with it.

We choose which two coordinates are to be affected by clicking in the viewport with the coordinates that we wish to affect. For example, if we move an entity in the Top view, we can affect only the entity's X and Z coordinates; the Y coordinates are unchanged.

To change the Y coordinates, we must choose a Left or Front view and move the object again. That's why all the exercises, in this book and others, specify the view in which the editing operation must take place.

Another way to think of this 2D limitation is that our editing operations are constrained to a flat plane in space. In our example above, we moved our entity on the XZ plane, normal to the Y axis.

The User Viewport to the Rescue ... Sort Of

With this new mental model, we're ready to think about editing in the User viewport. When we edit in the User viewport, we're still on a flat plane, but now we are not constrained to an orthogonal orientation. Instead of being stuck in the XY, XZ, or YZ planes, our surface can face any which way.

Imagine the User view is a movie camera, floating in space. Now imagine our mouse pad is always oriented so the movie camera is looking straight down on it, so all we ever see is a perfect overhead view of the mouse on the pad. The mouse pad surface is the plane along which we can move (or edit in general) our entities. That means when we want to change the direction of the plane, we have to rotate our User view. It also means that it's sometimes quite tricky to get the User view aligned so our editing plane is arranged as we want it.

The power of editing in the User view can be very useful, and it's usually difficult. We'll use it when we have to, but editing in an orthogonal plane is usually easier.

Using User View for Editing

We can use the User view for more than just seeing what we're working on. We frequently need a view that is not simply orthogonal to accomplish our work. Let's work on an example of this.

Orienting Two Objects in Space

Use the User view to align two randomly oriented cylinders in space:

1. Starting with a new drawing in 3D Studio, click in the User view and orient it to a random direction. Create a six-sided, one-segmented smoothed

Designing 3D Graphics

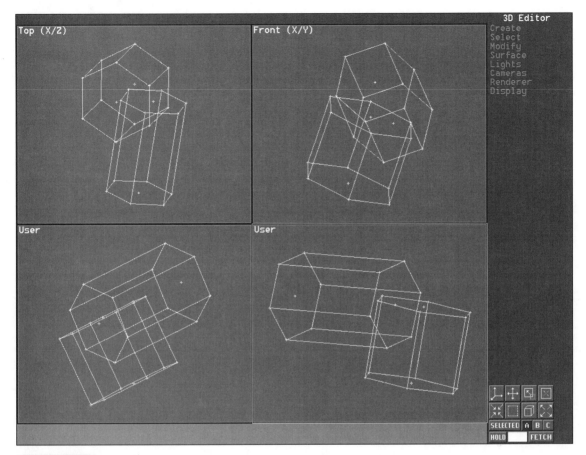

FIGURE 5.19   Alignment exercise model.

cylinder by clicking in the User view; make it approximately square.
Name it CYL01.

2. Repeat step 1. The second cylinder should be near, but not aligned with, the first one by spinning the User view before creating the new cylinder. Name this object CYL02.

3. Spin the User view some more, then zoom all views to extents.

Our screen should now look like Figure 5.19.

Now that we've set up the problem, our first action is to align the User view with one of the cylinders.

4. Choose Display/User View/Align. Click on one of the verts at the center of one of the cylinders. Click again to select one of the end faces (it doesn't matter which one because they all point the same way).

CHAPTER 5 • **Advanced Tool Studies**   **101**

The User view is now aligned with the cylinder we selected. This, all by itself, can be very useful—for example, if we wanted to change the cylinder's diameter, we could use 2D Scale in this aligned User view. The same goes for other edits that require a 2D surface. There is no other convenient way to perform a 2D edit on a randomly oriented 3D object in 3D Studio.

5. Choose Modify/Object/Align and click on a center vert on the unaligned cylinder. Click again to choose any face. Click on "facing towards" in the following dialog.

We should see that the object has been aligned with the User view; thus, both objects are now resting on the same plane. If they ended up crossing each other, we could easily move them without disturbing their alignment as long as we don't rotate the User view.

This little stipulation can be inconvenient during heavy modeling; we often want to spin the User view to visualize our object, but we need it aligned for editing. We have two solutions to this problem. We can store the User view's position with the [key, spin it around, then restore it with the { key when we're done. We can also replace one of the other viewports with a second User view. When we have two User views, they are totally unrelated to each other. In this way, we can use one User view for visualization and the other can be aligned with our geometry.

Designing 3D Graphics

MAPPING

This chapter covers probably the most difficult part of real-time 3D modeling in 3D Studio: mapping. We'll start by explaining what mapping means, work through some simple examples, and then explore 3D Studio's mapping tools in detail. From there, we'll work through some more examples of mapping, and then we'll wrap up by resolving some of the sticky situations that mapping can bring up.

 # Prologue

As we discussed in Chapter 2, the family tree of computer graphics splits early between raster and vector, and 3D modeling involves both. Mapping is how we connect the two types.

 # The Many Meanings of Mapping

Mapping is a confusing word because it's commonly used with several related, but not identical meanings. Let's take a look at the common meanings. When we talk about *mapping* in general, we mean the process by which we associate 2D raster-based art with 3D vector-based geometry.

But *mapping* can also mean the UV coordinates that we generated during this mapping process. For example, "Don't weld verts because you'll destroy the mapping" refers to the actual mapping data in the ASC file (no, welding verts cannot destroy the actual concept of mapping!).

Other Kinds of Mapping

In the context of real-time modeling, *mapping* almost always is used by textures, but in 3D Studio mapping is used for other effects as well: reflection mapping, bump mapping, opacity mapping, and so on. Though we won't discuss it, the basic principals shown here work for most mapping-based effects in 3D Studio as well as our focus: texture mapping.

 # Why Is Mapping So Difficult?

Mapping is a frustrating and seemingly irrelevant step in the eyes of many artists, especially 3D Studio users. Frustration occurs partly because 3D Studio's mapping tools are not very flexible or powerful; in addition, because 3D Studio does not offer a seamless RT3D engine built-in, it's not an interactive process—to see if your mapping worked, you usually have to render the scene.

But the problem runs deeper than just the lack of good tools. Mapping is conceptually one of the hardest steps in 3D modeling—in a way, it's the point at

Designing 3D Graphics

which 2D meets 3D, and this is a tricky transition to make, both theoretically and in practice.

To further complicate the issue, 3D Studio's mapping coordinates are not always stored correctly, especially in .ASC files, and they can be damaged easily. This issue adds to the frustration (but, we hope, gives us a good reason to keep consecutive backups as we work! See the section in Chapter 5 about backups for some strategy and suggestions for dealing with backups).

Put your thinking cap on and jump in!

 # Simple Mapping Example

Let's start off by looking under the hood. We'll build a cube and put an example texture on one face, then look at the mapping coordinates in the .ASC file.

Explore a simple exercise in texture mapping:

1. Ensure that the example texture maps that come with this book are in the Map Paths, so 3DS can find them (see "What's on the CD-ROM").

2. Press F5 to go to the Materials Editor and click on the Texture 1 Map button. Choose TEXRTEST.TIF which comes on the CD-ROM. Drag it to the View Image button and make sure it looks like Figure 6.1.

3. Put the material in the library using the name Texture Test by typing P. (Note—don't save the material library unless you want to add this useless example material to your 3DS material library.)

4. Return to the 3D Editor (F3) and create a box (Create/Box). Type 0<Enter> 0<Enter> 0<Enter> to define one corner of the cube. Then type 1<Enter> 1<Enter> 1<Enter> to define the other corner. Give the cube the name TestCube01.

5. Zoom all windows to their extents (right-click on the Zoom Extents icon).

6. Click on Material/Choose and select the material we just created from the list. (To quickly navigate a listbox in 3D Studio, type Alt plus the first letter of the name.)

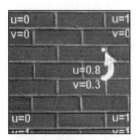

FIGURE 6.1   Texrtest.tif.

7. Assign this material to the cube (Material/Assign/Object).

8. Activate the Front view by clicking in it.

9. Choose Material/Mapping/Scale from the menu. Move the pointer to the Front view, hold down Alt, and click on the cube. This does two things: It aligns the mapping icon with the active viewport, and it scales the icon so that the object barely fits inside it.

10. Note the appearance of the mapping icon, which is the yellow and green box with the small line on top. In the Front view, the icon overlaps the cube's edges, and in the User view we can see the icon is aligned with the front face. Now visualize our test texture inside the mapping icon—imagine the mapping icon is a picture frame.

11. Assign the mapping icon to our cube by choosing Material/Mapping/ Assign and clicking on the cube.

12. Save the cube as the ASC file TESTCUBE.ASC and load it in the text editor. You should see the following code:

```
1.     Ambient light color: Red=0.039216 Green=0.039216 Blue=0.039216
2.
3.     Named object: "TestCube01"
4.     Tri-mesh, Vertices: 8      Faces: 12
5.     Mapped
6.     Vertex list:
7.     Vertex 0:  X:0      Y:0      Z:1      U:0      V:1
8.     Vertex 1:  X:1      Y:0      Z:1      U:1      V:1
9.     Vertex 2:  X:1      Y:1      Z:1      U:1      V:1
10.    Vertex 3:  X:0      Y:1      Z:1      U:0      V:1
11.    Vertex 4:  X:0      Y:-0     Z:0      U:0      V:-0
12.    Vertex 5:  X:1      Y:-0     Z:0      U:1      V:-0
13.    Vertex 6:  X:1      Y:1      Z:-0     U:1      V:-0
14.    Vertex 7:  X:0      Y:1      Z:-0     U:0      V:-0
15.    Face list:
16.    Face 0:    A:0 B:1 C:2 AB:1 BC:1 CA:0
17.    Material:"TEXTURE TEST"
18.    Smoothing:  1
19.    Face 1:    A:0 B:2 C:3 AB:0 BC:1 CA:1
20.    Material:"TEXTURE TEST"
21.    Smoothing:  1
22.    Face 2:    A:0 B:4 C:5 AB:1 BC:1 CA:0
23.    Material:"TEXTURE TEST"
24.    Smoothing:  2
25.    Face 3:    A:0 B:5 C:1 AB:0 BC:1 CA:1
26.    Material:"TEXTURE TEST"
27.    Smoothing:  2
28.    Face 4:    A:1 B:5 C:6 AB:1 BC:1 CA:0
29.    Material:"TEXTURE TEST"
30.    Smoothing:  3
31.    Face 5:    A:1 B:6 C:2 AB:0 BC:1 CA:1
32.    Material:"TEXTURE TEST"
33.    Smoothing:  3
34.    Face 6:    A:2 B:6 C:7 AB:1 BC:1 CA:0
35.    Material:"TEXTURE TEST"
36.    Smoothing:  4
37.    Face 7:    A:2 B:7 C:3 AB:0 BC:1 CA:1
38.    Material:"TEXTURE TEST"
```

```
39.    Smoothing:  4
40.    Face 8:     A:3 B:7 C:4 AB:1 BC:1 CA:0
41.    Material:"TEXTURE TEST"
42.    Smoothing:  5
43.    Face 9:     A:3 B:4 C:0 AB:0 BC:1 CA:1
44.    Material:"TEXTURE TEST"
45.    Smoothing:  5
46.    Face 10:    A:4 B:7 C:6 AB:1 BC:1 CA:0
47.    Material:"TEXTURE TEST"
48.    Smoothing:  6
49.    Face 11:    A:4 B:6 C:5 AB:0 BC:1 CA:1
50.    Material:"TEXTURE TEST"
51.    Smoothing:  6
52.
53.
54.
55.
56.
57.
58.
59.
60.
61.
62.
63.                                    Page 1
```

Notice that starting on line 7, the vertex entries now have U and V coordinates in addition to their XYZ coordinates. These are called the *mapping coordinates* (or *UV coordinates*). 3D Studio uses UV coordinates to figure out how to place the texture map on the faces.

Conceptually, UV coordinates are like the XYZ coordinates in 3D Studio, but not really. Calling them coordinates is technically accurate, but a little misleading because most people associate coordinate with Cartesian coordinates (that is, points in space). These are really quite different because they refer to a unitless location on a texture map, not a point in space.

Intro to UV Anomalies

The observant and curious will have noticed that some of the UV coordinates have a value of -0. Obviously, negative zero is not that meaningful and would be better expressed as zero, so why did 3D Studio write -0?

The answer is known only to the creators of 3D Studio, but probably it occurred due to rounding problems. It is not the only problem with mapping coordinates and .ASC files; in many cases, mapping coordinates are written imperfectly (and sometimes wildly inaccurately!). In particular, Modify/.../Mirror seems prone to damaging mapping coordinates.

What's a UV Coordinate?

Look back at the example texture map and notice the UV coordinates written on it. These labels are intended to refer to the corner to which they are closest; for example, u=0 v=0 refers to the upper left corner.

Note that UV coordinates start in the upper left corner of the texture, unlike the XYZ coordinates' lower left corner. Also, UV coordinates have no units—they always range from 0 to 1, no matter how large or small the texture. They are not a hard unit like pixels or inches.

This second point has some important implications, so let's look at an example. Figure 6.2 shows two texture maps. The white dots on both of the textures indicate the same UV coordinate.

Because they have no units, think of UVs as a percentage (or a fraction—whichever is easier for you to work with). For example, a U coordinate of 0.31 means 31 percent (about one-third) of the width from the left side, and a V of 0.875 means 87.5 percent (seven-eighths) down the side of the texture.

How Do UVs Work Exactly?

As stated earlier, 3D Studio uses UV coordinates to figure out how to place the texture map on the faces. Let's follow the exact steps used to accomplish this, using face 2 from the listing as our example.

When the graphics engine (or 3D Studio) has to draw a face, it gets the UV coordinates from all three vertices and uses them to define a triangular mask on top of the texture map. It then copies this triangular chunk out of the texture and stretches it to fit in the triangular region defined by the face onscreen.

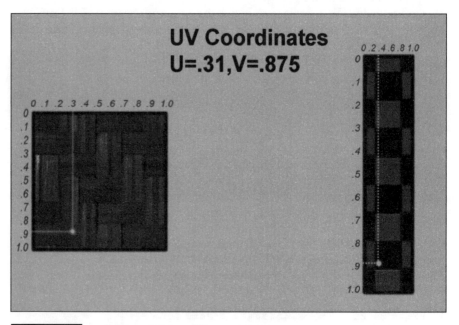

 Same UVs, different textures.

Designing 3D Graphics

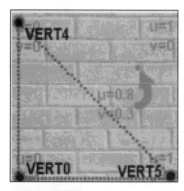

FIGURE 6.3   Triangular piece of texture.

In our example, face 2 uses verts 0 (u=0 v=1) and 4 (u=0 v=0) and 5 (u=1 v=0). If we plot them on top of our texture map and connect them with dotted lines, we'll get something like Figure 6.3 (they're not at the actual corners of the texture for clarity).

This triangular piece of the texture is then stretched to fit the shape of the face and is put on the screen, as shown in Figure 6.4. In our example, the face's geometry corresponds with the texture's shape pretty well, but that's not always the case.

That's the basics of mapping in a nutshell. Now, let's go deeper into the tools we use, and study how we create mapping in 3D Studio.

FIGURE 6.4   Textured face on screen.

CHAPTER 6 • **Mapping**   **109**

● Exploring 3D Studio's Mapping Tools

3D Studio's documentation attempted to illustrate the different types of mapping on a beautifully printed but utterly confusing card, named "Mapping Coordinate Methods," that comes with the manuals. It shows four rows, each row containing a box, a cylinder, and a sphere. Each row uses a different kind of mapping, but the mapping type is not labeled and it's unclear which kind is which unless you already understand mapping (the other side of the card—keyboard shortcuts—is quite useful. In fact, this card is so confusing, especially in its choice of a cylinder, box, and sphere as example objects, that it may actually hinder understanding of mapping, rather than advance it.

Mapping is confusing territory, even to the people who wrote the documentation for the program. Here, we will attempt to improve this woeful state of affairs. Let's review what mapping abilities 3D Studio has to offer and see how they suit our needs.

3D Studio offers a few basic types of mapping: Planar, Cylindrical, Sphere, Lofted, and Face mapping. The three types of planar, cylindrical, and spheroid are related—they're all projection mapping; the other two are oddities that we'll deal with separately.

Projection Mapping

The weirdest thing about planar mapping is the idea of projection (Figure 6.6).

The term *projection* comes from the idea of a movie projector sending an image in a long, mapping-icon-shaped, thick laser beam. Figure 6.5 shows two mappings being projected onto a 3D model of a table.

FIGURE 6.5 Projection mapping example.

The map icons (shown as icon-like boxes with the texture map inside them) in space above the table, but because the mapping is projected (illustrated by translucent striping from the map icon to the table), the table still receives mapping coordinates.

Like the movie projector, the mapping icon hits the mapped object no matter how far away it is. And, like the projector, the mapping icon has to be aimed at the object correctly, but there is one difference: unlike film projectors, the mapping projection doesn't get larger as it gets farther away from the projector. That's the "thick laser beam" part—it's a laser, not a flashlight's expanding cone.

The key thing to understand is that moving the mapping icon along its normal (the laser-beam line that it points along) doesn't matter. Referring to Figure 6.5 again, the left mapping icon is much farther along its axis of projection than the right one, but the mapping orientation and scale are identical for both.

If you want, you can load the project file that this illustration came from (MAPP01.PRJ), use Mapping/Adjust/Acquire, and see that the table uses the left icon's mapping everywhere except for the extended table leaf element, which uses the right icon.

Planar Projection Mapping

Planar mapping is probably the easiest to understand, and the most generally useful, of all the mapping types. With *planar mapping*, the mapping icon physically resembles the texture map—it's a rectangle, floating in space, that frames the texture map we're applying (see Figure 6.6).

We can edit it easily; to make the texture appear smaller, we simply scale the icon, and so on. Note that it's quite easy to distort the proportions of the texture

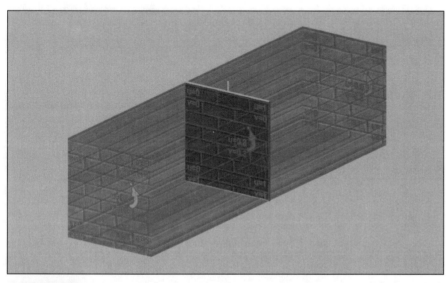

FIGURE 6.6   Planar texture mapping illustration.

if the mapping icon's shape doesn't match the texture. Fortunately, 3D Studio's designers thoughtfully gave us the Surface/Mapping/Adjust/Bitmap Fit command for this very purpose. It adjusts the mapping icon's aspect to match any existing bitmap on the disk.

Cylindrical Projection Mapping

Cylindrical mapping is best understood if we imagine taking the planar rectangle and bending it into a circle, so the two vertical edges touch each other. Now, the projection occurs like radiation from the center of the circle, as shown in Figure 6.7.

No longer is the analogy to a film projector accurate—looking along the cylinder's axis, we see a radial projection like fluorescent light, emitting rays of light from the center of the circle. This simple change triggers an entirely different situation when you are trying to place the mapping icon correctly.

When we scale a mapping icon, we might expect a larger, but correctly proportioned mapping to result. Not so! Scaling a cylindrical mapping icon causes the vertical size and the diameter to change, as Figure 6.8 shows. The cylinder appears to grow uniformly, but unlike planar mapping, the outer mapping has a different width-to-height ratio from the original. This occurs because the horizontal sides of the texture form a circle, and the circle's diameter doesn't matter because the projection radiates from its center.

In other words, making the circle's diameter larger won't make the texture map repeat more times around the diameter. Imagine a roll of patterned toilet paper, but the pattern had to always fit around the outside exactly once. When the roll is new, the pattern will be stretched out around the large circumference,

FIGURE 6.7   Cylindrical projection mapping.

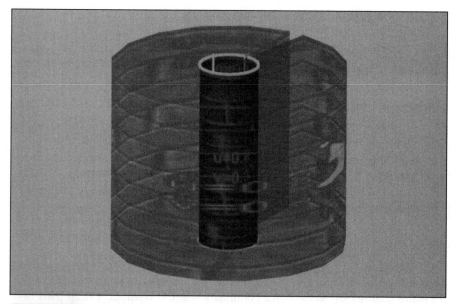

FIGURE 6.8 Cylindrical mapping icon.

but when the roll's nearly gone, the pattern will be scrunched (if you look closely in Figure 6.8, you can see a tiny, scrunched inner texture).

It is possible, though not easy, to avoid this distortion when using cylindrical mapping. See "Preventing Distortion with Cylindrical Mapping" later in this chapter.

Spheroid Projection Mapping

Spheroid projection mapping is simply the next step from cylindrical mapping. With *spheroid mapping*, we convert the straight-line height of the cylinder to a circle, leaving us a sphere.

This is getting really weird to understand, but the basic idea is used in cartography: Take a flat map of the world and wrap it around a sphere. In 3D Studio, we can stretch the map so we don't end up with creases or folds, but the top and bottom of the map are severely compressed, while the middle is stretched out. It is also similar to drawing on a balloon, then blowing it up. The top and bottom of the drawing don't grow as much as the center does; in fact, with spheroid mapping, the top and bottom shrink.

It's tempting to compare spheroid mapping to painting on a light bulb, but this is misleading. If we were to paint on a light bulb, we would paint on the curved 3D surface directly. Because we don't have any way (using 3D Studio) to paint in 3D space, we must make a flat painting and then have it stretched and squashed onto a sphere.

Spheroid mapping is not regularly used in RT3D modeling, though there is no technical reason not to (if you can find a use for it!).

Non-Projection Mapping

As promised, here are the two methods of mapping in 3D Studio that don't involve the projection concept. They're not pretty, nor are they very versatile, but at least we don't have to mess with the mapping icon.

Lofting Mapping

There's another way to get mapping coordinates out of 3D Studio without using projection mapping. It's possible to generate mapping coordinates when creating an object using the 3D Lofter. The procedure is fairly straightforward, and it is quite handy for certain complicated lofted shapes. 3D Studio, however, doesn't offer much control over these coordinates—you pretty much have to live with what they offer or use normal mapping methods.

Face Mapping

Face mapping in 3D Studio is a material switch that, if activated, bypasses all the normal mapping tools and methods such as UV coordinate assignment. Instead, it fits the texture map to each face's boundaries, and if possible, it finds pairs of coplanar faces that share invisible edges and fits the texture map in them. The only real changes that can be made to this process are hidden under the Settings button for the texture in the Materials editor. In there, we can change the tiling and the rotation of the texture, and these controls will affect the face mapping.

Many graphics engines do not support face mapping, and the ones that do frequently can't parse 3D Studio's data to figure out which faces should be face mapped and which should not.

Face mapping can give very impressive results, very quickly. When the shape of the faces should be emphasized, it's a handy shortcut for doing so.

 Messier Mapping Issues

This section contains some advanced concepts in working with mapping in 3D Studio.

Changing UV Coordinates by Hand

As you can imagine, it isn't too hard to change the UV coordinates by changing the values in the ASC file, and doing so is very informative about how mapping works (as well as occasionally useful!). Note that this is true for very simple geometry like our cube because we can easily figure out where each vertex goes; once we get a 200-vert model of a hand, it's another story.

Change the UV coordinate of one corner of a cube, and observe the result when we render:

Do the exercise in the section "Simple Mapping Example." You should now be in the text editor, looking at the ASC file you just created.

1. Change line 12 from "Vertex 5: X:1   Y:-0   Z:0   U:1   V:-0" so it looks just like this: "Vertex 5: X:1   Y:-0   Z:0   U:1   V:0.5" (in other words, change vertex 5's V coordinate from 0 to 0.5).

2. Save the file, return to the 3D editor, and load the ASC file, replacing the existing data.

3. Adjust the ambient light by sliding Lightness to 220.

4. Render the User view. You should see something like the view shown in the monitor in Figure 6.9.

So, what happened? We should have expected face 2 to change so that it looks like the single triangle in the center of the illustration, but the other faces changed as well. That's because UV coordinates are stored with the vertex, and more than one face referred to the vertex. If you look at the code listing, you'll find that faces 3, 4, and 11 also refer to vertex 5.

This is a very important point! If you want to change the mapping on a face, you have to be sure you aren't going to mess up the mapping on other faces that share vertices. The usual way to solve this problem is to detach the face from the current object, which creates new vertices (in the same XYZ location) for your face.

There's one other interesting area of our example cube. We've all seen mappings that turn out like the top of our cube (some call that "striping"). It's usually seen as a mistake, though there's nothing really wrong with it technically. How does it happen? It's obvious if we look at the three vertices that form one of the top faces.

The top face is easy to find in the listing because all the Y values of its verts will be 1.

First, we locate all verts with ASC-Z=1, then find a face that uses three of these verts.

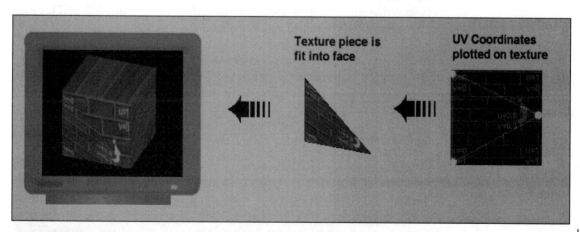

Texture piece is fit into face

UV Coordinates plotted on texture

FIGURE 6.9 Results of UVs changing.

```
1.    [..]
2.    Vertex 0:  X:0     Y:0     Z:1     U:0     V:1
3.    Vertex 1:  X:1     Y:0     Z:1     U:1     V:1
4.    Vertex 2:  X:1     Y:1     Z:1     U:1     V:1
5.    [..]
6.    Face 0:    A:0 B:1 C:2 AB:1 BC:1 CA:0
7.    [..]
```

As we can see, face 0 uses verts 0, 1, and 2, which all have a Z value of 1 in the .ASC file. The strange thing about this face is that verts 1 and 2 both have the same UV coordinates. Let's look at how this causes the striping effect (Figure 6.10).

Notice that the dotted "triangle" on the texture forms a single line. This tiny slice of the texture is stretched across the face, creating stripes from single points in the original texture.

Another way to visualize what's going on is to imagine the texture as a carrot, and the textured face as a thin slice from it. When the face isn't aligned with the cross-section, we get a striped effect—like cutting the carrot lengthwise instead of the easy way.

Striping is not an all-or-nothing process; in fact, most mapping involves some amount of striping because most faces aren't likely to be perfectly parallel with the mapping icon. Striping is not noticeable usually in small amounts.

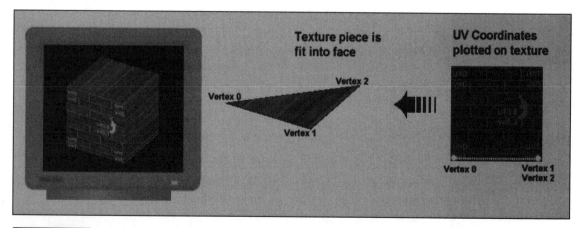

FIGURE 6.10 Striped mapping.

Mapping and Elements

Elements have some special properties in 3D Studio. Most importantly, 3D Studio allows us to assign mapping (UV coordinates) to elements. What does it mean to assign mapping coordinates to an abstracted concept like an element?

Remember the definition of *element*: a collection of faces that share verts. Because mapping coordinates are stored with the verts, it makes sense that mapping should be applied to elements; if we applied mapping to anything smaller (like a single face or vert), it would disturb the mapping of the neighboring faces that shared its verts.

The problem with elements is that they're abstract entities; we can accidentally create and destroy elements within objects as we edit. It's hard to depend on their being correct when we're ready to map. Remember that the only thing that defines elements is whether verts are shared. Therefore, to create a single element out of several faces, we make sure they all share verts. To divide an element into two pieces, make the dividing faces have their own, unshared verts. See Chapter 2 for more details on elements.

When we use Mapping/Apply Object, we apply mapping to all the verts in the object. This ignores the natural boundaries of shared verts vs. unshared; it's cruder than applying mapping to elements. As a side point, because verts can't be shared across objects, Mapping/Apply Object won't ever disturb the mapping on other objects.

Thought Experiment: "Map Ghost"

All this hassle about shared verts is a big drag, isn't it? Let's think, for a minute, about how we'd make mapping work in a more perfect world, and then we'll see if we can make it happen in real life.

First, the dream: Imagine something called "a map ghost": a different way of applying mapping coordinates. It would be made of spline surfaces that contained the mapping coordinates.

CHAPTER 6 • **Mapping**

To use it, we would take a few surfaces and arrange them around our object, like gift-wrapping with super-stretchy rubber sheeting, printed with our texture. The result would be a smooth-surface model somewhat similar to our polygonal model—a "ghost." Once we set up the map ghost, we could then mess up the verts, add and remove faces, and generally edit without worrying about messing up the mapping coordinates.

The cool thing about this scenario is it's backward-compatible. Once the model was finished, we'd do the equivalent of Surface/Mapping/Apply and our model would be a normal 3DS model with plain-jane UVs.

So, what's the problem? Here are the potential problems:

- There are times when we *want* the mapping to change with our vertex edits (for example, when we move the object) and times when we don't (welding verts, for example).

- We'd have to deal with multiple mapping surfaces conflicting—what if a vert could get two different sets of UVs because the mapping surfaces overlapped?

- We'd need good ways to convert ghost-map surfaces to and from UV coordinates, to make editing easy by extracting UVs from an existing object.

The map ghost's data would be stored separately from the UVs. For example, when we looked at the ASC file in the first exercise, if we used ghost mapping, we might see something like this:

```
1.      - WARNING - FAKE ASC FILE! - Ghost mapping thought-experiment
2.      Ambient light color: Red=0.039216 Green=0.039216 Blue=0.039216
3.
4.      Named object: "TestCube01"
5.      Tri-mesh, Vertices: 8      Faces: 12
6.      Mapped
7.      Ghost Mapping Used
8.      Vertex list:
9.      Vertex 0:   X:0      Y:0      Z:1      U:0      V:1
10.     Vertex 1:   X:1      Y:0      Z:1      U:1      V:1
11.     Vertex 2:   X:1      Y:1      Z:1      U:1      V:1
12.     Vertex 3:   X:0      Y:1      Z:1      U:0      V:1
13.     Vertex 4:   X:0      Y:-0     Z:0      U:0      V:-0
14.     Vertex 5:   X:1      Y:-0     Z:0      U:1      V:-0
15.     Vertex 6:   X:1      Y:1      Z:-0     U:1      V:-0
16.     Vertex 7:   X:0      Y:1      Z:-0     U:0      V:-0
17.     Face list:
18.     Face 0:     A:0 B:1 C:2 AB:1 BC:1 CA:0
19.     Material:"TEXTURE TEST"
20.     Smoothing:  1
21.     Face 1:     A:0 B:2 C:3 AB:0 BC:1 CA:1
22.     Material:"TEXTURE TEST"
23.     Smoothing:  1
24.     Face 2:     A:0 B:4 C:5 AB:1 BC:1 CA:0
25.     Material:"TEXTURE TEST"
26.     Smoothing:  2
27.     Face 3:     A:0 B:5 C:1 AB:0 BC:1 CA:1
28.     Material:"TEXTURE TEST"
29.     Smoothing:  2
```

```
30.    Face 4:     A:1 B:5 C:6 AB:1 BC:1 CA:0
31.    Material:"TEXTURE TEST"
32.    Smoothing:  3
33.    Face 5:     A:1 B:6 C:2 AB:0 BC:1 CA:1
34.    Material:"TEXTURE TEST"
35.    Smoothing:  3
36.    Face 6:     A:2 B:6 C:7 AB:1 BC:1 CA:0
37.    Material:"TEXTURE TEST"
38.    Smoothing:  4
39.    Face 7:     A:2 B:7 C:3 AB:0 BC:1 CA:1
40.    Material:"TEXTURE TEST"
41.    Smoothing:  4
42.    Face 8:     A:3 B:7 C:4 AB:1 BC:1 CA:0
43.    Material:"TEXTURE TEST"
44.    Smoothing:  5
45.    Face 9:     A:3 B:4 C:0 AB:0 BC:1 CA:1
46.    Material:"TEXTURE TEST"
47.    Smoothing:  5
48.    Face 10:    A:4 B:7 C:6 AB:1 BC:1 CA:0
49.    Material:"TEXTURE TEST"
50.    Smoothing:  6
51.    Face 11:    A:4 B:6 C:5 AB:0 BC:1 CA:1
52.    Material:"TEXTURE TEST"
53.    Smoothing:  6
54.
55.    Ghost Maps:
56.    [b-spline surface definition]
57.    [b-spline surface definition]
```

The Mapping Icon Revisited

Well, guess what? 3D Studio has a crude version of this scenario already implemented.

We already know about the mapping icon, but let's look at it in comparison to the scenario we described above. The mapping icon's three types of surfaces (plane, cylinder, sphere) could be thought of as simple versions of our "ghost map" surfaces: they are continuous mathematical surfaces, independent of the UV coordinates in the object's verts.

Also, like the "ghost map," the mapping icon is stored independently from the UV coordinates, one for each object. Note that the mapping icon is not stored in the .ASC file; it's stored only in the binary files .3DS and .PRJ.

It's important to emphasize that the stored mapping icon is completely separate from the UV coordinates. Effectively, two sets of UVs are stored with every object: one real set, stored with the verts, and a virtual one that is simply the position and orientation of the mapping icon.

This feature can be very useful, but only when we're editing verts whose UV coordinates are generated straight from the mapping icon. For example, imagine we've got a 3D model of a human hand, and a photograph of a hand that we're texturing onto the model. We want to make edits to the hand model, but we do not want to mess up the mapping coordinates. If we're lucky enough to have a model that requires only one application of mapping, we can accomplish this.

First, we use the background-trace technique outlined in the car exercise in Chapter 9 to get a basic correlation between the model and the texture, then

map the object. Now, imagine that we need to fine-tune the alignment. Once we set up our mapping icon, we can make changes to the object (such as tapering the fingers more, or welding verts) that damage the mapping coordinates and reapply the mapping to the object quickly.

Of course, a single object may have many elements, each with its own mapping, but 3DS stores only a single mapping icon per object. In our example, imagine that we have a bracelet on the hand with different mapping (cylindrical, for example). If the bracelet is not a separate object, we won't be able to reapply its mapping coordinates quickly because we can't use Surface/Mapping/Adjust/Acquire to get its mapping icon.

Also, the mapping icon has the same drawbacks. If we make basic edits and we *want* the mapping icon to follow along, there is no way to do this automatically. If we move the hand, the UV coordinates don't change: We don't need to remap, but our cool quick remapping is messed up. If we want to keep the mapping icon aligned, we have to move it separately.

The single-icon-per-object limitation is something to keep in mind when creating new objects and merging objects together. When we merge objects (using Create/Object/Attach or Create/Face/Detach with faces from multiple objects selected), we get rid of any mapping icon stored in the object whose name is gone (remember that we are not talking about the actual UV coordinates; we are only talking about the mapping icon itself).

To store a mapping icon with an object, we simply apply mapping to the object with the icon arranged as we want it stored. This could be a problem if we want to store the icon, but not actually modify the object's mapping, but that situation rarely arises. To retrieve the mapping icon from an object, use the Surface/Mapping/Adjust/Acquire menu option.

As you can see, the mapping icon is not a perfectly designed tool, but with a little massaging, it can really be helpful in a day-to-day labor-saving way.

Preventing Distortion with Cylindrical Mapping

Whenever cylindrical mapping is discussed, someone inevitably mentions the analogy of a soup can label. The idea is that the texture map is a piece of paper—the label—and the cylinder object is the can. This analogy is good for getting the basic idea across, but it doesn't go far. What happens if the can gets bigger?

Intuitively, we'd expect cylindrical mapping to behave like a patterned toilet paper roll: As the diameter changes, the pattern stays the same shape but it repeats fewer times around. However, 3D Studio doesn't offer any easy way to accomplish this. Instead, the default action is to stretch a single copy of the texture all the way around the larger can.

The best 3D Studio offers is tiling to cause repetition around the X repeat (X was the horizontal direction in planar mapping; now it's the circumference) with the Surface/Mapping/Adjust/Tiling command. The real question is, how many times should it repeat around the cylinder to keep its aspect right? The usual method is to guesstimate, render, and revise the tiling until it looks "good

Designing 3D Graphics

enough," but once in a while we must map a cylindrical object and simply must get the aspect right. It's not easy, but we *can* figure out the correct number of times to tile.

Calculate the correct number of times to tile:

1. Measure the circumference of the cylindrical object we are mapping. It's easy if we measure the diameter and multiply by pi (3.1416).

2. Divide the circumference by the cylinder's height. This gives us the desired aspect.

3. Divide the texture map's width (in pixels) by its height. This gives us the texture's aspect.

4. Divide the desired aspect by the texture's aspect. This is the correction factor. If it's greater than 1, that means the texture map is taller than the cylinder. If it's less than 1, it means the texture map is wider than the cylinder. If it's exactly 1, it's a perfect fit.

5. We can do two things with the correction factor, depending on whether we want the texture map to have an uneven height or circumference. If we want the circumference to be too long (or short) but the height correct, we enter the correction factor in the X repeat space in the Surface/Mapping/Adjust/Tiling dialog. Or, we can make the texture map uneven in height, but it will wrap around the cylinder exactly once. To do this, we invert the correction factor (that is, divide 1 by it) and put it in the Y repeat field.

For example, imagine we have a texture of 512 × 256 pixels, and it must keep its proportions while being mapped on a 2-meter-tall cylinder with a diameter of 1 meter.

First, we figure the circumference: 3.14 meters. Then, we divide it by the height, giving us a desired aspect of 1.57. The texture map's aspect is 512 divided by 256, or 2. Dividing 1.57 by 2 gives our correction factor of 0.785, which means that the texture map is too long to wrap evenly around the cylinder. So, let's make it repeat a little bit in height but wrap around the cylinder evenly. That means we put 1 in the X repeat and 1 divided by 0.785, which is 1.27, in the Y repeat of the Surface/Mapping/Adjust/Tiling dialog.

Paste-Mapping

Paste-mapping is a special kind of non-tiled texture mapping. *Paste-mapping* involves taking a single texture that is a painting of the entire object and using simple mapping to put the entire texture onto the object. For example, imagine we've got a 3D human hand model and a photograph of a hand. When we map the photo onto the model in a single Surface/Mapping/Apply Object command we're paste-mapping.

Paste-mapping contrasts with the classic texture-mapping concept of using various different repeating textures such as brick, grass, and so on, and assigning

them to different pieces of the model. This doesn't usually work too well for low-poly RT3D models because it requires that faces start and end at the material's boundaries, and because it frequently requires different mapping coordinates at shared verts. In normal working situations, we probably won't have enough faces to model boundaries between materials, much less unique details. That's when paste-mapping begins to look really good.

Why Use It?

Paste-mapping helps make objects look unique without adding faces. With a single texture that covers the whole object, we can make unique asymmetrical details in the texture. We can't do this with "normal" mapping methods because any change we make to the repeating texture will repeat wherever the texture wraps around.

Paste-mapping really shines when we are simulating surfaces or special effects that the real-time engine doesn't support. For example, we can model a series of buildings that cast shadows on one another, render the Front and Side views for each building, and have what looks like shadows in the real-time model.

When Doesn't It Work?

Of course, we can't use paste-mapping when we're representing effects that must change—for example, reflections of clouds in car windows look bad because they don't change during run-time; because they don't move when the car does, they look as if they were dimly painted on the windows.

Also, paste-mapping usually requires a lot of texture map memory; we usually can't reuse a paste-map because it's unique to a specific object (unlike tiling textures, which can be reused all over the model).

And, of course, paste-mapping can't show details that are 3D in nature very well. Door knobs don't look very convincing (though better than nothing), and attempting to paste-map a statue against a wall would look really fake. Designing a good map—one that shows detail but doesn't require any 3D thickness to show it—can be difficult.

How Do We Do It?

Imagine we have a building modeled as a simple bottomless cube. We want the top half textured with brick, the bottom should be a continuous glass window storefront, and we'd like to add some unique details if possible.

First, let's think about how we'd map it normally. Because we can't assign the two different materials to the same face, we'd have to divide the faces to use a repeating brick texture on top and glass on the bottom. We'd use textures like the ones in Figure 6.11 A and B.

A better solution would be to make a new texture that is half-brick and half-glass—effectively, a vertical strip of the building—and apply this to the building. Figure 6.12 shows this new texture.

Designing 3D Graphics

A

B

FIGURE 6.11 Separate, repeating textures.

FIGURE 6.12 Combined texture of brick and glass.

Designing 3D Graphics

Because we have this arrangement, we know where the brick will align vertically on the building. That is, we know that the top edge of the texture is going to meet the top of the building. We want to put something in the middle of all that brick—a window, for example.

The problem is, we don't know where the left edge of the texture will go until we map the texture onto the model. If we put a window in the middle of the brick, and then we apply mapping that has the texture ending halfway through the side of the building, we'll get a half-window on the edge of the building.

But, if we take this concept one step farther, we will simply paint the entire side of the building and then apply the texture to each of the four sides. That's paste-mapping (even though it is repeated on the four sides for economy of memory). With this complete side of the building, we can add details that we couldn't add normally, such as a small sign on one side, an entrance area, and so on. We could even use a photo of the side of a real building.

Special Effects with Mapping

These effects depend on the way the graphics engine works, so they may not work for everybody. Warning: Experimenting with strange uses of texture-mapping like these can cause crashes or strange behaviors that take a long time to debug, but sometimes the results are worth it. Here are some ideas:

- When texture-map memory is tight (and it usually is), it's possible to use the same texture in a bunch of different ways by using creative mapping. For example, imagine we're building a virtual lobby and we have a texture that includes the logo, company's name text, and a subtitle. We can use the same texture and, with careful mapping, effectively cut and paste the pieces over the whole object. We could have the logo on the floor, the company name text on the front doors, and the backdrop could have the whole original texture. We would accomplish this by choosing the area on the texture, then assigning mapping coordinates that include only the area we want.

- For somewhat varied color fills, map a small area of a low-contrast texture on the whole entity (that is, the mapping icon should be huge in relation to the entity). This will probably make large, square, crisp pixel borders, but as long as that look is acceptable, it makes for an interesting variation on the normal solid-color scene.

- For random sparkly effects, make the mapping icon really tiny. If the entire texture map fits within a single screen pixel, the graphics engine will choose pixels from the texture mostly at random. This one could definitely result in some crashes because the UV coordinates may be too huge for the graphics engine to handle.

- Striping, which occurs when a face is mapped with a single row of pixels from the texture, can be used to good effect once in a while. It can be especially cool with a gradient. Striping has become synonymous with

poor mapping ability among 3D artists, but the public doesn't worry about that, and neither should we. If it looks cool, who cares how we did it?

- By hand-editing the UV coordinates, we can really make some twisted mapping situations. For example, imagine swapping the UVs for two corners of a square. What would happen? Something interesting, to be sure (possibly a graphics engine crash, but probably not).

CHAPTER 7

CREATING TEXTURES

This chapter is about creating texture maps for real-time 3D models. It doesn't really teach you how to make realistic, lifelike textures because those skills are purely artistic. Instead, we'll cover how to keep the technological bottleneck as wide as possible for your artistic visions.

Prologue

Creating textures is a big deal in real-time 3D modeling—it's frequently what really makes a model shine because it's the most visible part of the model. The 3D model's shape is important, but when face count is at a minimum, the geometry often just acts like a "carrier," a canvas on which we paint the texture.

The most important part of good texture mapping is having artistic painting ability—being able to make an image that causes viewers to "get it," to see and feel what we intend them to. Let's assume you can make beautiful images when you don't have to worry about technical issues. We'll concentrate on this question: What should we know to make these beautiful images work as real-time textures?

We need to know how to take our artistic ability and squeeze from it all the requirements that a real-time application demands. Specifically, we need to make a beautiful texture that doesn't flicker, uses as little memory as possible, doesn't have banding problems, doesn't have resolution that is too low, works with the lighting model, and uses the master palette if we are working in 8-bit color.

General Editing Tips

This section is a collection of tips for creating texture maps that apply in lots of circumstances.

- The general technique of doubling an image's size, performing some slightly destructive edit like Gaussian blur, then scaling the image back down, helps preserve the image's quality in many different circumstances. This one is a really good basic idea, and it is closely related to the next one.

- Make the texture maps larger (as much as twice as big) than the final intended size, then save a scaled-down copy of the high-res image in the graphics engine. If it turns out that we can use a higher resolution than we originally planned, our large texture will make use of this detail (instead of being an expanded version of the low-res one). Even more importantly, all this detail makes for a much richer texture if an insignificant detail is on the verge of being lost—wood grains, for example. Also, if we find that our model needs more detail, we can quickly regenerate the detailed textures from the detailed source, instead of having to add detail to crude textures.

- When working with paletted color, create the textures in 24-bit, but use only colors from the game's palette. The conversion from 24-bit to 8-bit

should not cause any image quality loss, but certain editing commands will do much better on a 24-bit image than an 8-bit; in fact, in some bitmap editors, many editing commands will work *only* on 24-bit images. This tip is more sketchy than the others—some artists are really good at working within an 8-bit palette and can produce better art than if they work in 24-bit, then reduce. You know which approach is better for you (or you will after trying them both a couple times).

Choosing the Right Size of Texture

One of the hardest technical decisions to make when creating a new texture is determining how big it should be. We don't want to waste precious memory on a huge texture that will never be seen, and we definitely don't want those massive, blocky pixels we get when our textures don't have enough resolution.

The moral to the story: When we design our objects, we make our texture maps as close as possible to the size they'll be seen on the screen. Even if we had texture map memory to burn, we would actually get worse-looking models if we doubled all the texture maps' size in our application. The reason? These huge textures still have to be scaled to fit in the rendered viewport, and the graphics engine does a bad job of that compared to Photoshop. It's better to keep the graphics engine out of it, as much as we can, by trying to make the textures the right size.

Here's what we need to know to figure out the right size.

How Closely Will the Texture Be Seen?

Ideally, we will create textures that will be seen at their full resolution when the user is closest to them. We assume that the user will always be as close as possible to our textures, and we create the texture at the size that will map one-to-one with the screen pixels at that distance. The problem with this scenario is these answers indicate that our texture maps must be enormous, which usually runs us up against the memory budget. A better answer will attempt to compromise by choosing the most common position the user is likely to take, with the understanding that the texture will start looking bad if the user gets any closer. However, in most RT3D environments, we don't know what the user will do, so we don't know how close they'll get to our objects. For an example of this, see the car exercise in Chapter 9, where we discuss how to decide the size of the textures for the grille.

What Does Our Graphics Engine Support?

If the engine is limited to three texture sizes, then that makes our decision much easier (though not better; of course, we prefer to have many texture sizes to choose from). Once we know this, we pick the size closest to the first question's answer and continue. We need to know how many different size textures we can have (usually, the number of pixels on a side must be a power of 2: 16, 32, 64,

128, 256, 512), what color depths (usually either paletted 8-bit or 24-bit), and what aspect ratios (some engines allow only square textures: 16 x 16, 64 x 64, and so on). Note that if these sizes don't align with what we need, we can do some tricks explained later in this chapter.

How Much of Our Texture Memory Budget Should We Use for This Texture?

Once we have our object's texture memory budgeted, we'll break it down for each texture we plan to use. This is also where we weigh the relative importance of each texture, factoring in such issues as:

- How commonly is the texture seen
- How noticeable is its (lack of) resolution
- Whether it is a focus for the user's attention

We hope the memory budget allows for the "closest-to-the-user" size, but if it doesn't we'll have to make a compromise. Here are some of the compromises we can make:

- We can live with a smaller texture than would be ideal. This is the usual solution. The downside is that there will be times during the game when the texture is "blown up"—each pixel in the texture will fill several pixels on the screen, creating a blocky, jagged, undetailed appearance.
- We can sacrifice a different texture somewhere else and use its allocated memory to allow the larger texture. This is a simple trade-off.
- We can combine the textures into a single file. Later in this chapter we will cover how to do this.

How Much Memory Does Each Texture Map Use?

When considering texture size relating to memory usage, as we must do when we are trying to determine our texture map memory budget, we must know how much memory each texture uses. The best way to find this out is to consult the programmer to determine how to calculate it.

The theoretical formula is bitmap height (in pixels) multiplied by width, multiplied by color depth (bits per pixel), divided by 8. This tells us how many bytes of memory our bitmap uses.

For example, if we have a texture that's 512 pixels wide and 256 pixels tall, and it's an 8-bit (that is, 256 color, paletted) bitmap, we would figure:

512 pixels (width) × 256 pixels (height) × 8 bits per pixel / 8 bits per byte = 131,072 bytes

Where we'll need the programmer's help is in figuring how many of the textures will fit in memory. It's not always a simple addition exercise; sometimes the bitmaps must fall on even increments of powers of 2; at other times there are other factors that they must tell us.

If you find that you're constantly asking the programmer about texture memory constraints, you might want to find out what all these factors are and determine how to calculate the answer yourself, rather than simply getting "yes, 16 bitmaps will fit" answers. If we can figure it ourselves, we won't have to constantly bug the programmer with various "what-if" scenarios. What you want to ask is "How do I *figure out* how many textures will fit in my 2.5MB of texture memory?"—not "Will 16 128×128 textures fit?"

Dealing with Compression in Memory

One of the factors that the programmer may mention is compression. First, it's important to be sure you're not talking about compression on the storage medium (CD-ROM or hard disk); that's a different issue.

If the graphics engine allows for bitmap compression in memory, the good news is we'll have more texture memory than we might otherwise; the bad news is we don't know how much until we actually create the art. The most common type of compression is called RLL (run-length limited). It's a simple concept: If there are 128 white pixels in a row, RLL compression stores a "repeat this pixel 128 times" code. A normal bitmap simply stores 128 identical pixels. In this case, RLL saves lots of memory, but if there aren't a lot of identical pixels in horizontal rows, it doesn't do as well.

Knowing how we're using RLL compression, we keep this in mind (as a relatively minor issue) when we make our textures cooperate with the compression scheme and save a maximum amount of memory. For example, if we have created a striped texture, and we rotate the texture so the stripes run horizontally, it will compress beautifully. In general, we want to arrange any large blocks of similar colors so they fall in horizontal rows.

Tricks: Combining Maps for Efficiency

There are times when our texture map sizes don't align with the possible range of sizes that the graphics engine offers us. In this case, we can combine the various sizes into more palatable groupings, then carefully map each piece of the texture onto its face.

For example, let's say we have some long, thin textures (256×64) that we've drawn, but we can only make square texture maps. In this case, we can add four of these textures together to fill out the 256×256 texture. Then, we map one-fourth of the total mapping icon onto the area that we had mapped previously with the entire icon.

The most annoying thing about this trick is that it requires different mapping coordinates. However, if the graphics engine supports only certain size textures and we need something in between, this trick can sometimes buy us enough flexibility to accomplish what was previously impossible.

This trick is demonstrated in Chapter 9, where the robot's detail textures are combined.

Gouraud-Shaded Surfaces

Textures tend to destroy the illusion of Gouraud shading because though the lighting is smooth across two surfaces, any linear details in the map fold sharply across the face boundaries, exposing the surface as two flat surfaces instead of a single curved one.

This is different from 3D Studio because it stretches the texture to appear curved when it crosses a group of faces that have been assigned to the same smoothing group. This means we have to be careful not to depend on the way a Gouraud-shaded textured object looks in the 3D Studio editor—it may not be the same way it'll look in the real-time environment.

This doesn't mean we shouldn't use textures when we're using Gouraud shading. We just have to be careful of any linear details in the texture, or at least be aware that it will reveal the two faces as flat, contradicting the smooth lighting that Gouraud shading will give.

Perspective Angle

Perspective angle is a secondary factor, but it is frequently overlooked entirely. When we design a texture, we need to consider the following question: What is the common perspective angle at which the texture will be seen?

This question is hard to answer because we don't know how the user will be using the application; all we can do is guess if the texture will commonly be seen from an edge-on view, like floor tiles, or face-on, like walls and signs.

If we're building a texture that will frequently be seen from an edge view, it is much more likely to be distorted and to flicker because real-time graphics engines generally have a harder time when they have to portray a severely distorted image.

Compared to a sign texture that will usually be seen front-on, our edge-on textures should follow the guidelines that are outlined for flicker-free texturing, but to a greater extent in the "short" direction.

● How Textures Are Scaled in RT3D

Real-time applications must constantly scale the original textures to fit them onto the objects as they move around on screen. Getting our textures to look good at any size is quite tricky. This section will discuss the basic principals of why it's a problem, then explain what we can do about it.

Figure 7.1 portrays the basic scaling issues. At the left, we see the original texture (denoted with the gray border around it). The texture to its right was created by simply throwing out half the rows and columns of the original texture. This leaves one pixel where there were four in the original image. That's how real-time graphics engines handle the problem when the textured object occupies only a few pixels on the screen—it just tosses out most of the texture's pixels and plots the rest. This is a pretty crude way of handling it, but that's all it has time to do—texturing is already slow on most graphics engines.

Designing 3D Graphics

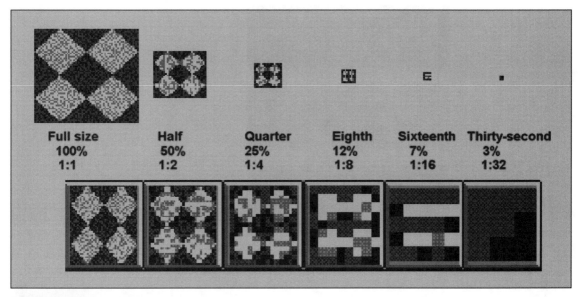

FIGURE 7.1 Texture with one-half, one-fourth, one-eighth reductions.

The second row of images are copies of the textures, scaled up so we can clearly see them.

Halves of Areas

It can be confusing to talk of the texture's dimensions being halved, but losing three-fourths of the pixels. Think about it this way: If we cut the bitmap in half left to right, we get half of the original bitmap, but the height didn't change. If we cut both the width and the height in half, we get one-fourth of the original texture.

This reduction has been repeated to the next texture to the right, leaving 1 pixel where there were 16 in the original image, and so on until the rightmost texture is a tiny dot—almost all the pixels were thrown out.

Obviously, scaling the bitmap means a massive loss of data. This scaling problem is unavoidable: The building is tiny on the screen because it is far away. We must show the bitmap as a tiny spot on the screen, but we can buffer the blow.

Let's go back to the first reduction, where the original texture was reduced in half in each direction. Obviously, losing this much data will damage the image quality, but we also know that using Photoshop's scaling techniques will yield very little image quality loss. When Photoshop reduces the size of an image like this, it considers the problem carefully. Its algorithm takes the four original pixels, perhaps even looks at the surrounding pixels, and calculates an average color for the single new pixel. The difference in quality is obvious, as is shown in Figure 7.2.

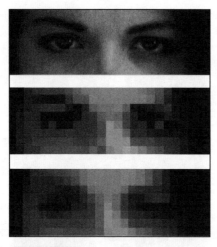

FIGURE 7.2 Size reduction—unscaled original, averaged and "chopped" reductions.

● Understanding Flickering

Flickering is a common problem in real-time 3D. It's easy to understand flickering once we know how scaling happens in our real-time application.

Let's take a look at an example. Our application portrays a scene like the one shown in Figure 7.3. On a building far away from the user is a checkered texture (Figure 7.4), and it naturally appears small on the user's screen because it is so far away.

In order to show the texture on the far-away building, the computer must resize and stretch the texture, very quickly. During this process, the computer starts with the original texture, but then puts only a small percentage of the pixels on the screen. It decides which pixels to put up in the quickest way possible, not knowing if it has left out important detail within the texture.

For our example, let's assume the computer chose a black pixel from near the border between a black and a white pixel.

A different problem comes when the user changes the viewing angle slightly. Now the computer must redo the rescaling of the textures on the screen. When it does, it chooses slightly different pixels. For example, this time it might choose a white pixel on the other side of the border instead of the black pixel. On the screen it appears that a black pixel changed into a white one. As the process continues, the user will see parts of that texture flash back and forth between black and white. This crude animation is what we call "flickering," and it's a major problem for most real-time texturing applications.

Perhaps you are thinking, "Flickering appears to be a problem with the graphics engine," and in one sense that is true because it could be solved with a better (but slower) texture map resizing algorithm. However, it's not one that's

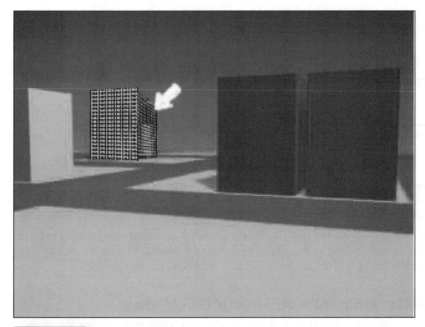

FIGURE 7.3   3D Scene with texture.

going to be solved without a lot more computing power. In the mean time, it's
more productive to think of flickering as a limitation that we must work around.

How to Make Flicker-Free Textures

Let's think from the perspective of the programmer who came up with this
method of choosing a pixel. It is written this way purely for speed. This method
of taking a bitmap and choosing individual pixels assumes that the neighboring
pixels aren't too different, so if it chooses a pixel from that region, it doesn't
matter too much which one it chose.

This is a silly assumption for most highly detailed textures, but if we work
backward and accept it, then we can build textures for which it holds true. Thus,
our first guideline: *Non-flickering textures have pixels that are relatively similar to
their neighbors.*

FIGURE 7.4   Blotchy checkered texture.

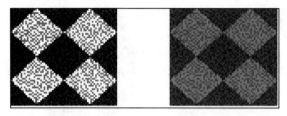

FIGURE 7.5 Two versions of the texture—one high contrast, one low.

Keeping the contrast down in the bitmap is a way of hedging our bets: When the pixels are picked from two different areas, if they aren't too different from each other, then the flickering won't be as pronounced. Of course, the detail will also be less noticeable because the contrast is lower, but that may be preferable to the alternatives. Take a look at Figure 7.5 for an example. The high-contrast texture on the left will flicker more noticeably than the one on the right.

Low Contrast: Not Always a Good Idea

The low-contrast guideline is not a rigid one, and frequently it is not worth the sacrifice in art quality that it requires. If we are portraying tiny detail, it is a good way to reduce flickering. An important point is that the contrast does not have to be lowered throughout the whole texture—only on sections that have intricate, high-contrast detail.

For example, we have mottled pavement that has lots of white specks in it. On that pavement are large, bright yellow stripes. We want to prevent the white specks from flickering, but we don't want the yellow stripe's color to be dulled. We can reduce the contrast of the pavement part severely, but leave the stripe as a bright yellow; this will reduce flickering just as well as if we had dulled the whole image.

Another important note is that the colors have to be close to only each other, not to gray. If we use the old-style Contrast slider to reduce the contrast, it will cause our colors to approach a 50 percent gray. This isn't necessary—the "target" color can be light or dark, gray or saturated. The only important thing is that the variations aren't too different from it.

This can be easily seen on a histogram. If the neighboring pixels are far from each other on the histogram, the texture is flicker-prone. What we need to do is move them closer to each other, but not necessarily to the middle of the histogram. They can be clumped down in the dark end of the spectrum, up in the light area, or anywhere else. The important thing is that each pixel's neighbors are near it on the histogram.

Blurring to Prevent Flickering

The more brute-force way to prevent flickering is to make large or blurred details in our textures. We especially avoid bright one-pixel-wide lines or dots.

Gaussian blur is an excellent way to create smoothed images that are very flicker-free, but it also blurs the image, which we may not want to do because we can lose valuable detail.

One technique that can help prevent severe blurring is this: Scale the image by 200 percent (that is, double the height and width), blur the large image, and scale it by 50 percent to its original size. This will allow the Gaussian blur filter to work with more pixels, losing less detail (but inevitably losing some), and still getting smoothed edges that won't flicker as much.

Anti-Flicker Guideline Summary

To summarize: high-contrast (black next to white), tiny detail is the most flicker-prone type of texture. Textures that don't flicker are low contrast, with large details that fade smoothly into each other and the backgrounds.

 # Paletted Color

Paletted color is the foundation of many graphics engines. It's difficult to work with, but in return, we get small, efficient bitmaps, special effects, and generally improved performance when compared to true color.

Making good use of paletted color is a really subtle issue and warrants a full book all by itself. Other books and articles discuss this, mainly in the context of 2D artwork; here, we'll just do an overview and touch on some topics that frequently occur when dealing with paletted color in RT3D environments.

How Is Paletted Color Different from "Normal," Non-Paletted Color?

Paletted color is really different from "normal," non-paletted color. Essentially, paletted color carefully throws out two-thirds of "normal" color data—instead of using 24 bits per pixel, we are storing only 8. To do this with any reasonable results, paletted color can't really use the same approach. As you probably know, 24-bit color uses three bytes—one each for red, green, and blue—to represent each pixel's color. This makes for a great range of possible colors, but uses a lot of memory by comparison.

Paletted color names a set of 256 certain colors (each color is called an *entry*, and the set is the *palette*), and the bitmap's pixels refer to any one of them, much like a face refers to a vert. Each entry in the palette can be pretty much any RGB value we want, but 256 slots aren't really enough to make a reasonable representation of all the possible colors. Somebody must choose which colors are available in the palette, and then all the bitmaps must refer that palette.

Creating 24-Bit Art with the Palette in Mind

When we create artwork, we are creating 24-bit images, and then we map those images to an 8-bit palette. This is dangerous if we don't keep the palette in mind

when we're making the 24-bit image. We can draw an image that doesn't use colors in the palette. Then, when we convert the image to paletted colors, these colors are approximated with the nearest match from the palette, which can look awful. We must be careful to use colors from the palette (or very similar to them) so that when we convert to paletted color, we don't see our art get mangled.

One good way to do this is to have the palette open, even just as an image, and use the dropper (sample tool) to use only colors from the palette as we edit our 24-bit image. The feathering from the airbrush and other similar tools will use other colors, but at least the base colors will be right. Keeping the palette open also serves as a visual reference, a reminder of the available range of colors.

Artistic Look Limited by Palette

Often, the bitmaps in a game tend to look similar because they're all using the same palette, so it becomes a challenge to create art that looks good (uses lots of colors in the palette) but doesn't look like everything else. It's possible to change palettes during the course of the game, and there are a lot of cool tricks that can be done (such as transparency and color cycling) with palettes. These are always unique to the graphics engine, and they vary enormously, speculating on them here is pretty useless. These tips are discussed a little more in Chapter 13.

Color Reduction

Reducing the color depth (converting to paletted color) is often difficult and confusing. The exact procedure for remapping from 24-bit to 8-bit paletted color varies widely from program to program, and some programs don't do it at all.

To remap, we need a source palette. This is an 8-bit image that uses the correct palette, and it is usually supplied by someone else. For the exact procedure, see the exercises in Chapter 9.

● Using the Histogram

All high-quality photo retouching programs like Photoshop have a feature similar to the histogram. The concept behind a histogram is to show which colors are used most often in the image. It's really just a graph of lightness versus amount.

Along the bottom is the range of colors (usually shown as a gray scale, ranging from black on the left to white on the right), and along the side is the "frequency" scale (the bottom means the color isn't used much and the top means the color is very common).

Audio buffs will probably see a strong similarity between a histogram and a "spectrum analyzer"—those fancy LED graphs commonly seen on multiband equalizers and flashy stereo equipment. Like a histogram, they show frequency along the bottom (bass on the left, treble on the right), and the side measures loudness.

FIGURE 7.6 HIST3.TIF: Wood grain texture.

There is a problem with using a histogram on a color image: Colors don't really rank from black to white. A pure red is not any brighter than a pure blue, at least when using the RGB color model employed in computer graphics. The histogram simply ignores everything about the color except its lightness, unless the user specifically requests the red, green, or blue channel. Using the histogram isn't that helpful. It would be more useful to pick a certain hue, then see a histogram of that hue's usage.

Let's describe a simple case. If we draw a picture with only two colors, we'd see two sharp peaks in the histogram, at those colors' point in the lightness table, and nothing else. Or, if we have an image that uses all the colors, like randomly chosen colors for each pixel, we'd see a mostly flat line across the histogram.

How do we use a histogram?

Try to imagine what the histogram for the image shown in Figure 7.6 will look like before turning the page.

If we thought about the image correctly, we would realize that there were no occurrences of pure black in the wood pattern, so there wouldn't be anything happening at the left side of the histogram. Similarly, there is no pure white in the image, so the right side is empty as well. All the action is in the center, where the wood shades are appearing. Figure 7.7 shows this.

Also, notice that the colors are in noticeable slices; there are a good range of colors, but not a continuous range. That can be caused by a lot of things, but most commonly it's the result of 8-bit color; it's showing the fact that 8-bit images aren't really continuous tone.

Now, if we crop the empty areas off the ends of the histogram, stretching the colors to fill the spectrum, we'll see a change like the one shown in Figure 7.8.

In a pure data sense, these changes to the histogram make wider use of the color range we have. Visually, this edit results in higher-contrast images. For

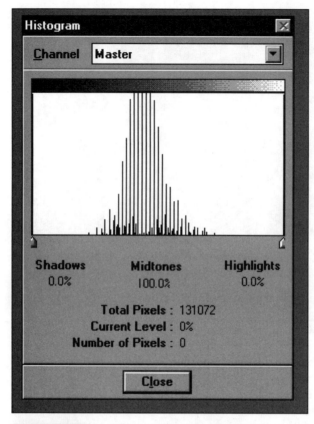

FIGURE 7.7   Histogram of HIST3.TIF.

FIGURE 7.8   HIST4.TIF: Wood texture expanded to full range of contrast.

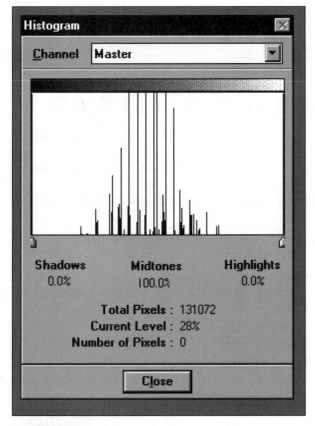

FIGURE 7.9 Histogram of HIST4.TIF.

example, for a 24-bit image, we have 256 levels of red, green, and blue. Each of the 256 increments is spread evenly from pure color (for example, solid red) to no color (black). Our image will have more increments to choose from if it covers a large contrast range. In other words, if we took a grayscale image and lightened it so it uses only the 16 lightest shades of white, then there are only 16 increments between lowest color range and the highest. Each pixel in the image must pick from one of these limited choices. If we allowed the image to use the full spectrum, each pixel could be any of 256 shades. This is also reflected in the ease of viewing—humans have an easier time discerning imagery if it is high contrast, for much the same reason.

Of course, there are problems with high contrast images: They tend to flicker more, as we noted earlier in the chapter. But, let's not lose sight of the forest for the trees.

Most importantly, and most commonly, the image may simply need to be at one end of the spectrum to look right—in that case, definitely don't make it high contrast for these technical reasons! The most important thing is that the image looks good in the game. This wood texture is a good example of that.

Regardless of whether the image is high contrast, histograms are a very powerful way to quickly understand the color levels in an image and to adjust contrast without damaging the image as much as the usual contrast-adjusting tools do.

● Generating Textures from 3D Models

We may also build complicated 3D models whose sole purpose is to generate texture maps for the real-time 3D model. This perhaps sounds needlessly labor-intensive, but it can really pay off if we must produce very realistic, high-quality artwork—especially if the textures have lighting built into them.

This technique works very well in conjunction with paste-mapping. Here's how it typically works:

- First, build a detailed model. Use all the tricks—shadows, translucent glassy reflective windows, and so on.

- Next, build a vastly simplified version of the model. This can be a simple silhouette, but any parts that really need to be 3D should be modeled. For example, a porch on a house should probably be modeled, but the doors, windows, gutters, and trim shouldn't be.

- To create the textures, simply render the complicated model and edit the resulting bitmap to fit the simple model with an image editing tool.

- Apply the textures using simple mapping on each side of the simple object.

- Render and look for places that are mapped poorly.

One of the toughest problems that this approach causes is alignment. When two different textures are aligned along an edge, making sure all the details inside the texture meet can be difficult. In theory, alignment can be fixed by establishing a certain number of pixels per meter, but in practice this is difficult to implement. To make use of that approach, we have to make our mapping icon a certain XYZ dimension for each bitmap.

If possible, an easier solution is to eliminate or reduce details along the edges of the texture that have to align. In the easiest case, the entire edge is the same color, which solves the alignment problem entirely. In reality, keeping aligning details near the corners of the texture goes a long way to simplifying this problem; we can then use the corners of the mapping icon to determine where the two aligning details should meet.

Designing 3D Graphics

CHAPTER 8

RT3D MODELING STEP-BY-STEP

As artists, we've all faced a blank screen and taken the first step in the creative process: getting started. This chapter will help break the ice by working through each step in creating a real-time 3D model, from the making first design decisions through implementing that design.

● Summary of Steps for Building RT3D Models

In the most formal representation, there are three basic stages of model creation: preparation, design, and implementation. During preparation, we gather (or maybe create) the basic data we'll need to create a solid RT3D model design. In the design stage, we take the basic data and create a solid blueprint-like plan for building the model. Then, in implementation, we follow the blueprint and create the object.

Preparation Stage

The preparation stage involves these tasks:

- Get source art (make or understand design, get vague concept sketches)
- Gather technical information

Design Stage

The design stage involves these tasks:

- Plan how model will be created (draw a construction sketch)
- Choose a modeling method (lofted, Boolean, or normal 3D shaping)

Implementation Stage

The implementation stage involves these tasks:

- Build the model geometry
- Create the textures
- Map the textures on the model
- Import to the real-time application

The Danger of Step-by-Step Explanations

Experienced real-time 3D modelers may read this and snort in ironic amusement at the naïve idea that a model can be built in a series of neat little stages and steps. They have a valid point in doing so because for those of us who are

actually building real-time 3D models in 1996, there is no step-by-step procedure. Ideally, we'd say that these steps blur together as we integrate them into a single, seamless process of modeling, but really it's more like a wild torrent of information rushing in, out, and through all the members of the development team in a seamless flow of activity. Each of these ordered steps is eventually covered, but often not in order, and there are lots of variations (to say the least!) on the methods described here.

Partly, this lack of order occurs because this type of work is so new that there are no established ways of dealing with the many unique situations that crop up. This results in last-minute problem solving that doesn't fit into a rigid procedure. There's something else, though, that must be admitted: If we stick blindly to any set of procedures, including the ones below, we'll end up in trouble. This real-time 3D modeling business is a new field, and it requires some flexibility, creativity, and willingness to stray from the known path to solve problems.

Writing a list of steps like this one can be dangerous because novices might follow them blindly. Instead, use them as you would follow a foreign recipe: cautiously, and trusting your own instincts. If you realize that you're being asked to add eight cups of fish sauce (an absurdly huge amount of very strong sauce, for the cooking-ignorant), skip it and use your own common sense.

That said, these steps do work, and they can be valuable even to experienced, professional artists. For new or complicated projects, they can serve as a reminder of the work that goes into a model and of steps that we often forget or don't consider important.

● Details for Each Step for Building RT3D Models

Here, finally, is the complete breakdown of each step.

Preparation: Get Source Art

Our first step in building a real-time model is getting source art.

Source art: Drawings, blueprints, photos, and other information, usually graphic, that define the shape of a 3D object. Source art describes both real-life objects and made-up designs.

What Kind of Source Art Do We Need?

The most basic source art we'll need is a blueprint-style sketch that shows views like top, front, side, or isometric. We'll also need some basic info about the materials used in our object.

No matter what kind of object we're modeling, drawing the sketch helps us understand its form. A good designer will think about how the design will be

constructed as they design, and not create features that are impossible to model; however, the blueprint sketch does not typically have specific technical data on it. Details such as what the mesh looks like and exactly how many faces are used in the torso should be saved for the second sketch.

On the other hand, some experienced modelers merge in other modeling steps as they create the blueprint sketch—leaving out details they don't plan to model, superimposing a grid of triangles where they plan to build the mesh, thinking about the modeling method, and so on. For them, it becomes more than just a sketch—it is the entire planning stage, condensed into a single drawing.

An example of a simple blueprint sketch is shown in Figure 8.1.

How Much Detail?

Once we get used to the process that we're learning now, we'll learn what we need to know about a model and what we don't. Knowing what to define clearly and what to ignore saves time in the designing process, but it's not something to be stated categorically.

Obviously, we don't need to define details that will never be represented in the model, and we do need basic forms fully defined, but learning where to draw the line between these two extremes simply comes from experience.

Source Art for Fantasy Designs vs. Real Objects

If our assignment is as wide-open and freely defined as "Make a vicious but cartoony, dragony sea lizard," we'll need to do design work: Create specifics about

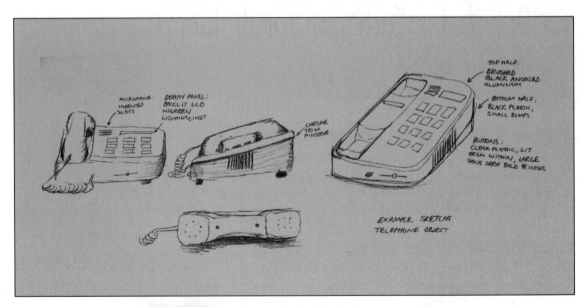

FIGURE 8.1 Hand-drawn sketch of top-front-side view of phone.

Designing 3D Graphics

the shape so we can build it. However, if we are modeling something that really exists, getting source art is an entirely different task.

There are multiple sources for information on real-life objects. We can take photos, go look at the thing ourselves, take measurements, and maybe even get blueprints of a solid object. For made-up designs, our only source of information on the object is the designer (often ourselves).

Imaginary designs are usually in a constant state of flux, whereas solid objects are not. Whoever designs an imaginary object will be tempted to change the shape; this is less true for real-life objects.

It may seem obvious, but real-life objects are possible—there won't be any Escher-like design mistakes where one part impossibly intersects another, which happens with imaginary objects.

Designing Imaginary Objects

If we're modeling an imaginary object, the first step is to design the object. Usually, we have a vision in our head of the object we're building—pure creative process, blue-sky, imagination.

The really hard part is getting this fantastic vision clear, on paper, as a doable model. Among the many ways to accomplish this, one good way is to sketch pseudo-blueprints of our idea, starting with vague, messy drawings and refining, rejecting, and accepting variations on the idea as we go. This sketching can be annoying and slow, but it's the most important part of the design process. The resulting blueprints are the key to making the transition from free-form design to real-world modeling.

Think of the blueprint creation process as forcing our nebulous designs out of our wild-eyed designer's imagination and onto paper, where we can examine them from the pragmatic modeler's point of view. We may discover conflicts or problems with the design idea, and we may spend time revising quickly and easily on paper rather than painfully and slowly while halfway through building it.

Someone Else Is the Designer

If someone else designed the object, our task is a little different. We must concentrate on clear communication: We need to know what the designer has in mind.

For projects with time constraints, the designer hopefully will have produced an intricate, fleshed-out, thought-out shape and drawn some good, but incomplete, sketches. These can't be fully detailed due to lack of time, and so the designer has some of the details in his or her head still.

For projects with plenty of design time allocated, the designer will supply detailed renderings and blueprints of the object we're creating. This simplifies our job a lot and cuts down the amount of communication we need to have with the designer. Still, we may need to talk to the designer after studying the design to verify that our vision matches theirs.

To head off potential problems as we explore our source art, we should note and discuss the areas that the designer is inclined to change or seems unsure about. We should note these areas as less settled, attempt to resolve any major unaddressed issues, and keep the rest in mind as possible problems.

We almost always have to communicate with the designer and try to get more information about the design we're building. One way is to meet with the designer for a half hour, perhaps marking up the blueprint sketch with jotted notes like "gray/blue dirty, scratchy aluminum" or "no riveted panels."

Another way is to compare conceptual understandings, drawing on cultural references like movie characters or sets. A small library of popular and design magazines to flip through and discuss can come in handy for this. If we use this method of understanding, we must keep focused on our goal: a solid, reliable understanding of what the designer wants. Try to get specific details agreed upon as well as the overall mood or look for the model. This is important because it's often easy to find a couple of concepts that you and the designer agree on ("yeah, Jetsons retro-futuristic, but with a dark Blade Runner slant, cool!") but when it comes to converting this to specific details on our object, we'll definitely want to get the designer's agreement for the first few implementations.

Once we think we understand the design, we should test this knowledge by proposing new details ("OK, just for example, what would you think of some thick pen-stroke Japanese characters on this side panel, dark blue, embossed into the door's frame? Does that kinda match your vision for this object?") and seeing if the designer agrees. If we really understand, the designer will agree to the concept, even if we don't end up doing it.

Proposing of new features is quite hard to do—it's putting your design and communication skills to the test, right out in the open, with no room for mistakes.

For more about communicating with designers, see Chapter 1.

Anticipating Design Revisions

Because almost every modeler has done some design work, we know that in the design process, revisions are natural and free-flowing. This is in direct conflict with the non-revision-friendly nature of modeling.

If we have a choice it's wise to put off modeling revision-prone areas, in hopes of the designer resolving their issues by the time we work on them. Note that if we're designing our own models, this still applies—we usually have areas we're unsure of, and we should be aware of them.

Preparation: Get Technical Information

This step has several parts. We start with information gathering, in the form of a Question and Answer session. The Q/A format makes sense because this information often comes from the programmer, so we usually end up asking a list of questions not unlike the ones here. When we have an entire list like this, it's wise to ask in a written form (email is ideal) so we can remember their answers, and so the programmer has time to research their answers, if necessary.

The list of questions below represents the technical issues we may need to resolve to build our model. This list makes a lot more sense with an example; be sure to look at the examples in Chapter 9 (and the simple example later in this chapter) to make more sense of these questions. Of course, the answers to some questions will

affect which other ones we ask. For example, if our environment doesn't support texturing, we won't be asking what resolution the texture maps should be.

What's the Face/Polygon (or Vert) Budget?

This question reveals our basic geometry budget. Like most budgets, it is usually approximate because its purpose is to guarantee a certain frame rate. It often makes sense to specify a number of verts, rather than faces, if the graphics engine is limited by the math, not the screen-drawing.

What Kind of Polygons Are Supported?

This simple question should be easily answered by the makers of the graphics engine. The usual answer is either "Only three-sided faces are supported," or "Convex planar polygons with any number of sides are supported." There are other possibilities as well.

How Are the Polygons Created from 3DS Faces?

Obviously, this question is asked only if polygons are supported. Sometimes polygons are created from faces with an automated procedure in which a preprocessor program accepts the 3DS file, looks for coplanar faces that share edges, and replaces them with polygons. In other cases, the program depends on a different method, such as reading the edge visibility setting to determine if two faces should be combined.

What Tolerance, If Any, Is Used When Deciding that Two Faces Are Coplanar?

This question applies if the preprocessor program has the ability to accept slightly non-coplanar faces as coplanar when forming polygons. This can save a lot of unnecessary editing in 3D Studio because it's common to have slightly non-coplanar faces during normal construction and it's hard to make all faces perfectly coplanar in 3D Studio.

Are T-intersections Allowed?

The hardest part of this question is agreeing on what a T-intersection is. Briefly, T-intersections occur when a face touches another face, either in the center or at an edge, without sharing any verts. Once both we and the programmer agree on this, the answer is usually a simple "yes" or "no." If the answer is "no," we should be sure to understand the reason; there may be cases where we need T-intersections, and we need to know if we can live with the resulting problem.

Are Intersecting Faces Allowed?

This question may be asked instead of the sorting question, but it's better to understand the various sorting options instead of getting a "yes/no" answer to

this. Be sure that the programmer agrees on the definition of "intersecting faces"; what we mean is two faces that cross each other, forming a line (or a plane, if they are coplanar) of intersection.

What Kind of Sorting Is Used? (Z-Buffer versus Face-by-Face BSP-Tree Sorting)

The main purpose of this question is to determine whether intersecting faces are supported (Z-buffering allows intersecting faces, but most other sorting methods do not). Other issues can be resolved once we know the answer to this question.

Are There Any Special Shapes that Should Not Be Built?

This question reflects the fact that some graphics engines don't cope with strange faces, such as a line-face, which uses only two verts, or a point-face, which uses only one vert. Also, some engines don't handle long, thin faces (for example, a triangle that fits in a 1000×1 rectangle) well. This is the question that should bring out all these special cases, if there are any.

How Will This Model Be Seen?

This is a pretty tough question because frequently constraints are placed on the user's movement that don't translate easily to a limited range of viewing positions. The purpose of this question is to determine what parts of the model will be scrutinized, and which parts (if any) are very rarely seen. The answer should include a min, max, and typical distance, which will be used to determine the size of the object onscreen. Obviously, the programmer may not be the best person to ask this of; the person who is designing the overall game would be more likely to know, especially early in the project.

What Are the Surroundings Like?

This vague question's purpose is to get a sense for what "look" to use—photorealisic textured, smooth futuristic shading, cartoony, flat shading, or something else—and also to determine what kind of detail is necessary for the object to be in sync with its surroundings.

What Kind of Animation Will This Model Be Able to Use?

Usual answers include hierarchy, animated bitmaps, 3D morphing, or "none at all." We'll also want to ask exactly how we import the animation data. For example, do we supply a string of 3D models as keyframes (LEAD01.3DS, LEAD02.3DS, LEAD03.3DS, and so on), or can keyframes be imported directly out of the 3D Studio animation data?

Designing 3D Graphics

Will Any Moving Objects Always Be Moving?

For objects that have moving parts, such as spinning wheels on a car or propellers on airplanes, we need to know if the spinning object will ever be seen still. In that case, a different method of modeling would be required for the animated part.

What's the Screen Size on Which This Object Will Be Shown?

This very important question tells us what resolution the textures should be, and it can also be used to determine the amount of detail our object will need (though the usual answer is "More! More!").

How Many Colors?

The maker of the graphics engine should know this. The usual answers are 8-bit, 16-bit, or 24-bit.

Palette Issues?

This question applies only if the application will use 8-bit (hence, paletted) color. We want to open a dialogue with the graphics engine programmer about palettes. We need to know as much as they can tell us (and as much as we can understand!) of how palettes work in the application. Specifically, we'll need to know how many (if any) of the colors we can dictate values for, how the fade tables work (if they exist), and what happens when the lighting changes the colors.

Any "Special" Colors?

This refers to colors that are handled by a special method. For example, some graphics engines consider any pixel that is pure black (RGB = 0,0,0) to be transparent if the material has any filename under the "opacity map" setting. Other palette-based systems use certain palette entries for flashing colors, color cycling, and numerous other effects.

What Kind of Lighting?

This question is pretty obvious. Aside from knowing the lighting type (point-source, directional, ambient) we'll want to know how to set these lights and whether they are animated. If they are, we'll need to know how to animate them.

What Kind of Texture Mapping (If Any)?

Several kinds of texture mapping are possible, each with a different trade-off between rendering speed and distortion. At the quick-and-dirty end of the spectrum, we have basic affine, and at the other end, we have perspective-corrected bilinearly interpolated. If our graphics engine supports more than one kind, we

may have the luxury of deciding which one our object will use; however, that option is not very common.

If the texture mapping is affine, we must be careful not to use large faces that will appear edge-on, or nearly so, to the user. That's the worst case for affine mapping, and the bizarre warping that results can be really horrifying. To solve this, we divide the faces up, keep the faces reasonable sizes, use textures that don't accentuate this, or use any combination of these approaches.

What Kind of Shading?

Almost every graphics engine is capable of flat shading from a fixed directional light source. Most can also handle Gouraud shading (a.k.a. smooth shading).

What Are the Allowable Combinations of Shading, Lighting, and Texturing?

This important question is often missed in the confusion of technical answers, but it's important to know. For example, many graphics engines won't smooth-shade a textured face, and ambient lighting may behave differently for flat-shaded (as compared to smooth-shaded) objects.

How Are Gouraud Shading Borders Determined?

Most smooth-shading graphics engines assume that any faces with shared verts should all be smooth-shaded together. 3D Studio has a way of forcing creases in a group of faces, even if they share verts at the crease (using the Surface/ Smoothing/... tools). Very few, if any, graphics engines support this, but if they did, we could save verts by using this instead of detaching faces (thus forcing them not to share verts) to form creases.

How Much Texture Map Memory Is Budgeted?

This question is covered in detail in Chapter 7.

What Size and Shape Can the Texture Maps' Dimensions Be?

This question is covered in detail in Chapter 7 as well.

Design: Creating Construction Sketch

The first part of this step involves making an analysis and conclusion sketch (Figure 8.2), in which we come up with some basic facts about the way we plan to build the model. These conclusions are drawn from the information we gathered during the questions, as well as from the source art. This sketch is pretty vague—basically, we're just outlining the details we think are important.

FIGURE 8.2 Example conclusion sketch.

The next step is creating another sketch, called the construction sketch. It's basically a triangular grid overlaid on the source art, showing where we'll build the faces and verts, what will be modeled and what won't, and so on, as shown in Figure 8.3.

In a way, this second sketch is where the rubber meets the road; it's where we propose what faces to build, where. Despite this, we should remember that this is just a sketch—if we change it when we actually build the model, that's okay. The purpose is to get the basics right—to meet our face and/or vert count target to establish a concrete target to shoot for when we sit down to model. This step is described in detail in the examples throughout this book.

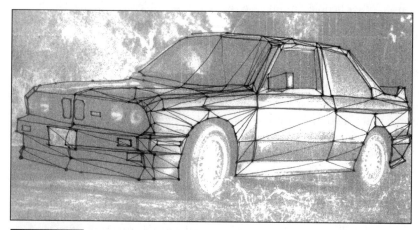

FIGURE 8.3 Example sketch.

Design: Choosing the Building Method

This step is simply about deciding how, exactly, we'll build our construction sketch. It's a quick step, usually just a few seconds of thinking, but at first it can be daunting because we must consider lots of issues simultaneously. Refer to the list of issues at the end of this chapter.

Various methods of creating a 3D object in 3D Studio are outlined throughout the book, but to summarize, we can loft a 2D shape into 3D, we can start with a 3D object and modify it to become what we want, and we can combine these two techniques, if reasonable.

Depending on the object we're building, we will have to choose a specific method of construction within the general idea of starting with 3D objects. See Chapter 9 on modeling particular kinds of objects for some basic approaches. Note that combining two different techniques in the same 3D model without lots of careful planning is usually time-consuming.

In all this vague talk we are really saying that this step requires experience, but once you have that, weighing your options and choosing a method will not be too hard.

Planning for Revisions

A good modeling method will allow for quick revisions, so we should think about this as we choose our modeling method. If we're sure our model won't require major revisions once we're done, we may choose a modeling method that calls for lots of time spent finishing "by hand." On the other hand, if we expect a long string of revisions, we may wish to emphasize a modeling method that is easily repeatable.

Communication and Revisions

Unfortunately, sometimes we don't have much choice in our modeling method, and we anticipate lots of requested revisions in time-consuming, difficult areas coming from other people. In this case, as soon as possible, we will involve the person who will be revising. As soon as we realize the scope of the problem (usually after we've started modeling), we can show them the model on the screen, maybe produce still renderings of the incomplete model, and demonstrate which areas are going to be easy to revise and which parts are likely to be problematic.

In other words: When in trouble, communicate! Let both the reviser (the person requesting revisions) and the project manager know your dilemma early and clearly; that way they can at least plan on having difficulties (there are few things a project manager hates more than unforeseen difficulties). If we get the reviser to understand *why* the requested changes are problematic, then we can get them in a much better mood to compromise or work around the requested revisions.

If the project manager is really under tight time constraints and is smart, they'll scope the revision process to items that can be quickly changed (And in the worst case, you'll at least be recognized for the massive amount of work you'll do during the painful revision process!).

Implementation: Building the Model

Once we have the source art, the technical info, the sketch, and the building method, we're ready to sit down at the computer and build the model. At this point, we've defined the model thoroughly, and it might seem that the construction would be pretty easy.

That is the goal—to make the actual time spent with 3D Studio quick and easy—but it doesn't always work out that way. Plenty of things can still go wrong: Mistakes in the sketches, changing designs, and unforeseen problems all emerge during the actual construction.

Unforeseen Problems When Building

There are always times when we simply don't know how we're going to build a certain part of an object. We have a good guess about an approach, but if we have never done it before, we may get halfway through and realize that our approach simply isn't going to work.

It's good to be philosophical about this. Working on the forefront of technology, where not all issues are solved ones and there isn't always a step-by-step procedure to follow, means we sometimes get stuck. The bottom line, however, is that when we get caught in this situation, we'll have to decide whether to back up and redo some work or (if possible) try to keep working on the flawed approach.

Starting over is a touchy issue. Its associations of failure and waste may cause us to avoid it. Remember that, in real-time 3D modeling, it frequently pays to start over. From a time-management point of view, it usually takes longer to work with a bad mistake, especially a bad strategic decision, than to simply restart.

From an artistic point of view, starting over is healthy because it allows us to experiment more freely, alternate techniques, and constantly learn. If we can learn to overcome our natural resistance and just chuck the flawed work and start over when that needs to be done, we'll usually have better models as a result. And, we will probably save time, compared to plugging ahead and trying to make the model work.

Decision Points

The time to decide to start over is *before* we've spent two weeks on details that can't be reused! Look at the whole approach carefully before investing lots of time in a specific detail or step that can't be reused.

Think in terms of the time spent on the project, as well as progress. For example, imagine we're about to spend half a day hand-building 60 complicated faces to solve some modeling problem. This half-day is a commitment to the modeling method we're using. If we're unsure of that modeling method, the time to decide whether to start over or continue is before investing those four hours, not after!

The decision point is something that has to be kept in mind throughout the construction process. Every time we look at the next step we should think, "Is this step going to be a wrong turn—am I going to end up redoing it—and if so,

can I reuse the work I'm doing now?" Of course, many times the answer is "No, I've got to go ahead and hope this works out," but if we can avoid an unnecessary round of painful edits, we win.

When making a tough strategic decision in the middle of constructing a model, use backups! Save the 3DS project with a different name before going ahead. This is our "undo"–it will make it easy to come back and start over if we took the wrong path.

Implementation: Create the Textures

In this step, we start up our paint program and draw the textures we decided we need for this model. Because we usually can't decide if the new texture needs re-editing until we map it on 3D model, we may repeat this and the next step several times. If our design is good, we may not have to repeat much, if at all.

If we paint the textures by hand, we may not leave the paint program, but there are many ways to create textures. For example, we sometimes build complicated models, simply for the express purpose of generating good texture maps. Once the textures are created, we convert them to the correct size and color-depth, if necessary, and then we're ready for the next step.

Implementation: Map the Textures on the Model

This step is a really hard part of modeling to do well. Part of the problem is that 3D Studio doesn't offer a very rich tool set, but in reality it is a culture clash: We have to negotiate harmony between our 2D raster-based textures and the 3D vector-based model, and that's not easy. That's why we've devoted an entire chapter, Chapter 7, to this step alone.

After we finish this step, we often render the model in 3D Studio to be sure it's complete; then we are ready to test it.

Implementation: Import to the Real-Time Application

In this final step, we take our completed draft model and load it into our application. It's a hard step to describe because the process is not standardized at all; each environment handles it differently. However, it's probably safe to say that most RT3D development environments have some kind of "preprocessor" code. This is the thing that accepts the 3DS files and their texture maps, perhaps asks some questions, and then spits out a processed version of the model that the graphics engine can digest.

The preprocessor can be in many forms. It's commonly a standalone program that is run at the DOS prompt command line, with a cute name like 3DS2MOD.EXE, or it can be a custom-written 3D Studio plug-in; sometimes it's an integral part of the graphics engine itself.

We'll use a VRML v1.0 browser as our example graphics engine. Several possible preprocessors are available; we'll use a free 3D Studio plug-in that does the job. As preprocessors go, it's really simple to use. We make sure the object is oriented and scaled correctly, save the file as VRML using the plug-in, then use our VRML browser to open that VRML file.

Whatever the preprocessor's form, it will (we hope) come with directions on how to use it. We'll work through an example from a major commercial graphics engine in the following section.

Example: Basic Chair

Now we have a rough idea of what each step of modeling is like. Let's work through a hypothetical example: a basic model of a chair. We'll only do the steps up to the actual modeling here.

Get Source Art

We must now create a sketch of our chair. In this case, we'll just use an existing chair as our sample; see Figure 8.4.

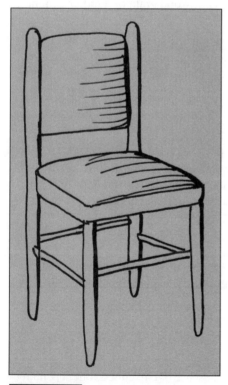

FIGURE 8.4 Basic chair.

Get Technical Information

As we discussed earlier, this is the stage at which we get answers to the technical questions we need. The questions here are not a complete list, suitable for any model; instead, they are the minimum questions we'll need answered to design our chair.

Note that some questions that seem obvious, such as "Does this model use textures?", have not been asked here because they were answered in the "assignment" statement.

Q: What's the face budget?

A: Use 25 faces or less.

Meaning: With a 25-face budget, we're going to be doing a very minimal chair—no fancy anything!

Q: What's the texture map budget?

A: One unique 128×128 texture can be used, in addition to any other textures already in use in the scene.

Meaning: A single unique texture of 128×128 is pretty big; this is a relatively generous budget. Being able to use other textures in the scene is good (and an easy trick because they're already loaded in memory); it allows us to save our unique texture for detail instead of wood grain or another common texture.

In this exercise, we aren't going to be doing any actual texturing, but if we were, we'd need to get copies of all the textures available to us, design our unique texture to complement them, then map whatever textures are appropriate onto the geometry.

Q: Is any animation of the chair possible?

A: No.

Meaning: This means we don't have to worry about the chair folding or changing in any way—no surprise, given what kind of chair it is. It's important to be sure of this because animation can require substantially different modeling methods. See the next section for more detail on this.

Q: What color depth can we use?

A: 24-bit color is available.

Meaning: 24 bits of color is good news—no yucky palette issues to deal with. This allows us to use subtle color variations that are difficult with 8-bit paletted color.

Q: What shading methods are available?

A: Gouraud and flat shading are available, but only non-textured surfaces can be Gouraud shaded.

Meaning: Gouraud shading gives a great sense of curvedness, but depending on our chair design, this may not do us much good. Also, the fact that the textures can't be Gouraud shaded means that we'll have to think about this decision—Do we go with smooth, untextured, curvy-looking materials, or sharp-edged, textured materials? We'll need to know more before answering this.

Q: What kind of lighting is used?

A: A single, stationary directional light.

Meaning: Though it sounds like a shortcoming, the simple lighting actually makes our job easier since we don't have to wonder what the object will look like in various lighting environments.

Q: Are transparent textures possible?

A: No.

Meaning: Transparent textures would have been handy if we wanted to portray lots of intricate woodwork that has holes and non-square edges, but since we can't, we won't.

Q: Are T-intersections allowed?

A: No.

Meaning: Using a T-intersection can simplify designs, thus saving modeling time; however, they are sometimes disallowed because they can cause "ripping" (slight cracks that appear and disappear during run time) with certain graphics engines.

Q: How will the model be viewed?

A: It will be seen only from a standing position, but it can be seen from any angle—not partially hidden by the table.

Meaning: This is good news—it means we don't have to worry about correctly modeling the underside of the chair (because we'll always be standing above it, and because it doesn't animate).

Q: What will the rest of the room look like?

A: Textured hardwood floor, textured wooden table, flat-shaded walls with textured paintings.

Meaning: Our chair will look a little funny if it isn't mostly textured, next to the textured table and floor, so we better not use untextured Gouraud shading for most of it.

Analysis

With the knowledge gained from our questions and answers, we can determine that the chair is to be textured, with no bottom side modeled, and we should concentrate detail on the upper half because that's what we'll see most often.

Specifically, we'll take the wood-grain texture that the table is using and apply it to the lower half and back of the chair. On the backrest and bottom, we'll make a unique texture showing leather padding with metal rivets and possibly a design embossed on the leather.

Plan How Model Will Be Created and Choose a Modeling Method

Now it's time to start the construction sketch. For this example, we'll work though several possible designs, and for each one we'll discuss the steps we'd go through to build the design shown. In this way, both the planning and method-choosing steps are demonstrated several times.

This iterative approach is commonly done when the object being modeled has a very tight face budget; in that sense, this approach is realistic and normal, not just for demonstration reasons.

For the sake of comparison let's build a chair with a simple, easy-to-grasp modeling method and no concern for polygon count. Conceptually, it's pretty easy to imagine a chair as two flattened cubes that form the L of the seatback and the seat itself, and four thin squares for legs. This simple construction, using 12 faces per cube, gives us 72 faces, as shown in Figure 8.5.

We could easily erase the 16 faces that form the tops and bottoms of the legs, reducing the count to 56 faces. Combining the seatback and seat with a chamfer joint instead of letting them butt against each other saves another 4 faces, leaving us with 52 faces.

Erasing the bottom of the seat brings us to an apparently minimal 50 faces, which is still a lot. Worst yet, the model is full of T-intersections because the connecting ends of the legs do not share all their vertices with the seat. This

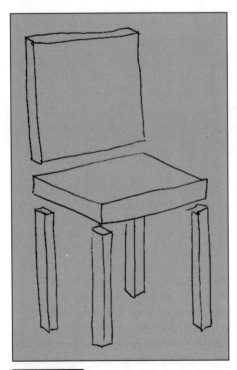

 FIGURE 8.5   Inefficient chair design.

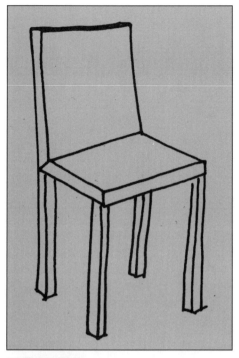

FIGURE 8.6   Slightly improved, inefficient chair design.

model is shown in Figure 8.6. We can do better than this!

Let's explore our options by starting as simply as possible, then adding details.

The chair shown in Figure 8.7 is conceptually as simple a "chair" as can be modeled. Obviously, this is a pretty lame chair visually, but it's a simple, understandable starting point and serves its purpose as such.

Construction-wise, a cube forms the seat and legs, and touching it is a two-sided square, forming the backrest. The cube is missing its bottom faces because these would rest against the floor and would never be seen. That leaves 5 square sides, or 10 faces. The backrest takes 4 faces because it is two-sided. Therefore, this chair uses 14 faces total.

The second attempt at our chair (Figure 8.8) is visually the same except for the addition of two triangles, one on each side, that are "wedged" between the front and back sides of the backrest. This accomplishes two things: first, the backrest now has thickness from the side view, improving the "solid" look of the chair considerably.

The second benefit of the triangles is more subtle: The long side of the triangle allows us to use a single square on the back side of the chair where there used to be 2 squares; thus, our new chair actually uses the same number of faces as the first one did: 14 faces. It's still looking lame, though—the problem is the solid "legs."

The third attempt begins to address the "lack of leg" problem, as we can see

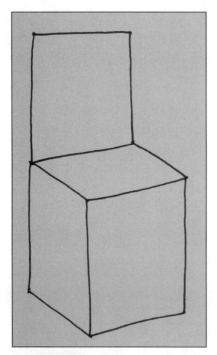

FIGURE 8.7 Super-simple chair shape.

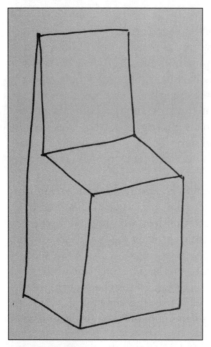

FIGURE 8.8 Thickened-back chair.

Designing 3D Graphics

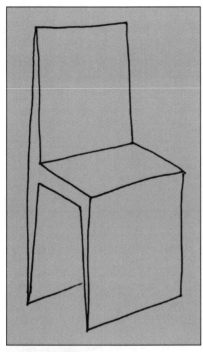

FIGURE 8.9   Separate front and rear legs added.

in Figure 8.9. The construction is different only in the bottom half, but it's quite different down there, and it's easier to think of the whole thing as being an extrusion than a modification of the last chair.

We'll picture the side of the chair as a 2D outline, composed of straight line segments. Two segments compose the pointy front leg, two compose the top and bottom of the seat, and the back leg and backrest together take three. That makes 7 segments, which makes 14 faces when extruded. That's a lot, so to reduce that number, let's not create faces for the underside of the seat. This removes 1 segment, thus 2 faces, bringing us to 12 faces in the extrusion. Much better!

We still haven't accounted for the "caps" to the extrusion—the sides of the chair. Counting out the triangles it would take to fill in the 2D outline of the side of the chair, we see one in the front leg, one in the back leg, two in the seat, one in the backrest, and one where the backrest, back leg, and seat all come together. That makes 6, which must be doubled (for the other side), totaling 12.

This chair, therefore, uses 24 faces, and looks considerably better as a result, but it's still got some problems. Mainly, the legs are ugly as extrusions–they'd look a lot better if they were divided into individual legs.

As figure 8.10 shows, chair version 4 has indeed improved, sporting exciting individual legs as we desired (but unfortunately it's also grown complicated to describe its construction).

Starting with the extruded chair, we erase the two extruded "insides" of the legs (that is, the faces that point toward the floor and the other leg). That leaves

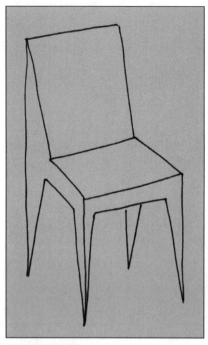

FIGURE 8.10   Separated legs.

only the two outward-pointing faces and the caps of the original extrusion to form the legs—but we're not done.

We then divide the bottom edge of the aforementioned outward-facing extruded faces twice and move the resulting two new vertices up toward the seat of the chair and toward the top of the nearest leg, as though we are lifting a skirt. At this point, the front and back of the legs should look like the sides: triangular legs with thin horizontal bars connecting them. We now have two of the three sides of the legs defined, so to complete the operation, we hand-build new "inner" faces from the four verts that form each leg (leaving out the one that is shared by the seat surface).

In the resulting chair, the legs together use 12 faces, the edges of the seat use 8, the seat itself has 2, and the seatback has 6, totaling 28 faces.

This is a major improvement in face count over the baseline chair with 50 faces, especially when we consider that this chair has no T-intersections. In all fairness, this chair does look strange because its legs are pointed, but other than that, it's comparable in appearance.

The Rest of the Steps...

At this point, we have built the 3D object itself. To finish the steps outlined in the first section, we would design, create, and apply the texture map, then test the model in the real-time application, and revise if necessary, but, as promised, these steps will be covered elsewhere.

MODELING SPECIFIC TYPES OF OBJECTS

In this chapter, we'll exercise our knowledge by actually building some RT3D models. First, we'll work through one lengthy, detailed exercise using 3D Studio to build a sports car model. Once we have that exercise under our belts, we'll work through several other exercises to acquire modeling techniques that are particular to common types of RT3D models.

In particular, we'll cover open environments (an urban street scene), closed environments (houses, tunnels, and so on), some super-low-poly character modeling, and we'll close with a look at some texturing techniques used in *Descent*, the popular RT3D action game.

 # Prologue

When learning how to build models, most people assume that because we can theoretically model absolutely anything, there is no point in learning techniques for modeling a particular category of objects; we assume it's better to concentrate our learning energy on understanding tools and acquiring general knowledge about modeling. In a sense, this is true; however, several categories of objects are so commonly needed that knowing how to handle them is an advantage.

 # Modeling Vehicles

Vehicles is a very commonly requested modeling category for commercial RT3D modelers. We could be asked to model plenty of vehicles: airplanes (especially jet fighters), ships, spacecraft, and submarines; sports cars seem to crop up more frequently than some of these.

Let's work through the steps we outlined in Chapter 8, then get into a step-by-step exercise once we are ready to build the actual real-time model of a BMW M3 sports car in 3D Studio.

Step 1: Get Source Art

Getting source art is pretty easy for sports cars. We can find source art in lots of places: books, magazine articles, manufacturer's literature, and even the real thing, but the best source art of all is a 1/25 scale plastic hobby model. These not only give us the 3D shape of the body to examine closely, but they also provide important details like dashboard layout, coloring, and painting directions for the variations on the model. Also, the instructions and outer box contain many various line-drawn views of the car. Unfortunately, hobby models aren't made for every car.

TABLE 9.1	BMW M3 Basic Statistics	
Length	171.1 inches	4.35 meters
Width	66.1 inches	1.68 meters
Height	53.9 inches	1.37 meters
Frontal area	20.0 sq feet	1.86 sq.meters
Wheelbase	100.9 inches	2.56 meters
Track, Front	55.6 inches	1.41 meters
Track, Rear	56.4 inches	1.43 meters
Ground Clearance	5.0 inches	0.13 meters
Wheel *rim* diameter	15.0 inches	0.38 meters
Wheel *rim* width	7.0 inches	0.18 meters
Wheel diameter (est.)	25 inches	0.64 meters
Wheel width	7.0 inches	0.18 meters

(Source: November 1987 Car & Driver Magazine review)

After doing some research, we found that there is no existing plastic model for the BMW M3; we'll have to use more humble source art. For this example, we'll work from the following source art.

For those not familiar with the terms used above, refer to Figure 9.1.

Figures 9.2 through 9.6 constitute our source art. They are included on the CD-ROM. These pictures are basic, but if we are going to be modeling the exterior only, they're reasonably complete. If the underside or the interior were to be featured, then we would need more source art. Also, if you can't get a good idea of what this car is really shaped like from these pictures, visit a BMW dealer (be sure you're looking at the same car! There are several types of M3s).

The next step is to find out what, exactly, we'll be modeling.

Step 2: Get Technical Information (Q & A Session)

We have a lot of questions that we'll need answered. Some of them are technical, but many of them simply deal with the circumstances in which this model will be seen. Note that these questions are a subset of the list provided in Chapter 8—the excluded questions obviously are unnecessary. Also, if you want a more general explanation of any of these questions, refer to the discussion in Chapter 8.

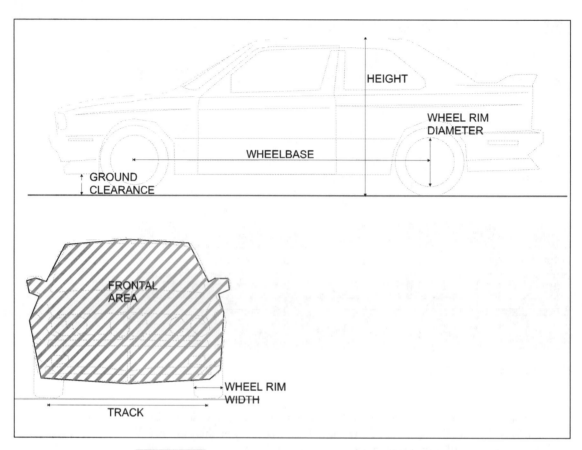

FIGURE 9.1 Terminology used in describing car.

FIGURE 9.2 BMW M3 photograph.

Designing 3D Graphics

FIGURE 9.3   BMW M3 photograph.

Q: How will this model be seen?

A: This car will be seen driving on the highway, only seen from chase helicopter views. It won't be seen from underneath, though it may be seen briefly from a chase car position. It will sometimes fill as much as the full screen width, but the user won't usually get any closer than that.

Meaning: This means that we don't have to model the interior or the engine, so we don't need any more source art than what we have. The model should be quite detailed since it's being featured prominently (filling the screen), but we don't have to worry that the camera will zoom in really close. That's good to know; it'll help us decide how much detail to model.

Q: Will the car always be seen on the highway? Will it ever be seen stationary?

A: It will always be moving.

FIGURE 9.4   BMW M3 photograph.

CHAPTER 9 • **Modeling Specific Types of Objects**   **169**

FIGURE 9.5   BMW M3 photograph (rear).

FIGURE 9.6   BMW M3 photograph (front).

Designing 3D Graphics

Meaning: This tells us that the wheels, one of the hardest parts, should be modeled to appear in motion; we don't have to worry about trying to show them in a stationary position. That's handy for us.

Q: What is the environment like when the car appears?
A: The car will be seen in a summer day's lighting conditions. The situations will be various driving scenarios where a real car is likely to be: race tracks, city streets, country roads, and freeways.
Meaning: This knowledge will help us make texture maps that fit in. If the situation were to take place at night, we might design our textures to fit that situation more closely.

Q: What kind of animation do we have?
A: The tires will not spin, but they will move up and down with the suspension, and the front tires will steer left and right. No other animation will be possible.
Meaning: This animation makes our tire modeling trickier, but the car will certainly look better than if the wheels didn't move, so we shouldn't complain.

Q: What are the graphics engine's capabilities?
A: It supports rendering at 320×200 with 256 colors, Gouraud shading, texture mapping, and dynamic point-source lighting.
Meaning: We'll have palette issues to deal with, but other than that, the engine sounds good. Gouraud shading is good news, and the moving lights could show off our model to good advantage.

Q: What's our face budget?
A: 300 polygons.
Meaning: 300 triangular faces is a good-sized budget for a car, especially if we have Gouraud shading and texturing available, but "polygons" means that we can use even more if some of our triangles can be combined into planar polygons. We'll need to know more about this.

Q: What kind of polygons are supported?
A: Any polygon using from 3 to 256 sides. All polygons must be totally, perfectly flat and convex (no inner holes or cavities).
Meaning: These are typical requirements. If the answer wasn't so clear, we might press the issue on "flat"—sometimes it's not that important that the faces be perfectly flat, and that can save us a lot of hassle (it's hard to be sure a polygon is going to be flat).

Q: How are the 3D Studio triangles combined into polygons?
A: If two faces share an edge, and the edge is invisible, the faces will be combined into a single polygon.
Meaning: This is a common way of doing this, but there are other methods. Sometimes the development environment includes a utility that does the combi-

CHAPTER 9 • **Modeling Specific Types of Objects**   **171**

nation step, and some game companies have written a 3D Studio plug-in that combines faces into quads, puts the new model in a proprietary file format, then saves that file to disk.

Q: How much texture memory do we have?
A: 256 KB for this object maximum; it would be good if you could avoid using that much because there are many other objects that could use more textures.
Meaning: This will mean we don't have tons of texture memory, so we probably shouldn't texture the entire body (we use Gouraud shading of a solid color instead).

Q: What kind of constraints do we have for the textures?
A: They have to be either 64 × 64, 128 × 128, or 256 × 256, and they have to be 8-bit color images that use a supplied palette (CARPALET.TIF). Transparency is available—just use color 255, and it will be transparent when the model appears in the environment.
Meaning: This is a bit of a pain for us—it's nice to have the flexibility of using a non-square texture (64 × 256, for example). The 8-bit color is nothing new. The transparency is good news; that can really help.

Q: Anything special about the palette?
A: No, palette control is actually handled at run time by the game engine.
Meaning: This means our common-palette problems will be out of our control.

Step 3: Plan How Model Will Be Created

We now know enough to start thinking about the construction of this car.

With our car model, we are in danger of portraying a generic car. Cars look a lot alike, and this car is especially hard to distinguish from many similar models—for example, Ford Mustangs, tricked-out Nissans, the BMW 325, or even a fancied-up Escort. We need to make sure this car is recognizable as what it is: a BMW M3, not any other sports car. If we accomplish this, car people take one look and say, "Hey, it's an M3!" instead of "Nice car—is it a Mustang?"

The car is basically symmetric, so we should design and model half, then mirror it. This sounds like an obvious observation, but it's surprisingly easy to get sucked into meshing the whole car instead of the smallest unique piece (in this case, half). It's important to save time and annoyance by taking a look and recognizing symmetry anywhere we can, early on.

Car Terminology

We need to agree on some basic terms for the pieces of the car. Listed below is a letter, a corresponding definition for a term of a major body piece, and sometimes a discussion if the piece is non-obvious or confusing. In the following

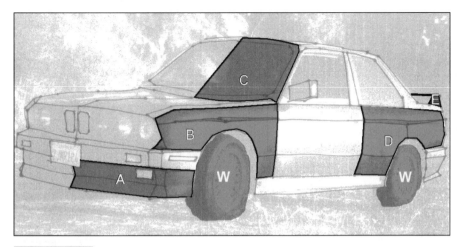

Car part names.

series of diagrams, the car is laid out with the body pieces in the picture identified and labeled with a letter.

W: Wheel. This refers to the tire and rim together. Outside of this book, it can also refer to the metal part only, but here it always means the whole wheel.

A: Air Dam. Also known as "chin spoiler" or "front skirt." This is a fiberglass extension of the original body.

B: Front Fender.

C: Windshield. Includes the trim.

D: Rear Fender. This area is also called the "quarter panel" sometimes.

E: Spoiler. Also known as "wing" or sometimes "fin."

F: Grille. Includes headlights and BMW kidney grilles.

G: Door.

FIGURE 9.6B   Car part names.

FIGURE 9.6C Car part names.

H: Rear Skirt. This term is not well established, but it's the best we can do for now.

I: Tire. This refers particularly to the rubber part, not the metal center of the wheel, and not to the combination of the two.

J: Front Bumper. Note that it wraps around to form part of the opening for the front wheel.

K: Hood.

L: Side Window. This includes the trim and the side edge of the trunk lid.

M: Side Skirt. This trim piece spans the bottom edge of the car between the wheels.

N: Rim. This is the metal part of the wheel, and it excludes the rubber part.

Other terms not visible in the illustrations above are now defined:

Wheel well: This is the area of the body that is usually hidden behind the wheel. It's the unpainted inside of the fenders, where ice and snow accumulate.

Nose: Hood, front fender, air dam, bumper, all combined together.

A pillar: The thin metal bar-shaped piece that connects the roof to the rest of the body, between the windshield and the front door. There are two A pillars; one on each side of the windshield.

B pillar: The metal post that connects the roof to the body, between the door window and the side window.

C pillar: The wide bar that connects the roof to the rest of the body, between the rear window and the side window.

How Much Detail Will We Be Able to See?

Our source material tells us that the car is 4.3 meters long, and the question-and-answer session tells us that, in the worst case, its length fits in a 320-pixel-wide screen. How many pixels per meter does this model use?

The answer is 320 pixels / 4.35 meters = 74 pixels per meter. Well, that's nice (and hopefully some math teacher somewhere is jumping around shouting, "See, word problems *are* useful!"), but what does it mean for the size of details in the geometry?

To answer that, let's look at this issue another way: Our questions told us that the whole car could fill the 320-pixel width of the user's rendered view, maximum. That means we have to represent the car's length (4.35 meters) with 320 pixels. If we divide 4.35 meters by 320 pixels, we get 0.0136 meters per pixel. This means that details smaller than 0.0136 meters (1.36 cm, about one-half inch) are probably going to be pointless to worry about—they are smaller than a pixel and so can't be seen. This is the closest the car will ever be seen; even details at this size will be visible only when the car is filling the screen, so we may want to go with a more typical viewing range and say that any object smaller than 1.9 cm (three-quarter inch) is going to be barely visible. This is partly a judgment call; some things, like the edge of a windshield, could be this thin but still clearly visible. We've only got 300 polygons, so we're going to be pressed to represent the big stuff, let alone this kind of detail.

Handling Curves

We must pay special attention to anything that's obviously curved or circular in our model because these are always a source of difficulty when modeling with polygons. The gentle curves of the sheet metal aren't usually the problem; obviously circular curves like the wheels, wheel well arches, and the headlights are a bigger issue. We have a couple of choices on how to handle these curves.

One way to handle curves is to avoid modeling them and put in a texture map instead. Portraying a nice curve with textures is easy, but, of course, it won't work if the object is basically 3D. The headlights are a good example of something that would look good textured because a 2D image is a reasonable approximation. On the other hand, the wheel well arches could not be done with a texture because they are a 3D hole in which the tire goes.

We can also model curves as polygonal objects, which has the obvious disadvantage of having flat-looking edges. We can counter this by using the method we use for the tires (described below), thus making sure that we have enough edges to make the object appear circular—this could add up to a lot of faces. Still, for many situations it's our only option, so we use it.

Modeling the Wheels

We have 300 polygons to use for the whole model. As the most prominent curves on a car model, the wheels always consume a lot more faces than we might think, so let's start with them.

First, we should recognize that we probably don't have enough faces to model any detail on the wheel other than the roundness—no inset rims, no sidewall curvature. We can get a lot of detail by texturing, so our wheels will look good even though this detail is not modeled.

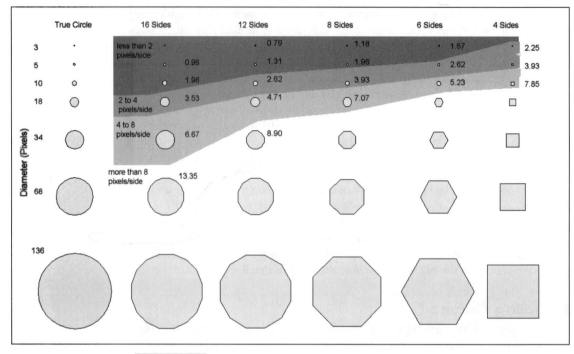

FIGURE 9.7   Pixellated circle chart.

Let's figure out how many sides we'll need to make the wheels look round. This question is related to how large the wheels appear on the user's screen. The first thing we need to know is how many pixels the diameter of our wheels will use. The wheel diameter is 0.64 meters. When we divide this by our figure of 0.0136 meters per pixel, we find that our wheels are 47 pixels in diameter.

So, now that we know the diameter, how do we find the number of sides we should use? The number of sides necessary to show a circle depends on the number of pixels. This will make sense if we refer to Figure 9.7.

The purpose of this figure is to show that as the size of the polygon reduces, it looks more and more like a circle. Examine it by looking at the bottom row first. For all the polygons, we can see they are composed of straight sides connected in a ring shape, as compared to the true circle on the left. Visually travel up the column for each object and compare each smaller polygon to the true circle on its left. At a certain point, we will see that the polygon's shape is indistinguishable from the true circle's shape. Note the pixel diameter for that circle (the vertical scale on the left). That's our target size.

Think of it another way: we're trying to portray a circle, but we can't make any true curves because we can use only straight-sided entities. This chart shows us how small the sides have to be for the polygon to look just like a circle.

For our wheels, we start by looking along the vertical scale and choosing the nearest pixel size—34. We then follow the row of polygons to the right until we see a polygon that looks circular enough for us. We can see that the 12-sided polygon looks pretty good, but we can begin to see facets with the 8-sided polygon. Because our wheel is somewhat bigger than 34, we should go with approximately 12 sides if we want perfectly curved wheels.

So, our wheel starts as the standard 3D Studio 12-sided cylinder that uses 48 faces (see Figure 9.8). Multiplied by four wheels, that's a lot, but by optimizing and remembering to count polygons, not faces (that is, by mentally combining the coplanar faces into polygons), we realize the count is quite a bit lower than it might seem.

Each pair of triangular faces on the tire's surface combines into a single 4-sided polygon because they are planar and share verts. Twelve such combinations can be done. The rest of the faces form two planar flat surfaces that share verts. These surfaces can be represented by two 12-sided polygons. That means we're

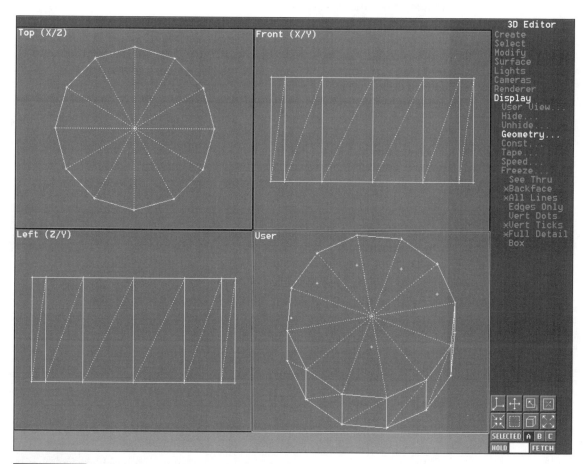

FIGURE 9.8   3D Studio 12-sided cylinder.

using 12 polygons on the tire's curved surface and 2 for the flat surfaces, for 14 polygons total per wheel. For all four wheels, we use 56 polygons.

We will also use 96 verts in the four tires. We don't have a vert budget, but if we did, we'd worry about that—that's kind of a lot.

Is there anything else we should do to optimize this model? Well, we can eliminate an unnecessary vert in the center. We'll just weld it to any other vert with which it shares an edge.

We can consider reducing the number of sides on the cylinder even further. When we try to portray roundness, it's a good idea to get far away from parallel-sided objects. Eleven sides would be far less parallel than 12, and the viewer's eye would be slower to recognize the shape as a polygon. We'll decide this once we get to that modeling point, but for now let's assume we're building 12-sided wheels.

That's a solid plan for the wheels' polygonal model, so let's think now about the other issues we'll have to address when we build the entire wheel model.

Deciding the Wheels' Textures

What, if any, textures are we going to use for this object? Textures with linear details usually destroy the illusion of Gouraud shading (for more discussion on why this occurs, see Chapter 7). Because portraying the outside of a spinning tire surface (the part that touches the road) will definitely involve straight lines, and because we really need to portray the tires as curved, let's not texture the outside rubber surface; this will be only Gouraud shaded.

The sides, on the other hand, could definitely use a texture. We'll make a blurred spinning rim texture and put it on the 12-sided polygons. When we actually do this and see the result in the real-time application, we may find a problem. The border between the textured and the untextured faces may be visible and obvious—the Gouraud shading may not "bridge" from a textured face to a non-textured surface. If that's the case, we'll build large triangular faces that slightly overlap the 12-sided polygons and put our texture, with transparent edges, on that. We won't assign textures to the 12-sided polygons; we will allow them to be Gouraud shaded seamlessly with the other faces.

That should do it for the wheel models.

Planning the Construction of the Car's Body

For the rest of the car, we will have to try a couple rounds of drawing faces on the source art, counting how many faces we've used, and redoing it if we didn't hit our mark. We used 56 polygons in the four tires, so that leaves us 244 faces for the rest of the model. Let's start by drawing a mesh that we'd be very happy with, as far as detail goes, without worrying about the polygon count to see how many polygons that uses.

Exactly how do we draw a mesh? There are lots of ways, many simpler but less organized than the method described below. This method is good for mostly convex objects, like the car body.

We start by taking a source art picture and creating a "traceable" version of it on which we can draw. This is done by increasing the brightness of the source art until it is a light background, then printing it out. The image quality can be

FIGURE 9.9 Traceable car drawing.

pretty bad (though, of course, it's better if the quality is decent); the purpose of this print is to serve as a template to draw over. See Figure 9.9 for an example.

Next we draw on the printout we just made. Using a fine felt-tip pen that bleeds when it's held still can be handy; we can use the bleeding to make vert location markers as we draw. Also, using a colored pen can be helpful.

Our goal is to trace the important parts of the car that we plan to model with a series of straight lines. We aren't worried about how the lines will connect to form faces; what we really want to think about is which details are important to model in polygons and which ones are not.

When trying to decide which parts of the car to outline, remember that the important details are the ones that define the object—that form its shape. In other words, the big, basic, overall, general shape is the most important.

That said, it's also important to capture the unique details that differentiate this car from the many similar cars. This is the time to do that, so we will make sure to model the flared fenders and other racy bodywork, the shape of the grille and nose, and, of course, the spoiler.

Once we're done with this sketch, we should end up with something like Figure 9.10.

Notice that, as promised, the areas that are curved, prominent, or unique have a lot more lines than the normal areas of the car. For example, the shape of the nose is very important for identification, so it has a lot of detail drawn in. The curve of the fender flares is somewhat uncommon, so they are carefully outlined. On the other hand, the very normal-looking door is drawn simply, as is the rear window.

FIGURE 9.10 Rough traced car.

Notice that the grille doesn't have lots of details outlined. That's because they are likely to be in a texture, not modeled as polygons.

Note that our source art doesn't show the roof, the back end, the spoiler, the underside, or the trunk top. We'll ignore these areas for now, after noting their absence. We'll also notice that this drawing shows lines on the left half of the car's nose; this means the artist got carried away while tracing. These lines are unnecessary because the car is symmetrical.

From this sketch, we can compose a mesh over the drawing we just made. This is when we decide which face goes where, which may sound like a daunting task. By way of reassurance, remember that this is only a sketch. We are not married to the decisions we make here, and we will probably redraw this before building the actual 3D model from it. The real purpose is to start thinking about

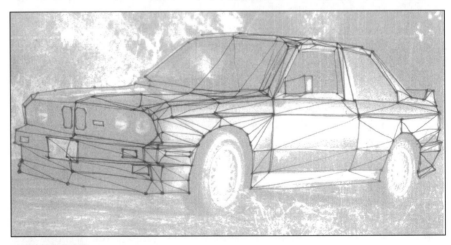

FIGURE 9.11 First draft of sketched tri-mesh.

the mesh's layout, and to get a ballpark estimate of our face count.

During this step, we'll rely on our first line drawing, basically just connecting the lines we drew into triangles that together form the mesh over the vehicle's surface. As we work, we'll have to decide which details to skip, which to texture, and which to model. Making notes about these details on the drawing is a good idea if we have trouble remembering them.

Some details aren't symmetric, though, like the "M3" badge on the grille and the license plate. For these, we'll make exceptions as we count, and we will also handle these specially when we actually build the model. It's important to note which faces are not symmetric.

Work carefully but quickly; don't linger for long times over a certain, nit-picky face arrangement. Instead, lay out the whole car in an approximation of the real mesh, with the primary goal of counting the faces we are using.

We end up with something like Figure 9.11.

Let's take a look at where the faces are used in this model. The nose and the front fender have a lot of faces in them. The door is pretty simple, and the windshield isn't very complicated either, though the trim around the windshield uses quite a few faces.

TIP

It's important that we do not see this kind of unfaithfulness to the original as a mistake; it's a positive (but surprisingly difficult) thing to improve the model as we work. We do this by deviating from the original drawing. This is another one of those seemingly obvious hints, but when we're down in the trenches, drawing triangle after triangle, it's easy to forget that the red lines we drew earlier aren't carved in stone— they were our semi-guessed judgment calls, and they should be freely revised as necessary.

Note that there is no mesh drawn for the headlights and the front grilles. That's because they will look much better as a texture, as we had decided when we drew the outline sketch.

When the chrome BMW trademark "kidney" grilles were outlined with red, they were intended to be modeled as 3D objects, but when the second, meshing step was taken, we realized that the grille could be part of the texture that includes the headlights.

If we look at it, we'll also notice that the mesh doesn't line up with the underlying artwork in some places. This is especially noticeable around the door's window frame. That's fine; this is only a rough sketch to help us plan the face layout, not an artistic creation! As long as we end up understanding how we will lay out the faces, we've accomplished our goal. Our drawing is slightly messy but still legible, and we saved time by not drawing a gorgeous, unnecessarily detailed mesh.

Take a look at how the marker lights and fog lights are sketched. They don't share verts with the surrounding faces; instead, they seem to be somewhat unre-

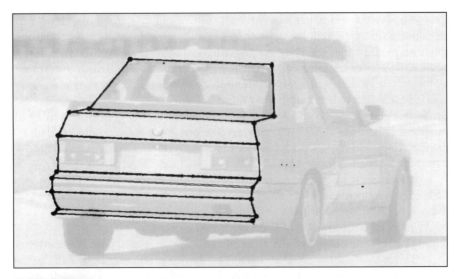

FIGURE 9.12 Rear end of car, with existing mesh sketched in.

lated, perhaps floating over their intended location. There are two reasons why we would suggest such an arrangement: to save faces and to keep the Gouraud shading smooth. For more information on this basic issue, see the section on floating faces in Chapter 5.

The Back End
So far, we have covered most of the bodywork except for the back end, which isn't visible in the view we've been working from. We'll have to work from a different

FIGURE 9.13 Rear of car with basic mesh.

Designing 3D Graphics

view now to cover this area. Let's sketch a mesh over the source art that shows it, just as we did for the other view (Figure 9.12).

There is a difference, though, between this art and the previous view—now we have existing meshes that our sketch must match. Figure 9.13 shows the existing points, connected by horizontal lines to form a string of basic surfaces over the back side.

This pretty much defines our basic mesh surface, but we will model some small details, like the license plate and taillights, as floating above the basic mesh. We've also cut out a piece of the rear skirt for the exhaust pipe area.

What about the Areas We Can't See?

Now we have to plan the construction of the areas that aren't visible on the source art. If the areas that aren't covered were full of detail, we would either have to get more source art or decide the detail wasn't important. For the missing areas we have, we really don't need source art. We can figure out what kind of mesh and how many faces we will have in the missing areas just from the mesh we've already drawn.

There aren't too many unique areas that we can't see. Specifically, there is the roof, the underside, and the wheel wells.

Let's start with the roof. If we follow the topmost edge that is shared with the roof from the corner of the windshield to the edge of the back window, we'll see that there are about four line segments through there. Tracing along the windshield from the centerline to the aforementioned corner at the windshield, we see two line segments, approximately. It's hard to tell, but what's important is not the lines we drew, but our budgeting.

In other words, if we had to build the roof half with 2 line segments along the width, would it look okay? The answer is yes; because the roof is practically flat, 2 segments along the width and 4 segments along the length are plenty—perhaps excessive, but we'll go with it for now. Two segments multiplied by 4 segments makes 8 four-sided polygons, thus 16 faces, that will be used for the roof half.

Next, we have the wheel well—the inside of the fender area. Why are we bothering to model this seemingly unimportant area of the car? We'd love to be able to use those faces elsewhere, but unfortunately, if we leave out the wheel wells, the gaps between the wheels and the wheel wells would look like raw holes in the model, allowing the background to show through. We have to put something there that blocks the holes but doesn't intersect the wheels, and that's why it'll be as simple as we can make it. Basically, we have to connect the edge of the fender to a simple four-sided vertical surface behind the wheel.

As a side note, it is possible to try to model a simpler box that butts up against the inside of the fender, not sharing any verts with the fender itself, but this approach is generally problematic. The problems stem from the small gap between the wheel well and the fender; it is almost impossible to make that seam disappear entirely. Let's not mess with that approach; instead, we'll go with the method described previously.

We are modeling the underside even though it's unlikely it'll ever be seen because it doesn't add much overhead to the model and it makes the model

much more versatile. If we simply connect the bottom edges of the existing body faces, we create no new verts, which means the math shouldn't be too bad. Also, in most graphics engines, faces that point away from the viewer are backface-rejected (that is, immediately ignored for rendering) without costing much of the computer's time. Even though it increases our face count, it's important to remember the bottom line: Frame-rate-wise, it probably won't hurt much at all.

Totaling the Face Usage

Now that all areas of the car are accounted for, we add up the face count and figure out whether we can build this model within our polygon budget.

As we count, we should be counting polygons, not faces. To do this, we'll need to note coplanar faces that combine into polygons, and we will not count these combined faces.

To figure the face count in the wheel wells and underside, we count the number of edges of the wheel wells because one face has to connect to each of these edges. Then we add 3 more polygons to fill out the square wheel well in the back, and 3 or 4 more for the bottom underside. There are 24 faces in the drawn wheel wells, which means we'll use 31 polygons for the bottom and wheel wells.

Here's a summary of the face usage in the first draft of the car model. The counts are for the whole model (not just half, due to symmetry):

- 60   Wheels
- 46   Front end: front spoiler, grille, bumper, air dam
- 70   Front fender
- 10   Hood
- 46   Windshield
- 28   Door and side skirt
- 34   Rear fender and side of rear skirt
- 14   Side window, rear window, trunk lid
- 8   Roof
- 19   Back end: rear skirt, bumper, tail light area
- 31   Underside and wheel wells
- **366   Total**

The total is not too far over our budget, and not at all bad for a first draft. We can trim some faces here and there as we model, but that's close enough that we don't have to make a second pass at the overall approach.

If this had totaled to a number like 450 polygons, we'd resketch the mesh with a less detailed model. For example, we would skip the trim on the windshield and door windows, the exhaust pipe hole on the back, and we would simplify the mesh on the roof. Once we had simplified enough detail, we could meet our polygon budget.

Texture Budgeting

Texture budgeting is simpler than face budgeting for this model. So far, we've noted that we'd like to texture the front grille, the wheel, the M3 badge and the BMW logo. That's a lot, but they don't all have to be detailed—we will work with some tricks to get them all in.

Choose a Modeling Method

It's always a little surprising to get to this step, after having carefully explored the mesh on the object, and realize that we haven't yet decided how to make the mesh! Now is the time to look at that.

We can take a couple of different modeling methods, but there's only one good choice. For an example of a bad choice, we could build this car from 3D objects like cubes and spheres, moving the verts into the forms we want. Arranging these primitive objects into the face layout we've drawn on our sketch would be very tedious. There are other equally useless approaches, but what makes the most sense is to draw the side of the car, extrude it, and then edit it to match our mesh sketch.

Create the Model

We're now ready to build the 3D mesh of our car model in 3D Studio. Our basic approach is divided into groups of steps, called "phases" here. Phase I is creating a 2D side view and extruding it into a pseudo-3D object. After that, we embark on Phase II: adding the information from the front view into the model we have. From there we do Phase III: build the secondary models (wheels, underside), then clean, tweak, and tune the model into perfection.

Phase I: Creating an Extruded 2D Model

Our first job is to create the faces that will form the side of the car. This is most easily done in the 2D shaper if we put the source art as the background, so let's set up the side view of the car as the background.

1. Choose Configure from the drop-down menus, click on Map Paths, then choose Add. Add the directory (listed in the next step) that contains the source art for the M3 to the Map Path list, then click OK on all the dialogs.

2. In the 3D Editor, choose Renderer/Setup/Background and choose the side view source art (the file CAR-S3SI.TIF from the CD-ROM) for the bitmap entry.

3. Press F1 to go into the 2D Shaper. From the View drop-down menu, choose See Background.

Our screen should now look like Figure 9.14.

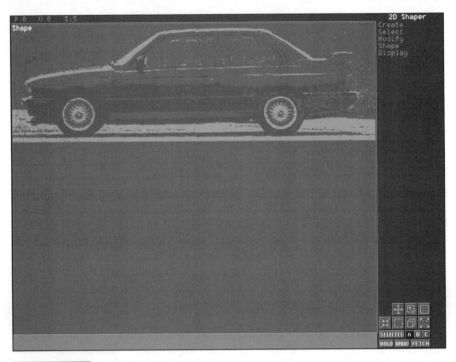

P:0   U:0   S:5   2D Shaper
Shape   Create
                                                         Select
                                                         Modify
                                                         Shape
                                                         Display

FIGURE 9.14 Ready to trace.

As we can see, this makes it pretty easy to create a basic mesh that matches the car's outline—all we have to do is trace the silhouette of the car. Also, notice that the image quality is pretty bad. Part of this is the fault of the original image, but 3D Studio only uses three shades of gray to represent the image shown. If our source art didn't show up too well here, we could try to adjust it (View/Adjust Background), but we might need to go back to Photoshop and edit the art to suit 3D Studio.

Background images are tricky to trace because there is absolutely no association between them and the vector-based art we are creating. If we zoom or pan while we trace, we immediately lose the alignment of our geometry with the image; we'll have to go back, if we can, or restart the tracing. To prevent automatic panning if we move the mouse off the edge of the display, we'll disable it, then we'll start tracing.

4. Under the Views drop-down menu, choose Scroll Lock.
   The mesh sketch we made earlier should be nearby for this step so we can look at it as we work.

5. Choose Create/Line and carefully trace an outline around the M3's silhouette, using approximately the points we chose when we drew the mesh sketch. Skip the wheels and wheelwells; instead, choose the points where the fenders meet the bottom of the car.

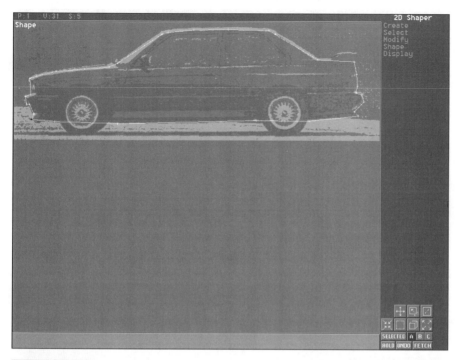

P:1 V:31 S:5
Shape
2D Shaper
Create
Select
Modify
Shape
Display

FIGURE 9.15 Initial outline.

When we've clicked all the way around the car's silhouette, our screen should look like Figure 9.15

6. Choose Display/Freeze/All.

7. Trace the car again. This time, trace the vertical side of the car, not the silhouette. For example, trace the line where the fender meets the hood, not the centerline of the hood, which sticks out farther. In some areas this trace will overlap the first trace path, such as along the bottom of the car and near the back section, but mostly it should be inside the area traced by the first line.

Now the screen should look like Figure 9.16 (except this figure has everything unfrozen so we can see the original line).

Now we need to add the wheel wells to the outline, but we can't see them in our source art very clearly. We'll adjust the image to show that detail.

8. From the drop-down Views menu choose Adj. Background and move the Dark slider to 17. Move the Light slider to 50. Click Display to see a thumbnail of the results. Experiment with different slider settings until the wheel well area can be seen more clearly.

9. Choose Create/Line and click in the middle of the line segment that crosses the rear wheel. Place verts around the edge of the fender one by one, and right-click when there are the correct number of verts (accord-

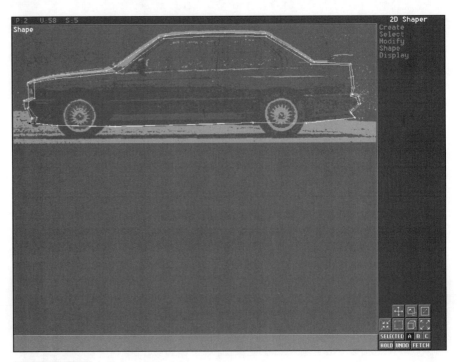

FIGURE 9.16 Two tracings.

ing to our sketch). If the placement isn't perfect, that's OK—the important thing is to create the right number of verts.

10. Create the front wheel arch in the same way.

11. Choose Modify/Vert/Move and adjust any verts that are out of place on the wheel arch. Take a look at the other source art to get a clearer idea of the correct shape and size of the arches.

12. Choose Create/Line and trace the door window with verts in the same approximate position as our mesh sketch. Close that polygon, then trace the side window the same way.

13. Use Modify/Vert/Adjust to move any verts that aren't in the correct location anywhere on the unfrozen polygons.

We're just about ready to bring the outline into the 3D Editor, as Figure 9.17 shows.

14. Choose Shape/Assign/All.

15. Press F3 to return to the 3D Editor. Click in the left view and choose Create/Object/Get Shape. In the ensuing dialog, enter the name 2D-Side, set shape detail to low, and cap shape to on.

16. Zoom all views to extents and verify that there is a flat mesh of the side of

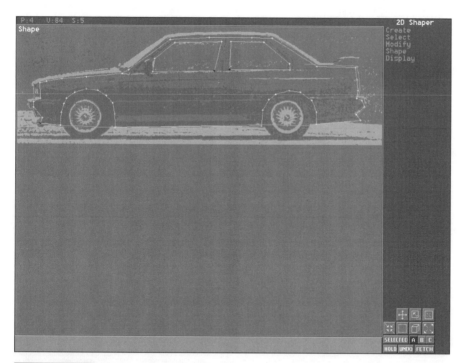

FIGURE 9.17 Edited outlines.

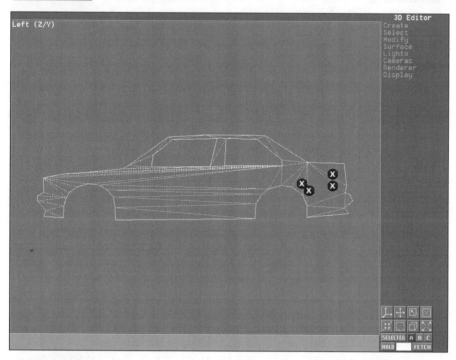

FIGURE 9.18 2D mesh outline in 3D Editor.

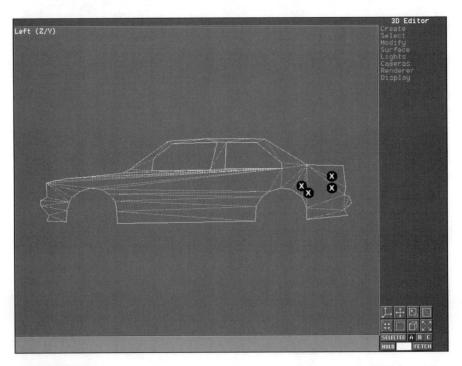

Left (Z/Y)

3D Editor
Create
Select
Modify
Surface
Lights
Cameras
Renderer
Display

SELECTED A B C
HOLD   FETCH

FIGURE 9.19 Edges to be turned are indicated, and more are marked.

the car, with holes for the windows. Type W to make the Left view fill the screen.

The screen should now look like Figure 9.18.

We're now at a decision point. If we start editing the object we just made, we won't be able to revise the 2D shape. We need to decide if we are going to build the rest of the model from this basic mesh, or if we should add more detail in the 2D shaper before going ahead.

Our decision is based on the easier way to accomplish what we need to do. The 2D shaper is the fastest way to create a new area (like an antenna or mirror) quickly, but it doesn't allow much control over the resulting mesh's shape. The 3D Editor makes it pretty easy to move and add verts in the middle of an existing mesh without creating a hole, but it's hard to add entirely new features.

Of course, what the 3D Editor really allows us to do is get the 2D shape into a 3D form, but we aren't worried about that right now—the first step is to get the right number and basic layout of verts in the mesh, then we can form them into a 3D shape.

Comparing this mesh to the mesh sketch, we see that we've got a lot of details that aren't shown here, even ignoring the nose, roof, and other parts and concentrating on faces that are mainly on the side of the car.

For example, our sketch shows verts along the edge of the door, where the fender flares meet the body. We'll have to add some verts in the middle of the mesh to model that seam. It makes sense to do this in the 3D Editor—all we have to do is divide an edge and move the resulting vert.

We also need to add the verts for the mirror and side marker lights. These float above the surface of the car, as discussed earlier, so we don't want to put them in our outline here. We'll add them once we have the basic car's model done.

All factors point to making the decision to progress into the 3D Editor and abandon our 2D shape, so that's what we'll do. The next step is to refine the design of the mesh that 3D Studio created by turning edges.

What's the Point of Turning These Edges?

We're setting up the mesh so that when we can add verts for the fenders and pull them out to make a 3D curved surface, the triangles will be correctly arranged to represent the smooth curve of the surface (Figure 9.19).

Turn the edges:

1. Choose Modify/Edge/Turn and click on the edges marked in Figure 9.20. Compare the results to the rear end of Figure 9.23.

The next step is really tricky—if the wrong edge is accidentally selected, the results can be extremely confusing. Remember to save backups along the way. Also, refer to the discussion of Modify/Edge/Divide in Chapter 5 if you are

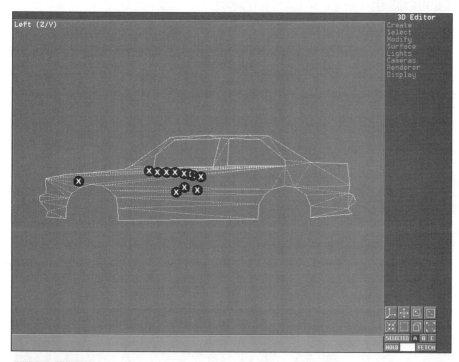

FIGURE 9.20   Indicated edges have been turned.

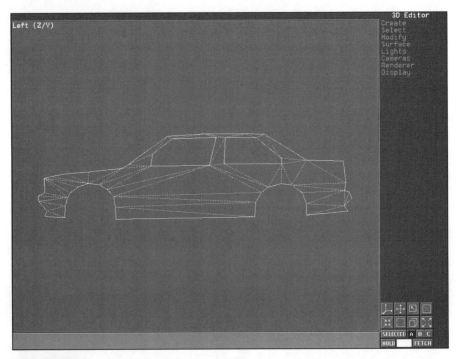

FIGURE 9.21 More edges turned.

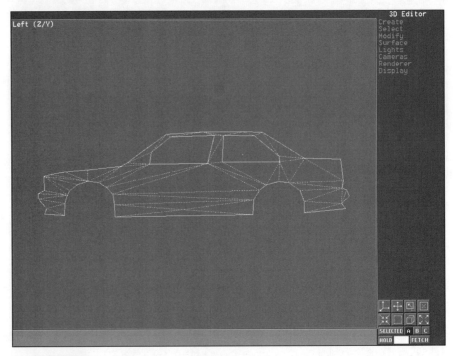

FIGURE 9.22 First door edge divided.

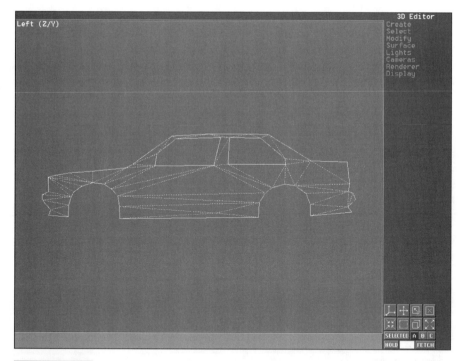

3D Editor
Create
Select
Modify
Surface
Lights
Cameras
Renderer
Display

Left (Z/Y)

SELECTED A B C
HOLD FETCH

FIGURE 9.23   Lower trailing corner of door formed.

unfamiliar with edges. You should correctly predict the results of each edge turned before you do it. If 3D Studio doesn't do what you thought it would, be worried! Restore the backup and try again—when turning edges, the "hey, nothing happened" extra clicks can come back to haunt in a big way.

2. Turn the edges that are indicated in the illustration above so the mesh looks like Figure 9.21.

The next step is to add verts in the middle of the mesh that will form the lower corners of the door. This car is a little unusual in that the door's shape can be seen in 3D because the flared fenders stop at its edges. On lots of cars, we don't bother putting verts at the corners of the doors because the entire side of the car is smooth and doesn't need any verts in the middle.

3. Choose Modify/Edge/Divide and click on the lowest shared edge in between the wheel holes. Compare the result to Figure 9.22.

4. Choose Modify/Vert/Move and move the new vert to the corner of the door, as shown in Figure 9.23.

5. Choose Modify/Edge/Turn and click on any horizontal edges between the lower corner of the side window and the new vert, as shown in Figure 9.24.

6. Divide the edge that runs between the new vert and the rear corner of the front fender. Move this new vert to form the lower corner of the door.

CHAPTER 9 • **Modeling Specific Types of Objects**   **193**

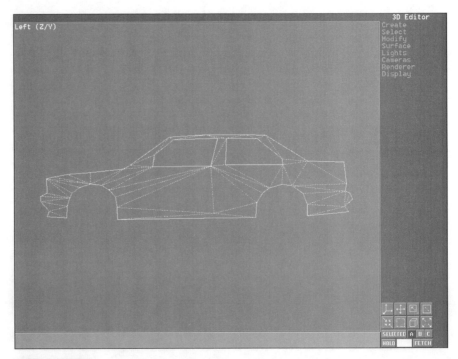

FIGURE 9.24 Edges turned to form door edge.

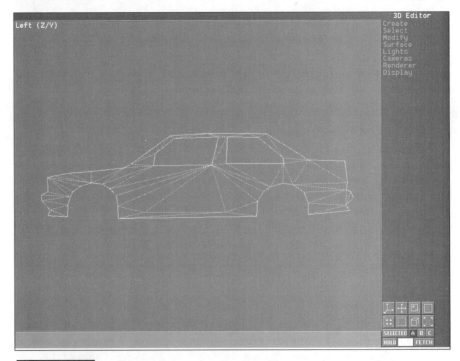

FIGURE 9.25 Added point for leading lower corner of door.

Designing 3D Graphics

The previous step should obviously be the same basic procedure we did for the rear door edge.

7. Divide the little edge that connects the door window to the trailing edge of the hood. Turn the edge above it.

The mesh should now look like Figure 9.25.

8. Turn edges until the leading (hinge) edge of the door is straight, as shown in Figure 9.26.

Take another look at the mesh sketch. We've now got the verts on the corners of the doors, but we need to add the ones in between, along the vertical edges of the door. That's what comes next.

9. Choose Modify/Edge/Divide and click on the leading and trailing edges of the door. Turn the edges so these two new verts are connected by a horizontal edge. Move the rear vert so the door edge is vertical.

10. Turn the edges that connect the door window to the rear fender, so there is a single edge connecting the side window to the vert we just moved.

> **TIP**
>
> One thing to be learned from this constant dividing and turning of edges is that the number and location of the verts are important, and the mesh that connects them is fairly fluid.

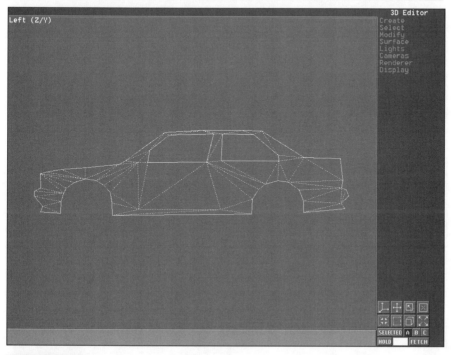

FIGURE 9.26   Turning edges for leading edge of door.

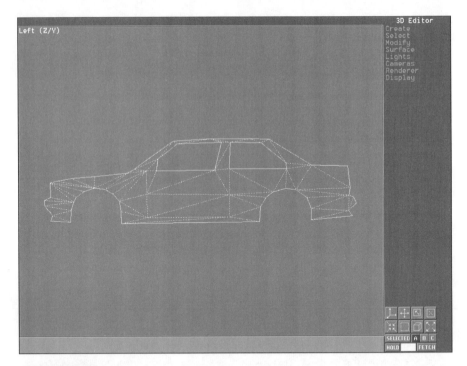

FIGURE 9.27 Door's middle verts added.

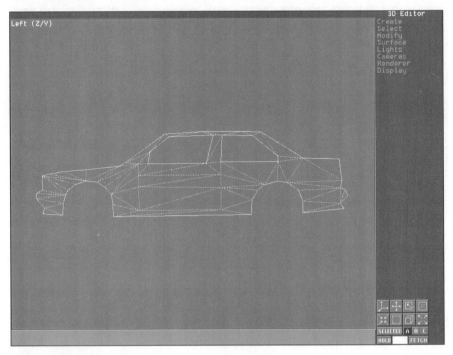

FIGURE 9.28 More middle verts in door.

Designing 3D Graphics

The mesh should now look like Figure 9.27.

11. Choose Modify/Edge/Divide and click on the two vertical edges of the door above the verts we created most recently. Turn the edges between them, so these two new verts are connected by a horizontal edge.

Comparing our sketched mesh to the one on the screen (see Figure 9.28), we see that the meshes at the fenders don't really match.

The onscreen mesh has long, thin triangles connecting the lower corner of the door window to the rear fender. This occurs partly because we don't have any verts above the center of the wheels, in the middle of the flares, so we'll add those now.

12. Divide the edge that connects the top of the front fender arch to the hood.

13. Divide the edge that connects the top of the rear fender arch to the rear corner of the side window.

14. Divide the edge in the back end that forms the vertical part of the trunk corner.

Our mesh should now look like Figure 9.29

At this point, we have verts in place that pretty much set up the fender definition. We don't have the small verts that stick off the body to form the flare of the fenders, but we'll add those once we start making this curved in 3D.

The verts onscreen roughly correspond to the ones we sketched, but the meshes at the fenders don't really match. Our model has triangles zigzagging

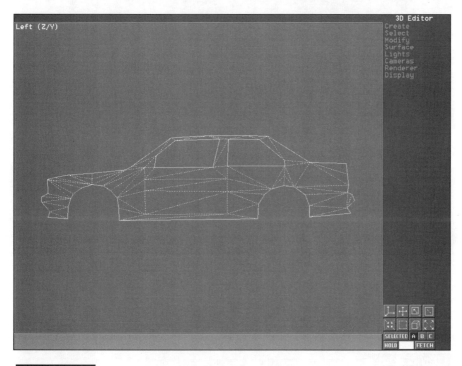

FIGURE 9.29   Fender flare edges added.

across the horizontal upper edge of the flared fenders, where our sketch has nice neat triangles. Next, we'll turn edges to more closely resemble the mesh we drew.

15. Choose Modify/Edge/Turn and turn edges that are not in line with the upper edge of the flared fenders.

Though it sounds like a step-by-step procedure here, in reality the last few steps would be part of a "diagnostic" time. The modeler spends a half-hour or less examining the whole model, looking for problems. This working style is the iterative puttering and preening of making a flower arrangement, compared to a step-by-step procedure of assembling a bookshelf.

What kind of problems? In this case, we're mainly looking for edges that cross a feature of the model (for example, a diagonal line across two areas that will have different materials, or a straight edge that crosses a bent surface), but we also keep an eye out for edges that make two triangles unnecessarily long and thin.

We turn this, tweak that, and work in a vague fashion, referring to our sketch from time to time to judge our progress. Of course, the sketch isn't gospel; in some cases we'll just ignore it and build a better mesh.

16. Look at the sketched mesh and the modeled mesh as described above. For example, the rear bumper is sketched with horizontal lines connecting all points to rear side of the fender. Turn those edges until they match Figure 9.30.

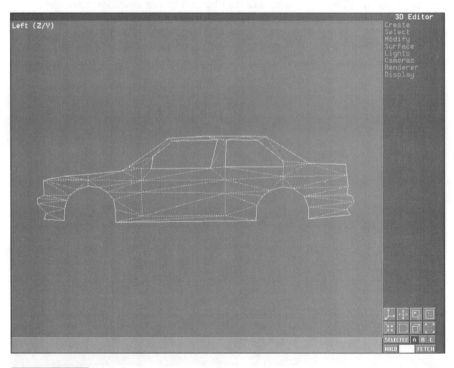

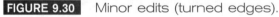 **FIGURE 9.30** Minor edits (turned edges).

Taking a look at our model compared to the sketched mesh, we see that it's looking pretty close. There's some differences, though. A minor difference is the lack of verts on the body where the spoiler will attach.

A larger difference is in the nose. The model has a very simple grille where the sketched mesh has many verts around the edge of the nose. Though this may look like a problem, it's not. This modeled mesh is totally flat, and those verts are there to define the unique curves where the hood, fender, and nose merge. So far, our mesh has been strictly 2D so we haven't gotten involved in creating those verts yet.

17. Choose Modify/Object/3D Scale and scale the object until the length of the car is 4.35 meters.

18. Use the tape measure (Display/Tape/Find) combined with the Zoom Extents to find out the length of the car.

19. Choose Create/Face/Extrude and type Alt-A to select all faces. Extrude all the side faces 0.77 meters. Choose "outward" for the extrusion direction.

20. Extrude the selected faces again, but this time only 0.10 meters.

21. Hide the selected faces. Redraw the viewport.

22. Delete the faces that frame the side and door windows (shown selected in Figure 9.31). Answer "yes" to the "Delete isolated vertices?" prompt.

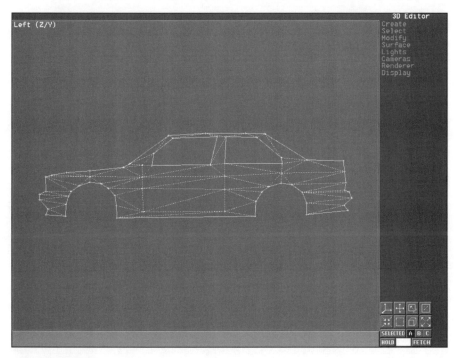

FIGURE 9.31   Erasing side-glass faces.

Redraw the viewport.

23. Select the faces that frame the wheel wells and the three horizontal sections that touch the wheel wells. Choose Create/Face/Detach and detach the selected faces into a new object named Bottom.

24. Hide the new object by choosing Display/Hide/Object and then typing H to choose Bottom from the dialog. Choose Display/Unhide/Object and click on the object onscreen. The selected side faces are now visible.

25. Type W to see all viewports. Spin the user view around and examine the object you have so far built. Compare it to Figure 9.32, which is what you should have.

Our examinations tell us that we have a very square-looking half of a car, with the wheel wells missing. It's very rough, but it's a 3D object, and it will serve nicely as a raw model to tune.

Phase II: The Hard Part

Now we'll modify our cookie-cutter extruded 2D outline into a true 3D shape. This phase always involves a certain amount of head-scratching. The basic idea is that since we already have two of our three dimensions modeled, we try to add in the missing third dimension, along the extrusion axis. Our 2D sketch did not fully capture the car's shape—we chose the outer surface of the side of the car,

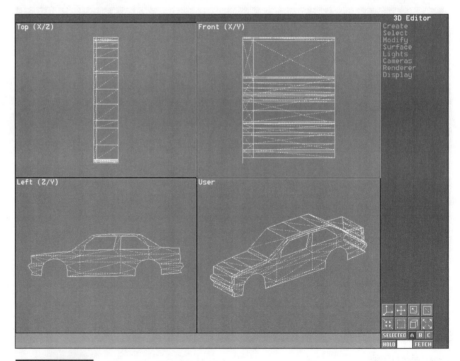

 FIGURE 9.32 Crude 3D car.

not the center line section, to trace. As we define the 3D shape, we'll be correcting that as well.

Our basic approach will be to manipulate the verts in small groups. We'll work around the various areas of the car one by one, moving, adding, and removing verts until the 3D shape is properly defined.

We start with one of the hardest areas of the car: the front fender/headlight area. It's harder because it's a 3D curved area that defines the shape of the car to the eye, and there's no convenient way to get that 3D curve—it's not a simple spheroid curve or even a lathed spline curve—it's a unique, complex curved corner, fading smoothly into the hood, fender, and grille, that must be implied from source art. We'll want to refer back to the source art, especially the photographs, as we work to keep in mind the shape of the curve we're trying to achieve.

The "good" news is we don't have to define the curve that precisely because we don't have enough faces to do so. On our sketched mesh, we have a lot of faces in this area, and though it may seem that we need these faces to clearly define the curve, we're going to remove some faces from this area because we're over our face budget. Our sketched mesh is 65 faces more than our budget and though this corner is important, it's a small area on the screen. We don't need too many faces to show its shape, so it's a good area from which to remove faces.

26. Select and hide all faces except the ones in the nose of the car that face forward. That's the grille, the bumper, and the fairing below it.

If we zoom to extents, the screen should look like Figure 9.33.

The left view shows that we have isolated a group of faces that are a continuous mesh that doesn't bend more than 180 degrees.

Compare this to a sphere. Spheres' surfaces wrap 360 degrees, so we must be very careful when we edit verts by clicking on them because they could be either on the front or the back of the sphere. If we're not careful when we click, we'll accidentally select a vert on the far-away side of the sphere. With the shape we have here, we can see that there is no danger (in the front view) of picking a vert behind another one because they don't overlap. This allows us to edit quickly without worrying which vertex we're picking.

In 3D Studio when we move verts to which hidden faces connect, the faces move also. That means we can edit faces that we can't see! Actually, that's good because the alternative (hidden faces don't move) would cause us to leave gaping holes in the mesh.

27. Select the leftmost column of verts in the Front view. In the Top view, rotate them around their local axis 45 degrees. Move them until the edges that connect them to the verts to their right are parallel, and the shortest edge is a little shorter than it used to be.

28. Choose Display/Unhide/Object and click on any edge. Examine the model by spinning the User view slowly (hold down the Shift key while pressing the arrow keys). The screen should look like Figure 9.34.

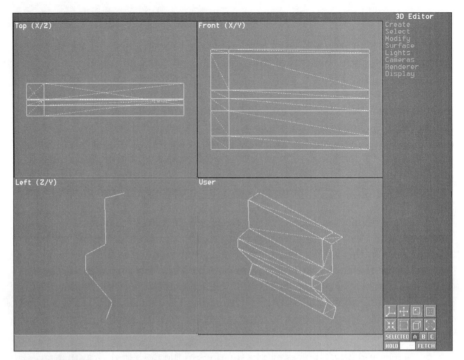

FIGURE 9.33 Only nose of car visible.

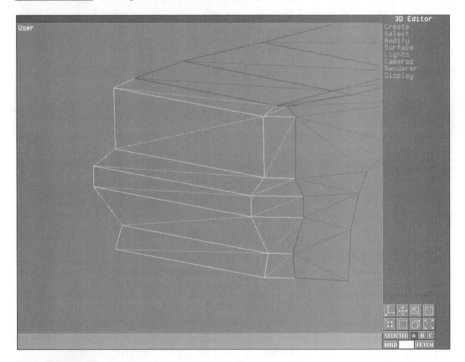

FIGURE 9.34 Editing corner of nose.

Compare the nose's shape to the source art, especially the front view. We should now see that the bumper looks pretty good, but the fender arch is not lined up with the bumper and the fender behind the corner of the nose has some problems. We'll get to those problems presently. Now look at the sketched mesh and notice that the grille surface has many rows of faces that meet along it. Our modeled grille surface does not; the two edges at the top of the fender ungracefully merge into a single corner. That's what we'll fix next.

29. Choose Modify/Edge/Divide and select the vertical edge of the grille that's not on the centerline. Divide it twice.

30. Turn the solid edge marked A in Figure 9.35.

31. Hide the selected faces, clear all selections, and select the verts we just created, as well as the one above them (circled in Figure 9.35).

32. In the Front view, move the topmost of the selected verts to the right. Move the middle vert up and to the right. Move the bottom vert up.

33. Adjust all three verts until they form a nice curve around the edge of the grille. Refer to the source art drawings to get the shape right.

When forming the curve, remember that the interior of the grille will be a texture map, so don't worry about modeling details on the inner grille area. The important thing is for the 3D silhouette to be right, and for the area to be textured to be planar.

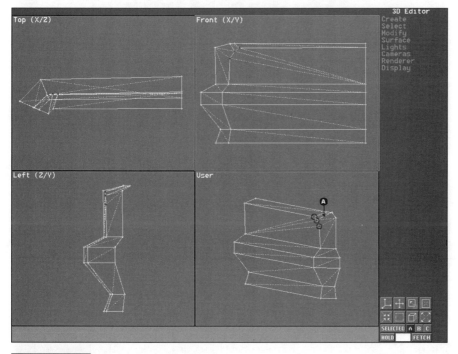

FIGURE 9.35 Corner of nose of car.

Now we'll reshape the next slice of verts along the body. This round is a little easier, because we've established a groundwork to work from. Figure 9.36 shows the intended result.

34. Adjust the next group of vertices so they define the corner as shown in Figure 9.36.

We're starting to touch the wheel arch area, and as this area comes into play, we'll realize that the bumper curve sticks out farther than the side of the car. This occurs partly because the side of the car doesn't have any curvature (from the Front view, this curvature would be approximated by an arc going through the top of the A pillar, the bottom of the A pillar, and the bottom of the door). Also, it occurs partly because of the mushy way we're modeling it. As we work through verts that form the fender, we'll work them into alignment while integrating the slight curvature of the car's side.

In the following group of verts, we're into the area that defines the fender flare (right above the top of the wheel arch). We need to build a sharp notch to define this clearly. We do this by dividing the vertical edge, then adjusting the resulting verts. Figure 9.37 shows the result.

Picking Up the Pace

From here, the steps are quite similar. Our basic approach is to work our way over the entire car, defining the geometry as we go. If this concept is daunting to

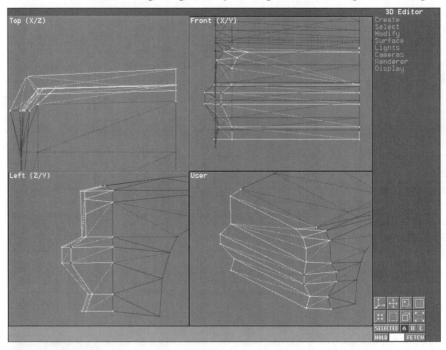

FIGURE 9.36 Corner of nose and leading edge of wheel arch defined.

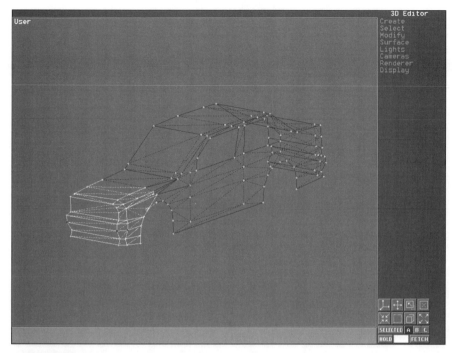

3D Editor
User
Create
Select
Modify
Surface
Lights
Cameras
Renderer
Display

SELECTED A B C
HOLD   FETCH

FIGURE 9.37   Fender flare definition.

you, practice a lot, following along the illustrations and loading the projects off the CD-ROM if you get really lost.

Figure 9.38 shows the roof area adjusted, and Figure 9.39 shows many of the faces reduced out of the roof area because they aren't doing much to define the shape.

35. Looking at the front fender flare, we notice the rearward edge that was created when we made the sharp little step so it is connected to the A pillar root. Turning this edge makes it nice and horizontal, connecting to the door's leading edge, as shown in Figure 9.40.

36. Next, we select the verts that define the rear wheel arch, the bottom edge of the rear skirt, and the middle of the door, and move them along the X axis (to the driver's left) until they line up with the front wheel arch. This leaves behind the lower corner of the doors (in fact, we should move those toward the middle of the car a little to accentuate this difference), the indented area of the rear skirt, and the row of verts that define the lower edge of the side glass and corner of trunk. Effectively, this move has created the curvature that the trailing edge of the door in our blueprint sketch shows. Our modeled door's trailing edge should now show this, too (Figure 9.40).

Actually, this model is looking pretty good. Next, we add the fender flare definition above the peak of the rear wheel arch, just as we did for the front.

CHAPTER 9 • **Modeling Specific Types of Objects**   **205**

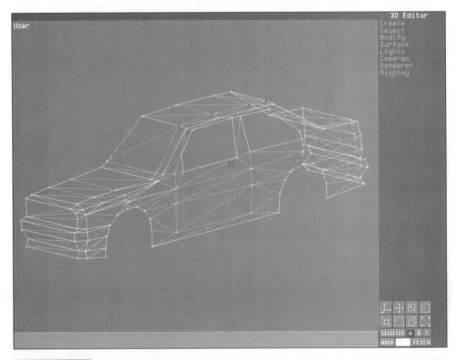

FIGURE 9.38 Revised roofline.

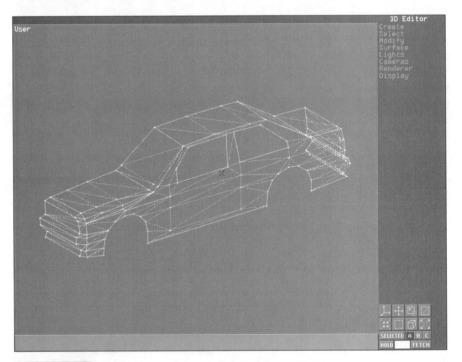

FIGURE 9.39 Welded verts in the roof area.

Designing 3D Graphics

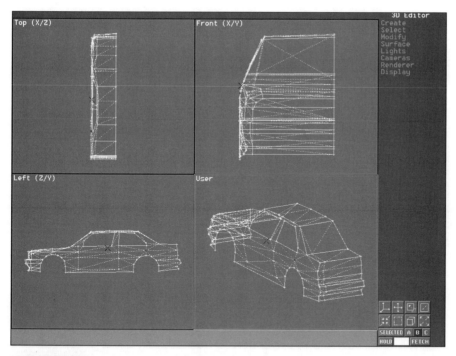

FIGURE 9.40 Side of car has curvature.

Then we preen a little more—perhaps refining the curvature of the fenders, adjusting the width of the B pillar, and modifying the shape of the roof. Looking at the rear end, we notice that a whole row of faces are unnecessary, and we weld them up to save faces. This creates a pretty boxy back end, which is what we want. We then move the rear verts around some to give a tiny bit of curvature across the width of the car. Next we adjust the A pillar, which is pretty wide, and weld up an unnecessary vert at the leading lower corner of the door window. A little tuning of the hood's curve, some adjustment of the front fender, and our model is looking pretty good (Figure 9.41).

This model looks good, but there is some unnecessary detail here and there. The lower edge of the windshield, for example, some of the roof, the undercut below the taillights, and the hood could all be simplified without much change to the way the model looks. Our model doesn't look much different (Figure 9.42) after these changes, but it's lost about 8 percent of its data (14 faces and 9 verts).

Next, we need to put some faces in the side windows and build the undercarriage. The undercarriage consists of four wheel wells and the bottom surface.

We need to delete the undercarriage that was created when we extruded (that's been hidden all this time). It's too dissimilar to what we are going to build, and it would take much longer to edit it into the correct shape than it will to rebuild it.

Add side windows and build the undercarriage:

1. Unhide and delete object Bottom.

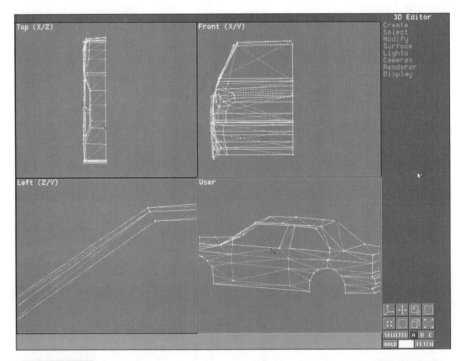

FIGURE 9.41 More tweaking and welding yields a nice half-model.

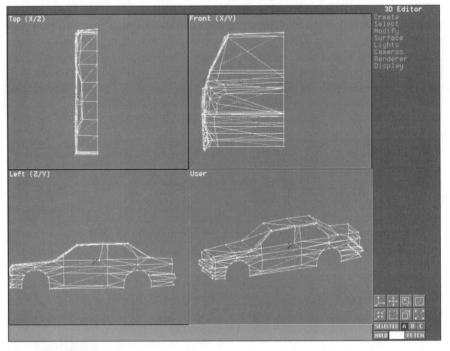

FIGURE 9.42 Car body half with 133 faces.

Designing 3D Graphics

Now, we'll build a new one. We could build it by using Create/Face/Build, but we'll save the time and hassle of clicking on all those verts around the wheel arches by extruding a copy of the entire "car-half" object.

2. Choose Modify/Object/Move, click on the car body, and click again without moving the mouse. Name this new object temp. Hide the car body object.

3. Select temp (Select/Object/By Name). Choose Create/Face/Extrude and extrude the selected faces inward, about 1/4 of the car's width. We should now have a strange mess on the screen, like Figure 9.43.

4. Move the selected faces up (+Y) until they are the same height as when they started.

5. Delete the selected faces, the faces that outline the side windows, and any face that is near the centerline of the car.

6. In the Top view, select the verts that don't align with the body's existing verts, and move them so the extrusion points straight to the right. Our screen should now look a little like Figure 9.44 (except we haven't fixed the edges yet).

7. Deselect the verts that are part of the wheel arches. That should leave five verts, all on the nose and tail edges. Move them toward the center of the car, until we end up with Figure 9.44.

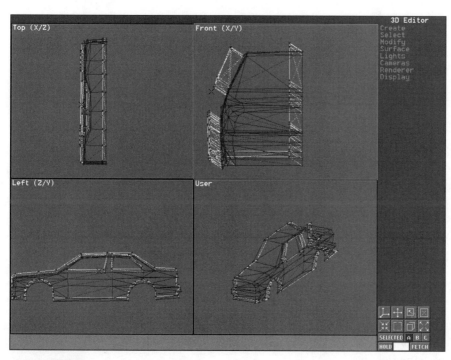

FIGURE 9.43 Extruded body (mess).

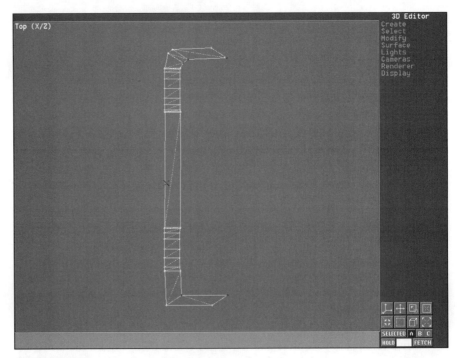

FIGURE 9.44   Pieces to form the undercarriage.

8. Unhide all objects, choose Display/Geometry/Backface. Choose Surface/Normals/Object Flip and click on temp. In the User view, examine the model and see if you can understand what the last step just did. Basically, we turned the faces so they are "inside" faces rather than "outside."

Now, we'll reduce the face count and put in the backs of the wheel wells.

9. Freeze the car body object, choose Display/Geometry/See Thru, and select all the verts that form the back of the wheel well. This is a little tricky, so be sure your selection set matches Figure 9.45.

10. Weld all the selected verts together, except the verts circled in Figure 9.45. Weld the other verts to these verts, so we form a box. Use Figure 9.46 as a guide.

11. Choose Display/Geometry/Backface, then choose Create/Face/Build and hand-build two faces that connect the four verts in the front wheel well. These faces should be visible in the Left view.

Be sure to pick the verts in the right order (counter-clockwise in the Left view); if we don't, the face will point the wrong way. If this happens, the face will be created with no warning messages, but it won't be visible. Spin the User view to verify that the face is backward, then use Surface/Normal/Face Flip to flip it back the right way.

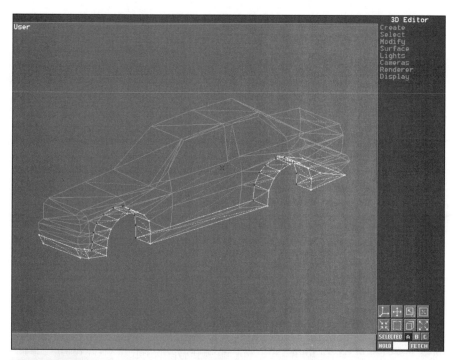

FIGURE 9.45   Selected verts that form the inside of the wheel wells.

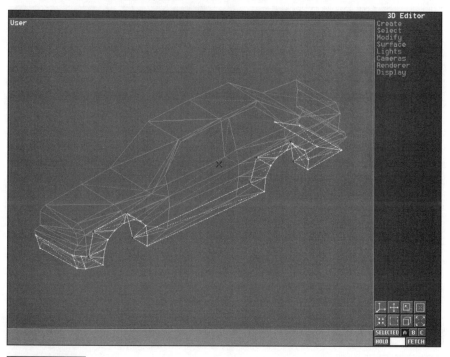

FIGURE 9.46   Wheel wells with insides welded into boxes.

CHAPTER 9 • **Modeling Specific Types of Objects**   **211**

12. In the Left view, deselect the lower verts (the ones that align with the bottom of the car). Move the selected corners until they more closely approximate the shape of the wheel arches.

Our model should look like Figure 9.47.

Now, we form the underside's large surfaces, using the extruded pieces as a starting point.

13. Choose a User view that shows the underside well. Select the verts that don't align with the body and aren't part of the wheel well (shown selected in Figure 9.47). Weld them to the nearest corner of the wheel well, being careful not to cause them to cross into the inside of the wheel well. The result should look like Figure 9.48.

14. Using Create/Face/Build, create four faces that connect the six vertices that are selected in Figure 9.48, thus filling in the rest of the underside surface.

15. Use Modify/Edge/Autoedge with a tolerance of one degree to set the flat faces invisible.

The screen should now look like Figure 9.49.

Note that the bottom is not fully planar. Normally, we'd flatten it out so all those faces could be combined into one large polygon, but the rear of the car is not flat, so if possible we'd like to keep that section slanted.

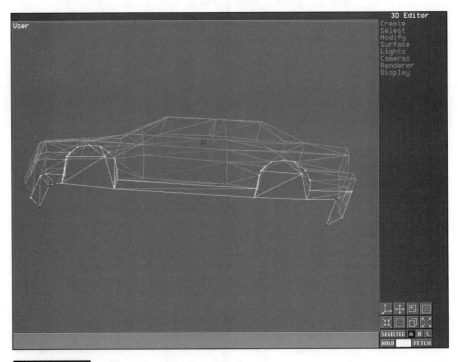

 FIGURE 9.47 Wheel wells finished.

Designing 3D Graphics

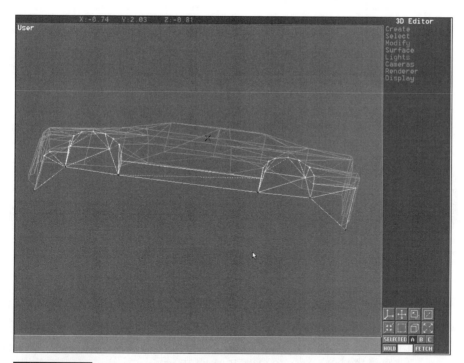

FIGURE 9.48 Part of underside surface created.

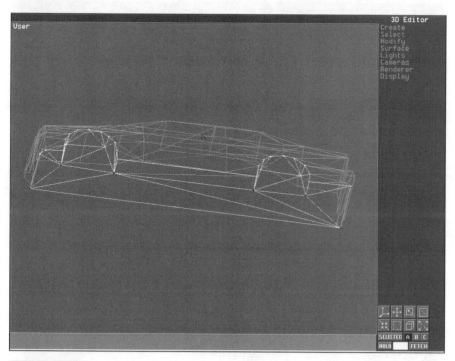

FIGURE 9.49 Finished undercarriage half.

CHAPTER 9 • **Modeling Specific Types of Objects**

Also, remember that our engine can't have concave polygons, which is what this would be. We'll need to divide this polygon up, and we might as well do that and preserve the model's definition (that is, keep the back slanted) as much as possible. The best way to do this is to wait until we build the full model (not just half).

16. Assign black matte to the whole underside object.

17. Attach the underside object to the car body object, select the resulting object, and weld selected verts.

We're nearly done with the body; now we need to be sure it is oriented, located, and scaled to real-world units correctly. Let's look at the scaling first.

18. Reset the axis (Modify/Axis/Home).

19. Create a box by entering coordinates from (0,0,0) to (-1.68,1.37,4.35). This second coordinate came from the width (X, negative so it'll be on the left), height (Y), and length (Z) dimensions in our source data. Name the box "car size."

Figure 9.50 shows this box with the car body. Remember that the box fits two halves of the car—it's the full width.

20. Scale the box by 50 percent in the width (X), using global coordinates (that is, leave the "local axis" button, the one with the boxed X, off). Change the box's color to make it easier to see.

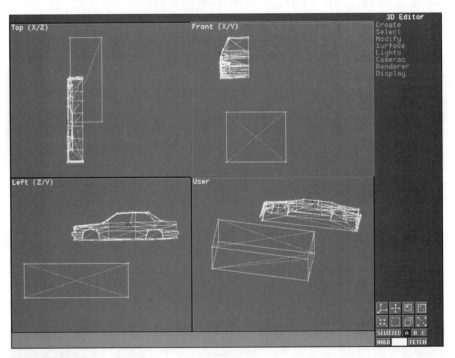

 Car with scaling box.

Designing 3D Graphics

21. Move the car so it fits in the box as closely as possible. Because it's missing its wheels, move the roof to the top of the box.

We'll probably find that it doesn't fit perfectly, so we'll adjust it to fit.

22. In the Left view, 3D scale the car until it fits in the box length-wise.

23. In the Front view, 2D scale in the Z direction only, until the width fits in the box. It should look like Figure 9.51.

24. Flatten the grille polygons by aligning the User view to one of the faces, rotating it 90 degrees so the grille faces appear to be in a line (but aren't quite, because they're warped), then using 2D Scale to smash the verts flat.

Now, we're ready to build the wheels. In the planning stages, we decided to build 11- or 12-sided wheels. Looking at Figure 9.52, which has the front wheel with 11 sides and the rear with 12, it should be clear that there isn't a big difference in appearance, especially when you consider how big they'll be on the user's screen. When in doubt, go with fewer faces! Eleven-sided faces are the way to go here.

We'll type in coordinates for the cylinders instead of clicking on the screen so we can enter the numbers from the source data directly.

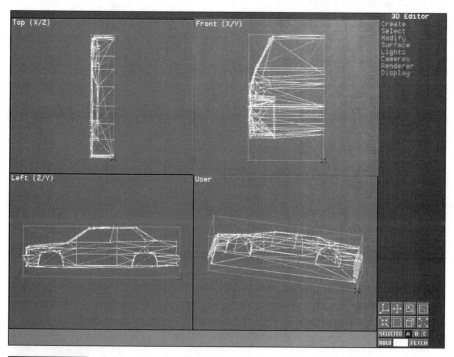

FIGURE 9.51 Car in the box.

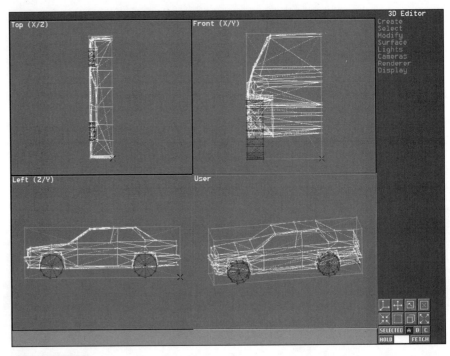

3D Editor
Create
Select
Modify
Surface
Lights
Cameras
Renderer
Display

Top (X/Z)

Front (X/Y)

Left (Z/Y)

User

FIGURE 9.52   Comparing 11-sided (front) to 12-sided (rear) wheels.

25. Choose Create/Cylinder, and set the values to 11 sides, 1 segment. Type in 0,0,0 for the center point, 0.32 for the radius, 0 for angle, and 0.18 for the length. Name it wheel01.

26. Move it to line up with the bottom of the size box, in the front wheel well. This will require two move operations: one in the Left view for Y and Z, and one in the Front view for X.

27. Get rid of the center verts by welding them to any vert on the edge of the wheel.

The next couple of steps will define the face that will hold the transparent-border texture map of the blurred spinning wheel.

28. Create a single face, using Create/Face/Build, that is approximately an equilateral triangle, using the verts on the front of the tire.

29. Detach this face, and scale the resulting object until it resembles the one in Figure 9.53. Move it away from the wheel (-X axis) a tiny bit. Attach this object back onto the wheel object.

We should have something like Figure 9.53.

30. Copy the wheel to the rear.

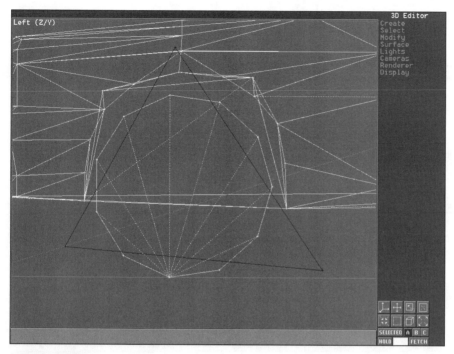

3D Editor
Create
Select
Modify
Surface
Lights
Cameras
Renderer
Display

SELECTED A B C
HOLD   FETCH

FIGURE 9.53 Completed wheel model, with rim triangle.

Now we're ready to consider mirroring the body half.

31. Choose Modify/Object/Mirror and mirror in the Front view along the X axis.

Take a long minute to examine this model now, before going any further. Hide the wheels, turn on backface rejection, and spin the User view for a while. This is our last chance to make edits once; after we commit to this mirror operation, we'll have to make changes to the both halves of the object.

Think of all the little things now, not later! Where's the spoiler? We'll have to build that. The side mirrors, marker lights, and taillights are missing too, but we just don't have enough faces to do them, so we'll skip them.

Also, if we have to reduce faces, now's the time. Let's think about face count. Using Modify/Object/Attributes, we can see the face count for the half-body object. It has 172 faces and 100 verts, and it's only half. With a budget of 300 faces, it looks bad!

32. Before we panic, remember that this is faces, not polygons. What difference will that make? Here's a quick way to check: Choose Modify/Edge/Autoedge with a setting of 1 degree (using zero degrees sets every edge visible regardless of angle) on the half-body object, as shown in Figure 9.54.

CHAPTER 9 • **Modeling Specific Types of Objects** **217**

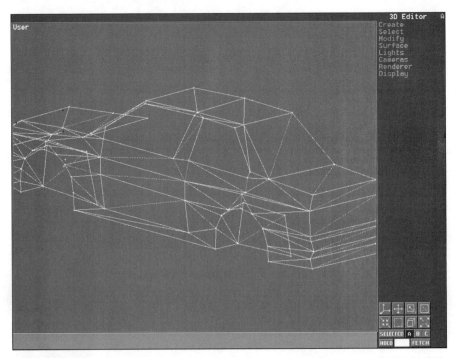

3D Editor   A
Create
Select
Modify
Surface
Lights
Cameras
Renderer
Display

User

FIGURE 9.54   Faces that will be converted to polys.

33. Count the dotted edges, subtracting one face for each one. We should count 25 dotted edges (not including the underside surface's edges; we're handling them separately). Each one saves two faces (because we're only looking at half), saving 50 faces total. Also, we can get rid of many of the faces at the centerline once we mirror the body, saving about 24 more polys there. And, the floorpan will simplify quite a bit—we'll save 17 faces by carefully combining it into a few large, flat polys. On the other hand, we'll need another 4 polys to make the side window glass, the spoiler will take another 6, and the taillight and license-plate overlays will take 3. Also, there are 56 polys in the wheels to consider.

So, in summary, we have 172 faces $\times$ 2 (because it's only half) giving 344 faces to start. 344 - (50 + 24 + 17) + (4 + 6 + 3 + 56) = 322 polys.

To reduce the final model by 20, we need to lose 10 faces (at least) in our half-model. Which faces can we get rid of? It's not easy but if we look, we can pick some places that won't suffer too badly. We can reduce the bottom of the A pillar a little more, simplify the roof and hood, and maybe edit the front airdam. It's tempting to try to reduce the number of edges on the wheel arches because we can save so many faces there, but it'll look really chunky if we simplify them any further.

Anyway, the changes we already listed should be enough to make our budget. To perform these edits, we simply do basic welds. We'll build the side-window glass and the rear spoiler as well. The step-by-step procedure is not shown here. The result is shown in Figure 9.55.

34. Now we mirror the object again. Choose Modify/Object/Mirror and mirror in the Front view along the X axis. Align the two centerlines as closely as possible. Mirror the two wheels.

35. Attach the two halves together and change the object's name to car body.

36. Weld all verts, then use Modify/Edge/Autoedge with a 1-degree tolerance. The screen should look like Figure 9.56.

37. Move the wheels up into the wheel wells a little more.

38. Fix the underside surface by turning edges. The goal is to connect the four wheel wells with rectangular pairs of faces. See Figure 9.58 for a guide line. Note that some the edges shown were manually set visible, separating the polygons into concave combinations.

39. Get rid of the centerline seam by welding the verts from the centerline edge to either side edge where they connect. Leave only the centerline edges for the front grille, the windshield, and the hood. See Figure 9.58 for an example.

Let's check our face count. We've got 310 faces in this model now. We will save 71 faces by polygon combination, making 239 polygons. With the wheels, we've got a total of 295 polygons. Great! We can put taillights in, which adds

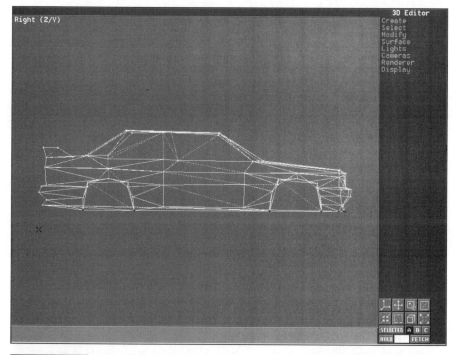

FIGURE 9.55 Somewhat simplified half-body with spoiler.

CHAPTER 9 • **Modeling Specific Types of Objects**   **219**

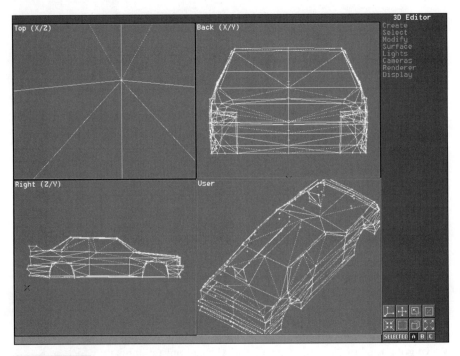

3D Editor
Create
Select
Modify
Surface
Lights
Cameras
Renderer
Display

FIGURE 9.56   Whole car body.

three polygons (though being this careful about hitting the polygon deadline isn't actually that realistic; most budgets can vary 10% without worrying anyone).

40. Divide the edge of the rear panel where the taillights fit into quarters horizontally, then half vertically. Turn the edges as you divide so the resulting faces are square. Figure 9.57 shows the result.

41. Select the faces that will be the taillights (see Figure 9.58) and weld the rest of the newly created verts back to the original ones. Change the edges around the taillights (and the horizontal edge between them) to visible.

42. Assign some basic materials to the object: red plastic to the taillights, black glass to the windows, black matte to the wheels, and black plastic to the rest of the body.

We're done with the geometry for this model.

Create the Textures

We need to create two textures for this model: a grille and a spinning wheel model. Both of these are easily derived from the source art.

Creating the Grille Texture

To make the grille texture, we'll examine our source bitmaps and look for a clear view of the grille. Obviously, CAR-FR.TIF is the best candidate.

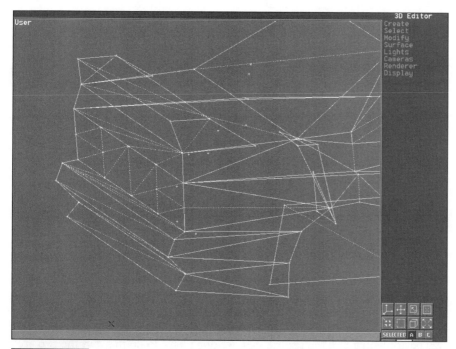

FIGURE 9.57 Making the taillights.

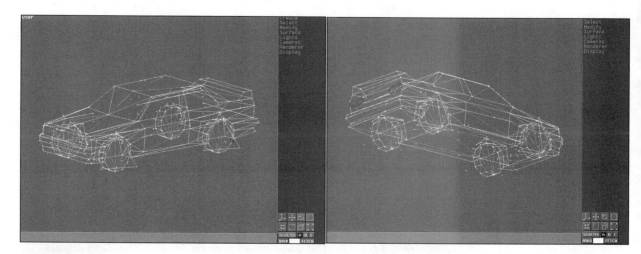

FIGURE 9.58 Final geometry for car (front/top and rear/back view).

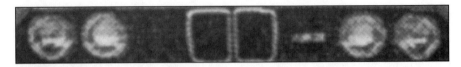

FIGURE 9.59   Cropped grille.

Create the grille texture:

1. Open CAR-FR.TIF.

2. Crop the bitmap to the grille.

When cropping, don't worry about the correct aspect or size. The important issue is what's in the cropped area. Keep the shape of the modeled grille in mind; imagine drawing a box around the polygons that define it. The upper corners are rounded, so that box would extend onto the body work. That's fine, just do the same thing when cropping the bitmap. Remember that the grille will be shown only on the faces that we assign the material to, so the bodywork won't have any stray bits of texture on it.

The cropped grille is shown in Figure 9.59.

Now we'll paint over the bodywork areas. If we map perfectly and our geometry perfectly matches the texture then we don't have to do this, but the two are sometimes different. This could cause a little bit of the bodywork in the texture to appear on the grille polygons. We could fix this by changing the mapping, but it's much quicker and easier to preemptively fix it here.

3. Sample the color of the black striped background of the grill. Use the airbrush with this color, 100 percent feathering, and paint over any bodywork that is visible.

Now we'll touch up any areas that need it. Let's brighten the red and blue parts of the M3 logo so they're more visible.

4. Choose pure red and airbrush over the red part of the M3 logo. Do the same for the blue part.

Now our texture should look like Figure 9.60.

5. Save this texture as M3GRILL.TIF

We need to convert this texture to square because our engine handles only square textures. We're using only about 10 percent of the texture. If we wanted to, we could go back and add a couple more faces to put textures on (like a hood

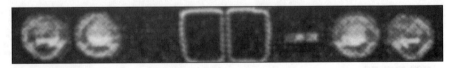

FIGURE 9.60   Retouched grille.

logo or separate taillight faces), then use the remaining 90 percent of empty space in this texture for these images. We'll stick with our original plan for now. There are two ways to make the texture square: either stretch it to fill a square or pad it with blank space. Stretching will make it slightly easier to map, but padding will make the image keep its aspect ratio in the texture map (which it makes it easier for us to work with). Also, padding will make it easier to return to add other images. Either is fine, but let's pad it.

6. Create a new image that is square, with the same width as the current texture.

7. Copy the current texture and paste it into the new image, at the top. Close the current texture.

8. Save the new image with the same name (M3GRILL.TIF) as the existing texture, overwriting the existing file.

This is our source texture. That means the rest of the edits are disposable. If we change anything in the texture, we'll edit M3GRILL.TIF, then redo the resizing and recoloring steps.

Why keep two versions? This 24-bit texture has more accurate data than the color and size-reduced version. Editing 8-bit images often doesn't work very well, so we need to edit 24-bit images. We could reconvert the 8-bit image to 24-bit, but it won't regain the original 24-bit data; it's better to edit the 24-bit source image and resize and reduce as the last steps.

Next, we'll approximate how the image is going to look in the application. Recall from the beginning of this exercise that the car's textures should be 74 pixels per meter, at best. If we measure the grill in 3D Studio (using Create/Box in the Front view and looking at the top status line as we drag the second corner), it fits in a 1.38 by 0.20 meter box. So, how many pixels wide and tall should the grille be? 1.38 meters $\times$ 74 pixels per meter = 102 pixels wide, 0.20 $\times$ 74 = 15 pixels tall. That means the best texture size is a 128 $\times$ 128 texture.

9. Resize the image to 128 pixels wide and tall, using anti-aliasing if your editor asks. Do not save the image.

If we've never done this before, our initial reaction to the 128-pixel texture is probably disgust and horror. Where did all our wonderful detail go? We can't even see the lines in the grille! We will probably feel an urge to use a 256-pixel texture instead. If so, remember that the grille will *never* be seen any larger than 128 pixels on the screen. That means that it will usually be much less (like 30) pixels onscreen. It would definitely be wasteful to use a 256 $\times$ 256 bitmap on this texture. This horrible image is the reality of our rendering situation: it's only a 320 $\times$ 200 screen, and the player will never be really close to our car. Remember the circle chart that we used to decide the number of sides for our wheel. That chart showed that the wheel onscreen is so low-res that users won't be able to tell a 12-sided polygon from a perfect circle; with that in mind, our 128-pixel grille is a luxurious amount of detail.

However, the best way to learn the futility of this is to experiment. If you still doubt the truth of this, you definitely should build both textures and try them out. The result should be that there is no difference at run time.

The reason this is so important is that if we always make our textures too big, they'll eat up all the texture memory, depriving other areas of textures, and thus hurting the overall quality.

10. Revert to the high-res saved image (we'll redo the sizing when we remap the colors).

Now that we can see what kind of detail we're going to have, we may wish to go back and edit the source bitmap a little, perhaps to emphasize detail. This is a good time to do that. Once the image is ready, save it.

Creating the Wheel Texture

The wheel texture is a little more challenging than the grille. What we need is to make a blurred, spinning wheel. Start with the source art photo of the rim (W-STILL.TIF, shown in Figure 9.61).

The first step should be to make sure it's not too huge, so we don't spend too much time worrying about totally tiny details. It's 289 × 278 pixels—a reasonable size, but it's not square. This probably occurred because the scanner is not calibrated. Resize it to square—we might as well make it 256 × 256 because it's close to that anyway.

Next, we make it blurred. There are a lot of different ways to make this into a blurred, spinning wheel.

• Use a smear tool in a circular pattern.

 Source art for wheel.

Designing 3D Graphics

- Copy, rotate, and paste additive and/or multiply, or with partial transparency.
- Use a special radial blur (spin) filter.

Do it any way you want; in Figure 9.62, the copy/paste additive was used many times.

Note that we didn't do a heavy blur on this image, leaving a few darker edges here and there between the spokes. We're anticipating that this will cause a slight flickering at run time as the darker pixels appear and disappear against a mostly gray surface. Normally, that's a bad thing, but in this case it is a special effect: slight flashing of light bouncing off the spinning wheels (of course, if everyone thinks it just looks bad, we can always change it).

We want to be sure this bitmap has transparency around it, which is determined by any color using pure black (RGB = 0 0 0). Use a point-sample to be sure that the outside of the circular is pure black, and make sure there isn't any inside the circle. This can be done by making a mask and slightly lightening the inside area (or any number of other methods).

Save this file as M3WHEEL.TIF.

Now, we'll reduce the color depth and size for the textures we created.

To remap, we need a source palette. We'll use CARPALET.BMP.

Sizing and Paletting

Reducing the color depth (paletting) is often difficult and confusing. The exact procedure for remapping from 24-bit to 8-bit paletted color varies widely from

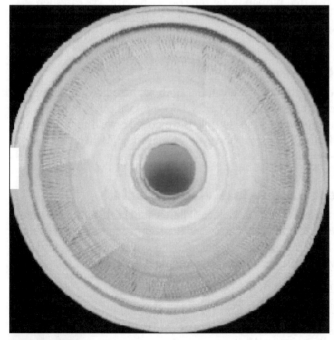

FIGURE 9.62 Blurred spinning wheel.

program to program, and some programs don't do it at all. For more general information related to palettes, see the section about palettes in Chapter 7.

The instructions here refer to Image Alchemy, a shareware image manipulation program, but use whatever you have. Many image editors have this function built-in (with varying degrees of usefulness). There are also stand-alone utilities that do this, including Hi-Jack, among others. On the Macintosh, there's a great program called Debabelizer that also does this.

We'll discuss Image Alchemy here. We'll use the DOS command-line directions, though it's also possible to do the same thing with the Windows-based interface that comes with it. This is one place where a command-line application works really nicely because it's designed for batch processing—converting a whole pile of textures into something else, all using the same palette (or size, for that matter). But we have only a couple of textures, so we'll do them one by one.

Here is how to reduce the 24-bit image M3GRILL.TIF to an 8-bit 128 × 128 version, using a specific palette. In MS-DOS, type (all on one line, with correct capitalization for the options):

```
X:\UTILITIES\ALCHEMY X:\EXAMPLES\CAR\M3GRILL.TIF -w -8 -X128 -Y128 -f \
X:\EXAMPLES\CAR\CARPALET.BMP
```

We're assuming your CD-ROM drive is X.

Here's what our command line did, translated to English: "Image Alchemy, take M3GRILL.TIF, convert it to a BMP format (-w), use 8-bit color using the palette from CARPALET.BMP (-8 -f CARPALET.BMP), and resize it to 128 × 128."

Image Alchemy will then generate M3GRILL.BMP, which is what we wanted: a 128 × 128 paletted bitmap using the correct palette. We can then repeat the command, changing the filename to M3WHEEL, and then we've got both bitmaps.

Batching the Conversions

In fact, if we end up doing this a lot, we can put both of these lines in a simple ASCII file, name it something like CONVERT.BAT, and we can just type CONVERT the next time we need to do this. If we do that, we'll find that we have to delete the old .BMP files first; however, we can force Alchemy to over-write them with the -o option.

Map the Textures on the Model

Now, we'll put these textures onto the object. There's some substeps here—creating materials that use the bitmaps we just made, assigning these materials to the faces that should have them, applying mapping coordinates, and the usual render-edit-render cycle, which is done once the model looks great.

Make the materials:
1. In 3D Studio, go to the Materials Editor (F5).

Now we'll add the folder that has the textures (M3WHEEL.BMP) to the map paths, so 3D Studio can find these textures when it tries to render.

2. Type *, click on Map Paths, and click on the window showing a list of paths (it may be empty; that doesn't matter). Navigate to the folder that contains the .BMP files we created, then click OK until we're back at the material editor.

Every graphics engine (or preprocessor code) handles the material settings differently. You'll have to find out how your graphics engine expects the materials to appear; for this exercise, we'll assume some common conventions: the material name has to match the texture name, in which case it is textured, or it is of the form COLORNNN where NNN is the palette entry number, in which case the face is Gouraud shaded with the color in that palette entry. We'll also assume that if the texture is intended to have transparency, we must put the bitmap in the Opacity Map section of the material. This won't make it render correctly in 3D Studio, but it will (we're assuming) make the graphics engine look for transparent pixels in the texture; without it, pure black pixels will be drawn as pure black, not transparent.

3. Type N to clear the library. Create a material that uses the M3WHEEL.BMP file we just created as its texture and opacity maps. Change the bitmap settings for both of these to decal, not tile.

Don't worry about any of the other material settings.

4. Type P to put the material into the empty library, with the name M3WHEEL.

Repeat this for M3GRILL, except don't put anything in the opacity map.

5. Return to the 3D Editor, clear all selected faces, and select the faces that make up the grille. Assign the M3GRILL material to them.

6. Clear all selected faces, then select the triangles that the wheel textures will go on, and assign the M3WHEEL material to them.

Now we'll apply mapping coordinates to the grille. This is pretty easy because these are the only mapping coordinates that the car body object is getting—we don't have to be careful not to overwrite some other mapping.

7. In the Front view, choose Surface/Mapping/Adjust/Scale and click on the car object while holding down the Alt key.

The mapping icon aligns with the Front view and is scaled to fit around the car body.

8. Choose Surface/Mapping/Adjust/Reset, and click Aspect Only.

Now it's square (1:1 aspect), just like our texture. Let's adjust it to cover the grille faces. As we do this, imagine the mapping icon contains the texture; we're trying to align the top bit with the faces that should have the texture on them.

9. Scale the mapping icon uniformly (don't change its aspect) so it fits around the grille faces from left to right.

10. Move the mapping icon until its top edge aligns with the top edge of the grille faces. Choose Surface/Mapping/Apply Obj and click on the car body.

Figure 9.63 shows the result.

We might be tempted to render now, but because rendering takes a while, we should apply the other mapping first, then render and check them both.

11. In the Side view, choose Surface/Mapping/Scale, and with the Alt key held down, click on the front wheel. Reset its aspect we did as before.

12. Move the icon until it encloses the round wheel (not the triangle) closely.

13. Scale the mapping icon down until it encloses the rim area on the wheel.

We can do this by a visual estimate, or if we want to be precise, we can create a temporary cylinder with the diameter of the rim (0.38 meters), and scale the map to that. Apply this mapping to both of the front wheels, then move the icon to the rear wheels and apply it to them both.

Let's render this. First we'll need some lights. We can use ambient lighting instead of building lights, but the car body won't show up well; only textures will be visible. Let's build a couple of Omni lights instead.

14. Choose Lights/Omni, and place them in the Top view at opposite corners of the car. Adjust them to be fully bright (L slider to 255). In the front view, move them up above the car.

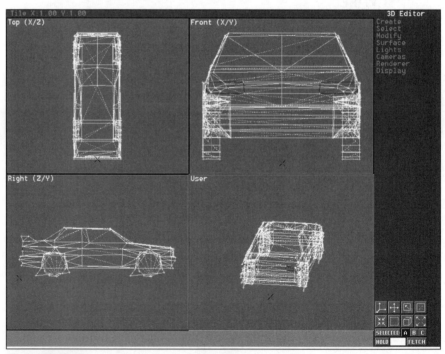

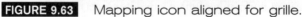

FIGURE 9.63   Mapping icon aligned for grille.

FIGURE 9.64 3D Studio test rendering of mapping for car.

15. Make sure the background is turned off (Renderer/Setup/Background).

16. Adjust the User view to an angle that shows both the grille and the front wheels.

17. Choose Render/Render view. In the following dialog, change the rendering type to Gouraud. Click on Configure and change the video driver to VGA320 × 200, and click on the 320 × 200 button. Click OK, then click Render.

Figure 9.64 shows the result.

Okay, it's critique time:

The mapping looks good on the wheel, but the grille has a white line at the bottom. That means the mapping didn't quite match, so the grille picture ended before the faces did, causing the white part of the texture below the grille to appear on the bottom edge of the faces. We can fix this by scaling the mapping icon up slightly or by editing the texture map.

The M3 logo on the grill is on the wrong side. We can simply rotate the mapping icon to fix that.

The materials on the car are pretty hard to see; let's choose something else for the body and glass.

The wheels have really sharp edges because they have smoothing information stored for them. We'll clear everything and assign it all to a single smoothing group since that's how the graphics engine will handle it.

On the other hand, there are some areas where we want sharp edges. The bumpers and the back end should have creases along their edges. To do this, we select the group of faces and detach them, then reattach them. This prevents this group of faces from sharing verts with the rest of the object, which prevents the Gouraud shading from blending them with the rest of the object. Unfortunately, this also makes a bunch of extra verts, slowing down the performance. This

trade-off depends totally on the graphics engine in question, but let's assume that it's not worth a performance hit to have the body correctly Gouraud shaded, and leave it as it is.

18. Choose Surface/Mapping/Adjust/Acquire and click on the car body.

19. In the Top view, rotate the mapping icon 180 degrees.

20. Scale the mapping icon 102.5 percent uniformly, then use Tab to change the direction to up/down. Scale it 104 percent, then move it so the top edge lines up with the top edge of the grille again. Apply the mapping to the car body.

21. Load the 3DS material library (Surface/Materials/Get Library).

22. Deselect everything, then use Show to select the faces that use black plastic. Assign blue plastic to these faces. Repeat, replacing black glass with black plastic.

23. Choose Surface/Smoothing/Clear All, then click on all the objects. Assign and click on all the objects.

24. Render the User view again. Zoom to extents, change the view angle if you want, and render again.

The result should look like Figure 9.65.

Once we've got the model this far, we're basically done with edits and we're ready to get the model imported into the graphics engine. Save the model as a project (for us) and a .3DS or .ASC file, depending on which one the graphics engine requires.

View the Result in the Real-Time Application

This stage is totally dependent on the real-time application in question. The people who provide it should also provide a simple, step-by-step procedure for importing the model. That's what you now follow. Of course, if the graphics engine is custom-written, you won't always have this nice, neat set of steps, but someone had better explain them to you!

FIGURE 9.65   Final real-time model of BMW M3, rendered in 3D Studio.

Designing 3D Graphics

Revise the Models and Textures as Necessary

This step is the easiest to describe—and the hardest to do. Once the model is loaded into the engine, we'll critique it, as we did at the end of the mapping step. We'll take notes on any and all problems we see, then return to the 3D Editor, make the changes, reload, and repeat until finished.

It's smart to write down the problems instead of trying to remember them because it's too easy to assume we'll remember something when we're distracted by the animated objects onscreen.

Finished!

Once the revisions are done, the artwork is considered finished. We can archive all the intermediate project files and large 24-bit textures we've been saving along the way (put them in a big ZIP file), delete temporary files, and leave only a single, final project file, texture maps (24- and 8-bit), and compiled 3D object in the car's directory.

In summary, our BMW M3 model has two 128 × 128 textures, 297 faces, and looks pretty good!

Open Environments (Landscapes)

Landscape modeling is as varied as landscapes themselves. The defining characteristics are in the name: *Open* means there is no roof nearby. No faces point downward. *Closed* environments, described later, have faces that enclose the user—roofs of some sort. *Environment* means the model is made to be walked on, flown over, or stood on. This is different from models of cars or humans.

Within the general concept of an environment, there are two broad sub-categories of open environments.

- Natural—These are models of land that have been formed by natural powers (wind, rain, and so on). Examples include mountain ranges, gullies, and plains. They are usually intended to be realistic; because most natural landscapes are notable for their intricate detail and complicated structures, they are often very difficult to portray well with the normal face budgets we have to work with.

- Unnatural—These are open environments (real or imaginary) that humans have formed or created. Examples include suburban neighborhoods, city streets, as well as fantasy environments of all sorts. Unnatural environments are usually easier to model because they tend to have lots of regular planar surfaces, but they too can be difficult if the environment is a familiar one, like a city street.

Of course, some landscapes have elements of both of these categories, like a terraced hillside, garden, or farmland, but most landscapes fit into one category or the other.

General Issues with Open Environments

From a real-time simulation point of view, open environments have some drawbacks. They are usually large and spacious, are notable for their detail, and have many objects (like trees) that all come into view at once.

Many objects onscreen at once is definitely not good for frame rate! When this situation occurs, the computer suddenly has to render a bunch of objects that it did not have to consider before; this makes the frame rate suddenly drop. A consistent number of polygons onscreen at once is preferred, but it's hard to arrange when we're modeling a wide-open field with clumps of trees scattered on it.

What can we do about this? We can make the trees scattered as evenly as possible, and use as few as we can while still giving the look we need. We can also use standard real-time 3D techniques like backdrops to add detail, creating 3D models of only the part of the landscapes that the player can reach. We can use LOD swapping—substituting an extremely simple model for complicated objects that are far away. For more information about LODs, see Chapter 2.

Portraying Detail on Natural Landscapes

As the last section indicates, it's really hard to show good detail in a landscape while maintaining a decent frame rate, especially for a natural environment. Using polygons to model natural environments is a pretty bad approximation in most cases; in general, we'll rely on texturing as much as possible: creating simple, unobtrusive models that mainly serve to represent natural landforms and provide something to put the textures on.

Texture mapping is our main method of showing detail cheaply. As we learned in Chapter 6, we can use two different methods of mapping: tiled and fitted.

With a tiled landscape, we'll create a "generic" ground texture, like a grassy flatland, rocky field, or icy snow. This texture must be fully tiling and should be at the maximum resolution we're allowed. Then, if we have enough texture memory available, we build variations on the original map to provide variety and reduce the possibility of the user noticing the repeating texture.

We then apply uniform mapping to the ground model and assign the varied textures to pieces of the model, mixing them up to reduce the presence of uniform patterns appearing and providing what passes for variety.

For fitted landscapes, we can generate detail that matches the 3D model. One way to do this is create an elaborately detailed 3D model whose sole purpose is to create a source texture map for the simple model. This process, called "paste-mapping," is described more fully in Chapter 8. This is commonly used for landscapes, and it usually yields good results.

If we're modeling a natural landscape that is real, it's common to use overhead photographs of the actual landscape if we can get them. Making the details in the photograph correspond to the 3D model can be difficult, but the results definitely can be worth it.

Transparency

If our environment supports sprites or simply allows transparency in textures, we can use this to mask our straight edges. This is most commonly used in conjunc-

tion with the "always-facing" feature for making trees with a transparent background, but it can also be used to portray other natural forms that have non-straight edges, if we can figure out clever ways to work with the non-square edges!

3D modeling of a natural landscape can vary widely. Usually, the task is made easier by the fact that most natural landscapes are continuous surfaces—not many holes or complicated shapes are common.

If we're designing our landscape from scratch, the simplest way to start is to take a regular meshed grid of faces and move the verts up and down. It's surprisingly easy to get a mountainous terrain this way. We can also use an application like Vista Pro to generate large, complicated terrains in an automatic way.

If we're building a landscape that must match an actual landform somewhere, we must somehow generate or obtain the 3D data for that piece of land. If the land is in the United States, 3D models, as well as paper maps, are available from the U.S. Geological Service. The digital maps are available in DEM files (the USGS's 3D terrain format) at: http://sun1.cr.usgs.gov/doc/edchome/ndcdb/ndcdb.html.

These paper maps have contour lines that show elevation; that's what the DEM files are based on. The paper maps also have buildings, rivers, and tons of other types of detail drawn over them. The USGS also has this information in some form on their site, but it's not clear if there's any good way to combine it with the DEM data. A company in New Mexico is dedicated to this idea, more or less:

Rapid Imaging
Fax: (505) 265-7054;
Email: tnrapid@pop.nm.org
Web site: http://www.nm.org/~landform/landform.htm

There are also numerous companies offering digitized landscapes for sale, with or without accompanying texture maps.

Using Stock 3D models

Depending on our project, these may be an excellent way to save time, or they may take more money and energy to get and convert than building the landscape from scratch. It's sometimes helpful to estimate how many hours of modeling time their price would buy, and if it would be possible to generate a comparable model (and don't forget that building the model from scratch means complete, unfettered ownership of the final product; this is often a large factor when working on commercial projects because many stock libraries keep partial ownership of their products).

● Unnatural Open Environments

As stated earlier, what we mean by unnatural open environments are human-created environments. Examples include city streets, football fields, race tracks, lunar bases, and space stations.

These are quite different to build from natural landscapes because most human-created shapes are made from relatively simple geometry (compared to natural shapes like mountains), like planes and simply curved surfaces. This is a closer match to the planar triangles we have to build with, which makes our job easier.

On the other hand, we have to create geometry that most people are very familiar with; we don't have the luxury of flexibility when we're placing street-lights, telephone poles, and other details that are generally more noticed when they are different from what people expect.

Let's take a look at the steps in building a basic unnatural outdoor scene.

Scale is a big issue when building outdoor scenes. It's easy to make things too big or small, so we'll be keeping reasonably close track of the dimensions as we work.

Preparation Stage

Step 1: Get Source Art

Remember, the purpose of this step is to make (or understand) the model's design, and to end up with vague concept sketches.

When getting source art for this kind of project, we can often find a lot if we identify a model that really exists. If it's a futuristic scenario, of course, we'll have to make it up.

Step 2: Gather Technical Information

We now get all the facts about our project that will affect the way we decide to build it. As usual, the exact questions we ask will vary, depending on what we need to know (and what we learn as we ask), but they will include, at least, the following questions.

What's the Face/Polygon (or Vert) Budget?

For this model, we'll have a 1,000-onscreen-poly budget. *Onscreen* means that the database is able to cull, or quickly ignore, the faces that aren't visible by the player, so as long as we can only see 1,000 faces or fewer from any angle, there is no over-all face budget. That sounds great, but it's not as free-form as you might think because we don't know what the user is going to look at. Therefore, we have to be sure there is no possible way they can see a lot of faces. Thus, we have to design our model very carefully and be very dependent on the far clipping plane (which is a distance from the player for which objects aren't drawn because they're too far away) to keep far-away objects from being counted in our face budget. We should verify with the programmer that we can rely on using the clipping plane to help meet our budget; it's not always assumed that the artist sets it.

What Kind of Polygons Are Supported?

We've got the usual convex planar polygons to work with.

How Are the Polygons Created from 3DS Faces?

Polygons are automatically combined by the preprocessor. They don't need to share edges, and the edges' visibility is ignored.

Designing 3D Graphics

What Tolerance, If Any, Is Used When Deciding that Two Faces Are Coplanar?

We can adjust the tolerance if necessary, but it defaults to 1cm (0.01 meters = 3DS units).

Are T-intersections Allowed?

Yes, they should render well.

What Kind of Sorting Is Used?

Our graphics engine uses static BSP-tree sorting for the landscape.

Are Intersecting Faces Allowed?

Because we're not using Z-buffered sorting, we can't have intersecting faces.

Are There Any Special Shapes That Should Not Be Built?

Long, thin faces are likely to cause problems, though theoretically they should work, so avoid building any huge (like quarter-mile-long) faces, and don't build any faces with more than a 1,000-to-1 aspect.

How Will This Model Be Seen?

This question is very important for landscapes especially. We need to know any and all constraints on the user's motion, in order to make the model look good from the allowed areas (and so we don't waste time modeling areas that no one can ever see).

For our project, the user will be driving a car and won't be able to leave the road surfaces (which the preprocessor code will identify).

How Will the Preprocessor Code Know Where the Road Is?

We, the artists, will set the material names of road surfaces so they begin with ROAD, and the preprocessor code will know from those materials.

What Is the Look Like?

This question tries to get at the basic feeling of the game—Is it realistic? Dark? Silly? The look is usually pretty well known from the earliest mention of the whole project, but for our exercise, we'll have to state it outright: We're making a racing-through-the-streets game that is realistic, but also has room for some adult humor (like sarcastic "Sale! Huge Sale! It's All On Sale!" signs in every single storefront) or other interesting touches.

What Kind of Animation Will This Model Have (Hierarchy, Morphing, None)?

There will be some color-cycling animations for stoplights and signs using palette tricks, but that's it.

What's the Screen Size That This Object Will Be Shown On?

It's a 320 × 200 rendered window size.

How Many Colors?

256-color paletted color is our graphics engine's capability.

Palette Issues?

Definitely! We'll be working with a palette that has been defined already, except for 16 colors left open for us to set as we need them for our world.

Any "Special" Colors?

Yes, color 255 is transparent, 252, 253, and 254 are red, yellow, and green, cycling between very dull and super-bright at traffic-light speed (that is, about 10 seconds for red and green, three seconds on yellow).

What Kind of Lighting?

Lighting will be of the static point-source variety. We can place omni lights in 3D Studio. Only the lightness value, position, and range will be used from the omni light settings. The game has a minimum lighting level of 10 percent lightness; we can't make it any darker than that.

    In our world, the lighting will only make colors darker than their original setting, so we should use colors at the brightest level they should ever be seen, expecting them to be usually darker.

What Kind (If Any) of Texture Mapping?

This graphics engine supports perspective-corrected texture mapping, so we shouldn't have any trouble with warping textures that some (linearly interpreted texture mapping) graphics engines have.

What Kind of Shading?

Gouraud or flat shading is allowed.

What Are the Allowable Combinations of Shading, Lighting, and Texturing?

Textured surfaces can't be Gouraud shaded, but all other combinations are okay.

How Are Gouraud Shading Borders Determined?

All the faces in each element will be smooth-shaded together, so in order to make creases, we must prevent the faces along the edges from sharing verts.

How Much Texture Map Memory Is Budgeted?

We have 1 MB of texture memory.

What Size and Shape Can the Texture Maps' Dimensions Be?

We can use textures of any aspect, but the sides must be 16, 32, 64, 128, 256, or 512 pixels.

What Should This World Be Like?

Because our model is more than just a prop in a scene, we need to know a lot more about the context in which it will be used. This general question is where we discover that information. The question really is a placeholder for a discussion with the game designer about what our model needs to be like. We need to know how it'll be used and what it's intended to portray visually to the player.

    In this exercise's game design, the player is a get-away driver in a bank robbery. The plot starts with an overhead view of a eight-block-by-eight-block area around the bank; this is what our model will cover. There are two important buildings: the bank and the warehouse where the robbers will change cars, which is where that level ends. The get-away plan is outlined, with a proposed route from the bank to the warehouse shown. Then, we're taken to the street in a first-person dashboard-layout view, parked in front of the bank. When the robbers come out and get in the car, the game begins. The street layout should allow for a wide variety of options, so for advanced levels we can strategically block the easy planned route (for example, a delivery truck could be parked in an alley), forcing the player to take another route.

Step 3: Plan How Model Will Be Created

This is a big step for this model. We still don't know much about our model, other than its basic idea. A lot of world design issues will come up here. For example, we should consider the FOV setting we'll be using (let's assume it's 45 degrees) and think about what the player will be able to see when they drive. The player may not be able to see across a four-lane street with an island in the middle and may miss a turn because of that, for example. Think about this in the vertical, as well. We should decide on eye height early on, and make sure that we build objects that work with it well. For example, we can put objects that prevent the player from seeing oncoming traffic until it's really close, but we can only do that if we know the player's eye height exactly.

Another common question at this stage is "Where should we put detail? Should we model gorgeous buildings or detailed cars?" This really depends on the focus, or goal, of the game. Our game is not about sight-seeing; it's about fast action: frantic driving through streets, dodging taxis, and so on. Staying focused on providing this experience should help set good priorities for deciding what to model. For example, exquisitely detailed 3D buildings would be nice but are unnecessary for this.

In driving games, anything that isn't touching the edge of the road should be modeled very simply. It's amazing how little the player can see when driving, and most of the stuff that's not on the road can be shown with textures on flat polys because the player can't get close to it. Really, the player mainly can see road, signs, streetlights, curb/sidewalk, sky, and other cars. The architecturally interesting things—beautiful buildings, bridges, and so on—are background art, and they can either be modeled simply or skipped entirely without hurting the game experience.

Finally, we should carefully consider performance-related issues. City scenes are notorious for having really bad frame rates, simply because there's so much detail to be shown, and the buildings overlap a lot, causing overplotting (often a performance problem).

We want to design scenes that don't overplot. To visualize our goal, imagine we shoot a super-laser-weapon from the camera's position, in any direction. Ideally, it should always penetrate only one face before going off into the atmosphere, but this is almost impossible to achieve. Our goal is to make sure that it hits as few faces as possible. Again, see Chapter 12 for more details on this very important issue.

When modeling urban environments, a common source of overplotting is the sides of a bunch of buildings in the same area. The problem sides are perpendicular to the street (that is, not the storefront side, or the back).

Figure 9.66 illustrates this by drawing the buildings with a glass material (with wireframe showing the faces' constructions) against a brick background.

FIGURE 9.66 Street scene demonstrating overplot.

Wherever the bricks are hidden through all the glass layers, a lot of overplotting is going on.

Backface rejection is hiding the faces that point away from the camera (i.e., the bottoms, tops, and backs of the buildings) because that's what the graphics engine does.

On the left, we see a row of cubes, and on the right, we have a unified clump of buildings that are all attached and missing most of their side faces. We can see that the buildings on the left are bad—they're completely obscuring the brick in most places, and generally are overplotting a lot. On the right, there isn't nearly as much overplotting (though there's still some, especially where the buildings are different heights); the bricks are visible through the whole area.

The difference in construction is apparent if we load the model (TOWN02. PRJ) in 3D Studio. We'll see that the building clump that doesn't overplot is all connected. It is made of overlapping cubes, then a Boolean Union on them to effectively remove the side faces where they overlapped.

Let's look at any problems with this solution. It makes a lot of extra faces because all the big, simple sides have to be divided to attach to the neighboring buildings, but these faces aren't too big a deal—they do not add any new verts, and their slight overhead is well worth the overplotting savings.

Another trade-off is that there is no space between the buildings, but that's a pretty minor loss. Lots of city buildings are constructed that way, so it's not unrealistic. Also, the driver will almost never be looking in between the buildings

because the camera is connected to the car's direction. The player will be driving straight down the street 99 percent of the time.

We can also reduce overplotting by using thin, pole-like detail objects, like streetlights and parking meters, instead of large objects like dumpsters. This is especially important for common objects.

We'll spend our detail on road-related areas, at the expense of a balanced, overall city model. We'll make a few urban street-side objects, as shown in Figure 9.67.

The street-side objects are as follows:

- Mail drop-box (18 faces, 12 verts, 0 textures)
- Streetlight (28 faces, 17 verts, 0 textures)
- Traffic light (48 faces, 32 verts, 0 textures)
- Café signboard (8 faces, 6 verts, 1 texture, 64 × 64)
- Parking meter (22 faces, 16 verts, 0 textures)
- Street and curbs (28 faces, 40 verts, 3 textures, 256 × 256, 128 × 128, 64 × 256)
- Buildings (50 faces, 24 verts, 2 textures, 128 × 128)
- One block (only buildings, street, and curbs) (74 verts, 78 faces, 5 textures)

We've also got a five-building clump (derived from the example in Figure 9.66), using 50 faces, 34 verts, and two 128 × 128 textures. It needs more textures, but the ones on it are good enough to design with; it's easy to make more and assign them to the faces. This building clump is one block long and is shown in Figure 9.68.

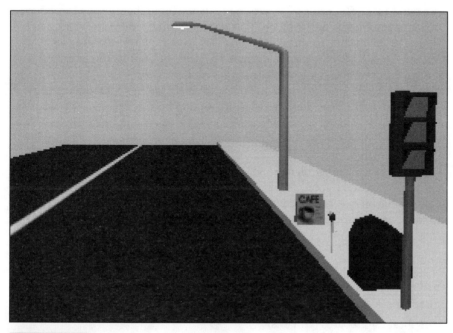

FIGURE 9.67 Detail for town.

CHAPTER 9 • **Modeling Specific Types of Objects**   **239**

FIGURE 9.68   Group of five connected buildings, and street/curb model.

We also have a street surface modeled, using two textures (one 256 × 256 general asphalt, one 64 × 256 stripe), 16 verts, and 12 faces. The curb object uses one 128 × 128 texture, 12 verts, and 8 faces. Note that the street faces are broken in the middle of the block. This occurs because we are attempting to prevent problems due to very long, thin faces, as our question/answer session told us. We may also have some of these problems in a few of the faces in the buildings, but we'll assume they're okay for now.

Next, we'll figure out how many of these details we can combine to keep our scene under 1,000 faces. Let's start by establishing how many blocks we want to see onscreen at once. If we show fewer blocks, we can use more detail, but if we have too few, it will be more annoying to play because the blocks will appear to pop into view.

Let's set the clipping plane so we allow the player to see three blocks maximum. That will take about 300 faces for the street, curbs, and buildings (allowing extra for intersecting street polys that may be visible), leaving 700 faces for detail. If we use

- 8 streetlights (224 faces)
- 8 parking meters (176 faces)
- 2 mail drop-boxes (36 faces)
- 2 traffic lights (96 faces)
- 3 café signboards (24 faces)

we've used 556 faces in detail objects, leaving 144 to spend as we please.

At this point, we would draw a basic plan layout and sketch in the number of buildings and details.

Step 4: Choose a Modeling Method

For this model, we'll use 3D editing construction techniques like the ones shown for the streetlight exercise in Chapter 4.

Step 5: Build the Model Geometry

Building the geometry for this model is pretty simple. First, we build the buildings. We do this by creating a series of overlapping cubes, the bottoms of which align at Y=0. The dimensions are pretty wide open, but they should be reasonable building sizes, and the heights should be in even one-story increments (we'll estimate one story as 5 meters for this exercise). Also, they should add up to 90 meters, which is what we'll call a block (not counting street width). If we build all the boxes' dimensions in increments of 5 meters, texturing will be much easier. Then, we'll move them in slight offsets to make varying storefronts.

Once they're all arranged, we use Create/Object/Boolean/Union to merge all the cubes, one to the next, into a big single object. As usual, the Boolean operation will create a bit of a mess—extra verts here and there, and some slight sliver faces, so we'll clean those up, delete the bottom faces, and then we're ready to apply mapping (Figure 9.69).

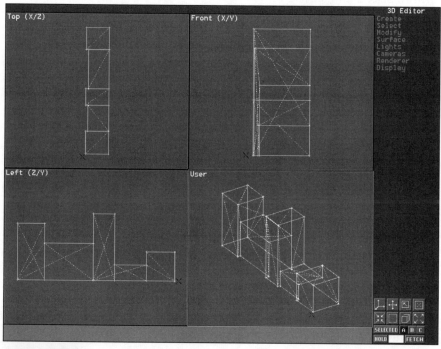

FIGURE 9.69 Building clump.

Because our buildings are in 5-meter increments, we can make our map 5 meters square and it should tile perfectly on the buildings. We don't need to apply mapping to each cube; a single mapping application, aligned at a corner, should do it.

Now we build the street. It's structure is trivial—two flat squares of faces, one thin for the center stripe, one wide for the lane. The textures are what we'll look at here. We have a stripe on the middle of the road, and we want a detailed, rich texture of asphalt on the road as well. We'll build a model of the striped area so we can assign a different, thin texture to it, then we'll put a tiling asphalt texture on the unstriped part of the road. We want to be sure to use the same pixel-per-meter for both textures, so they match nicely. To do this, we first determine a good pixel-per-meter for the general asphalt. We can experiment, trying a few different mapping sizes and rendering in 320 × 200 with all effects except mapping turned off to simulate our real-time engine's output, or we can attempt to measure the size of the asphalt in the texture and apply it at the correct scale. Either way, we'll get a mapping that looks good on the road.

Once we have that, we'll have a square mapping icon. If we know the dimensions of our striped texture (64 × 256), we can make our mapping icon match its aspect but keep the same long dimension as the plain asphalt (256 × 256) texture. Then we align this icon with the center stripe geometry and adjust the geometry to match the mapping icon's width. This is a frustrating step because every time we choose Modify/ … to move the verts, the mapping icon disappears! Once we've got it right, we apply mapping to it, and then we can merge the two objects into one.

The curb is built much the same way. We'll apply mapping that is a similar size to a single square of the sidewalk (about half the width). We'll make the sidewalk just wide enough to completely reach the storefront of the most recessed building, but no farther since this is overplotted by the other buildings' front faces.

From there, we build the various detail objects. Most of these are quite easy. The signboard started as a box, then the top two verts were welded together to form a triangle. The bottom was deleted, and then the two triangular side faces were also deleted, leaving four faces. We want to see the inside of the sign as well, but the faces are one-sided, so we'll make duplicates with normals that face the other way by making a copy of the object, flipping the copy's normals (Surface/Normals/Object Flip), assigning a dark material to it, and attaching it to the original object. Then we select the object and weld the selected verts, which eliminates the duplicates. From there, we apply mapping, create a cute little texture, and it's ready.

The streetlight is a reduced-face version of the one we built in the exercise in Chapter 3. We simply go through the object and weld lots of its verts together, leaving material boundaries where possible.

The mailbox started as a cube, and then had its top edges divided two times, the edges turned to be straight, and these new verts moved into an appearance of curvedness with one side flat (where the drawer goes).

Designing 3D Graphics

The other shapes are similarly simple. Triangular sections are used for the poles (except the streetlight, which gets a four-sided pole at the base).

Step 6: Create the Textures

Creating the textures for these objects is where the art is. The buildings are the hardest because they have the greatest dependency on their textures. We can use photos of buildings or paint them from scratch. They should be square aspect, and probably not any larger than 128×128 because they'll usually be a little ways from the player. For our exercise, we're using placeholder textures: R-BRICK.TIF and R-GLASS.TIF, with the understanding that we'll come back and replace them with fully detailed textures once we've had a chance to see how the game looks in the graphics engine.

The asphalt (ASPHALT.TIF) is easy to come by in any decent texture library, and painting a yellow stripe on a little chopped-off piece for the yellow-stripe texture (ASPH-YS.TIF) is easy.

The sidewalk texture is a light-gray noised, blurred texture with a dark edge on two of its sides.

The café sign (S-CAFÉ.TIF) is painted from scratch, using an airbrush with splatter and shades of gray, and the letters are made blotchy by putting down letters with a mask border, then using the same airbrush as a mask trace. A little noise filter and Gaussian blur, and it's ready.

Step 7: Map the Textures on the Model

This step is already done as we build, for the most part. What we can do is assign the materials to the model. We'll create a new material for each texture we made, using the same name as our texture, then assign it normally to the appropriate faces.

We'll also assign materials to the non-textured surfaces here. The streetlight gets its special materials: COLOR253, COLOR254, and COLOR255.

At this point, our pieces are all set to render. Before we import, we'll build a single street section so we can take a look at how it all works together. This is quite straightforward: simply copy the objects and lay them out according to our plan. The streets can be made to tile by pulling the center verts out until the street edge forms a 45-degree intersection with another street rotated 90 degrees.

Step 8: Import to the Real-Time Application

As the earlier exercise stated: "This stage is totally dependent on the real-time application in question. The people who provide it should also provide a simple, step-by-step procedure for importing the model. That's what you now follow. Of course, if the graphics engine is custom-written, you won't always have this nice, neat set of steps, but someone had better explain them to you!"

Now we are at the point where we decide what to do with this model. How does it look? Is it done?

Revisions

Obviously, we'll need to make better building textures, but what we really want to know is if it has enough detail and is good-looking. If so, we simply duplicate it in a 8 × 8 grid, adjust the building and street widths for variety perhaps, and we're done.

 # Closed Environments

Closed environments cover a lot of types of structures. Houses, caves, space stations, tunnels, and even a car's interior could all fall in this category. The basic requirement is that the player is enclosed in the model, and it has modeled walls, floor, and roof.

Performance Issues with Closed Environments

When modeling a huge environment, we quickly find that our target platform's computer has some problems loading the whole thing at once. RT3D applications always have this problem, but it's really emphasized with closed environments. In general, the overall face (or vert) budget is deemphasized, and the emphasis is placed on the number of onscreen polys.

The basic problems that we list here are very well-known to graphics engine programmers. Because of this, your environment may have unique innovations if you are working with custom-written graphics engines, so you may have options not listed here.

Clipping Planes Don't Work Very Well

In open environments, clipping planes are a way to keep frame rate high. This doesn't usually work very gracefully for closed environments because it's totally disruptive to have the far-away walls appearing and disappearing.

Some possible workarounds allow us to use clipping planes in a closed environment. We could set the clipping distance high, thus preventing the walls from getting clipped, but then we're including a lot of geometry, generally losing the benefits of clipping. We could build each room sized so it falls outside of the clipping plane, but this is very constricting to the design.

Instead, good gross culling arrangements can accomplish the same basic purpose, if the environment is designed with them in mind.

Partitioning

In general, the idea of partitioning is to break the scene into sections. Sometimes each section is an independent environment, and other times it is incomplete by itself. Independent sections allow the graphics engine to concentrate on only

that section—it can be the only scene in memory, and the user can't tell except when he or she changes between sections.

For example, if we have a large torus-shaped space station, we can divide it into air-tight sections and require a clean connection between the two (like an airlock that leads from one to the next).

We can keep all the sections except for the current one on the hard disk, and when the user opens the door to the next section, it is loaded from the disk in a relatively seamless way. In most applications, this is annoying because it usually involves a pause. The action will freeze for a second as the hard disk frantically loads in the new level, then the new scene will pop in. Most RT3D computer games ritualize this break into the concept of a level. Each *level* is loaded into memory, one at a time, as the player progresses through the game. There are other ways to design this transition into the environment gracefully, such as using an elevator (or anything else where the user will expect a delay before seeing a new area) instead of a door, but it's still an important design constraint.

When designing for this partitioning, we need to know which (if any) textures, special-effect animations, or other resources are always available and which will change from level to level. But more importantly, we need to be sure that each partition fits within our application's memory and performance constraints.

Subdividing Sections

If we continue to divide an independent section, we create subsections that require each other in order to make a complete scene. This is fully covered in Chapter 12 (under the Gross Culling step in the graphics pipeline). In closed environments, we often have some extra advantages that other environments don't have. Often we are working with rooms, and if we design them well, we can work with the gross culling to avoid drawing the neighboring rooms. The essential design concept is to prevent the user from seeing into the neighboring rooms. We can do this with doors or with a "bathroom entrance" type arrangement in which it is impossible to see around the walls, but there are no doorways.

For custom-written graphics engines, as are common with computer games, we can often work with the programmer and get involved with the behavior of this essential step. For commercial engines, there is a preset behavior around which we must design our world.

In any case, the bottom line is whether the faces in the neighboring room count as onscreen faces. In other words, does the graphics engine have to render them, even if the player isn't in that room? If we're not careful, the answer will be yes, and we'll see our face budget reduced severely.

LODs

Also, when we design a closed environment, we have to give a lot of thought to the number of onscreen faces. It's important to avoid making rooms that force the computer to display lots of faces all at once. That's a big constraint on the

design, and it really requires some talent to portray a large space without showing it all at once.

The concept of LOD (levels of detail), if supported by our application, can really help us here. As you may know from Chapter 2, the idea of LODs is to create very simple representations of the complicated models. These simple models are shown only when the model is far away from the user (because the user can't see it very well anyway).

For example, imagine we want to make a model of a huge ballroom, using 10,000 faces, but our engine can only show 4,000 faces onscreen at once. We divide it into four subsections and build simple, 200-face LOD models for each one (using large textures on simple geometry to portray most of the missing detail). When the user enters the room, the nearest 2,500-face section is loaded, and the simple LOD models are substituted for the rest. That makes an acceptable 3,300 faces (but some have lots of textures; we'll probably have a worse frame rate than we predict, so we shouldn't try to use up those extra 700 faces).

LODs are generally used for independent entities (such as a table or a car), but they can be used for dependent sections of the environment as well.

As an interesting side note, it's really hard to reduce a real-time model and throw away valuable detail. The artist can sit and stare at the seemingly "simple as it can get" model, wondering what to cut. However, if we have the assurance that the detailed model will load in when the user is close to it, we feel free to loosen up and hack away. The surprising thing is that the LODs frequently look good enough (and offer such performance improvements) that the original models are never used.

Example: Basic House Model

In this example, a supplier of linoleum has commissioned us to build a house model in a VRML environment. The purpose is to demonstrate different types of linoleum in the kitchen of the house.

Preparation Stage: Get Source Art (Make or Understand Design, Get Vague Concept Sketches)

Our source art for this house consists of some photos of linoleum and a pre-rendered 3D Studio model of the kitchen that the client has supplied us. It may seem strange to have a 3D model as source art, but this is not too unusual. Figure 9.70 shows the rendered view of CAMERA1 from the model we are given (KITCHEN .PRJ), and Figure 9.71 shows what the model looks like in 3D Studio.

Gather Technical Information

Because this is a VRML-based application, refer to Chapter 13 for more information on these technical specifics. Note that most VRML constraints are actually imposed by the capabilities of the browsers, not theoretical limitations, so these constraints are totally dependent on the browser that the user is using. Of course, we artists don't know what browser is being used, so we simply have to guess. We'll go with the assumption that our audience is running a pretty basic

Designing 3D Graphics

FIGURE 9.70 Rendered view of pre-rendered kitchen model.

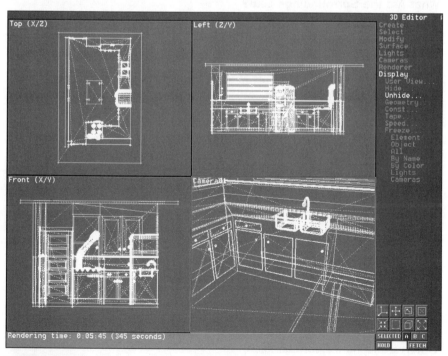

FIGURE 9.71 Screenshot of kitchen model.

setup: a 486/50 PC with 8 MB of RAM, and a basic 1MB SVGA video card in $1024 \times 768 \times 8$-bit mode. We'll assume that the software is Windows 95, a 14.4 PPP Internet connection, Netscape, and the Live3D VRML browser.

What's the Face/Polygon (or Vert) Budget?
We'll use a somewhat arbitrary face budget of 1,000 faces or less.

What Kind of Polygons Are Supported?
VRML supports basic n-sided planar polygons.

Are T-intersections Allowed?
Yes.

What Kind of Sorting Is Used?
This is totally dependent on the browser being used, so we should build for the worst-case (static face sorting). That means we can't have intersecting faces.

Are There Any Special Shapes That Should Not Be Built?
Not especially; VRML is quite versatile.

How Will This Model Be Seen?
VRML doesn't put many constraints on movement; in fact, there is no physics simulation or collision detection so we need to make sure the model looks vaguely understandable from the outside.

What Are the Surroundings Like?
The model is alone in the VRML universe, but the rest of the material is commercially clean, non-artistic, factual, but visually appealing with simplicity and white space.

What Kind of Animation Will This Model Have (Hierarchy, Morphing, None)?
VRML v1.0 doesn't have animation.

What's The Screen Size That This Object Will Be Shown On?
That's one of the hardest parts about VRML: We don't know. It could be anything, but it is likely to be 640×400 or larger. Compared to games, this is a huge amount of rendering area; we can expect our frame rates in 640×400 to be one-fourth that of a comparable 320×200 application. That's a big hit!

How Many Colors?
We'll draw as though it's 24-bit, but this varies. Most PCs will be 8-bit, though they may not have to be.

Any "Special" Colors?
No, there aren't.

What Kind of Lighting?
VRML offers a decent selection of lighting capabilities for a RT3D application. Omnis are supported, for example.

Designing 3D Graphics

What Kind (If Any) of Texture Mapping?

There is a fairly extensive variety of texture mapping available. The exact type (linearly interpolated, and so on) depends on the browser being used, so we should design our model to work with the worst case: linearly interpreted.

What Kind of Shading?

Gouraud shading is possible.

What Are the Allowable Combinations of Shading, Lighting, and Texturing?

All combinations are possible.

How Much Texture Map Memory Is Budgeted?

Budgeting texture memory for VRML is very tricky. VRML itself doesn't put any constraints on the number of textures, but if we use too many, most people's machines won't be able to show them all. The limits really come from our target platform. We have to know what machine our VRML world should work well on, and keep in mind that there may be people who will be seeing the world without textures.

In general, we should use as few textures as possible, both to improve download times and to allow as many people as possible to view our model, but we should also keep the quality of the model in mind. We don't want to throw the baby out with the bathwater; we'll use what we must to make a decent-looking model.

Design Stage: Plan How the Model Will Be Created

Because we've got such clear source art, we know quite accurately what we want the model to look like. What we need to do now is examine the model and decide how we'll make it work for VRML. Looking back at Figure 9.71, we can see that some objects have a lot of detail, like the refrigerator and the stove, and others are fairly simple, like the cabinets and floor. Using the viewing techniques we learned in Chapter 4, we explore the model and discover more about its structure.

We'll see that there are a lot of faces (13,000) in this model, but most of them are in tiny details like the knobs of the cabinets. That makes sense for a pre-rendered model, but we can get rid of this detail. The walls are fairly simple, though modeled a little messily, and the roof does not share verts with the walls.

Where will we need textures? Obviously, we'll need to texture the floor, but we may not need any texture anywhere else. The countertop could use one, but it's not a big deal. That's good—we'll use a really detailed texture for the floor. Looking at the rendering (Figure 9.70), we see that the floor has a light grid on it, but there is no modeled grid, so that must be a bump map (or something in the texture).

Basically, our approach is to simplify the complicated objects, clean up geometry that overlaps, and erase any detail that we don't need.

Choose a Modeling Method

For this model, our modeling method will be editing the existing geometry.

Execution Stage: Build the Model Geometry

Because we're not really building anything here, we'll go through the model object-by-object and adapt the objects for use in a RT3D environment.

Let's start with the sink. It's full of complicated curves that we don't need. We can simplify it to two inset boxes with a rim, with a simpler faucet. We'll make the faucet non-curved to avoid having to approximate it with crude straight sections. Figure 9.72 and Figure 9.73 show the result.

We'll do the same thing to the refrigerator now. The existing one is very curvy; we'll take the liberty of putting a nice, square modern fridge in its place (Figure 9.74).

The stove follows suit, losing its rounded vent tube entirely. Because it's not critical to the model, we have chosen to get rid of the vent tube entirely, rather than try to approximate it.

Next is the cabinetry. After deleting the knobs, we're left with some tricky geometry. First, the countertop needs all the bottom faces deleted, and then the corners where the sink goes need to be welded into squares, eliminating all those extra verts. The cabinets are all built in a typical 3D Studio fashion: a large block with doors placed over them. This will cause overplotting problems for our graphics engines, so we've got to cut in the cabinet doors into the cabinet.

The only automated way to do this is to use the Boolean operation, which doesn't work for this geometry. So, we have to delete the cabinet wall faces, then hand-build faces that connect the corners of the doors to the corners of the cabi-

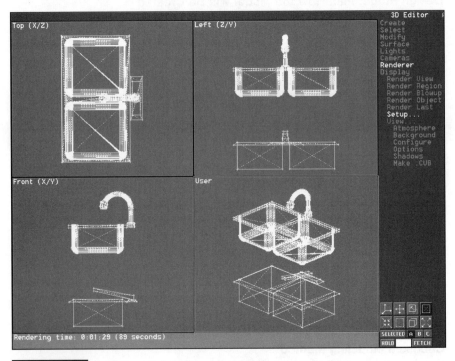

FIGURE 9.72 Sink—old and new, 3DS screenshot.

Designing 3D Graphics

FIGURE 9.73 Sink—old and new, rendered.

FIGURE 9.74 Old and new refrigerator.

netry (remembering to pick them counterclockwise to make their normals point outward). This takes about two hours, even if we're pretty fast at clicking on the three verts, so we're looking at a lot of work. Before doing this, we should give some thought to its payoff. In this case, it's pretty clear that most of the cabinetry would be overplotting, and in most views, the cabinets would take up a large part of the screen, so this performance penalty is significant. Therefore, we should go ahead and do all the work. Once we're done, we do some test renderings to be sure we didn't miss any faces, then assign the cabinet's blue color to the new faces. The result should look something like Figure 9.75. Note that this figure shows them without texturing, which saves rendering time.

The dishwasher is modeled as a black cube that intersects the cabinetry. This is not very well modeled—it's intersecting the cabinet door, as we can easily see, and it is a pretty bad model (just a black cube). This kind of problem would be something to ask our manager about if it was important that this model be perfectly accurate, but we don't have to worry about accuracy for this display-only model. To fix it, we can either shorten the cabinet door or shorten the dishwasher. Because the cabinet door is smaller and less noticeable than the dishwasher, we'll revise it. Also, we'll make the dishwasher cut into the cabinetry instead of intersecting (to prevent overplot), and add a little detail to it, in the form of a silver control panel.

An initial rendering will show that the glass-door cabinets are all colored the glass color, instead of just the glass inset part. Upon fixing that, we should have a cabinet model that looks like Figure 9.75.

The walls are kind of messy, too. There's a two-tone design that was apparently made by simply copying all the walls, scaling the copy down, and reducing its height so it is at the trim-line in the middle of the wall. We'll redo this mod-

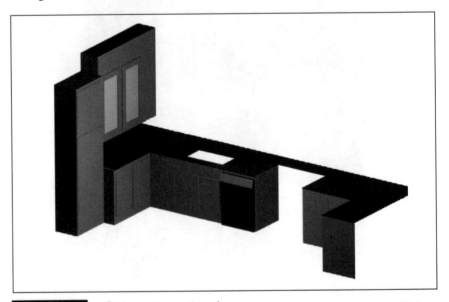

 FIGURE 9.75   Cabinets, revised.

eling by erasing that copy, cleaning up the original (which has lots of overlap, among other problems), then rebuilding the upper/lower split without overlapping faces.

In the cleanup process, we start by deleting the lower wall half. This can be selected via elements or by showing the material it's made with (HP LITE GRAY). Then we clean up the doorways, which are fairly messy. There's a modeling mistake above DOOR01; there aren't any faces up there. We'll also iron out the walls so they're perfectly planar.

Next, we'll adjust the walls so they don't stick down behind the cabinets (preventing more overlap). After looking at the cabinetry, we can see that the entire back wall is covered, except for an area between the glass-door cabinet and the backsplash and around the door. We build little patch pieces for these two spots, then delete the whole back wall. The window wall's bottom edge can be raised to the top of the backsplash, and the wall behind the stove can be matched to the cabinets and stove profile.

Overplotting versus Adding Faces

You may realize, as we make these edits, that we're adding geometry; essentially, we're trading faces for overlap. How do we know when to make this trade? The answer to this question depends on the bottleneck in your graphics engine. For most PC-based machines, the bottleneck is clearly the graphics pipeline; specifically, the actual pixel-by-pixel rendering step. That's where overplotting costs so much (and that's why it's worth a few extra faces to prevent it). This isn't necessarily true for a hardware-accelerated graphics workstation, for example. In their case, the limitations may be in the number of faces, so we'd be building this model differently if that were our target platform.

The second question is harder: how much overplot savings (how many overplotted pixels) is worth an added face? The only way to answer this question definitively is to try some tests with our target platform. For this model, we're guessing that the trade-off is somewhere around 200 overplotted pixels, if they're seen more than 25 percent of the time. This time constraint acknowledges that if the user constantly sees the overplotted pixels, it's more important than the occasional drop in frame rate from a glance in a bizarre corner. For example, the burners on the stove aren't cut into the stove surface because it wouldn't be worth the cost of the extra faces for the slight overplotting that they will cause.

Now we simplify the doors. They are pretty, but they have extra faces and lots of overplotting, so it's simpler to rebuild them than to try to edit them. We'll make a box that encloses the door, then make a beveled box that cuts out an indented area, Boolean-subtract the two, and then delete the backward-facing faces.

The floor comes next. It's a nice surprise—it's already cut out to avoid overplotting, for the most part. We'll just edit around the stove and a few other places, and it's basically ready to go.

Now, let's make the wall divide so we can color the bottom slightly differently. We really need to do this only on the wall opposite the window and

around the doors because that's where we can see the division. We do this by copying the pieces of the wall object, then shortening both the original and the copy so they meet at the trim line.

The ceiling is a simple box shape, totally unconnected to the rest of the model. It would be better modeled as a set of faces using the verts at the top of the wall object.

The window is a little tricky. It's modeled as a hole, which is structurally fine as long we don't mind blackness outside. We now make a design decision to delete the Venetian blinds object, which saves about 100 verts at a loss of detail that we'll agree is acceptable. If we do want Venetian blinds, we should consider using a texture instead of modeling them.

The table is fine, except for some faces on the bottom of the legs that can be deleted.

The geometry is finished at this point. In 3D Studio, our geometry looks like Figure 9.76, and Figure 9.77 shows it rendered from the same camera as the original rendering. We're using 798 faces (instead of 15,000!). This model is in KRT-GEOM.PRJ.

Obviously, what we're missing now are textures!

Create the Textures

Looking at the textures that came with the model (see the list below; these images are on the CD-ROM), we see that we have a few.

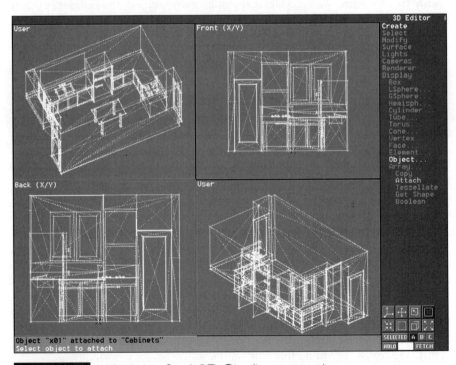

FIGURE 9.76 Kitchen, final 3D Studio geometry.

Designing 3D Graphics

FIGURE 9.77   Kitchen, rendered.

Looking back at our work assignment, we see that we are supposed to make all the linoleum fit on 12" tiles (with almost no grout space) on the floor. Some of the images here are not square, and they have other problems. We need to clean them up: Make them the correct size, color depth, and file type for use with a VRML browser.

What size should they be? The linoleum is the point of this simulation, and we'll have only one in memory at once, so we'll make it plenty big (256×256) under the assumption that the user will get close to it.

VRML browsers usually support JPEG (.JPG) images and often handle .GIF as well. We'll make these all JPEGs, powers of 2 in dimension. For example, see LINO-C-B.TIF, a 306×408 24-bit image of mottled gray, industrial-looking linoleum. We'll crop it to 256×256, then add a slight grout edge to compensate for the loss of the bump map. We'll rename the resulting file LINOGREY.JPG. We'll do this for all the rest of the files as well, except for the following:

FORMROSE.TIF is a 64×64, 24-bit image that is all a solid RGB value (87 percent, 70 percent, 65 percent). We should not use it as a texture because it offers us nothing over simply assigning an RGB color to the object. We'll discard it.

REFMAP.GIF is used only as a reflection map for the silver objects; we can discard it for our model.

MARBTEAL.GIF is a 320×200, 8-bit image of green marble. If we look at the mapping on the original model, we'll see that it's used in the countertops,

CHAPTER 9 • **Modeling Specific Types of Objects**   **255**

being squished to a 1-foot square. With our target window size of 640 × 400, we can probably use a 128 × 128 texture here and have it look fine, so we'll resize this to 128 pixels wide, crop it square, and add a grout surrounding (because it won't have a bump map as the original did).

GRID-1%.GIF is the bump map used in the original; we can discard it for our model.

AVODIRE.JPG is a 343 × 175, 24-bit wood JPEG image that is used on the table. We'll resize it to 256 × 128 and resave it.

We should now have the following files:

1.	avodire.jpg	5659	3-05-96 14:02
2.	linoblak.jpg	10916	3-05-96 14:42
3.	linoblu2.jpg	12931	3-05-96 14:41
4.	linoblue.jpg	11941	3-05-96 14:41
5.	linochek.jpg	8727	3-05-96 14:29
6.	linocorn.jpg	11445	3-05-96 14:31
7.	linogre2.jpg	13318	3-05-96 14:39
8.	linogree.jpg	12977	3-05-96 14:32
9.	linogrey.jpg	9712	3-05-96 13:59
10.	linogry2.jpg	12975	3-05-96 14:33
11.	linogry3.jpg	11922	3-05-96 14:40
12.	linonavy.jpg	13612	3-05-96 14:38
13.	linorang.jpg	12414	3-05-96 14:29
14.	linowhit.jpg	8770	3-05-96 14:30
15.	marbteal.jpg	4125	3-05-96 13:51

Back in 3D Studio, we create materials for each of these bitmaps. The materials should have correct ambient, diffuse, and specular colors; that is, the green linoleum should have green diffuse color. This is what the user will see if the texture doesn't load, so it's important that it be correct. We name each material after the filename it uses and create a new library from it.

At this point, we should go through the materials that the model is currently using (type F in the Materials Editor) and make sure that they aren't using any bump maps, reflection maps, or anything like that. If they are, we should replace them with new materials.

Map the Textures on the Model

Now we apply texture mapping to any object that has textures. The only textures are on the table, counter, and floor, so we'll apply mapping to them. The table's mapping coordinates are intact from the original model, so we don't have to worry about them.

Designing 3D Graphics

If we choose Surface/Mapping, we'll see that the mapping icon is already set up for the countertop, left over from the original mapping. We can simply apply this to the entire cabinet object, but we'll have to map the backsplash elements separately (and separate the backsplash into elements where necessary).

We'll set the mapping on the floor to a 12" square, so our linoleum tiles fit at the correct scale, and simply apply that mapping to the floor object.

Then we assign some of the new materials to our object and test render the model.

Import to the Real-Time Application
There are several ways to get a 3D Studio model into VRML, but for this exercise, we'll use the free Autodesk VRML plug-in. V1.2 handles textures strangely, from the 3D Studio user's standpoint. It requires that each face in a textured object be textured. That means that an object can't have untextured faces or faces with a different texture. Our cabinet object will have to be divided between countertop and untextured cabinetry. Once we do that, we load the plug-in (see Chapter 14 for how to do this) and select each object that is textured from the list, one by one, click on texture, and type in the name of the texture that goes with that object. Then choose Convert, and select all. Deselect the cameras (which don't import correctly). Save the .WRL in the same directory as the textures.

The model is now ready to load in the VRML browser.

 # Human Figure

Building realistic, low-face-count humanoid characters is possibly the most difficult form of real-time modeling. Players have very high expectations for realistic humanoid figures, and computer hardware, powerful as it is today, just isn't ready for truly realistic, real-time human animation. To make a decent human shape, we'll compromise and corner-cut like crazy.

Let's go through an example of character modeling. We will create a generic 100-face untextured human figure from a supplied 2D illustration.

Get Source Art
Our first step is to get source art. In reality, this means we've either got to draw a character to model or work from existing artwork.

For our example, we'll use Figure 9.78 as the source art.

Gather Technical Information
The next step is gathering information.

Q:	What's the face budget?
A:	Use 100 faces or fewer.
Meaning:	This is a tight budget for a humanoid, which means we're going to be doing a minimal model (as usual!)

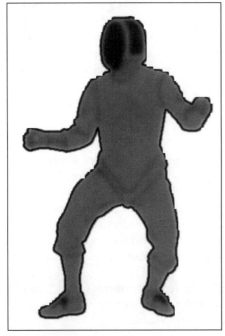

FIGURE 9.78 Human figure—faceless.

Q: What's the texture map budget?

A: No textures are used.

Meaning: This is odd, but conceivable for a background or secondary character.

Q: Is there any animation? What kind?

A: Yes, there will be morphing animation.

Meaning: Morphing animation is good news for the modeler—that means we don't have to build any special joints—but we'll have to make sure that the faces around the joints can bend without destroying the shape of the object.

Q: What color depth can we use?

A: 24-bit color is available.

Meaning: 24 bits of color is good news—no yucky palette issues to deal with.

Q: What shading methods are available?

A: There are Gouraud and flat shading, but only non-textured surfaces can be Gouraud shaded.

Meaning:	Gouraud shading gives a great sense of curvedness, especially handy for human figures that are morphing. Because we don't have any textures, we'll definitely be using Gouraud shading.
Q:	What kind of lighting is used?
A:	A single, stationary, directional light.
Meaning:	This is a simple, but common, solution. Note that smooth shading requires some kind of light source.
Q:	Are T-intersections allowed?
A:	No.
Meaning:	Using a T-intersection can simplify designs, thus saving modeling time; however, they rarely are allowed since they can cause *ripping* (slight cracks that appear and disappear during run time). So, it's slightly bad news, but should be expected, that we can't allow T-intersections.
Q:	How will the model be viewed?
A:	It could be seen from any angle, but it will usually be seen from another human's viewing height, standing up. It might be seen up close sometimes, but usually it will be seen so its onscreen height is 100 pixels or less.
Meaning:	This is bad news—we'll have to model all sides, including the soles of the feet, to keep the model looking right from any angle. The good news is that it mostly will be seen from at least a little distance—this allows us to approximate a few details.

Analysis

In light of this information, let's take a look at our figure. The source art shows a pretty generic-looking humanoid—sexless and faceless, good for architectural "sketching" or for far-away shots. Aside from normal arms, legs, and head, the only noticeable features are where the clothing attaches. (With textures added, it could look much more realistic, but this exercise won't go into that—we'll skip the detail on the clothing and just go for main features: basic body form.) We'll be using Gouraud shading and morphing, and we can't have T-intersections. All three of these requirements mean that we must make the model share verts as much as possible.

Why does Gouraud shading require shared verts? To answer this, we'll have to know how Gouraud shading works. Gouraud shading averages the normals of all faces that share a vert, then instead of determining the light level by using a single angle on each face, it interpolates the angle across these faces surfaces, approximating a curved surface by changing the lighting level continuously. If two adjacent faces don't share a vertex, the Gouraud shading algorithm doesn't know that the two faces are adjacent, so no interpolation is done across that boundary.

Sketching

The next step is to sketch the model. Here we will go through the model more thoroughly, deciding how many faces to use for each piece and what it will look like.

For this model, the head and torso are more able to "flex" their face counts—they could add or drop a couple of faces without a big change in appearance. By contrast, the arms and legs will be modeled as simply as possible; we won't be able to do any adjusting on those.

We choose to keep the arms and legs simple because there are four of them; any face we add to the design means four faces in the final model. This is a pretty arbitrary decision, however. If we knew that our model was going to be used where its limbs were the focus and the head and torso were relatively unimportant, we'd change our approach.

Cross Sections

Cross sections are an easy way to evaluate the number of faces in an object that is *linear*—that is, an object that has a definite axis (Figure 9.79). The idea is to cut through the body of the object and count the number of edges, then multiply by the number of sections the object has. The section showing flat construction uses just four faces per straight section. This type of model looks very non-solid for the two faces it saves over triangular sections. It might seem that it

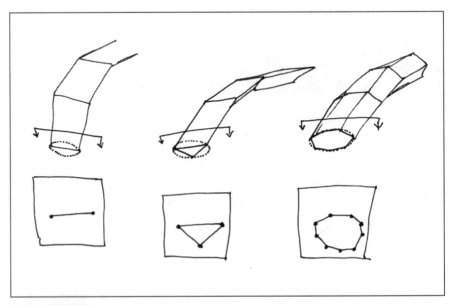

FIGURE 9.79 Cross sections: straight (flat), tri, square, arbitrary with face counts labeled.

Designing 3D Graphics

would use only two faces per section, but because faces are one-sided, we'll need four faces to make it visible from both sides.

Let's use triangular cross-sections for the arms and legs. That means we'll have six triangles per straight section. Each limb will have:

2 sections (forearm and biceps)	12 faces
cap the end of the limb	1 face
joints	4 faces
Total, per limb:	**17 faces**
Total, four limbs:	**68 faces**

That's about right for our face budget.

The next step is to sketch out how we'll use our budgeted faces on the arm.

Figure 9.80 shows a crude pencil sketch of the arm we will model. Let's walk through its construction, starting with the striped triangular attachment point where the arm connects to the body. No face is drawn here because this is inside the body. These three verts are the only ones that join the arm to the body.

From that triangle, two triangles attach, forming the shoulder joint. The purpose of these two small triangles (and the two in the elbow) is to flex and bend when the shoulder moves—without them, the arm's cross-sectional shape would drastically change as it moves. The shoulder joint could stand a couple more of these because the shoulder is a sphere-based joint; the elbow will be fine with the two it has, but that's getting ahead of ourselves.

The shoulder joints form another imaginary triangle inside the body, a cross section at the top of the biceps. From this, the upper arm from the bottom of the shoulder to the top of the elbow is defined by extruding the imaginary inner triangle, then rotating the three new verts we just created around the extrusion axis until one edge aligns with the hinge axis of the elbow. This is shown in Figure 9.81.

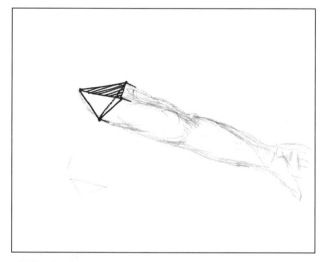

FIGURE 9.80   Sketch of forearm, with three body-connecting verts and shoulder joint.

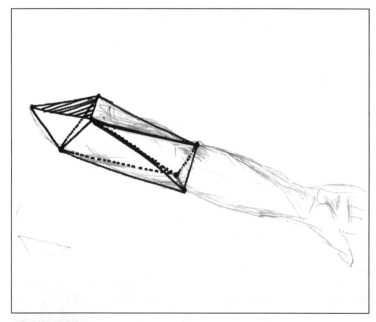

FIGURE 9.81 Arm with biceps/upper arm faces overlaid.

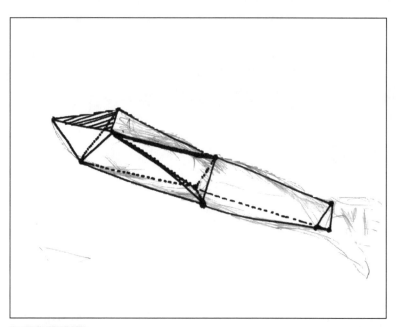

FIGURE 9.82 Arm model sketch.

Designing 3D Graphics

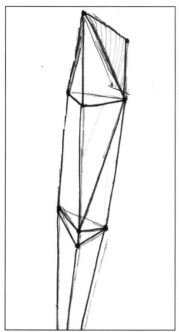

Sketch of leg design.

The twist we just described has two purposes. First, because we know which way the elbow will bend (unlike the shoulder), the edge aligned with the bend axis helps to prevent horrible distortion of the arm's shape. Second, the twist keeps the faces in the extruded walls from being coplanar and thus looking flat. This arm should approximate round, not flat, so it's good to mess up the flatness that an extrusion gives us.

From there, we have the two elbow faces that are much like the shoulder joint, then we continue the triangular extrusion to the wrist (Figure 9.82).

It would be nice to have some kind of hand, but we didn't budget faces for even the simplest of hands, so we'll just cap the arm and hope that we can add hands later, if we have enough faces in the end.

Similarly, we will now sketch out some possible leg designs (Figure 9.83).

The legs are designed very similarly to the arms, perhaps with more attention paid to the shape of the body connection site, since the two legs will touch each other (unlike the arms), thus limiting what we can build in the torso. Even with this extra consideration, we'll probably have to rework this sketch a little when we actually build the model, but it's a fine place to start.

Next comes the torso, as shown in Figure 9.84.

The concept for the torso is simple: start with the connection triangles where the 4 limbs connect, and join them with as few faces as possible. That's what we have here. We may notice that the connection triangles' shape has changed some from the one on the limb, in order to keep the torso's shape reasonable. This kind of flexing is what sketching is for; we shouldn't feel bound by our previous sketches if they constrain the rest of the model horribly without good reason.

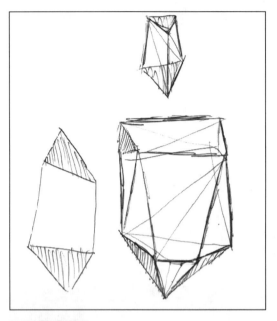

FIGURE 9.84 Sketch of torso design.

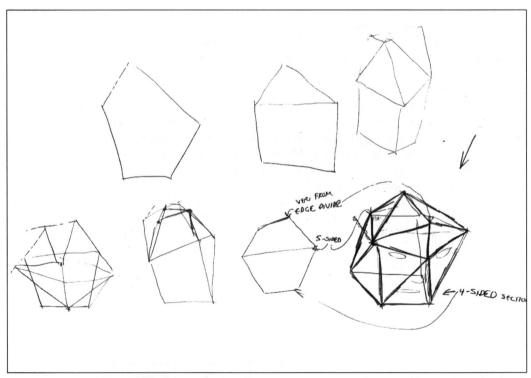

FIGURE 9.85 Sketch of head with 17 faces, with numbers.

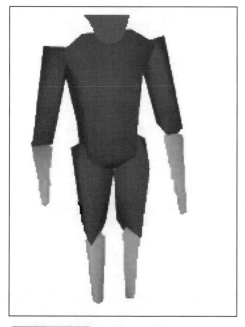

FIGURE 9.86   Sketch of whole body.

This torso design uses 15 faces. With the limbs, we've now used 83 faces, leaving a paltry 17 faces for the head. That's not many—the head's going to be pretty ugly, or we're going to have to go over our polygon budget.

Let's try the ugly head first. A sketch is in Figure 9.85

The basic shape is spheroid, but the construction isn't a simple 3D Studio Create/Sphere. Start with an extruded pentagon shape, sitting like a tin can. Twist the can so that the top and bottom pairs of 5 verts are not aligned. Scale the top verts around their local axis about 120 percent.

Create by hand 5 new faces that cap the bottom end, like a bottom on the can. Weld one vert to another in the bottom section, creating a four-sided bottom, connected to a five-sided top. The edge that was formed by the weld operation is the nape of the neck. Create a five-sided pyramid to cap the top of the pentagon.

We are now using 18 faces in this head model, and it needs 2 more. Divide the edge in the pyramid cap that is farthest from the nape of the neck—this should be the middle of the forehead. Move this new vert, along with the pyramid peak vert, in the Side view until the head is a little rounder looking.

We're now using 20 faces, which puts us slightly over our face budget. Our model, completed, looks like Figure 9.86.

Finished

That's it for the minimalist human body. It's really rough-shaped, but it is recognizable, and it has very near the minimum number of faces possible. With a larger face budget, we would add hands, feet, and lots more detail.

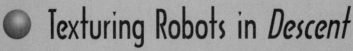

Texturing Robots in *Descent*

In this section Adam Pletcher (lead artist for Descent; *see biography at end of section) describes techniques he uses when he textures his RT3D models.*

As you might guess, good texturing of real-time 3D objects is very different from that of pre-rendered ones. The end result needs not only to be pleasing to the eye, but must fit within the speed and memory limitations of the application. Some of the limitations that a real-time texture artist may expect to encounter include low-resolution bitmaps (often no more than 64 × 64), low color depth (256 colors or less), low object detail, and the constant threat of memory requirements. While creating the various 3D robots and objects appearing in the games *Descent* and *Descent 2*, I've been able to uncover a few techniques and tricks to make this process much less intimidating.

TEXTURES

Before starting, you must have a good idea how much memory is available for the textures of your object. *Descent*, for example, uses an average of five or six 64 × 64 × 256 textures per object. This equates to about 20K of memory per object. If the object you're designing is for an interior game, like *Descent*, you will need to account for the memory needs of the surrounding wall textures as well. Space simulator games, taking place in open environments, can usually afford more memory and detail per 3D object.

Also take into account the relative size of your object. A tiny alien robot object is going to occupy much less space onscreen than a large boss-type robot. It makes sense to remember this when deciding how many textures to use on the object. If you use too many textures on a small object, much of the detail will be lost. Likewise, using too few textures on a large object will give it an undetailed, blocky look. For this reason, it is important to be consistent with respect to the other objects being used in your game or application.

Mapping Coordinates

Once you have an object ready to be textured, you need to consider how the mapping coordinates will be arranged. If you are using 3D Studio, or a similar package, you will probably have three methods immediately available: planar, cylindrical, and spherical. The shape and detail level of the object will determine which method is best for each of its parts. I'm going to use a robot object from *Descent* to help illustrate things further.

You should start by visually breaking down your object into different shape categories. Figure 9.87 shows an untextured version of the SuperHulk Boss robot object from *Descent*. Because real-time objects like these tend to be low detail and "blocky" looking, the task of applying mapping coordinates is actually made easier. Even though I've used cylindrical and spherical mapping on occasion, they often require more work than they're worth for real-time model use.

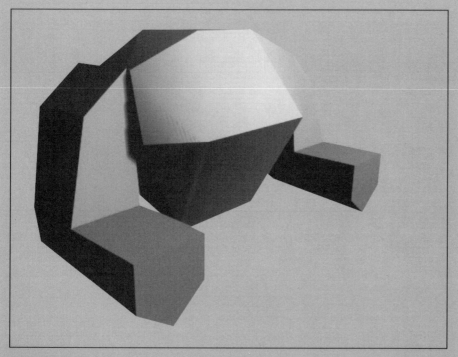

FIGURE 9.87 Untextured Boss object.

I've found that for most of my real-time texturing needs, planar mapping offers the easiest and quickest results.

Figure 9.87 shows the untextured Boss object. Notice that it can, for the most part, be broken up into a series of square shapes. If your 3D object consists of several smaller objects, you can use Alt-B to turn on Box mode. This will show bounding boxes for all objects and may help you visually break things down.

The first texture application will be for the all-purpose "body" texture (Figure 9.88). This is a low-contrast background texture that will appear on most of the robot's body. Details will be added to it later. It's important that this body texture tiles well with itself when it's laid side-by-side across its body. Depending on your object, this texture could be a green metal texture on an army tank or a wood grain texture for a treasure chest.

Basic Mapping

The next step is to apply mapping. We'll separate the model into three objects: front facing, side facing, and top facing. Front-facing polygons are, quite simply, the polygons that face mostly forward or backward, while side-facing are those facing left or right.

Let's start with the front-facing polygons. Press Alt-N (the keyboard shortcut for Select/None) to clear everything from the current selection set. Use the

FIGURE 9.88 General texture for robot.

Right or Left viewports to get a side-on view of the object. Choose Select/Face/Fence from the menu. Use the fence to highlight all polygons that fall into the front-facing category. It may be necessary to temporarily hide different parts of the object as you do this (such as the robot's arms) in order to get a clear view of the polygons you're after. When you've selected all front-facers, choose Create/Face/Detach to remove them from the surrounding geometry. Name this new object FRONT.

Note: If you're not using 3D Studio, you may be able to assign these faces coordinates without physically separating them. In 3DS, however, it is necessary initially to do this in order to assign unique mapping coordinates to the different areas of the object.

Next, from the Front viewport, select Surface/Mapping/Type and verify that you have planar mode selected. Choose Adjust and center the mapping icon over the object. At this point, you may wish to consider the desired pixel size of the object's textures. Let's say you're using 64×64 textures, 10 pixels = 10 meters, and your object will be 30 meters across. You should use Surface/Mapping/Adjust/Scale to change your mapping icon to roughly one-third the size of your object.

Next you must orient your mapping icon. You want to orient it as parallel as possible to the assigned faces. Look at the Right viewport again. Does the FRONT object contain many polygons that face slightly downward (such as the lower torso in this robot object)? If many of them face up or down, you may wish to rotate the mapping icon slightly to account for it. Likewise, look from the Top viewport to see if many faces in the FRONT object are oriented right or left.

If you're happy with the orientation of the mapping icon, go ahead and use Surface/Mapping/Apply Object onto the FRONT object. Once you've done this, use Display/Hide/Object on the FRONT object. Follow the above steps for the side- and top-facing polygons until you've applied coordinates to all of the object's faces. With a more complex object, it may be necessary to create more mapping groups due to differing orientations.

For background textures like the one we're doing here, the edges will probably not align perfectly with each other. For example, the texture on the LEFT object won't end at the edge of the face, so the texture on the FRONT object probably won't start at the same place. I've found that for most 320 × 200 real-time applications, no one usually notices (especially if the corners are nearly 90 degrees). If you have a high-contrast texture it will be more apparent, though.

Once all faces have mapping coordinates, you should use Surface/Material/Assign to place the body texture on all faces. If you need to make any further mapping adjustments, you can detach the problem area and reapply the coordinates.

Creating Details

When you're satisfied with the object's basic mapping, we can start with the details. The first will be the eye. If you have advanced mapping software such as Meshpaint 3D, the addition of details can be accomplished in the texture (without increasing much of the geometry). For the purposes of this exercise, I'll assume that we don't have the software and will rely on the built-in 3DS tools.

The easiest way to do a detail like this is to create a few detail faces specifically shaped to take the desired texture. By using only two faces, we can give the robot an evil-looking eye, as seen in Figure 9.90. Note that the 3D application will almost certainly render faster if such detail faces are cut into the body geom-

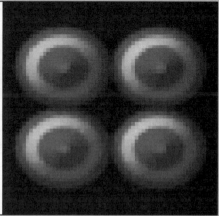

FIGURE 9.89   Detail textures.

etry (not just attached). By eliminating overplot in this manner, you will probably get more speed out of the 3D application.

Once you have a set of faces you'd like to apply the details to, simply use Surface/Mapping/Adjust/Move and /Rotate to position your planar mapping icon over the detail faces and apply them. This may take a few tries to get it oriented correctly. If you haven't already, use Create/Object/Attach to bind the object and its detail faces together.

Figure 9.89 shows a few of the detail-textures used in *Descent*. Notice that more often than not, several details appear on the same texture. By carefully adjusting the position of your mapping icon, you can utilize only a portion of one texture per object. The other details can appear on different parts of the same object or on totally different objects. This can provide great memory savings, especially if the texture uses several frames of animation.

Apply the same methods to the remaining texture details. Also remember that simple geometry details can be added as well. A good example of these are the gray "spikes" I placed on the robot's shoulders. These are simply three-sided pyramids attached to the shoulder geometry. A close fit can be achieved by using Create/Object/Boolean/Union. This will eliminate any intersecting geometry and leave you with the rest. The final result is shown in Figure 9.90.

FIGURE 9.90   Final model.

These instructions provide only the most basic techniques. As you create more objects, you'll soon pick up many tricks and shortcuts of your own. As with anything else, practice is the key to easy real-time 3D object creation.

For the past two years Adam Pletcher has worked at Parallax Software, developers of the award-winning action game Descent *and* Descent 2. *He created many of the real-time 3D models in both games, primarily using 3D Studio and a few proprietary tools used to integrate them. Adam's background includes computing as well as 2D art, but he remains self-taught in the workings of 3D modeling and animation. He's currently located in the Champaign, Illinois office of Parallax Software, and he is working as 3D artist and project leader for the upcoming game* FreeSpace. *Adam Pletcher can be contacted via email at adam@pxsoftware.com.*

Descent, *for those of you who don't know, is a very popular RT3D action game that simulates a small spacecraft traveling through hostile mining tunnels. Technically, it is known for its real-time lighting, animated transparent textures, network play, and AI simulation, while sustaining a very high performance level.* Descent *runs on PCs, Macintosh, and the Sony Playstation. There are shareware versions for some platforms available on Interplay's net site:* **http://www.interplay.com.**

All objects and textures shown in this chapter are Copyright © 1994–1996 Parallax Software Corporation, all rights reserved. Descent *and* Descent 2 *are registered trademarks of Interplay Productions.*

CHAPTER 10

CONVERTING NORMAL 3D MODELS TO RT3D

This chapter discusses the basic techniques we use and issues we face when reducing a complicated model to a simpler model suitable for real-time rendering.

Prologue

There's a myth that real-time modeling consists mainly of taking pre-rendered 3D Studio models and simply reducing the face count. Though we real-time modelers do this, it's not usually our day-to-day job.

Why don't we use existing models instead of rebuilding so much? When we design and construct our real-time model shape from scratch, it is usually faster and results in better-looking models. However, there are times when it makes sense to convert existing models.

What Scenarios Require Us to Convert?

There are many scenarios that would require us to reduce a complicated model to a real-time version. Here are some examples:

- We have a beautiful but complicated model, and we fear losing its beauty if we rebuild it from scratch.

- The model was created automatically from digitized video or is from some other hard-to-replace source art.

- We built a real-time model that has too many faces, so we must go through and remove some of them.

When Converting, Should We Reduce or Rebuild?

Once we've decided to convert a complicated model to a real-time version, the first question we must ask is: Would it be better to build a real-time model from scratch, based on the geometry we have, than to edit this geometry into the real-time model we desire?

A very weak rule of thumb for this decision is that if the old geometry has more than twice the budgeted face count, it's a good candidate for rebuilding. The theory here is that if we have more than twice the correct face count, we will spend a lot of time welding verts, and that time will probably be better spent building the model correctly from the start. Of course, if we're using an automated tool (like Optimize), this rule may not apply.

Ultimately, this decision must be made by each modeler on an individual basis. Beginning artists will get a sense for the speed of each approach as they work and be able to judge for themselves, as long as they try both methods.

If it is really important to know (for example, if our project needed 200 car models built from pre-rendered versions, and we needed to give an estimate for this work) we could find out by reducing and rebuilding the same model, comparing the speed and ease of each method. Obviously this is overkill for most cases, but occasionally it might be necessary.

Rebuilding

If we plan to rebuild it, we'd start with the advantage of excellent source art (the old geometry), and if we built the first model, we'll have a good idea of how we're going to construct the new one (or maybe which techniques we're not going to use, if the first one didn't go well!). This second point is important—like the return trip when hiking, it's amazing how much faster our task is when we are familiar with it.

When rebuilding, we use the old 3D object as a "reference model"—like a 3D sketch or even a 3D framework, a form to build from. When we do this, 3D Studio has a handy command: Display/Freeze. This causes the reference model to be "frozen"—it's drawn on the screen only as a convenience for us. We can't accidentally change frozen objects in any way other than to unfreeze them. This is a good feature because we can use commands like Select/All without constantly having to deselect our reference model.

Staying Focused on Frame Rate

When reducing a model, it's easy to get obsessed with the face count. If we really start getting into our work, the face count can become the score of a game—we win when it's lower. It's also common for managers to use face count as a handy index to quality: If the count's low, they're happy. While no one will argue that a low face count is always a bad thing, it's really important to remember our goal: good-looking models at a high frame rate.

Many factors to a model besides face count affect the frame rate. If we're being asked to reduce an existing real-time model's face count, it often means there's a performance problem: the frame rate isn't high enough with the existing model.

Know Thy Bottleneck

It's important to know where the performance bottleneck is with our model, and what we can do to widen it, rather than just blindly reducing face count and ripping out valuable detail in hopes of fixing everything.

We'll need to find out, probably from the programmer, what performance bottleneck is keeping the frame rate low. Is it the number of textures? Usage of multiple light sources on Gouraud-shaded surfaces? Number of vertices? Depth cueing code being overwhelmed by too many objects? Morphing animations taking too much CPU time? There are many possibilities.

If the programmer doesn't really know if the frame rate problem is due to face count, but we're still being asked to reduce the face count, it would be a

smart idea to find out if our work will pay off or not. We can find this out fairly easily if the application is developed enough to load objects. Here's how:

We create a dummy object, like a sphere, with the face count we plan to have in the final model. We then load the dummy object into the real-time application in place of the model we're about to build and see if the frame rate is improved.

If the dummy object didn't improve things, we call this to the attention of the programmer; we hope the programmer will research it and figure out the real performance bottleneck.

For more information about bottlenecks, see Chapter 11.

Vert Count versus Face Count

Besides face count, there's another common measure of the simplicity of a model: vert count, the number of vertices in a 3D model.

Vert count is a good way to measure the likely performance of the model. For each vert, the computer has to perform several math steps; depending on the hardware platform, this may be a large percentage of the computer's time.

Because of this, reducing vert count is often more important than getting the face count down. On the other hand, some hardware-accelerated graphics machines can breeze through vertex math quickly. In that case, we may be encouraged to use plenty of verts, but perhaps textured faces are slow to render, so we try not to use many textured faces.

Usually when we remove verts, we also have to remove faces, and vice versa. This isn't always true, though—especially for small models (under 50 faces), we can affect the model's vert count either way if we're aware of the need. This trade-off is usually made by sacrificing dissimilar texture mapping coordinates at a single vertex.

Figure 10.1 shows a simple car model. Imagine that we have unique textures for the front and side views. This car would normally have 16 verts, but since we need to have different mapping coordinates along the seams, we'll need duplicate verts along all the shared edges. There are several ways to put textures on all the surfaces, and if the problem is vert handling, we can lessen the vert count by using a mapping technique that doesn't require separate UVs for each vert (like cylindrical mapping). This will probably require more texture map memory or other resources.

Ownership of Reduced Models

There is an unresolved legal issue that pertains to reducing face count. The situation is this: If we create a new model that is based on a model we don't own, do we own the new model or not?

On one hand, imagine taking a commercial model, scaling it 10 percent, and claiming ownership. Because we modified it, it's ours now, right? Obviously, this is not a fair claim.

On the other hand, if we simply look at a 3D model that is owned by someone else as source art, like a photo from a magazine, and build every face in our

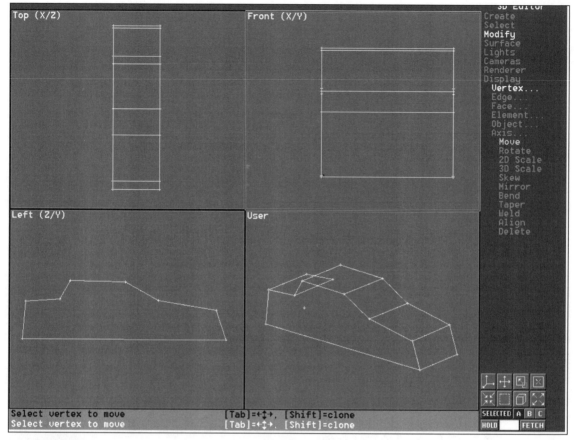

FIGURE 10.1 Picture of simple wireframe extruded car, Lincoln-hat-shaped.

new model from scratch, it's unreasonable for the original model's owner to claim ownership of our new model. And, if we use a small part, like a single face, from another owner's model, he or she probably won't be able to claim our model.

Where to draw the line? When have we made enough changes that we can claim ownership? Unfortunately, there are no concrete guidelines; the safe thing to do is consult a qualified legal advisor when in doubt. Because most artists can't afford to consult a lawyer for this kind of issue, some simply use common sense and ask themselves, "If someone else were using my model this way, would I take issue with it?"

Tips on Reducing

If we are reducing a model, we have to decide which parts are to be reduced and which ones will not be disturbed. This decision is messy, but some general guidelines bear mentioning. These should be considered as suggestions, not rules.

Some of these will appear very obvious, but they are listed here just in case they are forgotten and to form a checklist of factors to weigh when approaching a new model.

- Reduce little faces over big faces.

This simple rule suggests that large faces are more important because they are more noticeable if they are erased than are small faces. For example, a 3D doorknob looks nice, but it cost a lot in terms of faces and verts; if it comes to a decision between the sidewalk and the doorknob, obviously the doorknob should go first.

- Reduce faces that are in dusty corners.

As compared to faces that are prominent to the viewer, faces that are not often seen are less valuable to the model; if we have to get rid of faces, we should remove ones that aren't prominent.

- Reduce verts that do not define sharp edges.

A vert in a smoothly curving foothill is less important than a vert at the peak of a mountain.

- Reduce the inside of surfaces, as compared to the edges of a surface.
- Obviously, having verts on the middle of a flat surface is unnecessary, but there are other circumstances when we can get by with a very simple modeling of the interior.

This suggestion is true when we're working with a curved, Gouraud-shaded surface: Very few faces and verts are necessary to portray the center of a curved Gouraud-shaded surface.

For example, take a look at the two curved hexagons in Figure 10.2. The left object uses 7 verts and 6 faces; the other one uses 13 verts and 16 faces. Looking at the Front view, these extra verts may seem justified: The right object has a decently defined curve to it, where the left one looks pretty bad—it's a pyramid.

Now check out this smooth-shaded rendering of the User view, shown in Figure 10.3.

There's hardly any noticeable difference between the two! As long as the two objects aren't going to be seen from the side too much, the simpler model works fine.

Reducing with Automatic Tools

A plug-in called Optimize can reduce face counts in 3D Studio. The idea of improving face count by using an automatic tool to get rid of faces is a very appealing prospect to real-time modelers, and it's quite useful for many kinds of models.

After using Optimize for a while, most people discover that it does not solve all problems. While it works well for reducing models that have many faces defining continuously curved surfaces, it can do very poorly at reducing models that are already optimized.

Designing 3D Graphics

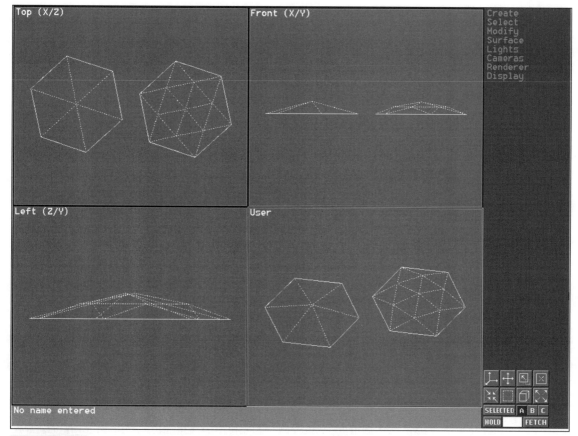

Top (X/Z)   Front (X/Y)

Create
Select
Modify
Surface
Lights
Cameras
Renderer
Display

Left (Z/Y)   User

No name entered

SELECTED A B C
HOLD   FETCH

FIGURE 10.2   Two hexagon models.

In other words, it's good when the decisions regarding what to keep and what to save are obvious and a lot of tedious execution of those decisions is required. It usually doesn't work very well when the model requires some hard decision-making regarding what detail is important and what isn't—weighing trade-offs.

Obviously, an automated program won't be aware of many issues that should be included in a decision to delete a face. That's unfortunate, but not surprising. Until the tool is improved, it means we'll still have to do much of the work by hand.

Despite this limitation, Optimize is a very useful tool and is well worth exploring.

Exercise for Optimize

Start by loading the file DUCK.3DS that came with 3D Studio. Change the Camera view to a User view and examine the model a little. Note the model's

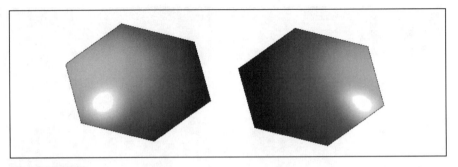

FIGURE 10.3   Rendering of two hexagons.

size: 304 verts, 564 faces, with 3 objects. If we select the objects, we'll see that
we have a body and two separate eyes.

Merge these three objects all into one by selecting all faces, then detaching
the selected faces. Use a logical name for the object, like "duck." Some unused
verts remained behind in a separate object. Delete this object.

When using Optimize, we should start by setting a targeted face/vert count
for our reduction. Let's set a goal of 100 faces or fewer. That means we'll be
erasing four out of every five faces, roughly.

Load Optimize by pressing F12, then choosing optimize from the list. Pick
the first object on the list. Turn on Show All Lines, click on the Render On
checkbox, and spin the model around. Notice that there's a missing face in the
bottom.

Explore the dialog a little; see Figure 10.4. Optimize is useful for much more
than reducing face count, as we will notice as we use it. For example, notice the
face normal controls—they allow us to modify face normals in a more interactive, obvious way than the usual "now you see it, now you don't" methods that
are built into 3D Studio.

The Auto-edge function is very handy, too. We can set it slightly higher than
the optimization angle to preview what edges are likely to be deleted if we
increase the optimization angle. The many other functions of the dialog are
important, but the documentation covers them quite well.

Now that we're familiar with the dialog, let's optimize. Set an optimization
angle of 25.03 degrees and click Optimize. This yields a pretty rough model, but
it meets our budget with only 81 faces.

Note that there are some obvious problems with this model: The tail is
strangely modeled—one side is fairly different from the other, and the eyes have
been heavily modified. It's not bad, though, and these problems are easily
repaired with standard 3DS editing commands. Try using a different optimization angle and compare the trade-off between quality and face count.

Think of Optimize as a form of compression, like JPEG image compression.
As in JPEG, some detail is lost during the process of compression. Also, like all
forms of compression, Optimize handles simple needs best. Optimize works best

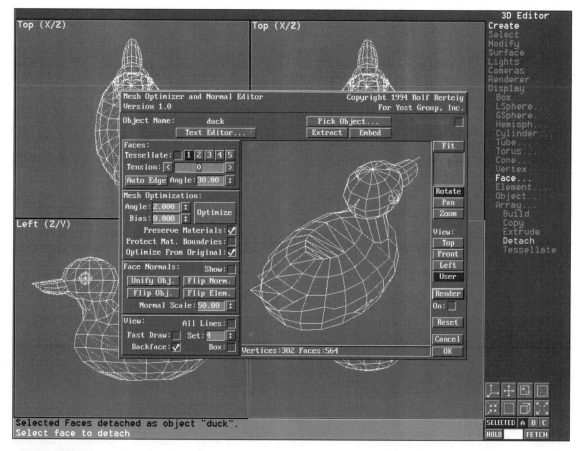

FIGURE 10.4 Optimize dialog.

with clear-cut cases, just as an empty bitmap compresses wonderfully, but a complicated, detailed bitmap does not.

What is a "clear-cut case" for Optimize? It loves coplanar faces with shared edges best. For example, extruding a square that is composed of five edges on each side generates a lot of unnecessary faces. Optimize will easily smash those all into large, flat faces. On the other hand, it has a harder time keeping decent-looking results for curved surfaces.

Optimize is great, but it doesn't help with a lot of the problems we artists face when we reduce a model. We must handle these cases because we have more information about the reduction problem than Optimize does. We know the likely viewing angles for the model (for example, "it will never be seen from below"), and we know what details are critical to keep and which ones aren't.

Optimize doesn't know about special cases. For example, if we have a jointed human figure, and we need to keep the limbs from collapsing into flat faces, we

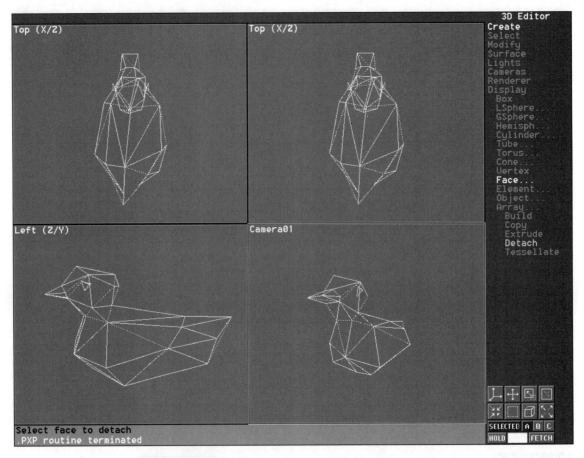

FIGURE 10.5 Optimized duck.

can add that to our mental list of requirements, but, of course, we can't reprogram Optimize to be aware of this.

The Future of Optimizing Tools

Right now, there are very few tools that automatically reduce face counts in models. As demand for real-time models grows, this will change, we hope.

As the tools improve, we hope they will allow more thorough—possibly interactive—control over decisions made during the optimization. With this control, the usefulness of these tools will be greatly extended and could possibly change the entire field of real-time 3D modeling.

Once the decisions about face reduction have been made, some additional problems often arise.

Common Problems (and Solutions) Related to Converting a Model to RT3D

We often have to deal with problems when we take a normal 3D Studio model and revise it for use in a real-time application. Many of these problems come up when we convert models to real-time environments because 3D Studio can handle some conditions that most real-time renderers don't. That means that we modelers must fix them beforehand.

It's tempting to think of these conditions as sloppy modeling, and perhaps curse the errant fool who built the original with the intersecting faces, but in the interests of justice, remember that there is no "right" way to model; the overall goal is simply to make an image appear on the screen. If that's more easily done with shortcuts, then why not use them?

Of course, if the model is purchased or was designed to be used in many different environments, the expectations may be different, and we may be justified in cursing the builder. Regardless, we must fix it.

Following are some modeling problems that pertain to real-time 3D modeling. For each problem, there are several sections. First is a detailed description of the problem, with an example, if necessary. That is followed by a description of the conditions in which that problem will arise, and some solutions to working around it are discussed.

Remember that problems are opportunities in disguise. Some of these problems can be turned into useful tools for solving certain problems; where this is possible, it is discussed.

Intersecting Faces

This is the condition in which one face sticks through another one. 3D Studio handles this without a problem, and some real-time rendering engines handle it effectively as well, but many do not.

An example of intersecting faces is an extruded cross. Imagine drawing two lines that cross, then extruding those lines into four faces. The faces cross each other, but there are no verts at the intersection points.

When Is It a Problem?

The symptoms of intersecting faces are shared with other problems. During run-time, the intersection line won't be visible. Instead, the intersecting faces will appear entirely in front or behind each other.

If the rendering engine supports Z-buffered sorting, it will generally be able to handle intersecting faces. Most other sorting algorithms don't support intersecting faces, and they will require the modeler to avoid creating them.

How Do We Fix It?

Often the intersecting faces must be fixed because we are working with a model designed for jointed hierarchy-oriented animation. For this case, be sure to read "Intersecting Objects" later in this chapter.

To fix intersecting faces, start by putting points on the intersecting edges of the faces, then revise the faces to use these points. This technique usually adds faces to the model, though if we can tolerate T-intersections (described in this chapter), we can avoid adding faces. For our cross example, divide the two original lines so they both have a vert in the middle where they cross. Extruding these lines will make the non-intersecting extruded cross shape.

The hardest part of fixing intersecting faces is placing the intersecting verts. Probably the easiest technique is to use the Create/Object/Boolean command (see "Intersecting Objects" for an example), but there are other methods.

Using the Orthogonal Views

When either of the intersecting faces are orthogonal (that is, they look like a line in either the Top, Front, or Side view), we can use this fact to place the intersection vert by hand.

Placing an intersection vert by hand:

1. Make a copy of both faces, in a new object. Freeze this new object.

2. Divide one of the penetrating edges.

3. There should be two viewports that show one of the faces as an edge. Choose one of these, and zoom in until the view shows the new vertex and the intersection point.

4. Move the new vertex to the intersection point, using the frozen edge as a guide. We can use Modify/Vertex/Move, or we can place the axis at one of the orthogonal faces' verts, then use 2D Scale to move the intersecting vert into place.

5. In the other viewport, verify that the new vertex is on the frozen edge (and move it if necessary).

6. Repeat steps 2–6 for the other penetrating edge.

7. Unfreeze and delete the duplicate faces.

Using the User View

For cases where the intersecting faces aren't orthogonal and we can't use the Boolean method to get the points, we can use the User view in combination with the techniques described above.

Use the User view when placing intersection points:

1. The procedure is to align the User view with one of the faces, then rotate the User view 90 degrees exactly.

2. We can now see the intersection point more clearly. If this isn't clear enough, we can change one of the other viewpoints into a second User view, and align it with the second intersecting face.

Designing 3D Graphics

3. With both of these views, we should be able to place intersection points using the steps described for the orthogonal intersection creation.

Intersecting Objects

Intersecting objects are similar to intersecting faces, but this problem involves entire objects crossing each other instead of a single face penetrating another. The line is fuzzy between the two (in a sense, it's really just a different way of looking at the same problem), but different approaches are called for when we're dealing with a large group of intersecting faces instead of a single face.

Even more than faces, intersecting objects are not usually considered to be a modeling problem for typical 3D Studio users. Intersecting objects are routinely created for jointed animations. The example objects on the World-Creating Toolkit CD-ROM and the exercises that come with 3D Studio provide ample precedent for creating intersecting objects. That is as it should be—3D Studio doesn't have a problem with it, so why shouldn't it make use of that ability? The problem is solely ours—it's real-time engines that can't cope with it very well.

When Is It a Problem?

Like intersecting faces, problems occur when the real-time rendering engine doesn't support Z-buffered sorting (and many do not).

For a real-life example, imagine we have a jet plane model to which we added landing gear. We originally built the model for rendering a normal pre-rendered intro sequence, but now we want to adapt the model for real-time use. When we built the landing gear, we created the landing gear vertical strut as a normal 3DS cylinder, deleted the top center vert, and placed it so it stuck inside the hull, through the faces that form the hull. That worked fine for the 3DS rendering, but now those faces are flashing on and off in the real-time environment. We'll discuss how to fix this below.

How Do We Fix It?

In general, we can use the methods described for fixing faces that intersect, but the Boolean function in 3D Studio can make this a lot easier.

If our objects are very clean, we can simply perform a Boolean addition between them, and our intersection will be nicely solved; however, this frequently does not work correctly, generates unnecessary verts and faces, or does both.

In the real-life example discussed earlier, we must first find the intersection points between the strut cylinder and the hull. We do this by making copies of both objects, then using Create/Object/Boolean to create the points where the two objects intersect.

Let's assume that the results of the Boolean operation are not useful (that is, the Boolean operation badly damaged the geometry), but it did generate verts correctly placed at the intersection, as is often the case. We then delete all faces and verts except these intersection verts that correlate with the original verts that form the top end of the strut cylinder. We can then merge this object with the

strut object and weld the verts at the strut's upper end to the intersection verts, creating a strut that appears to intersect the hull of the plane without disturbing the faces in the hull.

Note that this has created T-intersections, a separate issue that is addressed later, but the payoff is that no new faces or verts are created.

Extra Verts

This problem occurs simply when an object contains unreferenced verts; that is, some verts are not used by any face.

When Is It a Problem?

Extra verts are almost always a bad thing because they cause the real-time rendering engine to work without getting anything in return.

How Do I Fix It?

The obvious thing to do is to delete free-floating verts as we work, but this is both dangerous and unreliable. Sometimes an apparently unreferenced vert is being used by a face that is not drawn, often because of backface rejection (use Display/Geometry/See Thru to prevent this). Also, unreferenced verts may be hiding under good verts.

Probably the easiest way to find out if the model contains unreferenced verts is this: In a temporary copy of the model, select all faces, then use Create/Face/Detach to create a single temporary object from all the faces. This will leave behind all unreferenced verts. Thus, after detaching all faces, any remaining objects are made only of unreferenced verts. Unfortunately, unless we don't mind that the entire model consists of a single object, we can use this knowledge only to go through the original model and delete these verts one by one.

Holes in Geometry

Holes refer to missing faces, or undesired gaps between faces, in an object. Holes in geometry are a very general problem that all 3D Studio users face at one time or another, and they bear mentioning here only because they are really a symptom that is not cured by simply building the missing face.

In real-time 3D environments, holes can be caused by many of the other issues discussed here: sorting problems, warped polygons, and T-intersections. If the real-time environment allows it, holes can also be caused by accidentally setting a face to be invisible or using a texture that has an invisible section in it.

When Is It a Problem?

Holes are a problem when they are noticeable during the application's execution. Though we fix holes in 3D Studio, we really want to be checking for them in the real-time application.

How Do I Fix It?

The solutions vary: sometimes simply welding a vert or building a replacement face will fix it. Other times, we'll end up revising the entire model, depending on what's wrong.

A hole in geometry should never exist, so when we find one, we should take it as a sign of trouble. It's smart to figure out what caused it because whatever it was may happen again if we don't understand it.

Trying to figure out why a hole exists can be like looking for lost keys. One approach is to be methodical and work through a list of possible causes. Another (harder, but often more effective) approach is to mentally retrace the steps that led to the hole.

For example, if we just applied a texture to the model and all of a sudden there are holes, perhaps it was the texture that caused it—perhaps we should try removing the texture and reloading the model. (If you're thinking, "How could a texture cause holes in a model?" transparencies are sometimes set by using a certain "transparent color" value in the palette, such as 0 or 255.)

Faces That Depend on Two-Sided Rendering

3D Studio has a material and rendering option "force two-sided," which causes all faces to be visible from both sides (disabling backface rejection). When building pre-rendered models, this works nicely to save some modeling time when the situation requires us to see both sides of a face.

When Is It a Problem?

If the real-time rendering engine can support two-sided faces, then there is some hope that we won't have to change any geometry—we can simply figure out how to allow 3D Studio's two-sided setting in the material to be imported into the real-time 3D environment. However, most real-time environments don't support two-sided face rendering, so any time two-sided faces are used, it's a problem.

How Do I Fix It?

First, identify the faces that need to be seen from both sides. Then, we build faces that face the other way.

To identify faces that need a second side, simply look at the model in 3D Studio using backface rejection (Display/ Geometry/ Backface) and spin the model in the User view, noting faces that should be seen from both sides but are not.

Once we find the one-sided faces, we can either hand-build faces that point the opposite direction from the existing faces, or we can copy the existing faces and flip their normals. Obviously, hand-building faces is slow and error-prone. However, by copying the faces, we've created a bunch of unnecessary new verts that we must weld to the originals. This can take as long as hand-building faces, depending on the situation.

In either case, the result should be new faces with normals opposite of the originals, using the same verts as the original.

T-intersections

T-intersections are formed when two faces have touching edges but don't share the same edge. The faces will appear to share an edge, but they really don't.

The term is derived from a common situation, in which one large face has two small faces with edges that touch, as shown in Figure 10.6.

At first glance, there doesn't appear to be anything wrong with this, but there is.

We can see that the large face (face3) has a large horizontal edge, and face1 and face2 have shorter horizontal edges that touch it. Because face1 and face2 must have a vert to connect to, we know there is a vert at the point labeled T-vert. Remembering that each face can only have three verts, we see that face3 is using its three verts elsewhere, and we should know that face3 does *not* use the T-vert.

When Is It a Problem?

T-intersections are a common cause of several problems, both in real-time environments and in normal pre-rendered modeling.

The worst problem they cause is ripping, or small, sliver-like gaps between faces in the real-time application. These gaps usually appear and disappear irregularly, flashing on and off. It's often difficult to diagnose the ripping as being caused by T-intersections because it can occur for many reasons, including errors in the rendering code. In fact, some might argue that T-intersections should be properly handled by the rendering code at all times, but today, that's not how it works.

The problem is rooted in the way the real-time rendering engine converts vector-based geometry of verts and faces to raster-based screen images. To fully explain the nature of the problem is beyond the scope of this book, but a simplistic summary is that the two short edges are converted to pixels slightly differently from the long edge on which they are supposed to lie. This means they're drawn not quite on (or slightly over) the long edge, which results in a slight crack (or a slight overplotting).

If the real-time graphics engine is based on integer math (rather than the more accurate, but slower floating-point math), this problem can also occur from accuracy issues—imprecise handling of vertex coordinates can also cause T-intersections to be have ripping problems.

Also, because T-intersections are continuous surface with unshared verts, they will cause problems related to unwelded coincident verts. For example, smooth-shading algorithms are confused by unshared verts, which can cause odd dark or light patches in what should be a smoothly curving surface.

How Do I Fix It?

T-intersections can be fixed in one of several ways.

Designing 3D Graphics

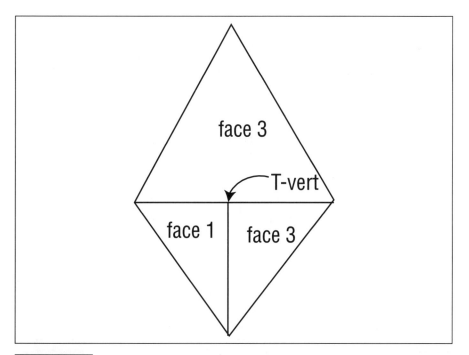

FIGURE 10.6 T-intersection.

The quick-and-dirty method is to move the T-vert slightly inside the big face, as shown in Figure 10.7.

This fixes the ripping problem by causing the slight variation in rendering to reveal the big face, not a big, ugly black tear.

The advantage to this fix is that it doesn't add any new faces, and it can be very quick to do. Also, it barely disturbs the mapping coordinates—the only disturbance comes from the slight movement of the vert.

On the other hand, it involves slightly distorting the geometry. That causes problems when the two smaller faces are not coplanar with the large face, or if they have different materials, making the change noticeable. Also, it fixes only the ripping problem—it doesn't fix the strange behaviors associated with unshared verts because the T-vert is still unshared.

The "correct" way to fix a T-intersection is to divide the large face and weld the resulting new vert to the T-vert.

The problem with this approach is that it adds a face (face4 in Figure 10.8) and messes up any mapping coordinates applied to the now-divided big face. The good news is that it doesn't add any verts to the model, and it fixes problems related to unshared verts.

Skinny Face

Skinny faces are extremely long, thin faces. Exactly how long and thin depends on the engine in question, but generally, if the longest edge is more than 100 times the length of the shortest edge, it's a skinny face.

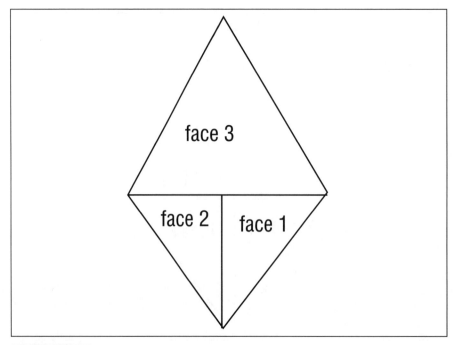

FIGURE 10.7   Overlapping T-intersection.

Once again, 3D Studio can handle this well, but real-time environments often can't, so this problem comes up when adapting a model intended for 3D Studio to a real-time environment.

When Is It a Problem?

Symptoms of skinny faces vary. One common problem occurs when they are part of a smooth-shaded object. The lighting values along the skinny face will be strange: too dark in the center, with a strange curved look along the skinny direction of the face. Other problems are related more to accuracy issues: If the rendering engine is integer-based, the small edge of the face may be accidentally collapsed, forming an invalid (two-sided) face. This step may occur at run time, but it can also occur during the translation from 3D Studio to the real-time environment.

Remember that this is an isolated problem in many cases. Many real-time environments can handle skinny faces, so don't worry about it unnecessarily.

How Do I Fix It?

To fix a skinny face, one must simply divide the face into less skinny pieces. It would be helpful to know what limits the real-time environment imposes for this

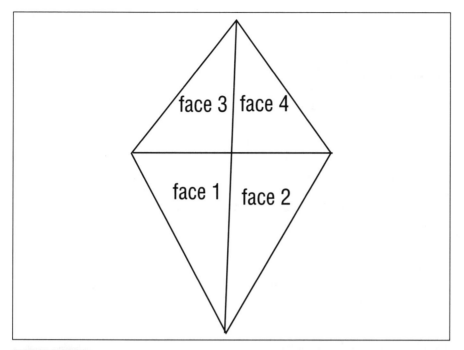

FIGURE 10.8   Fixed T-intersection.

type of face, but this is often more difficult for the programmer to find than using a trial-and-error approach to solving the problem.

Unwelded Vert

When two faces appear to share edges, but they have their own verts instead of using a common one, we have an unwelded vert.

Unwelded verts are a common problem when modeling for pre-rendered and real-time environments alike, but there are more problems related to them when working with a real-time application.

When Is It a Problem?

Ripping can be caused by unwelded verts in some real-time environments that have relatively low accuracy in their storage of vert coordinates.

Having unwelded verts are slow because the real-time environment must perform math operations for each vert. If the verts can be welded, we usually see a considerable performance improvement.

Smooth-shaded surfaces should not have unwelded verts (unless a sharp or strange transition is desired). This important limitation means that we can't have continuous mapping coordinates on any surface that must be smoothly shaded!

That can be an unpleasant surprise when we're designing an object; be sure to plan around it.

How Do I Fix It?

The simple answer is, weld the unwelded verts together (Modify/Vertex/Weld).

The real problem with unwelded verts is that, sometimes, they are necessary because of mapping issues. Often there is no easy way to fix the problem—we can't just weld the verts together because we'd damage our mapping coordinates.

Instead, we must balance the need for unique mapping with the need for welding verts. If we can figure out clever ways to map that don't require two sets of UV coordinates at a single vert, that is the best solution. Failing that, we must live with our unwelded verts and work the rest of the application around them.

Unsupported Material Attributes

This situation arises when a model is created using material attributes that are unsupported in most real-time environments.

When Is It a Problem?

This apparently simple problem can cause lots of work when the material attributes are extensively used in the actual construction. For example, when our real-time environment doesn't support transparency, but our 3DS model makes extensive use of opacity mapping to make windows in a wall, we must create geometry for these windows. That's a substantial amount of work, and it's worth mentioning that the resulting model will have an increased number of faces and verts.

In other cases such as bump mapping, it may not be missed if we leave it out. With those, we must decide if it's worth the time and energy to convert its effects.

How Do I Fix It?

The first approach is to see what the real-time environment can do. If possible, work with the programmer to make sure there aren't unknown capabilities that can be adapted to simulate the 3DS material attributes.

Once that option is exhausted (usually doesn't take long, alas), we must adapt. For each material attribute, we must decide if we will simply live without them or integrate an approximation of their effects in the texture map or the model itself.

When it's worth the effort to approximate the material attribute, the basic method is to render the model in 3D Studio, then use the resulting bitmap as the texture map on the real-time model. This is a form of paste-mapping, and it is surprisingly effective, but there are some issues to be aware of. See Chapter 8 for more description of this technique.

Coincident and Floating Faces

Coincident faces are simply faces that occupy the same area. For example, imagine we have a warehouse model, and we want to put a small, nonfunctional door on the wall. If we simply built the door as a pair of faces on the wall, we'd have coincident faces.

The usual solution is to move the door faces away from the wall slightly. This is called "floating faces."

When Is It a Problem?

Coincident faces are very problematic. First, they are very inefficient because they cause *overplotting*, which occurs when faces overlap each other during run time. This causes the graphics engine to work twice as hard to draw that area of the screen. This is a big deal usually, and often it's a good reason all by itself not to use coincident faces.

Also, overlapping coplanar surfaces are confusing to the polygon sorting algorithms, causing them to appear to be stuck in or behind the surface they float over. Though it's not common, this can also happen with floating faces due to tolerance issues (that is, the door verts' locations may be stored inaccurately enough to cause them to be coincident or inside the wall).

These problems are totally dependent on the specific rendering engine the model will be used in, and usually will only become apparent when the model is loaded into a real-time 3D environment.

The other issue with floating faces is one of smoothing. Because they don't share verts with the rest of the object, smooth shading algorithms don't take them into account when the lighting is calculated for that area. The floating faces are treated as unrelated, lighting-wise, to the surface they float above. This can be either a problem or a good thing, depending on the circumstances.

How Do I Fix It?

When we have a large surface and we want to put a flat detail against it, we can do one of two things:

- Put the detail into the texture map.
- Cut the underlying surface and make the detail share the resulting new verts.

Which is the best way? It's often better to model the detail, even though it adds faces, than to add more textures. Really, the correct answer depends on what our real-time environment can do best. If we have plenty of texture memory but we're already over our face/vert budget, we'll probably want to add a texture map instead of modeling. But if our environment doesn't handle texturing at all, we'll have to cut holes in the wall. This is a good question to answer with the graphics engine programmer.

CHAPTER 11

ANIMATION

This chapter covers the various methods of creating and handling animation data in real-time 3D graphics. It gives an overview of the various techniques, with an emphasis on hand-creating the animation data.

 Prologue

> *Animation:* Movement in the application that the user can see. This includes "fly-through" (camera motion in a static scene) as well as more typical examples, like a human walking or a car driving.

All real-time 3D models move on the screen, even if it's just the user moving around a still model a la VRML 1.0. To put it another way, if there is no motion whatsoever, then we could just pre-render the scene—forget RT3D entirely!

In general, animation is a relatively unstandardized area in RT3D; there are lots of ways to handle it, and each project seems to do it differently. Some projects rely totally on hand-created keyframes from the artist, while others (especially realistic simulators) don't use any hand-created animation data; instead, they use a simulation algorithm to generate the motion information directly.

Creating animations for RT3D is generally similar to animating normally: We create a series of keyframes using the normal 3D modeler's animation tools, then we export the keyframes to the graphics engine, which does the *tweening*, generating each frame's animation position. Simple implementations of animation only copy the keyframe to each run-time frame; fancier ones use a morph to create smooth transitions between keyframes. Obviously, we need to provide a lot fewer keyframes if the graphics engine will morph between them. We'll also need to provide a choreography sheet that shows how many frames of game time each step of the animation should get, including the computer-generated tweens.

Basic Types of Animation

There are several basic types of animation.

Camera Motion

The simplest method of animation is *camera motion*. In this scenario, the only motion in the scene is that of the user (whose viewpoint is often referred to as the "camera") moving around. No objects can be moved or modified, and nothing rotates or opens. For example, imagine that we're making a architectural fly-through. We don't have any moving objects like opening doors; we simply build the model and allow the user to move through it at will.

This animation data is usually provided from the user's input and generally does not require any work on the part of the artist, except sometimes setting up movement boundaries. Because of this, it's often not thought of as animation per se, but as any film student knows, a lot of animation possibilities are executed with camera motion alone.

This is the only type of animation that VRML v1.0 allows—it supports only camera motion as its animation. Almost every other real-time environment supports some of the other types as well.

Object Movement

Next complicated is *object movement*, the ability of objects in a scene to move relative to each other, but not move relative to themselves. For example, imagine a car-racing game where the opponent cars move relative to the ground and buildings, but their wheels don't bounce up and down; the entire car moves as a single unit.

This type of animation puts very few constraints on our choice of modeling method, though there may be some additional constraints, depending on how the graphics engine works. If the moving objects are allowed to intersect the non-moving ones, there may be problems that can be addressed only by building special, collision-friendly models.

Texture Animation

Texture animation is a relatively simple affair in which the texture maps are not static bitmaps, but are instead animated, often with a repeating pattern. Texture animation does not affect our choice of modeling method much, and if it's supported at all, it is surprisingly easy for the graphics engine to handle. The biggest problem is the amount of memory it takes to load the animation—it's very hard to justify even four frames of animation if they're using sorely needed texture memory that really could be used somewhere else.

Texture animation works really well when we're portraying motion that is faster than the frame rate (see the section on strobing in Chapter 14 for more information about this issue).

For example, we could use texture animation on a race car to portray spinning wheels. This would be especially appropriate because making the 3D model of the wheel actually spin would create horrible wagon-wheel strobing effects even if our frame rate was unbelievably high (above 60 Hz). The problem with animating the wheel the obvious way (by spinning it on its axis) is that we're missing an important motion cue: motion-blur. This is the visual anomaly humans experience when we see something that moves faster than we can really see. It's better to paint a blurred image that the user will recognize as motion, rather than try to simulate the motion itself. Of course, if our graphics engine can produce motion blur, this situation will be different, but few do.

Hierarchy Animation

Next up is hierarchy animation. In our racing game example, an example would be articulated, spinning wheels that are connected to each race car; a more common example is a human body with moveable arms and legs. *Hierarchy animation*

is very similar to object motion, but the difference is that the objects are connected in a hierarchy, which constrains their motion in logical ways. Also, the pieces in a hierarchic model are usually moving very close to each other and are sometimes intended to touch or intersect, requiring more careful planning in the model design as well as definition of the hierarchy.

3D Studio users are generally very familiar with hierarchy animation because that's 3D Studio's primary method of animation. It's great for certain types of motion, but it doesn't work well (by itself) for fluid, dynamic motions of organic shapes. The problem is that the motions are usually defined by simple rotations around a single axis, which very rarely happens in real life. It's possible, but very difficult, to define more complicated combinations of motion, without using other tools such as inverse kinematics.

Vertex-Based Animation (3D Morphing)

Vertex-based animation, also known as 3D morphing or vertex-level manipulation, changes some verts' XYZ values (relative to the rest of the object). It can be done in 3D Studio, and some graphics engines can do it at run time. As a form of real-time animation, it's a very powerful ability (though generally difficult for the graphics engine), and it allows us to do some amazing effects with very few polygons. As far as modeling goes, it means we'll have to pay careful attention to the number of vertices and their order, but this method of animation puts surprisingly few limitations on our motion.

3D morphing has several limitations. First, for it to work reasonably, the two models must have the same number of verts, and the same number of faces, connected in the same way. This restriction is pretty well known, and though inconvenient, it's possible to work with it. Because we often make morph targets by copying the original objects, we can usually not worry about this problem, but it greatly restricts our ability to make two dissimilar objects morph into each other.

Vert Order

When morphing with predictable results, the order of the verts and faces has to be the same. This is the weird one; it's one of the rare places that the concept even arises. The idea is that the order in which the verts appear in the list matters, even if the geometry is identical, between two morph targets.

In general, 3D Studio is not concerned with the order of the verts in the list (unlike some programs), so it doesn't offer any tools for controlling the order. A problem arises because morphing requires that the verts in the source and target objects have the same order. Some 3D Studio editing commands, such as mirroring and resetting the objects' transform, change the verts' order so it's very important that these commands are fully understood before we use them on a morph target. The best way to understand what these commands do is to play with them. Try out the various editing commands, using Shift to copy, then morph between them and see what happens.

Genus: Similar Types of Surfaces

We sometimes bump into a math concept when 3D morphing—a concept called genus, which is about similar surfaces. *Genus* means that if one object has a hole through it, like a donut, it can't cleanly morph into a sphere because the sphere doesn't have a matching hole. We can fake it by making the hole really thin, similar to how the hole in a fat bagel almost disappears, but we have to be careful to avoid closing it up or our geometry will get really funky (of course, if the goal is super-funky geometry, this may be just fine, but that's rarely the case).

Objects with no holes are said to be genus 0, while objects with one hole, like a donut, are genus 1, and so on. A ceramic coffee mug with a handle is genus 1—the cavity where the coffee goes isn't a hole; it's just a deep dent, topologically speaking. The handle, however, forms a hole.

If we make a polygonal sphere model and delete a face from it, we have not made a genus 1 object because the hole doesn't fully penetrate the sphere. Topologically, we've created an almost-closed bowl, which is genus 0. To make it genus 1, we'd have to Boolean-subtract a cylinder, like an arrow through an apple, leaving a hole that fully penetrates the sphere.

This area of math is called topology, and it's surprisingly relevant to our work. Topology also covers the air-tight concept, called closed surfaces. If this is new to you, it might well be worth while to study it a little (and enjoy already being familiar with many of the concepts after having played with them using our 3D tools!). For a starting point, see a book by M. A. Armstrong called *Basic Topology* (Springer-Verlag:1983) that has a relatively readable intro. Section 1.5 on classification sums up this information relating to genus and topological equivalence quite nicely in three pages, for the case of closed (air-tight) surfaces. Unfortunately, the author does not actually use the word genus in this section, but that's really the topic.

Skeletal Deformation

Skeletal deformation is animating objects by building and moving a skeleton inside them. It is very important to any project involving organic animation. Inverse kinematics and skeletal deformation, working together, are probably the best ways to animate organic models using 3D Studio. Best used for organic animation, skeletal deformation is a great way to animate people, animals, and aliens.

Skeletal deformation allows us to build a simple stick-man-like skeleton inside an organic model and connect them in some way. Then we can animate just the skeleton sticks, instead of the whole model. Particularly when we're working with contiguous models, skeletal deformation prevents us from having to make painstaking animation adjustments to the actual model itself. Some higher-end 3D software has this function built in, while most software (including 3D Studio) must rely on plug-in programs.

One quirk of this technique that adversely affects RT3D animation has to do with how it works on the geometry of the model. The bones of the skeleton are usually pencil-shaped boxes that exert an influence over the geometry of the model around them. This technology was developed primarily for use on models

with lots of faces and verts. Because of the low density of verts in RT3D models, the bones in a skeletal deformation structure do not have as many vertices over which to exert their influence. Therefore, to use this technique successfully with RT3D models, we will probably end up building busier skeletons than we would to animate the same kind of model with a greater density of vertices.

Animation Modeling Techniques

When modeling objects that are going to be animated in real-time, there are some additional concerns beyond the ones addressed above.

Collision Detection

Collision detection is the process by which the objects in a scene are made to interact realistically when they touch. Without collision detection, all the objects become ghost-like; they can drift through each other without any effect on each other (besides really messing up their appearance momentarily).

Most VRML browsers either don't have any collision detection, or allow the user to turn it off. It's worth playing with, at least once, just to see what we take for granted in most RT3D simulations. Without collision detection navigating becomes very difficult—we simply run through walls when we would expect to bump into them.

Graphics engines can calculate collision detection in several ways. The cheap way (cheap both in performance and realism) is to approximate the objects' shape with geometric primitives such as spheres and/or cubes. This makes it easy for the graphics engine to quickly figure out if the objects are touching each other, and where, but it's often difficult to reasonably represent a complex object with spheres and cubes. This can result in really weird collision interactions, or it can require a large number of spheres and cubes, offsetting the performance gain over doing full collision detection.

When it's more important that collision detection be accurate, we use the geometry of the object itself (as seems logical). The problem with this approach is that it can cost a lot of computation time to do.

Modeling RT3D Animation Joints

Joint: The place in a model where two separately moving pieces connect. Joints can be considered as points, surfaces, or even volumes. Examples include the human knee, a joystick's motion (both the stick and the buttons), cabinet hinges, or a car's power antenna.

Making realistic joints in RT3D is a major challenge, as anyone who's played modern RT3D video games can see. Several types of joints are commonly used for real-time 3D animation, and they all have pretty harsh drawbacks in one form or another. Let's go through them and explore their capabilities using a

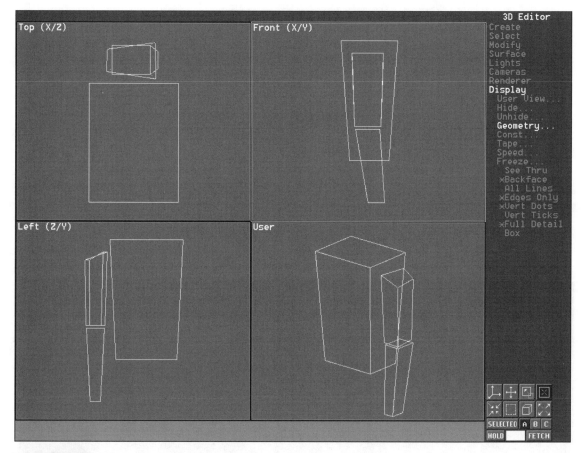

FIGURE 11.1   Example animated arm model.

simple animated arm example (Figure 11.1). This arm moves in a simple limbering-up motion, rotating the shoulder around two axes, and moving the elbow at the same time. You can see the motion in the JOIFLOAT.FLI animation on the CD-ROM.

Non-Intersecting Joints

Non-intersecting joints occur when the two objects never touch or intersect. These joints are simplest to design and model, but obviously, they don't work for every situation because there is a visible gap between the two objects. They solve a lot of problems when working with animation data that isn't precise or very controlled, such as motion capture-derived, because the two pieces don't have to have any kind of real alignment or constraints. Non-intersecting joints look rather strange if they are intended to represent a single, unified object like a human body.

The arm model shown in Figure 11.1 is an example of non-intersecting joints (though the elbow slightly intersects the biceps at one point). You can see the motion in the JOIFLOAT.FLI animation on the CD-ROM or by loading JOIFLOAT.PRJ into 3D Studio and examining the motion in the keyframer.

This model looks pretty weak—there are huge gaps around the elbows and shoulder. Part of this is necessary to prevent the object from intersecting, so let's take a look at a solution to this.

Overlapping Joints

Overlapping joints occur when any part of two objects cross each other at a pivot point, forming a shared volume in space, as the elbow/biceps intersection shows in Figure 11.2.

Overlapping joints are very easy to model, but unfortunately they can cause sorting problems for many rendering engines because most sorting algorithms assume that there are no shared volumes (that is, that no two objects overlap).

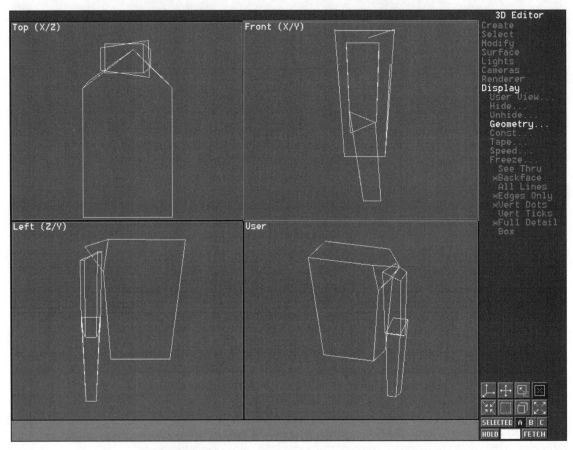

 FIGURE 11.2 Overlapping joints.

For some applications, the resulting inaccurate rendering isn't that bad—one object is drawn to appear completely in front of the other, and it can suddenly shift to appear behind the other— but it can be a problem if we require more fidelity in our model's appearance. Also, we won't have this problem if our graphics engine uses Z-buffering for its sorting method. 3D Studio uses Z-buffering, so the animation JOIOVERL.FLI shows this result.

Overlapping joints can also look funny even if they sort correctly— anyone can see that the joints do not bend seamlessly or perfectly—but this type of joint can be a reasonably good compromise for real-time animation. The joint appears solid, is simple to build (does not require too much special modeling or too many faces), and doesn't require any special code or excessive computing power to figure out.

Touching Joints

Touching joints occur when two objects have verts that don't move relative to each other. The joint can consist of a line of verts along an axis or a single pivoting vert like a trailer hitch ball.

The main criteria for a touching joint is that the two objects never overlap, but they do contact each other. This is shown in Figure 11.3 and demonstrated in JOITOUCH.FLI and JOITOUCH.PRJ.

Touching joints are relatively easy to design and model, and unlike overlapping joints, they do not generally cause sorting problems for the application. However, because they can only be pivots along a line or at a point, they are not useful for showing realistic portrayals of many kinds of "real-life" objects—for example, the shoulder modeled as a touching joint looks pretty bad, as we can see. On the other hand, it works fine for something like a spinning bicycle wheel or a door hinge.

Morphing Joints

When we're working with morphing animations, we have a very different problem when we make joints. The two pieces that moved separately are now a single object, and instead of one object moving relative to the other, a group of verts move relative to the rest of the verts. This causes the faces that connect the two groups to stretch and shift, creating a seamless joint without adding many faces for jointing. If done well, the result is a nice-looking, smoothly animating joint with no sorting problems, no creases, and no funny-looking gaps.

The bad part is that it takes a lot of math calculations to move verts like that—morphing is fairly slow, by real-time simulation standards—and it takes a graphics engine that supports the whole concept, and not all of them do. It can also cause distortion, sometimes severe, in the shape of the model because the verts are moving around. For example, one object may grow thin as it morphs; this doesn't happen with hierarchy-based animations because the objects themselves aren't changing shape.

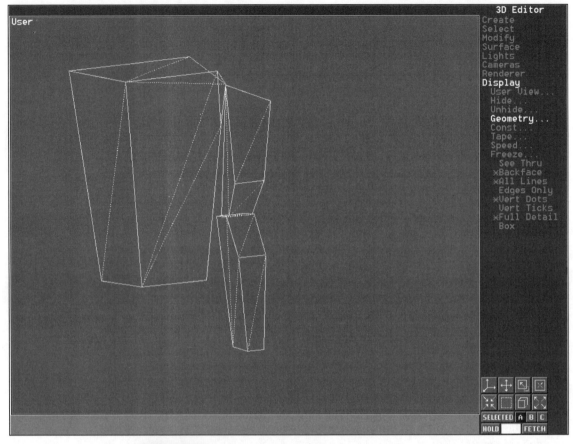

FIGURE 11.3 Touching joints.

Modeling joints for morphing mainly involves leaving enough verts and faces in the area so that when the object moves, it doesn't stretch out the surrounding geometry too much.

 Motion Capture

Motion capture is a really interesting area of animation. The dream is to scan motion in much the same way we scan textures out of the real world, thus extracting realistic motion straight from the source. It's still expensive and problematic for most animators as of this writing, but there's a huge demand for it, so we can expect it to get easier and less expensive very quickly. We'll briefly cover how it works here.

Motion capture technology uses several cameras (six, for example) to record the positions of reflectors in 3D space. These reflectors are attached to the vital parts and joints of an actor or athlete's body. The actor then goes through a series of motions, while the cameras record the positional information of the reflectors into a computer at 60 Hz or more. There are other ways of inputting the data besides the video-camera-reflector method, such as electromagnetic sensors and gyroscope-based methods.

Once the data is captured, the recorded tapes are analyzed (often not in real-time). To do this, the motion-capture software finds the reflectors on each frame of tape, correlates this with reflector's position on other tapes, and uses the locations of the cameras and geometry-oriented math to define a point in space from this data. As it works through the frames, it creates a list of 3D points for each reflector, thus capturing the motion. This animation data can then be applied to a model that has the necessary hierarchical data and control points already built into it.

Most of the motion capture animation for human forms in RT3D games uses segmented models. These models are easier to work with than contiguous morphing models because their basic parts have more freedom to move and rotate as necessary.

Motion capture is not a fully automatic process at all. There's potential for plenty of problems during the automated conversion of the video tape into 3D positions—for example, two reflectors may pass through the same spot, making the computer essentially guess which one is which in the next frame. Even when the motion capture data is applied correctly, usually some clean up work has to be done by hand. Specific keyframes of the animation might need tweaking, or the model itself may look strange here and there due to the way it was built. However, when it's done right, motion capture-based animation looks incredibly life-like.

ALL ABOUT
GRAPHICS
ENGINES

This chapter focuses on understanding graphics engines from a RT3D artist's perspective.

● Prologue: Why Read This?

We real-time 3D artists strive for the best tools and fewest constraints possible because if we don't, we'll unnecessarily compromise the quality of our art. To do that, we'll need to know where the limits can be pushed and what the consequences are.

The specific knowledge in this chapter directly affect the limits of the real-time 3D environment. When an artist ignores these issues, then tries to make the best models possible he or she may have a series of frustrating encounters with strange requirements like "all textures must be square." When the question "Why square?" is asked, the information in this chapter will be valuable.

Also, if we're expert RT3D artists, we'll be expected to know something about these issues regardless of our own need for the knowledge. Producers and managers will seek the expert artist's opinion on technical issues because the artist's perspective gives a technical view that isn't programmer-oriented. Without the general understanding of graphics engines that this chapter provides, artists may give some dangerously inaccurate technical feedback (like "Uh, I think we should be using 32-bit textures, cuz look what I could do in Photoshop with full alpha channels!").

● The Pipeline

The "graphics engine" as we've been using the term in this book is more precisely called the application's pipeline. What, exactly, is a pipeline? It's not a common term, even among game developers, but it's really an important concept to understand when we're thinking about graphics engines.

> *Pipeline:* In the context of RT3D, a pipeline is a list of steps that are done at run time for each frame.

The term pipeline comes from the somewhat dubious analogy of "graphics calculation = fluid flow": Each step in the graphics calculation can be seen as a section of pipe through which the answer flows. A better analogy is a factory that takes in raw materials (user input), consumes resources (computing power), and dumps out a finished product (rendered frames) in a continuous cycle. Pipeline is the accepted standard term for this concept, though, so we'll continue to use it here.

The pipeline is the heart of a RT3D application. It is the code that is working when the 3D action is happening; it doesn't have anything to do with the start-up screens, configuration, playing any cut-scene movies, or anything else like that.

Designing 3D Graphics

The definition says that there are a list of steps that are always done to create a frame on the screen. What are these steps?

A Computer's-Eye View of the Pipeline

Here is what goes on in a pipeline, in the closest possible approximation to plain English. In these steps, "we" refers to the computer (empathize with the computer to understand how it thinks!). Where we need an example, let's imagine it's a non-Z-buffered 3D driving game (see Figure 12.1).

All of these steps take about one-tenth of a second to do on a normal 486 PC, for a reasonably complex commercial RT3D computer game.

Pipeline Bottlenecks

> *Pipeline bottleneck:* Any single step in a pipeline that is consuming an unusually large amount of time. The term comes from the "graphics calculation = fluid flow" analogy: A wide-necked bottle, like a canning jar, flows faster than a narrow neck (like a beer bottle).

The obvious question from the definition of pipeline is: Which of these steps takes an unusually long time? This is a good question to ask, but it's very hard to answer. It depends on too many varying factors to be printed in a book, and it will probably have to be answered by the maker of the graphics engine (i.e., the programmer). For example, imagine that the programmer tells us that the sorting step is very slow with this pipeline; it's taking 40 percent of the processing time on that one step alone. In this case, the sorting is clearly the bottleneck.

Bottlenecks can be caused either by hardware or software. Hardware bottlenecks are the result of a limited graphics processing ability of the target platform, and software bottlenecks are the result of either poor programming or an intentional trade-off in performance for some other important benefit (like versatility). When we have a bottleneck, whether it's caused by hardware or software, the resulting problem will show up as a slow step in the graphics pipeline.

Artists Can Fix Bottlenecks!

Once we (we're artists, again) know which step is the bottleneck, the obvious thing to do is try to alleviate it. As artists, we can make a huge difference just by adjusting the way we model. If we keep the bottleneck in mind as we work, we can influence our modeling to make the problem less severe, thus improving the performance.

Let's look at each step in the graphics pipeline and figure out how each affects the way we make our artwork. For each step, a percentage estimate gives a rough idea of how much CPU time that step takes. These percentages are meant to be very rough estimates; each engine is different, and they're also heavily affected by every other part of the application, including the hardware capabilities, the rendering window size, and so on. That's why they don't add to 100 percent perfectly—they're vague estimates only!

Update camera

We start the pipeline by figuring out where the user's viewpoint (the camera) moved. This is where we gather the user input (like joystick movement) and use this in our physics simulation to calculate the camera's latest XYZ location and rotation in the 3D world.

Update opponents

For moving objects like opponent vehicles, we also need to update their locations. To do that, we have to run AI routines for the objects that we control, and if it's a network game, we query the network for network players' inputs.

3D object morphing/moving

This is where we update any animated objects in the scene. If the animation is scripted, we'd read the script and update the objects' position accordingly. If the animation changed depending on input (like steering the wheels of a car), we'd take the user's input and change the objects to match.

Collision detection

Now that we know where everything is in the world, we look to see if something hit something else. If we end up deciding that some objects hit each other, we take them and recalculate their locations based on our physics simulation, and trigger special effects like an explosion animation or a sound effect.

Sound dynamics

If we're doing cool effects like 3D sound and Doppler shifting, this is when we'd do it. Also, if the normal background/soundtrack music requires constant attention, we'd handle that at this stage, as well.

2D Animation

If there are any 2D animations playing, like an explosion, we load up the next frame and deal with it here.

↓

Graphics Pipeline

Now that we've got all the objects arranged and the housework done, we are ready to draw the scene. This step usually consumes most of the time, and it's where the 3D art affects things.

Here are the steps within the graphics pipeline.

1. **Gross culling:** First, we make a list of all the objects (cars, trees, track, grandstands, etc.), and then we remove the objects that the player can't see because they're off the camera or too far away.

2. **Transform to camera coordinates:** This step puts all the objects in terms of the camera's coordinate system, where one axis (Z, for example) points away from the camera. This makes it possible to quickly figure out which faces are in front of the others because we can simply look at their Z values to determine their distance from the camera.

3. **Culling:** Now we break our object list into a list of faces and get rid of any non-visible ones. Ones that point away from the cam era because they're one-sided are discarded. We check for any faces that are outside the camera's field of view. This may sound like the same thing as gross culling, but that step checked for whole objects; now we're checking each face in the object.

4. **Sorting** is the step when we shuffle our list so the faces that are farthest from the camera come first. This is important because we'll draw them first, then if other, closer faces overlap the far-away faces, we can just draw them in the list order, and they'll come out right: The closest faces will draw on top of the far-away faces.

5. **Projection:** Next, we flatten the faces to 2D outlines on the screen, making the far-away faces appear smaller (the programming term for this step is perspective projection).

6. **Render:** Finally we are ready to make the rendered frame. We start out by copying any background bitmaps onto a blank frame, and then we render each face in the list, overwriting the background as we go. We render faces by filling the 2D projected outline with a copied piece from the texture map. We have to do this pixel by pixel, and it usually takes a while. Here's what goes on: for each pixel that the face covers on the screen, copy the pixel out of the texture map, adjust its brightness according to lighting, depth cueing, and other effects, and then copy it onto the screen. On PCs without special graphics hardware, this step can take a relatively long time.

7. **Blit:** This step is where we take our completed frame and put it on the video card, where the user can see it. This sounds easy, but often this can take a very long time if the graphics hardware was not designed to handle it very well.

FIGURE 12.1   The pipeline.

CHAPTER 12 • **All about Graphics Engines**   **311**

Gross Culling (2 percent)

To summarize, gross culling operates on what we'll call pieces (similar to 3DS objects). It is not usually a bottleneck step; in fact, it is a step that saves lots of effort for the rest of the pipeline, but only if the objects are organized to cooperate with it.

For example, if we make a vast, 4,800-face racetrack landscape for a driving game and we divide it up into 16 simpler pieces of 300 faces each, the gross culling can toss out a lot of the model (perhaps 12 of the 16 pieces) without even looking at how many faces or textures the rejected piece used. That leaves 1,200 faces for the rest of the pipeline to deal with.

If that landscape had all been one piece, the gross culling could never reject it (because the camera would always be showing part of it), so then each of the 4,800 faces would have to be handled by the rest of the pipeline up to the face-level culling.

Some pre-processors automate the division of large objects into gross-culling-friendly smaller pieces, so this may not be anything we artists can control, but sometimes it's up to us to divide our model into these pieces. Usually that's done by separating large objects into smaller ones.

To make good use of gross culling, we should to understand how it works, and this varies a lot. Sometimes the engine approximates the pieces with a bounding sphere. Other times, a large rectangular prism is used; again, it's not done very consistently from engine to engine, so you'll have to ask the programmers how it works for yours.

Once this is known, we can attempt to divide the scene into pieces that will be easy and accurately represented by this sphere (or whatever) approximation. For example, with a spheroid approximation, the pieces should not have a very large aspect (i.e., not be skinny) if possible. Skinny pieces require large spheres that don't represent them well, so the gross culling won't do a very good job of deciding whether the object can be seen. How many pieces should you make? Generally, there is a trade-off point, but (surprise!) it totally varies depending on your graphics engine and model. Perhaps a good rule of thumb is no more than 300 faces per piece, but if you hear differently from the programmer, believe what they say.

If the gross culling isn't well organized, it just means that the objects will render more slowly, not that they won't be drawn at all.

Camera Transform (3 percent)

This stage acts on each vertex in the scene (not counting the pieces that have been culled already), and it is a somewhat difficult step for the computer. If we were to reduce our vertex count, it would benefit this stage.

Culling (6 percent)

This step acts on each face, and it's a pretty lightweight step, but if there are a lot of faces, it can add up. It's where backface rejection happens, as well as what's called *clipping*—dealing with faces that stick off the screen.

Sorting (8 percent)

Sorting acts on each face, and its performance price really varies, but generally it's not a huge deal.

Every graphics engine seems to handle sorting differently, but in general there are two basic types: polygonal-based sorting and Z-buffered sorting. In general, Z-buffered is slower but more accurate, and polygonal is fast, but problematic. Z-buffering consumes a lot of memory, but it handles intersecting polygons well.

Under polygonal sorting, there is another split between dynamic sorting, which means the computer thinks about sorting for each frame, and static sorting, in which the world is sorted before run time, and then only very simple sorting calculations are done for each frame. BSP-tree sorting, for example, is static.

Projection (2 percent)

Projection, the process of making 2D outlines from the 3D faces, is a relatively mild performance issue. Projection is related to the number of faces.

Rendering (70 percent)

Rendering is generally where the performance problems with PC-based graphics engines lie. It goes with the number of pixels on the screen—50 percent is true for 320×200 screens; it's more like 60–70 percent for 640×480 or higher screens.

It seems that the transparent parts of a texture map (for example, the area between the branches in a tree texture) should render faster than the areas with detail, but they don't usually. This occurs because the renderer is kind of distracted from its routine: It has to look at that transparent pixel, realize that it is transparent, and decide not to plot anything. On the other hand, the render can skip the lighting step and the pixel copy step, so theoretically this could outweigh the time to make the "don't render" decision.

Most issues with rendering are not anything we can help with, except for one.

Overplotting

One of the most important issues artists need to know about with rendering is overplotting. If there are any overlapping faces, the renderer generates those pixels twice, which is (obviously) really bad for performance. This problem is so common that it has a name—*overplotting*—and it is important to avoid, especially for machines that already have slow rendering.

Lots of times, we artists can do something about overplotting. For example, if we're modeling a forest scene, we have a lot of trees, and they all overplot over each other, causing horrible frame rates. What can we do? We can remove trees, of course, but we can (maybe, if we're clever) redesign the trees into clumps so they don't overlap within the clumps. If the user won't get in the area (for example, the user is looking at the forest from the road), we can make complexity in the textures and simplify the geometry in exchange. For example, with the trees, we can make a single texture that shows masses of clumped trees and put this on a far-away object. Then, in the relative foreground, we can put a few trees that will move against the complicated background and provide some sense of 3D-ness. They'll still overplot a little, but it will be a large improvement over a mass of overlapping trees.

For another example, imagine we have a row of buildings—it's an urban street scene. When our camera points down the street, all of the sides of the buildings pile up on top of each other, creating a massive overplotting problem. If we modify the sides of the buildings so they are like Hollywood sets—either the buildings meet at the edges or they have only short side walls that end a few feet from the front—then we can eliminate most of those side faces. Of course, for buildings that are taller than their neighbors, we'd keep their side faces. See the open environment exercise in Chapter 10 for a more detailed example of this.

Overplotting is generally a scene design problem, not an object modeling problem. Most objects aren't too bad for overplotting (though modeling a book with 200 textured page faces lying on top of each other should bring any renderer to its knees!). Because we don't know where the user's going to go in our scene, we have to be pretty tricky to prevent horrible overplotting problems from any arbitrary angle when our scene is prone to overplotting.

One way to do this is to limit what the user sees. If we know that the user is in a room, for example, and they definitely can't see beyond that room, then the programmers can make a special gross-culling that just gets rid of any object that's not in the room. With this design, we can make huge, complicated houses with side-by-side rooms that would normally have horrible overplotting problems, but it won't be a problem for us because our graphics engine is carefully designed to support it.

For this reason, many game developers write their own graphics engine instead of using a preprogrammed commercial library. They need the full flexibility of custom-written code to make the game passably fast and still have all the features (perspective-corrected texture mapping with dynamic lighting, etc.) that they want.

Blitting (6 percent)

There isn't much we artists can do about blitting. Platforms with specialized graphics hardware generally have solved this bottleneck, but PC developers can still face it, as we'll see below.

Hardware Bottlenecks

Most commercial PC-based games have a reasonably common computer, like a 486/33 computer with a basic VGA card, as their target platform. This computer is simply not designed for high-speed graphics rendering. This usually means there will be some really severe bottlenecks that are caused by the hardware.

For example, this 486 has to use its CPU to do the rendering step in the graphics pipeline; that's like paying a high-priced lawyer to address envelopes. The rendering step is much better done by a chip that is custom-designed for such a

task; however, until all our beloved users go and buy such a chip (like a fancy 3D graphics board), we have to make our application work with what they have.

The blitting problem is even more annoying. With a badly designed system, the CPU has to copy the screen bitmap from system memory to video memory, which is like making our lawyer go drive the letters to their recipients' houses one by one! It's such a severe problem that a lot of effort has been made to solve it—and it isn't as bad as it once was.

However, if we're making an application for a computer with dedicated graphics hardware, like a Silicon Graphics workstation or a Nintendo Ultra-64 game machine, the hardware may be quite well designed and offer no large obstacles. In this case, the limitation becomes the design of the hardware. For example, most dedicated graphics chips are made to process triangles, and many game developers output polygons with more than three sides. If they don't modify their graphics engine, these polygons won't fit through the pipeline and will either not work or be handled separately (i.e., very slowly). This is a very obvious situation, and most developers take care not to attempt what the hardware is designed specifically to do.

What if there is no obvious bottleneck, but there's still a performance problem? It's tempting to think that we don't have to worry about the way we model because there's no one clear cause of our slow frame rate, but that's not true. We simply need to improve all areas of our models more or less equally.

 # Graphics Engine Variations

This section will give a brief overview of the variations in features and capabilities that RT3D graphics engines offer today. Keep in mind that this information has a shelf life comparable to canned fish: Make sure it's still good before using it after a year or so. In other words, if you're reading this in 1998 or later, a lot of this information probably has changed.

Color: Paletted versus True-color

Graphics engines use either paletted, 8-bit-per-pixel color or true-color, which uses 16 or 24 bits per pixel. This is a big split—and not only because of the obvious fact that more color data means more work for the engine.

Palette Theory

The real difference is the concept of *palette*. This idea, born from the need to show more than 256 preset shades, is really quite powerful. Let's compare unpaletted color to paletted.

With unpaletted true color, the usage is pretty straightforward. To store a single true-color pixel, we divide its color into red, green, and blue components, then store these three numbers (see Chapter 7 for more on this). With this scheme, we don't care if that particular shade is used anywhere else in the picture.

With 24-bit color, each bit can choose from the 16,777,216 possible combinations of color. That is a heck of a lot of choice; 24-bit art does not suffer from the lack of just the right shade.

With 16-bit color, we are limited to five bits each for red, green, and blue (plus one left over, which is sometimes used as an extra green bit, and other times unused.). That means we have 32,768 (or 65,536 if we use the sixteenth bit) colors. That's still enough to show any color possible, though we may sometimes see places where we wish we had a shade in between two other choices.

With 8-bit color, we're down to 256 different combinations. That's just not enough to define any color possible; if we tried to represent the whole spectrum, we'd end up with enormous gaps in certain areas.

Inventing Paletted Color

Imagine that we were the first people to try to create artwork with 8-bit color. We'd sit down to draw our vision and quickly find that there is no way to create a beautiful pueblo scene because we only have six shades of brownish red. So, we go to the programmer and say, "Hey, I can't paint my pueblo scene without more brownish reds!" The programmer says, "OK, I'll change some of the shades from the lime-green area into more brownish reds." Once the programmer does, you now have 16 shades of brownish reds, and the art looks awesome. Sure, we can't paint any lime-green shades now, but who cares? Those colors are unnecessary, anyway, if we're painting a pueblo scene.

This is the logic from which palettes were born. Instead of trying to use 8 bits of data to represent any possible color in the world, we make a list of our 256 favorite colors and promise to use them, and only them. Each of these colors can be defined very accurately; with plenty of bits for red, green, and blue, but we can only use 256 of them. That's our palette.

From the programmer's perspective, palettes are look-up tables. Each pixel, instead of storing a red, green, and blue component, stores an index in a table (Figure 12.2). When the computer draws that pixel, it takes the index number and looks up the RGB values from the palette look-up table. This is an extra step, but it can offer some very cool payoffs.

This is the same idea behind having faces that use a vert's XYZ, instead of storing their own, and some of the same benefits apply. Just as moving a vert means all the faces that connect to it move automatically, if we change the RGB value of a certain palette entry, all the pixels that use that entry will change automatically. It's easy to do at run time, so we can do some cool tricks.

For example, let's say we want to make our pueblo painting (it's a 640 × 480 image) all dark and gloomy by cutting the lightness level of everything by half at run-time. If we're using 24-bit unpaletted color, the graphics engine has to edit all 300,000 pixels in the picture, but with paletted color, it can just change the palette RGB values, and there's only 256 of them. Because all 300,000 pixels get their RGB values from the palette, they'll all change color (Figure 12.2).

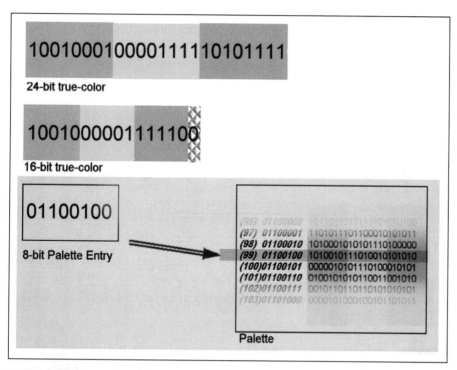

FIGURE 12.2 True-color compared to paletted color.

Palette Tricks

We can go farther with this idea by making certain entries in the palette really special. For example, if we want to have working taillights on a car, we can wire the brake on/off value from the simulation so it changes a certain palette entry from dull red to bright red. Then we use that palette entry only for the polygons or texture pixels that make up brake lights, and presto! Working brake lights!

The problem with this kind of trickery is that most image-editing tools don't support it. When the tool is converting a 24-bit image to 8-bit paletted color, these special palette entries look like a normal color to them, and they can get incorporated into the wrong area of the bitmap by accident. Because we have only 256 shades, we generally need every shade possible, and the image-editing tool has the same idea when it's remapping from 24-bit to 8-bit, or using the air-brush, or doing a Gaussian blur, or any editing where it has some choice in the exact color that's being used.

Ideally, we could just tell the image-editing tool, "hey, don't use palette entry 256 because it's not a real color; it means invisible," but it usually does not allow this kind of input. We have to lie to the program and set the color for that entry to something that is so disgusting that there is no way on earth the tool would find a use for it. Then, once we're done making the normal areas of our image, as a last step, we paint over the areas that are special effects with our gross special-

effect color. Somehow, we tell the graphics engine what the RGB values for the gross color should really be at run time.

Lighting

Graphics engines usually do lighting differently from each other. The following lists the basic categories of lighting. Some engines support dynamic lighting, in which the lights move around at run time, while others do not.

No Lighting

In a texturing graphics engine with no lighting calculation, it simply copies the pixel from the texture to the screen as it renders. Obviously, this is the quickest way to render but without any lighting, the scene can look pretty weak. There is a big exception to this, however. If we have a fully texture-mapped world (and plenty of texture memory), we can "pre-light" our textures and get a really nice-looking world without any lighting model. What this means is we calculate lighting into our texture (much as painters do), so the objects' shape is defined within the texture. This usually means doing a paste-map solution (see Chapter 7 for more information).

Static

When the graphics engine handles static lighting, it is first handled by the pre-processor. All the faces in the scene are compared to the light source and assigned a number that indicates how bright they should be. Then, at run-time, the brightness of each pixel is multiplied by that number as it is put on the screen. This is reasonably quick, but it's not dynamic lighting—the lights can't change as the game is played.

Dynamic

In a graphics engine that does dynamic lighting, it checks the direction of the light source as the face is being rendered. If the face needs to be darkened, the graphics engine adjusts the texture's color appropriately as it puts the texture on the screen. This is the slowest (but coolest) kind of real-time lighting.

Terms

Real-time lighting uses a slightly different set of terms and concepts than 3D Studio. Not all aspects of a light are necessarily available to the artist to control; it's a good idea to find out which parts of 3D Studio's lighting information are used, and which are not. The maker of the preprocessor should know this.

Directional

Directional lighting occurs when the scene's lighting is defined by a single direction and color value. There is no direct equivalent for this in 3D Studio, but it works something like ambient combined with a far-away omni light. This results

Designing 3D Graphics

in a lighting effect in which all objects appear to be lit from the same infinitely far-away light. This is good for sunlight or basic room lighting, not for local lighting effects like spotlights. If the light's direction is changed in real-time, the user sometimes gets a strange motion sense, like the world itself is spinning.

Point-Source

Point-source is what 3D Studio calls an omni light: a single point that radiates light in all directions. The fall-off distance is usually controllable. Very few real-time engines support 3D Studio-style spotlights; these lights are used instead.

Most real-time engines have at least directional lighting, and many also have point-source lighting.

Possible Range of Motion (DOF)

Most graphics engines have 6 DOF (remember, DOF stands for Degrees of Freedom; it means the number of ways the player can move in the world). 6 DOF is the maximum.

Some engines, based on technology used in Doom, have 4 or 5 DOF; they leave out rotation around the X or Z axis in order to improve the frame rate. These engines are based on a really different fundamental design; it's not just a matter of leaving out a couple DOFs. They are rooted in 2D maze game design, and they usually have a lot of limitations besides DOFs, when compared to 6 DOF games. That's not to say they are inherently worse; they just have a different set of trade-offs. They have better frame rates, and dropping a couple DOFs can allow for some other performance benefits, but obviously, not having full motion possible is a constraint.

Shading Type

Most graphics engines offer several shading types. Gouraud, or smooth, shading involves a very different set of calculations from flat shading, and it is slower to render. With flat shading, each *face* is assigned a normal, and its color is determined from that normal's angle and the light source.

In Gouraud shading, each *vertex* is assigned a normal. Of course, verts don't point in any particular direction because they're points in space, so their normal has to be averaged from the surrounding faces (or generated some other way—in 3D Studio, that's what smoothing groups do). Then, when the rendering engine renders each face, it gets the three normals from each of the verts (ignoring the face's own normal) and uses them to figure out how bright the corners of the face are. Based on this brightness, it makes a gradient fill across the face, which is very similar to how vertex coloring works.

Background

> *Background:* A bitmap that appears behind all other objects in the scene in the application. Also called horizon map.

Some graphics engines can show background, but they don't support full 6 DOF motion for it, even if they support 6 DOF motion for everything else in the scene. This improves frame rate, but it can give strange motion cues to the player. Also, these backgrounds cannot usually react to lighting changes. Other engines leave it to the artist to make background tents that surround the rest of the scene with a big textured sphere or hemisphere. These are usually slower than the first kind of engine because the background geometry is being processed more by the pipeline, but the motion and lighting are correct.

Memory Usage

Memory usage is an issue that permeates all aspects of real-time 3D modeling, but mainly it arises when texturing. Usually, artists can simply ask the project leader how much memory maximum is available for artwork, or how many textures and faces can be used. With any luck the project leader will have worked that out already, but sometimes they don't know either. And, all too often, it simply isn't considered until it becomes a problem.

In unorganized projects, this usually comes up when the artist builds the first complex scene with lots of textures, and it won't load. This is followed by a troubleshooting session, during which the problem is determined to be insufficient memory. Perhaps a slightly heated argument ensues, and finally comes the meeting in which a basic memory budget for each scene is hammered out. In a well-organized project this meeting will be held *before* the artist creates any artwork; regardless, this is an important meeting for the project.

You Shouldn't Have to Know This, But...

We artists should never have to get into technical memory issues this deeply, but sometimes it is necessary. So, here's how to figure out how much memory is available for artwork: First, we'll need to know how much memory we have maximum, and then we'll subtract the memory already used. If we didn't forget anything, and there aren't any strange memory tricks like DOS's 640K stuff, the remaining memory is available for game data.

At a minimum, memory will be consumed by the following:

- Operating system—Its memory usage is usually available from the OS itself. In DOS, MEM /C will tell you, for example. The graphics engine may also tell you this.

- Graphics Engine—If the application uses a prewritten graphics engine, its memory usage is usually in the documentation that came with the engine. This information sometimes accounts for memory used by the OS as well as the engine.

- Application code—This refers to the code written by the programmer that constitutes the application itself. It includes code to handle physics and motion of the user, AI behavior, history recording, and so on. How much memory it uses is a question for the programmer, and it will have to be estimated if you're doing this at the beginning of the project.

Designing 3D Graphics

- Sound code and game-play data—Sound is frequently a separate entity from the rest of the application, especially in computer game architecture, and can be overlooked when counting application code space requirements. If a sound library is used, the documentation will usually tell how much memory is required.

Given all the numbers above, we could theoretically figure out how many objects, faces, and textures the available memory translates to. To really do this, we'd need some really detailed knowledge about how memory is used and allocated that is beyond the scope of this book.

The programmer is often responsible for determining how much memory is allocated for the art, and will tell you how many textures, verts, and faces that will equal.

Specific Real-Time 3D Platforms

Now that we know more than we ever thought we would about how graphics engines work, let's take a look at some of the differences between graphics engines we are likely to encounter.

Types of Graphics Engines

There are two somewhat distinct categories of graphics engines. Full-featured products offer a wide array of features, such as physics and collision functions, complicated lighting options, advanced support for different hardware-accelerated video card, and a solid, well documented, easy-to-use programming interface. On the other end of the spectrum are simple, specialized 3D graphics libraries that offer high 3D graphics performance without complicated, extraneous functions.

In a general sense, the engines vary along the features/performance axis—if an engine gains versatility and ease of use, it's usually at the expense of performance or quality of support utilities—and vice versa. Price, oddly enough, does not factor in very consistently. Though generally full-featured engines are more expensive, some companies give away their graphics engines with ulterior motives (such as getting their related hardware widely supported by applications), while others charge tens of thousands of dollars. Usually, the price issue comes in when we look at such issues as technical support, and maintenance of the engine.

Comparing Performance between Two Engines

For most applications, performance (frame rate) is usually the most important factor. The question "how many frames per second does your graphics engine draw?" is a horrible question because frame rate is not determined by the

graphics engine alone—it's the end result of many factors, most of which are out of the engine's control.

For a fair comparison, the infinite quantity of outside influences should be identical between the engines being compared; however, this is usually impossible to do. If we understand how these differences affect the performance of a graphics engine, we can weigh any discrepancies with some idea of how they should affect the engine.

Obviously, to make a fair comparison, each factor should be equal; however, it's also important that the factors be as similar as possible to our intended application's basic design and target platform. For example, if we're writing an application intended to run smoothly on 486 PCs, it would be a mistake to compare graphics engines running on identical graphics-accelerated 586 PCs.

Scene Construction

In general, the RT3D art that's used has a huge impact on frame rate. Two scenes with the same polygon count can be very different in frame rate. When comparing engines, it's very important to use scenes that are as similar as possible to your planned application. If you plan to build an underground tunnel world, don't pay attention to demonstrations that show outdoor scenes! Specific issues that affect frame rate in scene construction are as follows:

- Shared vertices—Some engines can handle multiple UV coordinates per vertex or have other ways of allowing polygons to share vertices that 3D Studio does not.

- Type of polygons—Some graphics engines are optimized for rendering only triangles. If the database is composed exclusively of triangles, these engines will have an advantage when compared to their more versatile competitors. Depending on how your scene will be modeled, it may be helpful to use a comparable scene but composed of many-sided polygons where appropriate, and use this scene to see how the polygonal engine's performance improves.

- "Clone" objects—Tricky programmers can take advantage of multiple copies of the same object, improving rendering speed but putting limits on how the cloned objects can be manipulated.

This can be perfectly fine as long as the limits don't impede on your scene design; that is, if you plan for eight little mice to dance independent dances, don't base a frame-rate measurement on an example scene that shows eight mice with exactly the same movement.

Rendering Window Size

Rendering window: The area on the screen that is drawn by the graphics engine—the area in which the 3D action happens. This is opposed to the area of the screen that is devoted to dials, gauges, text, and 2D artwork in most applications.

Rendering window size and resolution combine to yield a rendered pixel count: the number of pixels that were created from 3D. Obviously, the two engines should be producing the same pixel count if possible.

Software—Commercial Graphics Engines

Here's a list of graphics engines that support texture mapping and 6 DOF, with some of their major features detailed. For a fully detailed list with links to the engines' Web pages, see the Web site: http://www.cs.tu-berlin.de/~ki/engines.html. The list printed here is meant only to illustrate the variations among features commonly available in commercial graphics engines; if you are looking for a comprehensive list or want more information about any of these engines, please don't use this list! Go to the Web site listed above for a really thorough, updated list that is intended for people shopping for a graphics engine.

OpenGL

OpenGL is a software interface for applications to generate interactive 2D and 3D computer graphics. OpenGL is designed to be independent of operating system, window system, and hardware operations, and it is supported by many vendors. OpenGL is available on PCs and workstations. OpenGL provides a wide range of graphics functions: from rendering a simple geometric point, line, or filled polygon, to texture mapping NURBS curved surfaces.

Among its features are the following:

- Geometric primitives (points, lines, and polygons)
- Raster primitives (bitmaps and pixel rectangles)
- RGBA (24-bit plus alpha channel) or color index (paletted) mode
- Hidden surface removal (depth buffer)
- Alpha blending (transparency)
- Anti-aliasing
- Texture mapping
- Atmospheric effects (fog, smoke, and haze)
- Polynomial evaluators (to support non-uniform rational B-splines)
- Stencil planes
- Feedback, selection, and picking

The OpenGL functions described are provided on every OpenGL implementation to make applications written with OpenGL easily portable between platforms. All licensed OpenGL implementations are required to pass the Conformance Tests and come from a single specification and language binding document.

RenderWare

RW is a portable 3D API for DOS, Windows, Mac and X-Windows.
Among its features are the following:

- Z-buffer and scanline renderer
- Multiple colored light sources (distant, point, and spot lights)
- Multiple cameras
- Gouraud lighted, dithered, transparent, perspective texture mapping
- Animated textures and environment mapping
- Object picking
- Materials support
- 3D Sprites
- Backdrop images
- Depth cueing
- Support for graphics accelerator cards like the GLINT chip
- Support for stereo glasses and headsets
- DFX, 3DS, and VRML converters
- 900 pages of documentation

BRender

BRender (Blazing Render) is a complete system with an applications interface, graphics libraries and device drivers.
Among its features are the following:

- Z-buffer and scanline renderer
- Hierarchical, linked objects
- Gouraud shading
- Multiple cameras and light sources
- Collision detection
- Sprite scaling and deformation effects
- 486PC, could very easily be ported to the 3D0, Saturn, FM Towns, or Jaguar
- A 32-bit library, with versions for Watcom or MS Visual C
- Support for hardware accelerators like GLiNT
- Planed: fog-effects, depth-cueing, anti-aliasing, and covered light sources such as spotlights
- 140 pages of documentation

Designing 3D Graphics

Reality Lab

RL is a commercial 3D library by Microsoft RenderMorphics. Version 2.0 has the following features:

- Wire frame, flat, Gouraud and Phong shading models
- Perspective corrected texture mapping in any shading model
- Environment and motion video mapping
- Full transparency, including alpha maps for textures
- Z-buffering
- Animated backgrounds with optional depth information
- Multiple, movable, colored light sources
- 4-, 8-, 16-, 24-bit color depths in both ramp and RGB modes
- SVGA and Windows 3.1/95/NT, X11 on RS6000/SunSparc/SGI, System 7 on Mac and PowerMac (both planned, no port yet), Sony PSX support
- Multiple instancing of objects and hierarchies
- Multiple viewports, devices, and cameras
- Bezier patches with subdivision on the fly
- Depth cueing with atmospheric effects (fog, haze)
- Projected shadows
- Stereoscopic capability
- Free-form deformation toolkit
- Complex spline interpolated motion
- Collision detection toolkit
- Immediate mode that allows low-level control over polygon lighting and rendering through direct access to vertices and normals
- 70 pages of documentation
- C-based API
- Support for hardware accelerators like GLiNT, Matrox MGA Impression, and 3D device standards like Intel 3DR, Microsoft 3DDDI

Virtek 3D Ware

3D Ware is a comprehensive 3D graphics library that allows high-speed 3D graphics applications to be written using your favorite compiler.

Among its features are the following:

- MS DOS, C++, based on F29 Retaliator engine
- Multiple viewports
- Autoscaling sprites

- Motion tracker support
- Support for HMDs and flicker glasses

3DRender

3DR is Intel's scaleable, real-time 3D graphics library that has been optimized for the Pentium processor.

Its features include the following:

- Up to 16 light sources
- Texture mapping, environment mapping, modulated textures
- Sprites and bitmaps
- Atmospheric effects
- Optional Z-buffering, anti-aliasing, transparency, alpha blending
- Windows 3.1, Windows 95, and Windows NT support
- Free of charge, no royalty fee

Quickdraw 3D

QD3D is a cross-platform application program interface (API) for creating and rendering real-time, workstation-class 3D graphics from Apple.

Its features include the following:

- Support for hardware acceleration boards
- 3DMF meta file format, with free available parser

World Toolkit

WTK is a commercial VR environment manufactured by Sense8. It is intended for single users running on a single workstation—although version 2.0 does have some low-level support for networking. It runs on IBM PC compatibles, SUN and Silicon Graphics workstations.

Its features include the following:

- Support for many I/O devices
- C library
- Multiple viewport and light sources, 3D paths, portals, 2D texts and shapes, object animations
- Support for graphics hardware

Cyberspace Development Kit

The CDK is a library to create VR application under Windows 3.1 or Windows NT. CDK is from Autodesk Inc.

Its features include the following:

Designing 3D Graphics

- C++ class library
- Color dithering
- Support for many I/O devices
- Support for graphics hardware
- Physical simulation classes

SuperScape

SuperScape is a commercial PC-based, single-user VR system manufactured by Dimension International Ltd.

Its features include the following:

- World, object, texture, and sound editor
- Support for joystick and 6D spaceball controller, trackers, and stereo-graphics glasses
- Sound hardware support
- Network support
- Script language based on C, no direct programming interface
- Virtual Clip Art (3D clip art models with additional properties, like sound and behaviors—like a desk calculator that actually works)
- Runs on Windows environments

Virtus Walkthrough Pro

VW is a real-time 3-D rendering and "walkthrough" engine for Macintosh and Windows from Virtus Corporation.

Its features include the following:

- Perspective texture mapping
- Transparency
- Dithered flat shading
- Modeling and editing tools
- Freeware "Virtus Player" to share 3-D models with clients, colleagues, friends, and family who don't have VWP software
- Planned VRML support

VREAM

VREAM is a complete solution for developing virtual worlds. It runs on standard PC platforms.

Its features include the following:

- Monoscopic and stereoscopic rendering

- World and object editor.

- Support for 3D input and output devices, like gloves, trackers, and HMDs

- Hierarchical objects with attributes like sound, motion, penetrability, throwability, weight, and elasticity

- Complex interactive cause-and-effect relationships

- 1,000 pages of documentation

- Script language, no programming interface

X-Sharp

X-Sharp is a 3D animation package for PCs by Michael Abrash (mabrash@bix.com) published in the Graphics Programming column in *Dr. Dobb's Journal*, as of the October 1992 issue, and in the Pushing the Envelope column in *PC Techniques* magazine, as of the August 1994 issue. The full source can be found on x2ftp.oulu.fi. The X-Sharp engine is also discussed in the book *Zen of Graphics Programming* (ISBN: 1-883-57708-X) by Michael Abrash.

Its features include the following:

- Linear textured, convex polygon mapping in mode X

- Flat shading

- ASM and C

DOPE

DOPE is a PC demo from the demo crew COMPLEX (complex@hut.fi). It shows very fast real-time 3D graphics with complex objects. The demo can be found on ftp.luth.se or on ftp.cs.tu-berlin.de.

Its features include the following:

- Phong shading with materials

- Phong shaded texture mapping

- Phong shaded bump mapping

- Phong shaded environment mapping

- Shadow mapping

- Metal shading

- Motion blur

SurRender

SR is from Hybrit Ltd. by Jouni Mannonen (Jouni.Mannonen@hybrid.org).
Its features include the following:

- Lambert, Gouraud, and Phong shading

- Texture and environment mapping with all shading models

- Multiple light sources with a realistic lighting model
- Lens flare, lens reflection, smoke, and glow special effects
- Inventive scanline buffering for efficient volume clipping
- Optional Z-buffering and polygon radix sort with 32 bits of depth
- Filtering and real-time image post-procession
- Motion blur and anti-aliasing
- Support for virtually any VGA or SVGA resolution
- Bitmap objects and 3D Sprites
- Mip-mapping for improved image quality and lower pixellation
- Stereoscopic 3D rendering, support for iGlasses virtual headset
- 100 percent ASM for 80x86 platforms, C/C++ API
- Compact code, run-time memory requirement of under 50 Kbytes
- IPAS plug-in for 3D Studio R4, allowing Phong shaded and texture-mapped previews of mesh objects to be manipulated in real-time with the mouse and even saved to SurRender format directly from under 3DS

CUBE

CUBE Technology is a full-featured 3D graphics environment for DOS and Windows, custom written by Image Space Incorporated. It features 3D textured mapped graphics pipeline (geometry, renderer) including the following:

- Real-time sorting
- Integrated hierarchical database management, including database feedback for terrain following and collision detection
- Animation support
- 2D graphics and font engine
- Ambient, directional, omni, fog, haze, and special lighting effects
- Resolution independence
- Integrated 3D Studio tools for world creation and object placement

CHAPTER 13

V R M L

This chapter explains the basics of VRML, which stands for Virtual Reality Modeling Language, and gives some resources that will help the beginning VRML artist. VRML is the first established, open standard for real-time 3D graphics on the Internet. As of this writing, Version 1.0 is widely adopted, and several major competing (and massively improved) designs for 2.0 are getting close to wide-spread adoption.

What Is VRML?

Unlike other forms of RT3D applications (for example, games, driving simulators, military RT3D), VRML does not have a single, obvious purpose. It's meant to be as open-ended as possible—a whole new paradigm in human/computer interaction. There isn't any prevalent style or even any widespread agreement on what a cool VRML world is like. For employed VRML modelers, that means our work assignments are likely to be all over the map: building realistic museums, cartoony microbacteria, advertising catalogs for mobile homes, super-abstract representations of data, or whatever the customer can dream up. Figures 13.1–13.3 show a few VRML worlds.

Right now, there aren't many known design themes or precedents for VRML art. Computer games have established genres (fighting, simulation, role-playing, strategic); VRML has nothing like that. The field is wide open, and if we're designing an unusual VRML application, it's possible that we'll be the first ones doing it, whatever it is. A common reaction from professional RT3D modelers is: It's obvious that it has great potential, but it's like an entirely new kind of metal: exciting, but what do we do with it?

Missing Pieces

VRML 1.0 is widely admitted to be an incomplete first effort at establishing Virtual Reality on the Internet. The most obvious missing piece in VRML is interactive objects (or what the VRML folks call "behaviors") in the virtual world. Currently, VRML does not allow objects on screen to move freely, and this lack becomes extremely obvious after exploring a few example worlds. Interactivity is acknowledged as important by the VRML designers many times, and VRML 2.0 promises to add that.

As we learn about VRML, it's important to remember that we're dealing with a very young technology. Many of the worlds that we can access look like experiments or beta versions, even though they are finished. This makes sense if we consider that VRML in general is in the early stages of full commercial development—when v2.0 comes out, we will probably see a lot more applications that are actually useful.

The Good News

The good news is that from a RT3D modeling standpoint, VRML is a good format. It supports all the basic things we need: arbitrary 3DS-style meshes, tex-

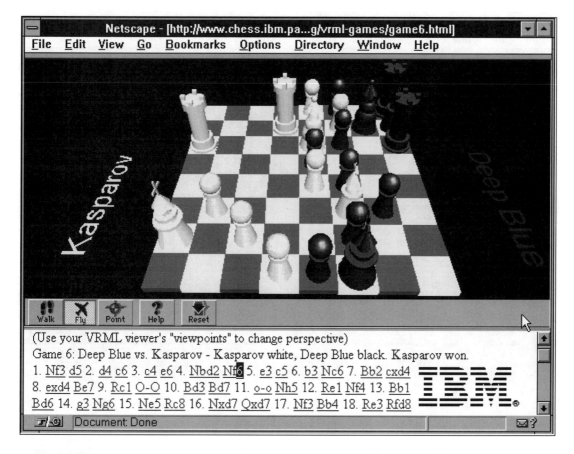

Netscape - [http://www.chess.ibm.pa...g/vrml-games/game6.html]

File   Edit   View   Go   Bookmarks   Options   Directory   Window   Help

Walk   Fly   Point   Help   Reset

(Use your VRML viewer's "viewpoints" to change perspective)
Game 6: Deep Blue vs. Kasparov - Kasparov white, Deep Blue black. Kasparov won.
1. Nf3 d5 2. d4 c6 3. c4 e6 4. Nbd2 Nf6 5. e3 c5 6. b3 Nc6 7. Bb2 cxd4
8. exd4 Be7 9. Rc1 O-O 10. Bd3 Bd7 11. o-o Nh5 12. Re1 Nf4 13. Bb1
Bd6 14. g3 Ng6 15. Ne5 Rc8 16. Nxd7 Qxd7 17. Nf3 Bb4 18. Re3 Rfd8

Document: Done

FIGURE 13.1   VRML chess game between Kasparov and
Deep Blue.

tures, and lights—and offers some powerful features as well. The addition of
animation capabilities should make it a strong contender for a general-purpose
RT3D modeling file format standard.

⬤ Required Knowledge

A basic understanding of the Web and the Internet is required to understand
VRML. The Web is not explained here (if there's one computer topic that is
well-documented, it's the basics of the Internet), but there are tons of various
sources for understanding it. There are literally hundreds of books on the topic,
as well as magazines, newspaper articles, and vast numbers of enthusiasts.

To make sense of VRML basic concepts, you won't need an extremely thorough knowledge of the Web or the Internet as it exists today. A simple conceptual introduction to the way the Web works will do.

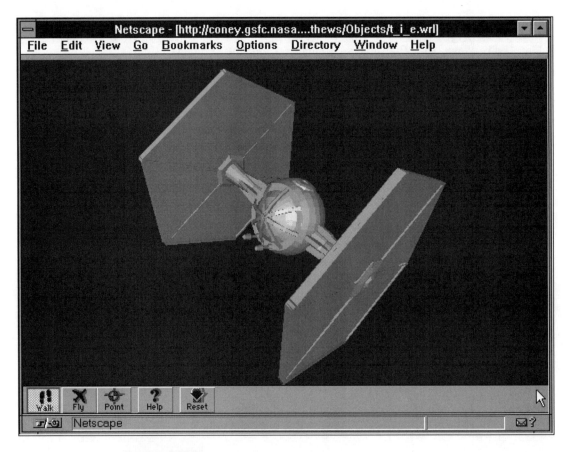

FIGURE 13.2   A VRML Tie fighter.

● How Does VRML Work?

From a content-independent, overall design standpoint, VRML works in the same way as HTML. There are two components:

Browsers are the applications that run on the user's local computer. They are composed of a RT3D graphics engine combined with a simple user interface and code that can request VRML files over the Internet. Like HTML browsers, VRML browsers subcontract other data types; for example, if the user chooses a link that plays sound, a VRML browser can refer this data to a sound-playing application, just as a normal HTML-based Web browser does.

Servers are publicly accessible computers that give out copies of the RT3D scene over the Internet. There's nothing too special on the server's end of things as far as we're concerned; it doesn't need to know anything about the 3D world. It just gives the browser the requested data.

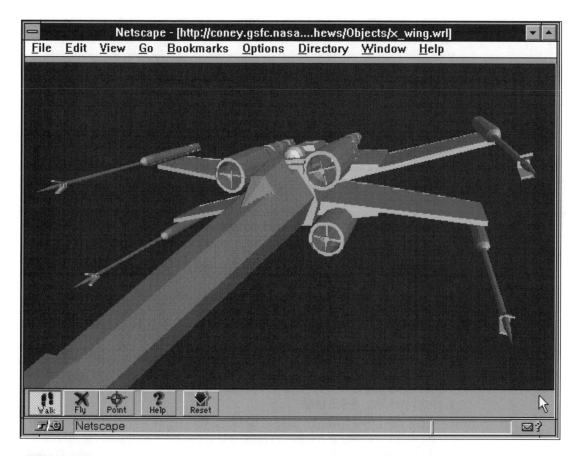

FIGURE 13.3   A VRML X-Wing fighter.

● Comparing VRML to "Normal" RT3D

From a pragmatic RT3D modeling perspective, VRML works like a simple, static-scene RT3D application that has specific behavior rules and some built-in Internet handling ability. We build models in much the same way (though generally we don't have as much capability to work with), and they're displayed on the screen in a basically similar way.

Performance Compared to Other RT3D Graphics

The most notable difference between VRML v1.0 and normal RT3D graphics applications (games, VR systems, military simulations) is the lack of capability—VRML browsers are generally weak performers compared to other RT3D applications. This generally means the worlds can't look as impressive—we're facing lower budgets for faces and textures.

Theoretically, there's no reason this must be true, but it's clear that high performance is not the total priority that other RT3D applications make it. Instead, VRML is focused on (as the v1.0 specification says) "platform independence, extensibility, ability to work well over low-bandwidth connections." That means it should run on as many computers as possible, be as upgradeable as possible, and not require any fancy Internet connection—a 14.4 modem is all the networking hardware the user will need.

On the other hand, the lack of interaction really reduces the need for superfast frame rates. When nothing much is moving, a 5 Hz frame rate is a lot less irritating than when you're trying to play a fast-action game. And, to be fair, some browser makers are emphasizing on graphics performance, making strong attempts to achieve excellent performance with the constraints they face.

The real performance difference is in the screen size. Users are generally running their VRML browser in full-screen Windows, often at 1024 × 768. That's about ten times the number of pixels of most RT3D applications (320 × 200); no wonder the frame rates are lower! We artists can't control this; either the users will live with the abysmal frame rates, shrink their screen size, buy fancy graphics hardware, or use a browser that will use tricks to avoid having to calculate 800,000 pixels per frame. It's hard to say what they'll do, and it's important to know because it definitely affects the way we design our world.

When we use an example in this book we'll assume our users will make their browser window 640 × 480, at the largest, in order to get a decent frame rate.

Hardware Limitations VRML Users Are Likely to Have

It's really hard to say who's going to be using VRML, and what kind of computers they'll be running it on, but a reasonable guess for a typical PC platform would be a 486/50 with 8 MB RAM, a 1 MB video card with no special 3D features, and a 14.4 Kbps modem with a PPP Internet connection. They'll probably be running Windows and have a browser like Netscape open as well as the VRML browser.

That means their machine will already be fairly busy running Windows and the browser, and compared to DOS-based games, we'll see a major performance hit, even if we disregard the difference in performance that comes from VRML compared to purpose-built games.

In fact, most VRML browsers have an option to degrade the quality of the image while the viewer is moving around in the virtual world. Without this option, even a user with a Pentium PC with 16 MB of memory can easily be reduced to frame rates well below 1/second.

 # Guided Tour of VRML v1.0

VRML Specification

VRML is essentially defined by something called the VRML Specification, a document that defines the structure of the VRML language; v1.0 is freely avail-

able on the Web. Most of the specification doesn't really pertain to modeling—it's written for programmers more than artists, but it might still be useful to take a look. It's broken into a few main headings:

- **Introduction**

- **Language basics**—Describes how VRML files work in a general way

- **Coordinate systems**—Describes the standard coordinate system for VRML, which is the same as the one used in this book and in 3D Studio

- **Fields and Nodes**—Describes the type of objects and data possible in a VRML file

- **Instancing**—Discusses making on-the-fly duplicates of objects in a VRML file

- **Extensibility**—Discusses adding other types of objects, not currently supported, to a VRML file

The specification ends with an example VRML file.

VRML File Structure: Programming Language or Data File?

If we're making VRML v1.0 worlds with the tools available in 1996, we will probably end up learning how the VRML file structure works. If that describes your situation, you should get a more detailed book about VRML's file structure. VRML is based on a file structure defined by Silicon Graphics called Open Inventor, but it's not identical to Open Inventor.

The structure of VRML files is a hierarchy of nodes. Nodes are very general; they can be almost anything. Some commonly used nodes are cameras, lights, spheres, textures, groups of faces, LODs, and Web links. They can also be abstract: a Transform node modifies another node's size, scale, and so on; a Separator node is a group of other nodes.

Each node can have some data that goes with it. For example, the DirectionalLight node has the following data: light on/off, brightness (intensity), color, and direction.

The Concept of "State"

For a RT3D modeler, one of the more confusing ideas in VRML is the idea of *state*: Each node is not necessarily self-contained. In a VRML file, some nodes affect any node that follows them. For example, if we put a light definition node in the middle of four sphere nodes,

```
Sphere node 1
Sphere node 2
light node
Sphere node 3
Sphere node 4
```

all four spheres would be lit. However, you can also use a Separator node to limit the effects of a light node. In the following example, only Sphere nodes 3 and 4 would be lit by the light node. The Cone node would not be lit because it has been separated from the Light node.

```
Sphere node 1
Sphere node 2
Begin Separator node
 light node
 Sphere node 3
 Sphere node 4
End Separator node
Cone node 1
```

This design is very different from normal 3D file formats, where the order doesn't matter at all. For example, if an ASC file had a structure of:

```
1. object 'sphere1'
2. object 'sphere1'
3. omni light
4. object 'sphere1'
5. object 'sphere1'
```

all four objects would be bright.

As you can see, the VRML file design is more closely related to a programming language than a data file format. It is defining more than geometry; it's also defining behavior, relations, and other aspects of the virtual world that most 3D file formats aren't designed to handle.

However, VRML v1.0 does have two nodes that map fairly closely to the ASC file's structure. The Coordinate3 node defines a list of 3D coordinates, and the IndexedFaceSet node refers to that list to define faces.

Let's compare the two file formats, using a triangle with a wheel texture from the car exercise in Chapter 9 as a simple example object. The VRML exporter plug-in from 3D Studio (explained below) generated the VRML file shown in Figure 13.4. Compare it to the ASC version of the same data shown in Figure 13.5.

The parallels are very obvious because both files have a list of 3D points followed by a list of faces, but there are some differences as well; for example, the material definition in the VRML file comes before; in the ASC file it is assigned to each face separately.

● What Can VRML Do?

What can VRML offer the 3D artist? As it turns out, VRML offers us quite a lot, but it's still difficult to take advantage of it because most 3D modeling tools don't support the features it offers. That will surely change as VRML becomes more wide-spread; in the meantime, let's look at what we can do with VRML now.

```
1.  #VRML V1.0 ascii
2.
3.  Separator {
4.  Info {
5.          string "Translated using (Autodesk, Inc. VRML Plug-In.)"
6.          }
7.          Material {
8.          ambientColor [ 0.2 0.2 0.2,
9.              0.000000 0.000000 0.000000, ]
10.         diffuseColor [ 0.8 0.8 0.8,
11.             0.000000 0.000000 0.000000, ]
12.         specularColor [ 0.0 0.0 0.0,
13.             0.000000 0.000000 0.000000, ]
14.         shininess [ 0.2,
15.             0.000000, ]
16.         transparency [ 0.0,
17.             0.000000, ]
18.         }
19.         DEF wheel11 Separator {
20.             Texture2 {
21.                 filename "m3wheel.bmp"
22.             }
23.         Coordinate3 {
24.             point [ -0.840520 3.092824 0.068570,
25.                     -0.840520 4.011435 0.148180,
26.                     -0.840520 3.620475 0.842183 ]
27.         }
28.         TextureCoordinate2 {
29.             point [ -0.526547 -0.092938,
30.                     1.358098 0.070391,
31.                     0.555996 1.494225 ]
32.         }
33.         MaterialBinding {
34.                     value OVERALL
35.         }
36.         Material {
37.             ambientColor [ 0.000000 0.000000 0.000000, ]
38.             diffuseColor [ 0.000000 0.000000 0.000000, ]
39.             specularColor [ 0.000000 0.000000 0.000000, ]
40.             shininess [ 0.000000, ]
41.             transparency [ 0.000000, ]
42.         }
43.         IndexedFaceSet {
44.             coordIndex [ 1, 0, 2, -1,
45.                     29264, 8559, 0, -1 ]
46.             textureCoordIndex [ 1, 0, 2, -1,
47.                     29264, 8559, 0, -1 ]
48.         }
49.     }
50. }
```

FIGURE 13.4   A VRML file called VRML-1.WRL.

Building VRML Files by Hand versus Using Modeling Tools

A large community of VRML users right now prefer to build VRML files by hand rather than use modeling tools. Thomas Van Putten, a VRML user and

```
 1. Ambient light color: Red=0.039216 Green=0.039216 Blue=0.039216 Solid
    background color: Red=1 Green=1 Blue=1
 2. Named object: "Light01"
 3. Direct light
 4. Position: X:1.07698 Y:4.580707 Z:1.660877
 5. Light color: Red=1 Green=1 Blue=1
 6. Named object: "Light02"
 7. Direct light
 8. Position: X:-1.220488 Y:-0.335213 Z:1.788636
 9. Light color: Red=1 Green=1 Blue=1
10. Named object: "wheel11"
11. Tri-mesh, Vertices: 3 Faces: 1
12. Mapped
13. Vertex list:
14. Vertex 0: X:-0.84052 Y:3.092824   Z:0.06857   U:-0.526547   V:-0.092938
15. Vertex 1: X:-0.84052 Y:4.011435   Z:0.14818   U:1.358098    V:0.070391
16. Vertex 2: X:-0.84052 Y:3.620475   Z:0.842183  U:0.555996    V:1.494225
17. Face list:
18. Face 0:   A:1 B:0 C:2 AB:1 BC:1 CA:1
19. Material:"M3WHEEL"
20. Smoothing: 1
21. Page 1
22.
23.
```

FIGURE 13.5   An ASCII file called VRML-1.ASC.

experienced 3D Studio user, says: "...I'd rather write a VRML scene by hand than use any of the available [modeling tools]. The best advantage of that is that it will be as small as it can be and relatively easy to debug. If you make use of the primitives, the DEF/USE, and the grouping abilities of VRML you can build everything you want. It's also very easy to write macros in your favorite editor or small (c) programs to produce the code and then check [it] in your VRML browser."

Though it surely is "easier" to debug hand-created models if you plan to immerse yourself in VRML code, it definitely cuts down on the ease, speed, and freedom of modeling if we can't interactively create our artwork. We'll assume that we are primarily using a 3D modeling tool to generate our VRML files here.

The specification is not very user-friendly, and it is not by any means a tutorial. To really learn VRML you'll need a book like *The VRML Sourcebook* by Andrea Ames, Dave Nadeau, and John Moreland (John Wiley & Sons, 1996).

Theoretical Capabilities and Limitations of VRML

Now let's look at what, exactly, we can represent in a VRML v1.0 file.

Supported Entities

Aside from the array of faces, the VRML file also supports a few interesting entities that don't have any equivalent in normal modeling software. The problem with these is there is no convenient way to create them unless we're using a VRML-aware 3D editor. If we're using 3D Studio, we use the kludge of building what we can in 3D Studio, then adding these entities in by hand during the export stage. Other VRML-aware editors, such as SGI's WebSpace or Caligari's Fountain, allow their users to place these special effects right in the model.

VRML has four *primitives*, or basic geometrical shapes: spheres, cubes, cones, and cylinders. Instead of drawing a circle one face at a time, you can simply use the Circle command, indicate the radius, and you have a nice circle. In VRML these primitives are defined as pure mathematical spheres, cones, and so on, but for a browser to draw the circle, it has to make it out of many small flat sides. Even though act as conveniences for those who write VRML code by hand, they pose a problem for us because different browsers will take the mathematically pure Circle primitive and render it differently (using different numbers of faces). So the downside to using primitives is that you lose some control over the precise, final look of your models. For us, there isn't much reason to use them if we are importing our art from a modeler.

VRML supports polygons, as long as they are planar and convex. These are the same basic requirements that most RT3D graphics have.

3D text is done very elegantly in the VRML file (three fonts, bold, italic), but it's not directly supported by most 3D modelers. Of course, VRML is not very practical for large volumes of text because it takes a lot of faces to form the curved letters.

URL links are an important entity that VRML offers. This is a way to assign a URL to an object so when the user clicks on it, it loads a different file. There are two types: WWWInline inserts another VRML world within the current one, and WWWAnchor replaces the current world with the new one. It's possible to link to things other than VRML worlds, such as normal Web pages.

Control over normals is another capability that VRML provides. Normal RT3D graphics figure the face's normal automatically; VRML allows us to define it specifically. It's also possible to enable automatic smoothing within VRML.

Mapping coordinates are separate from the verts.

A *shape hint* is a command that precedes a shape, letting the graphics engine know something about the nature of the shape it's about to draw.

Materials, Lighting, and Shading Capabilities

VRML supports a fairly diverse set of material attributes, by real-time graphics standards. It allows us to define ambient and lit colors for each material, as well as a decent selection of lights. There are no shading limits set by VRML itself, but most browsers support flat and Gouraud.

Textures

VRML texturing is handled in an essentially similar way to the methods described in this book, with one big exception: Mapping coordinates are not

directly stored with the XYZ coordinates of the vertices. Instead, a separate list of mapping coordinates acts as a peer to the XYZ coordinate list. The face definition calls out references to XYZ coordinates just like 3D Studio, but the mapping coordinates are also called out in the same way, which is unlike 3D Studio. With most graphics engines, as well as 3D Studio, the mapping coordinates are listed on the same line as the XYZ coordinates.

This difference allows opportunity for efficiency when building VRML worlds. We can have two faces that share a vert but do not share mapping coordinates. Effectively, we don't have to have duplicate verts to store multiple sets of UVs at the same point in space. That means we don't have to detach elements if we want different mapping in the same object! Of course, to do this, we need a 3D editor that supports this ability (not 3D Studio).

A slight difference between VRML texturing and other types of RT3D graphics is the convention of names for the mapping coordinates. VRML uses S and T for the labels of the horizontal and vertical axes. They are equivalent to the U and V labels that most RT3D graphics use.

● Building for VRML

So, what should be said about building objects for VRML?

General Design Issues

First, as with any other form of communication, we should know our audience. Who are we building this world for? Unlike computer games, which have a very clear, defined audience, there is a vast, largely unknown range of possible people who could potentially visit our VRML world. So, we need to decide who we want to impress, and from that we can decide what would impress them.

We should start by getting a functional VRML browser and a net connection, and then surfing around. Unless a massive influx of new worlds occurs after the writing of this book, the conclusion that there are not yet millions of interesting VRML worlds available will be inescapable. Why? There just aren't many people doing this yet, probably because the act of creating a VRML world is still prohibitive enough to prevent most people from dabbling. We can expect this to change, especially once interactions within VRML (i.e., VRML 2.0) arrive.

What worlds are out there? There are lots of open walk-around areas with pictures to click on that lead to Web pages and other worlds. There are several museums, which are somewhat interesting as experiments, but they aren't in danger of putting real museums out of business. Either the texture resolution is so low that 2D art hung on the walls tends to be horribly pixellated, or the frame rate is so bad that it's really hard to navigate. Not many people have attempted RT3D sculpture or other forms along those lines; most museums seem to be showing 2D art.

Designing 3D Graphics

There is room for improvement—that's very good news for us, though it's a little disappointing for the VRML surfer (but that will all change when we get our awesome virtual polka-dancing environment done, right?).

Specific Techniques

Like any other real-time environment, we should custom-design our models to our graphics engine. Unfortunately, we don't know which graphics engine (browser) our users will be using, so we can either "dumb it down" and make a simple world that will work everywhere, or make a world that is designed to work well with a specific browser, at the expense of the rest of the users.

Also, we should be sure to consider the way users will move through our world. That's to say, make sure the basic "fly/walk" concepts are appropriate for the design we're making because that's the only way our users can get around.

Textures in VRML

It should be obvious after exploring VRML worlds with a minimum Internet connection (14.4 modem with PPP) that textures are problematic with VRML. It can take longer to download the textures for a heavily textured world than it does to completely explore the world without them. Be sure the load times are reasonable for the textures you're using. How do you keep texture load times down?

Consider using LODs to swap in textures when the user gets close. This is a trade-off—it can make a big difference in frame rate because the textures won't be shown most of the time, and it can help download time by preventing all the textures from loading at once, before the world appears. However, it will also be a pretty dull-looking world if the user can see only one texture at a time, effectively, and it may be annoying to experience constant downloads while navigating the world instead of getting it over with all at once.

A low-res texture is better than a frustrated user; don't make users download a single 512×512 texture when they could be roaming around with 128×128 textures (downloaded eight times as fast) instead.

Use JPEG. Many artists tend to be resistant to using JPEG because it slightly damages the image quality, but its savings are so enormous that we can double our texture size (more than offsetting the damage) and still save space and download time. Better yet, almost every browser supports JPEG as a file format, so your textures will be accessible to the largest audience.

Of course, be aware that JPEG is "lossy." Your artwork should be stored in a normal bitmap, like TIFF, as well as in JPEG format, or you will lose date from your image! Consider JPEG to be a one-way format—you should use it to deliver, but not to edit, your art.

● VRML Browsers

Here's a general overview of the VRML browsers now available. This information was used with the permission of the San Diego Supercomputer Center's VRML Repository. You can visit the Repository at http://www.sdsc.edu/vrml.

AmberGL VRML Browser v1.0

This is a VRML browser (alpha release) built with DIVE Labs' AmberGL virtual environment tool kit for OpenGL. The alpha release of the Amber VRML Browser includes support for 65 K colors, multiple rendering modes (wireframe, flat/smooth shaded), and multiple lights. The browser does not currently support some features (that is, textures, cylinders, spheres, point sets), but they are continuing to develop the browser and are uploading new versions frequently. Future releases will include improved navigation, support for head-mounted displays and gloves, and other fun stuff! DIVE Laboratories, Inc.

Currently supported platforms:

- Windows NT (Intel)

Black Sun CyberGate

CyberGate 1.0 (Beta 1) is a VRML 1.0 compatible browser that provides extentions for avatar interaction via Black Sun's CyberHub server. CyberGate turns VRML worlds into multiuser chat spaces. CyberGate can be run as a standalone VRML browser or as a Netscape 2.0 plug-in. The beta version is available free for Windows 95/Windows NT.

Currently Supported Platforms:

- Windows 95
- Windows NT (Intel)

Dive—A Multiuser VR with a VRML Interface

The Distributed Interactive Virtual Environment (Dive) from SICS is an Internet (IP-) based multiuser VR system where participants navigate in 3D space and see, meet, and interact with other users and applications. Dive has a VRML interface, enabling VRML files to be imported as worlds or objects. These objects can then be shared and manipulated by several users (just as other objects) within the environment. However, objects with full interaction and behavior capabilities must still be defined with the Dive file format. Binaries for non-commercial use are freely available for a number of UNIX platforms. The first Dive version appeared in 1991. Olof Hagsand, SICS.

Currently supported platforms:

- SGI
- Sun
- HP/UX

Fountain (AKA Caligari worldSpace)

Fountain is a complete Windows VRML authoring solution that includes rapid modeling in perspective space, manipulation of texture-mapped VRML objects in real time, and interactive lighting. Fountain technology has been licensed by Microsoft for inclusion in Blackbird. Although Fountain is primarily an authoring tool, the ability to read VRML files will allow virtual world builders to take advantage of existing 3D resources on the Internet and to test VRML-specific features such as levels of detail, in-lining and hyperlinks to HTML, video, and sound files on the Web. Caligari Corporation.

Currently supported platforms:

- Windows 3.1
- Windows 95

GLView

GLView is a shareware VRML browser and 3D object viewer. It supports native OpenGL rendering on Windows NT and Windows 95, including hardware shading and texture mapping support. In addition to VRML, it also supports the following file formats: DXF, RAW, OBJ, GLView; texture formats: VRML inline, RGB, JPEG, GIF, TARGA, BMP/DIB. Holger Grahn.

Currently supported platforms:

- Windows NT 3.51 (Intel)
- Windows 95

i3D

i3D combines the 3D input and high-performance rendering capabilities of high-end virtual reality systems with the data-fetching abilities of network browsers. Using a Spaceball or a mouse, the user can intuitively navigate inside 3D worlds; selecting 3D objects with the mouse triggers requests for access to remote documents of any media type, from text to other 3D models. Time-critical rendering techniques allow the system to display complex 3D scenes at high and constant frame rates, making it possible to use it in the context of large-scale projects. i3D also supports stereo rendering for CrystalEyes LCD shutter glasses and the Multi-Channel Option. i3D was developed initially at CRS4, Caligari, Italy. Its development is now pursued at CERN by the VENUS group.

Currently supported platforms:

- SGI with IRIX 5.2 or later

Microsoft VRML Add-In Beta 1.1

Microsoft VRML Add-In Beta 1.1 is a fully integrated, plug-in VRML 1.0 viewer for Microsoft Internet Explorer 2.0. Using RealityLab technology, Microsoft VRML Add-In Beta 1.1 enables you to navigate easily through 3-D "virtual worlds" using a mouse, a keyboard, or a joystick. Microsoft, Inc.

Currently supported platforms:

- Windows 95

NAVFlyer 2.2b

This is a freely distributable, fully functional, interactive, and upgradeable flyer with LOD and adaptive viewing modes (faster modes when moving, then fully detailed and textured when stopped). NAVFlyer 2.2b is the first product capable of reading VRML models (along with DXF and 3DS). MicronGreen, Inc.

Currently supported platforms:

- Windows 3.1
- Windows NT (Intel)
- Windows 95

NeTpower Vizia 3D Viewer

When used in conjunction with a World Wide Web browser such as Mosaic, Vizia 3D displays and navigates 3D scenes with embedded hyperlinks to other VRML scenes or to HTML files. The Vizia 3D session automatically begins when the first hyperlink to a 3D scene is selected. For the duration of the session, Vizia 3D retains each scene viewed to allow a quick return to previously viewed scenes. NeTpower, Inc.

Currently supported platform:

- Windows NT

Pueblo Beta Client

The Pueblo Internet client is a multimedia game system that works with existing (multi-user dungeons) MUDs and media formats. Pueblo can display 2D and 3D graphics, music, audio, HTML, and plain text. It also includes a VRML browser that supports WWWAnchor, WWWInline, LOD, correct textures, and more. Chaco Communications, Inc.

Renaissance

Renaissance is a developing SG-based VRML browser running under Irix 5.2 (or greater). It is a powerful browser directly supporting the VRML 1.0 specification and offering some valuable features, including the following:

- Support for the Crystal-Eyes stereo viewing system, allowing true 3D browsing of VRML scenes
- A full-featured scene viewer, allowing full movement within and between scenes
- Integration with the Mosaic Web browser providing a full HTML/VRML browsing solution

- High-quality scene rendering facilities including full texture mapping
- Multiple rendering modes for optimizing performance and responsiveness in complex scenes

Renaissance is available free of charge and is freely distributable. A full support service is also provided without charge. Craig Hart, University of Leeds.
Currently supported platforms:

- SGI running Irix 5.2 or greater

Sony Cyber Passage

US Mirror Site CyberPassage is a VRML1.0 compatible browser with extensions to support behaviors using TCL scripts. An associated authoring tool, CyberPassage Conductor, is also available that allows quick development of animated VRML scenes, including support for sound and video. Beta version is available free for Windows 95. Sony Corporation, Inc.
Currently supported platforms:

- Windows 95

TerraForm

The TerraForm VRML browser, by Brilliance Labs Inc., introduces a new level of interactivity to 3D exploration by allowing direct manipulation of individual objects within the virtual world. It supports all nodes of VRML, with upcoming support for ActiveVRML. Multithreaded graphics and networking take full advantage of Windows 95 and NT. It is based on Intel's 3DR graphics engine, for top performance and quality. Brilliance Labs, Inc.
Currently supported platforms:

- Windows 95
- Windows NT

Virtus Voyager

Virtus Voyager may be used now as a standalone product or as a helper application for other 2D Net browsers like Netscape or Mosaic; it is soon to be a plug-in. In addition to VRML, Virtus Voyager will be expanded to import Virtus's own proprietary VMDL file format. This will be especially efficient for larger files. Future plans also include incorporation of other 3D modeling and rendering file formats. Virtus Corporation.
Currently supported platforms:

- Macintosh
- Power Macintosh
- Windows 95

VR Scout 1.1

VR Scout supports the entire VRML specification, including inlines, LODs, anchors, textures, and more. It supports gzipped files, zipped files, GIF/JPEG/BMP textures, DDE, internal HTTP if no DDE browser is available, and threading on Windows 95 and NT. VR Scout uses Intel's 3dr rendering library currently. Chaco Communications, Inc.

Currently supported platforms:

- Windows 3.1
- Windows NT (Intel)
- Windows 95

VRealm

VRealm runs as a standalone application or from Netscape Communications Corp.'s popular Web browser. It incorporates advanced image, video, audio, animation, and VR techniques. It also incorporates basic Internet functions, such as HTML. An alpha version is currently available for testing and evaluation. A supported version will be available in the fall of 1996 for $29.95. Integrated Data Systems, Inc., and Portable Graphics, Inc.

Currently supported platforms:

- Windows 95
- Windows NT version 3.51 (Intel)

Soon to be supported:

- OS/2 Warp
- IBM AIX
- Digital UNIX
- HP-UX
- Macintosh Power PC

VRML Equinox, Alpha Release

VRML Equinox supports the full set of the VRML 1.0 specification, using Apple's Quickdraw 3D technology to present realistic rendered environments. VRML Equinox can also communicate with Netscape Communications Corp.'s Navigator. VRML Equinox can instruct Navigator to retrieve new VRML files. Additionally, VRML Equinox can point Navigator to any Universal Resource Locator (URL), giving VRML Equinox the ability to be the front end to file servers and other information sources. Future plans for VRML Equinox include the support of behaviors and scripts. North Plains Systems Inc.

Currently supported platforms:

- Macintosh Power PC

VRweb

VRweb is implemented using OpenGL on SGI, DEC Alpha, and Microsoft Windows NT. For all platforms an implementation using the Mesa library (an OpenGL workalike) is available. It does not need or benefit from special graphics hardware, thus allowing browsing VRML scenes on ordinary X-terminals and PCs, too. Source code is now available for UNIX/X11 and Windows. IICM, NCSA, and the Gopher team.

Currently supported platforms:

- Windows 95

- Windows NT (Intel)

- Windows 3.x (with Win32S)

- UNIX (HP-UX, SUN OS, SUN Solaris, SGI IRIX, Alpha DEC ULTRIX, AIX)

An OpenGL version of VRweb, which takes advantage of any graphics hardware, is available for SGI, DEC Alpha, and Windows NT. For all platforms, a software-only implementation using the Mesa library (an OpenGL workalike) is available. This version of VRweb neither needs nor benefits from special graphics hardware and runs on standard X terminals and PCs.

Soon to be supported:

- Macintosh Power PC

- Macintosh 68000

WebFX

This is embedded VRML viewer for popular Windows web browsers such as Netscape, Spyglass, and Quarterdeck's Mosaic. In addition to providing full VRML 1.0 support, WebFX incorporates IRC 3D chatting, physics-based navigation with collision detection, and general-purpose, in-place authoring. Paper Software, Inc.

Currently supported platforms:

- Windows 3.1

- Windows NT (Intel)

- Windows 95

Soon to be supported:

- Macintosh

WebOOGL 2.0

This is beta release of the WebOOGL 2.0 software package, a public domain 3D Web browser. It is a "quasi-compliant" VRML browser: Most of the VRML spec is implemented, but a few nodes are silently ignored (most notably texture

mapping). The browser is built on top of the Center's 3D viewer, Geomview. The Geometry Center.

Currently supported platforms:

- SGI

- Sun

Soon to be supported:

- Linux and other X-Window system platforms.

WebSpace

WebSpace is a commercially available 3D viewer for the World Wide Web. Users can navigate to 3D Web sites through conventional 2D page viewers or simply run WebSpace standalone. WebSpace is a freely distributed product. Version 1.1 is now available. Silicon Graphics Computer Systems and Template Graphics Software.

Currently supported platforms:

- SGI
- Windows NT (Intel)
- Windows NT (MIPS)
- Windows 95
- SUN Solaris ZX/TZX
- IBM AIX

Soon to be supported:

- Windows 3.1
- Macintosh Power PC
- Digital UNIX
- HP/UX

WebView

SDSC WebView is a publicly available VRML browser for SGI/UNIX systems. WebView is released with full source code and is provided as a public platform for developing and testing experimental additions to the VRML specification. San Diego Supercomputer Center.

Currently supported platforms:

- SGI/UNIX

Whurlwind 3D Browser and Web Surfer

This is a PowerPC Macintosh QuickDraw3D VRML browser. Whurlwind is an application for viewing 3DMF and VRML models. Whurlwind relies on Quick-

Draw 3D for rendering, navigation, and URL picking. This first version of Whurlwind allows users to view 3DMF and VRML models from different camera positions and to jump to other Web sites (soon-to-be-released future versions will allow scene navigation, allowing users to cruise around 3D space). Bill Enright and John Louch.

Currently supported platforms:

* Macintosh models with QD3D installed

WIRL

The WIRL browser is the first VR browser to extend VRML functionality to include object behaviors, cause-and-effect relationships, and logic. Now available for free download, WIRL is a Netscape plug-in. VREAM.

Currently supported platforms:

* Windows 95

WorldView

WorldView enables standard personal computers and 14.4 modems to deliver the necessary power to support real-time applications. WorldView combines the rendering engine with its proprietary integrated networking functionality, delivering a browser that sets a new standard for high performance on standard PCs. InterVista Software, Inc.

Currently supported platforms:

* Windows 3.1

* Windows 95

* Windows NT (Intel)

Soon to be supported:

* Macintosh 68000—TBD

* Macintosh Power PC—TBD

Modeling Tools

There is a great demand for ways to build VRML worlds, and many companies are attempting to meet this demand. Their products are all very new, some of them having been built from scratch in a very short time, and their usefulness to professional RT3D modelers varies widely. It's worth pointing out, though, that they are more focused on the needs that we are likely to have (low poly counts, real-time rendering output) than normal modeling software.

This list largely was derived from the really well-organized, useful VRML resource site that San Diego Supercomputing Center maintains for VRML-

related information. You are encouraged to visit it directly: http://www.sdsc.edu/ SDSC.

Clayworks

Clayworks is a no-frills, MS-DOS modeling tool. As the Web page says, "Clayworks is a fully functional 3D modeling package offering you an easy and powerful way to draw in three dimensions. With an intuitive interface from a powerful GUI which is fast enough to allow opaque dragging and resizing of windows (no resize rectangle) even on a 386, clayworks will allow you to create complex objects quickly and cheaply."

A commercial version is planned for release in late 1996 that will offer a lot more features and abilities.

Contact: Tim Lewis (csc023@cent1.lancs.ac.uk, http://cent1.lancs.ac.uk/tim)
Platform: MS-DOS
Price: "Five pounds sterling (or equivalent)" for shareware.

Cyber Passage Conductor

A strange, "enhanced" VRML content creator, Cyber Passage Conductor was written to make a virtual society world that Sony has designed. Cyber Passage Conductor supports animations and interactive behavior, but only by using Sony's own improvements on the VRML standard. Note that Sony plans to support the Moving Worlds standard for VRML 2.0: "Sony is fully committed to Moving Worlds and will release a Moving Worlds compliant browser as soon as possible." When this happens, these products may become a lot more usable as general-purpose tools.

The Web page says: "The VRML browser, Cyber Passage, enables you to walk around the 3D space and is also equipped with the enhanced functions for manipulating moving images, movies, and sound. Another release at this time is the VRML editing tool, Cyber Passage Conductor. With this tool, you are able to create your own dynamic 3D world abundant with sound and images."

As of this writing, both products are in a beta stage of development.

Contact: Sony (vs_info@sm.sony.co.jp, http://vs.sony.co.jp/VS-E/vstop.html)
Platform: Windows 95, Windows 3.1
Memory: 16 MB RAM
Price: Free

Fountain

Fountain, from Caligari Corporation, is probably the most powerful free VRML editor available as of this writing. Clearly related in design to Truespace, Fountain offers a reasonably rich feature set for building 3D models, texturing them, and integrating other objects. More importantly, it offers a convenient interface for most, if not all, VRML-specific capabilities, such as placing links in the 3D world.

Contact: Caligari Corporation (sales@caligari.com)

Address: 1935 Landings Drive, Mountain View, CA 94043
Phone: (415) 390-9600
Fax: (415) 390-9755
Platform: Windows 3.1, Windows 95
Memory: 8 MB (16 MB recommended)
Price: Free

G-Web

G-Web is a virtual worlds authoring package for VRML. Specifically designed to meet the needs of VR and real-time graphics, G-Web provides both modeling facilities and the ability to import from all popular 3D CAD formats.

Contact: Virtual Presence (presence@presence.demon.co.uk, http://www.vrweb.com/gweb.html)
Address: it 6, New Concordia Wharf, Mill Street, London SE1 2BA.
Phone: +44 (0) 171 252 2922
Platform: Windows 3.1, Windows 95, UNIX (Sun)
Memory: 8 MB (16 MB recommended)
Price: Free

PhotoModeler v2.1

This tool allows the artist to use two photographs of the same object to extract 3D data from the object. It works essentially in the same way that binocular vision allows us to perceive 3D from two 2D inputs (our eyes).

PhotoModeler has been one of those looks-like-a-great-idea programs for a long time, but it is not meant to compete with normal 3D tools. Why isn't it used more? Possibly because of its unusual approach, combined with price: Artists want to explore strange tools and test their usefulness personally, especially if they're paying $795 for a helper tool.

Also, it's a fairly slow, involved process by 3D modeling standards. Users must take several good, clean photos of all sides of the object with a certain camera, develop them, then digitize the photos, and only then can they go through the steps in PhotoModeler. Though getting source art can easily take as long as this process, not everyone has the camera skills to do this kind of picture taking. On the other hand, this tool has the potential to make some kinds of modeling jobs a lot easier. Imagine building a model of a house without the blueprints, and without being able to measure it with a tape measure, or digitizing some new, secret-design show car simply from photos.

As the company's FAQ says, "PhotoModeler is best at measuring and modeling objects with well-defined visual features, whether they are the sharp, 3D edges that bound an object's surfaces or flat markings painted on the surfaces. PhotoModeler can measure objects of virtually any size. You do need to get around an object so all the surfaces you want in the model can be photographed from different positions and angles. Objects with smoothly flowing surfaces (like sand dunes or statues) or with edges having no distinct features (like curved con-

crete arches) will need to be marked or targeted before being photographed." Some accuracy issues are well documented by the makers.

Eos Systems reached out to the VRML community with a VRML-compliant update (v2.1), and a special Web page devoted to explaining it: "…The new PhotoModeler 2.1 release adds VRML with full surround texture mapping output."

Contact: Eos Systems Inc. (sales@photomodeler.com, http://www.photo-modeler.com)

Address: 205-2034 West 12th Ave., Vancouver, BC Canada V6J 2G2

Phone: (604) 732-6658

Platform: Windows 3.1, Windows 95, Windows NT

Memory: 8 MB

Price: $795

Lightwave 3D v4.0

NewTek's Lightwave3D is a professional-quality 3D animation system with roots in (and, still, a strong devotion to) Amiga computers. It creates VRML objects and VRML worlds with object references based on scenes created in Lightwave's scene layout module. Like 3D Studio, it's reasonably full-featured, including plug-in abilities, ray-tracing renderer, IK animation, and more, but it's not designed specifically for RT3D modeling.

Contact: NewTek, Inc. (http://www.newtek.com)

Address: 1200 SW Executive Drive, Topeka, KS 66615 USA

Phone: 1 (800) 847-6111

Platform: Windows 95, Windows NT, Amiga, UNIX (SGI)

Price: $995

Ez3D Series v2.0

Ez3D is a family of modeling programs that offer features designed specifically for real-time modeling, such as automatic face-count reduction as well as general-purpose modeling, texturing, and rendering abilities, plus NURBS-based surfaces. There are several specific products, including VRML-specific editors. It imports and exports from most popular 3D formats, including 3D Studio.

The VRML product, called Ez3d VR Pro 2.0, is described like this: "Ez3d VRML Author is a powerful, yet easy-to-use 3D modeling system for the Internet, pre-press image generation, and use with animation programs. Ez3d VRML Author offers 3D modeling, mapping, ray tracing, real-time scene composition, and VRML site creation in a tightly integrated environment. Ez3d Junior is a cost-effective solution for VRML authoring."

Contact: Radiance Software International (Ez3d@radiance.com, http://www.radiance.com/~radiance)

Address: 1726 Francisco Street, Berkeley, CA 94703

Phone: (510) 848-7621

Fax: (510) 848-7613

Platform: UNIX (Sun, Linux, SGI, HP, IBM), Windows 95, Windows NT (Alpha, NetPower, Intergraph, Intel)

Memory required: 16 MB
Current version: 2.0
Currently available: SGI, Sun
Available April 1996: Windows NT/95, IBM, HP
Available Summer 1996: Linux

WorldUp!

Sense8 is nearing completion of its simple modeling software designed for building real-time 3D models and locating them in space. It is part of "WorldUp!" (a $7,000 programming-free VR development environment), and it does support VRML v1.0 directly.

Contact: Sense8 Corporation (sales@sense8.com, http://www.sense8.com)
Phone: (415) 331-6318
Fax: (415) 331-9148
Address: 150 Shoreline Highway, Suite 282, Mill Valley, CA 94941

Virtual Home Space Builder (and Virtual Space Viewer)

Virtual Home Space Builder, written by Paragraph Software, is meant to be a "VRML for the masses" tool that allows quick, easy construction of Doom-like environments based on extruded 2D floor plans. It allows for a variety of materials to be placed in the world: textures, both static and animated, as well as sounds. Its interface allows for custom modification of textures with built-in airbrush and other bitmap-editing tools.

Contact: Paragraph (info@paragraph.com)
Address: 1688 Dell Ave., Campbell, CA 95008
Phone: (800) 810-0055
Memory required: 4 MB (8 MB recommended)
Price: $50

Strata Studio PRO

This is a full modeling, rendering, and animation system for Macintosh, including both spline-based and polygon-based (3D Studio-like) modeling. It can do real-time rendering within the modeling environment. It's not really designed for RT3D modeling, though it does have some support for real-time output formats, with full support for Quickdraw 3D, QuickTime VR, and VRML. It doesn't support 3DS or ASC file formats.

Contact: Strata Inc. (sales@strata3d.com, http://www.strata3d.com)
Platform: Macintosh (PowerPC-based)
Memory: 16 MB
Price: $1,500

TriSpectives

This program is a "3D for the masses" product, but it's much more powerful than most of that variety. It clearly has the corporate market firmly in mind. The interface is self-described as "Familiar user interface that's completely Windows® 95 and Microsoft® Office compatible." Experienced 3D artists are not the target audience for this product.

Still, it's worth checking out. It's got some interesting ideas, like collision detection within the editor, so that we can move objects around, not through, each other more naturally. Everything possible is oriented around dragging and dropping, and clip art figures heavily in the picture. It supports all kinds of import and export file formats, 2D and 3D, including 3D Studio.

The Professional version offers some more tools, like blending, chamfering, tapering, shelling, and capping capabilities; the ability to create CAD-like line drawings and dimensions; and even more import/export file types (AutoCAD's native DWG, IGES, Stereolithography, and more)

Contact: 3D/EYE Inc. (info@eye.com, http://www.eye.com)
Address: 700 Galleria Pkwy, Atlanta, GA 30339
Phone: (770) 937-9000, 1 (800) 946-9533
Platform: Windows 95
Price: $300 or $495 for professional ($10 for a 30-day trial)

WebSpace Author

This is the VRML world building tool from Silicon Graphics. It's considered to be the standard VRML tool by many, and it is widely used.

Contact: Silicon Graphics Computer Systems (http://www.sgi.com)
Address: 2171 Landings Drive, Mountain View, CA 94043
Phone: (415) 933-3900
Fax: (415) 960-0197
Platform: UNIX (SGI)

Virtus Walkthrough (and VRML Browser "Voyager")

To quote from the Web site, "Virtus Corporation introduces Virtus Voyager, the premiere VRML Web browser for the Macintosh/Power Macintosh and Windows 95 (Windows 3.1 not available). Virtus Voyager gives current users of Virtus WalkThrough Pro 2.5+ and Virtus VRML the capability of viewing their VRML files. Users can create 3D worlds with links to move across the Internet.

"Virtus Voyager may be used as a standalone product for viewing VRML files on your local machine and as a helper application with Netscape 1.1 (and later versions) for 3D browsing on the Web (and soon to be a plug-in module for Netscape 2.0).

"In addition to VRML, Virtus Voyager will be expanded to import Virtus's own proprietary VMDL file format. This will be especially efficient for larger files. We also plan to incorporate other 3D modeling and rendering file formats."

Contact: Virtus Corporation (info@virtus.com, http://www.virtus.com)
Address: 118 MacKenan Dr. Suite 250, Cary, NC 27511
Phone: (919) 467-9700
Fax: (919) 460-4530

Spinner

Spinner is self-described like this: "SPINNER is a $99 MS-Windows 3D Web (VRML) authoring tool. It outputs VRML 1.0 compliant files for viewing 3D files on the Internet. It supports VRML primitives, textures, embeds URL in objects, and will support VRML 2.0 once VRML 2.0 is completed.

"Spinner is an example of the variety of RT3D tools called placement editors. They do not offer low-level modeling tools like vertex editing; instead, they allow the user to construct their 3D worlds by choosing from existing pre-built pieces, then placing them and setting whatever interactions, etc., are possible. As such, they are a very different approach to modeling than full editors like 3D Studio offer, and the two types of tools can complement each other.

"Spinner offers real-time rendering in the editor, a hierarchy-based view of the scene, and VRML-related features like URL linking within the world. It also offers texturing control on a face level (unusual for this type tool)."

Contact: 3D Web Inc. (john@3dweb.com, http://www.3dweb.com)
Address: P.O. Box 410990 Suite 156, San Francisco, CA 94114-0990
Phone: (415) 956-9730, (415) 954-0963
Platform: Windows 95, Windows NT, Windows 3.1 with Windows 32s
Memory: 8M
Price: $99
Current version: Pre-release

CHAPTER 14

RT 3D
ENVIRONMENT
DESIGN

● Prologue

As this book's introduction said, professional real-time 3D modeling requires two abilities: an understanding of the technology's abilities and the freedom and power of artistic vision.

This entire book, except for this chapter, addresses the skills and tools required by the first part: the technological capabilities and limitations that we face and how to work around them.

This chapter addresses the other part: what to do with this knowledge. Because of this different focus, it overlaps with the designer's role. We talk about the introduction to the application, for example, which is not real-time 3D at all. It is, however, part of the world design, as we will see.

● World Design Theory

RT3D environment design theory has been studied and documented in the field of VR, so if you read this and want more, you should be able to find it. Look on the book's Web site, listed in the Introduction, for more info.

Let's go through a few of the basic principals that apply to designing an interactive 3D space.

Give Orientation

Providing a sense of direction and location to the user is very important. A new, different 3D world is a very confusing place, even to experienced VR veterans. Create objects that are easily identifiable, to help users understand the world around them.

This doesn't mean that the objects need to be familiar to the user already. For example, if we're building an alien spacecraft, we don't have to put green "exit" signs over the doors, but we could have exterior doors all with a certain shape, color, or other distinctive attribute. Consistency is the key, not normality.

If the environment is an outdoor one, this orientation can often be provided well in the horizon texture. The horizon texture is a very important, powerful tool for defining a scenario, but it can also provide landmarks and reference for users as they navigate.

Background versus Foreground Differentiation

One of the most basic ideas in world design is the differentiation of the foreground from the background. Like a theater, we want to accentuate the objects that are involved in the action and to let the background fade to an unemphasized part of the scene. We do this primarily by using low contrast colors, subtly repetitious patterns, and darkening the images used in the backgrounds.

Conveying Emotions with Polygons

Conveying emotions with the simple tools that RT3D offers can be a very daunting task, but it can be done. Now we must draw on our artistic vision, using techniques from film making and other emotionally powerful mediums, and keep clear in our minds the goal we have set. If there were no constraints, how would this environment look?

Once we have that clear, we examine this vision from the technology standpoint and decide the best way to provide that effect to the user. As is no doubt apparent from the rest of this book, the most important thing a RT3D world designer can do to make a successful world is work with (and around) the constraints of the graphics engine. Take a hard look at the limitations we face, and make worlds that aren't affected by them. Then, take a look at the capabilities we have at our disposal, and make worlds that are possible to show with those capabilities.

For example, fire is very hard to show well in 3D; building animating polygonal models of each lick of flame is a very challenging effort that probably isn't worth it. If we want to show fire, we can use an animated bitmap of flames on several overlapping polygons, together with some dynamic lighting (a red light that changes the brightness of the room). If our graphics engine is not able to do these things, we can either compromise (skip the dynamic light) or redesign the world to accommodate what we can do (replace the fire with glowing coals).

From both of these basic stances, we synthesize a world that is both a compelling experience and technologically possible.

Hint at It!

Let the user fill in details that are difficult to portray. This time-honored artistic trick is not only a convenience for the world designer; it also allows the user to become more involved in the world.

If that sounds like a lame justification, think about going to a photography exhibit. How much do the pictures say all by themselves? The photographer has provided a vision or is making a statement, but ultimately the photographs rely completely on their audience to derive meaning from the image. This is easy to forget in 3D world design because we have the power of an interactive medium at our disposal. The principal, however, still holds true.

It is common to use symbols and hint at detail in most RT3D environments, but the motivation is usually pure necessity. Symbols and hints are usually seen as bad things, to be replaced with excruciating detail as soon as the technology allows us. As designers, we should remember the power of the unstated—veiled hints can communicate ideas that are impossible to express explicitly. We should also understand our audience and know them well enough to guess where their imaginations will go when our visions leave off.

Define a Scenario

When a user is faced with a new RT3D world, there's no way to know most of the things we take for granted in the real world, like scale, location, time (both

past/present/future and the elapsed time in the virtual world), or even the user's own identity. These elements are all under our control, but we need to remember to make clear what we're defining.

Obviously, this information can be set up in the introduction to the application, but the environment itself should provide reminders as well. Show objects that the user is familiar with to set up some context. For example, a space suit hanging on a wall says something about the time (present or future, depending on the suit's style), place (somewhere near vacuum, presumably), and scale (how big does the suit look onscreen?).

Beyond the simple facts of the situation, we need to provide some idea of what the user is expected to do with this new world. There may be a few, odd cases where we simply turn users loose in an utterly mysterious universe with no clues about their motivations, but generally we want to provide them with some kind of context. Again, this is not really defined by the world itself usually, but it needs to mesh seamlessly with the world design. The themes established in the opening scenario need to be carefully, completely represented in the world. For example, if we're developing a gloomy medieval world in which the user arrives as a beggar in a city, we wouldn't want to design brightly lit, cheerful streets; that scene would clearly conflict with the world's design.

Integrate All Aspects of the Application into the Scenario

Once a scenario is defined (usually in the introduction to the application), every effort should be made to keep the user immersed in the scenario. For example, forcing the user to calibrate the joystick with an impersonal, real-world-based calibration screen after the exciting intro sequence is a mistake.

First Impressions Are Important

Be sure that the first few seconds in the environment are really impressive. The user should be immediately greeted—whether with opportunity, threatened by disaster, or embraced by strangeness undefined is up to the creativity of the designer. Don't plunk the user down on a big, empty grid and expect him or her to show interest. Give users something to do (or something to avoid!), and draw them in as quickly and deeply as you can. Most users have just gone through a lot of logistical annoyances (for example, a half-hour of software installation) to immerse themselves in your world, and they have (usually subconscious) expectations of immediate rewards.

Style as Well as Substance

Be careful to consider the style in which each model is built. This sounds obvious, but it's often overlooked (especially when using clip art) when it comes time to actually build the model. Use whatever hints are possible if limits prevent the actual construction of the usual details that would clue the user in. For example, if we're building a chair, we need to know what era it's from and as much as pos-

sible about its environment. Our model should reflect this knowledge in every aspect of the shape: The thickness of the legs; the height, width, and angle of the back; and the detail in the texture maps should all be representative of the era. Detail is critical in a sparse 3D world, and it should all communicate a consistent message to the user. If they see an ancient king's banquet hall with generic modern restaurant chairs, the scene's impact will be low, even if they don't notice the mismatched chairs.

Look to the Other Mediums for Solutions

Some things don't work very well when we try to model them in a straightforward, logical way; when we run into this situation, looking at how other mediums deal with that situation can be helpful.

For example, imagine we are trying to build a scenario where the user is standing in a night city street, about to be run over by a car. We want the user to be blinded by the headlights, so he or she can't see anything about the car except a vague silhouette. The problem is that when we model the car normally, we set the headlights to 100 percent lit, self-illuminating and all, but it doesn't cause the user to be blinded in the slightest.

To solve this problem, we need to step back from our technique and ask, "How does blinding actually work? What happens when I look at a bright light?" The answer is obvious if we look at a bright light captured on film or videotape. The camera has a limited range—a ratio of darkest to lightest objects that can be simultaneously captured. When the camera is set to automatically adjust to the lighting levels (as the human eye does), the range is dynamically set by the brightest object. This causes the dimmer objects to fall off the other end of the range when there is a very bright object within the range. Also, significant bleeding of the bright light onto the surrounding area of the film occurs.

To simulate a blinding effect, we need to remove the low-light detail in our scene and create a bright light area that's much larger than the actual lightbulb itself. We may be able to do this with palette tricks, by quickly adjusting the depth cueing distance, and by swapping in LOD models that have different flaring headlights, depending on their distance and angle to the user.

Color Usage

Use of color in RT3D is generally related to the game's feeling. Bright, saturated colors convey intensity and out-front action, where grays and muted tones generally feel moodier, slower-paced, and less indicative of intense action. It's part of providing a feel to the whole game.

Color can also provide a sense of unity and theme, both with the overall game and within a level or an area of a level. Users often identify areas in a virtual world by their color, and this is something that we should be aware of when we build the models. We can provide subtle connections between similar areas of the environment by using similar colors.

When working on 8-bit games, we should be aware of the palette when choosing color schemes. Be sure to use colors with variations that the lighting

model will be able to find, so when the color is darkened, the palette will be able to provide a reasonably darkened version of the color. In other words, be careful when using a single color that doesn't have any brighter or darker versions in the palette. If the graphics engine has to show this color as darker (because the lights aren't falling on it directly, for example), it will probably look bad.

● Story-Telling in RT3D

This section is pretty pure game design, but it's interesting simply because of the close link to our unique environment. One of the most challenging parts of RT3D world design is imposing a sense of linearity on a RT3D environment. RT3D offers its users freedom to wander at will, and that conflicts with the idea of telling a linear story. As anyone who has tried to tell a bedtime tale to a fidgety child knows, telling a story successfully requires the audience's attention and interest.

Most forms of modern storytelling are fully linear—a good book or movie creates a rich, vibrant world for the reader, but it can only show one path through it (unless the sequel revisits that world, showing another path). This severe restraint is lifted for RT3D environment designers, but that is both a blessing and a curse.

RT3D world designers are in a unique position in that we have a semi-captured audience. If we wish, we can force our users to do what we want by constraining their options, but after a certain point, we can't control their experience. Compared to art forms that provide a linear experience, such as film making, we will find this notion a little scary. What if the user misses the key piece of knowledge or never visits a huge area of our world?

This kind of "problem" is a trade-off of the RT3D medium, but that's little consolation to world designers. We can lead our users to water, but we can't make them drink. However, if the users are thirsty, the whole situation will solve itself; give them a world that invites them to explore, and they will! What we can do is provide hints to help our user fully explore our world. We can use lighting and sound cues to focus the user's attention on places that we consider important and de-emphasize areas that aren't relevant to the plot we're trying to show. This will happen naturally if we put our creative energy into the areas relevant to the plot; these areas will be more compelling to visit simply because they have beauty.

If providing encouragement in the vague, gentle way described above is not enough to meet the needs of the game's plot design, we can force the wandering user to leave the world and reenter it at a point on our linear plot. We can do this by using a time limit and stopping the action once it expires. Alternatively, we can divide our world into levels, rooms, or tracks and require them to achieve a certain goal (find a specific spot in the world, for example, or kill the boss) before continuing to the next piece.

● Field of View (FOV)

When designing a virtual world, remember that the field of view is much narrower than in real life. Humans can reliably see approximately a 120-degree-wide area, and a normal 14" (21 × 27 cm viewable area) monitor viewed from 42 cm only covers 32 degrees. It's important to understand just how little that is, so do this simple experiment.

Block out your field of vision until it matches a normal-sized computer monitor. To be fancy, you'd cut a 21 × 27 cm hole in a big piece of cardboard, or if that's not convenient, you can hold a ruler in front of you and pinch two big flat objects (manila envelopes work) against it, so they frame a hole 27 cm wide.

Hold this as far away as your monitor (about 42 cm), then look around the room.

In a normal 10 × 12 foot room, this means you can't see an entire wall from anywhere in the room! This experiment should demonstrate that what computer environments show is really different from natural surroundings.

Just for reference, a big 19" monitor helps some, increasing the arc to 40 degrees, and getting really close to it (an excruciating 25 cm from the 19" screen to the eye) makes a big difference; the 19" screen fills 78 degrees, even though it's hard to focus our eyes that close and not be claustrophobic.

The FOV (field of view) setting of the camera doesn't have to match the player's actual field of view. It's easy to experiment with this in 3D Studio, using Camera/Adjust/FOV, then moving the camera with the Camera viewport full-screen. Even if the field of view of the player's camera is fairly wide, like 60 degrees, this is still only half of a normal human's viewing area. You can get an idea of what this is like by repeating the experiment above, but holding the frame closer (24 cm or so).

Distortion

Also, as playing with the 3D Studio camera should show, some distortion occurs on the edges of screen when the camera's FOV doesn't match the player's.· In an extreme situation, this is what a fisheye lens does. The farther the FOV is from the player's actual FOV, the more distortion (fisheye or telephoto effect) will be evident. Of course, because we don't know how big the user's screen is, or how far they are sitting from it, we don't know what the user's FOV really is.

Deciding on a FOV

As you can see, choosing the correct FOV value can be really difficult. There are several competing factors. The lower FOV is, the higher the frame rate (because there are fewer objects to show), but the less the user can see. And, if the FOV is a long way from the player's actual FOV, distortion will occur. Common FOV values for commercial games are between 45 and 60 degrees.

In most graphics engines, changing the FOV is easy, so if the engine is working when the FOV has to be decided, we could just try a few common settings and see how they work.

Something not often considered is the perspective of the dashboard—the 2D art that overlays the 3D rendering in the game. In a driving game, this really is a dashboard, and with flying games, it's the cockpit gauges. Other environments like VRML browsers abandon the 3D illusion entirely and put plain icons and buttons there. Theoretically, this artwork should not only be drawn with perspective distortion (closer objects are bigger), but the amount of perspective should match the game's FOV. Realistically, it isn't horribly disorienting to have the dashboard essentially flat with no perspective warping, but the immersive feeling improves if all the onscreen artwork provides the same information to the user.

...Unless It's an HMD Application

This situation is really different if we're using a head-mounted display (HMD). HMDs can usually show a larger field of view. With them the distance from eye to screen is known, so we can be sure of the actual FOV of the player through experience. This makes setting the FOV a simple matter, and that's partly why HMDs look so good.

● How to Create a Feeling in a 3D World

Ready to get even more touchy-feely and vague? That's what we'll do in this section, where we'll look at ways to convey emotion and the like with a RT3D environment.

Portraying Speed in Driving, Falling

Speed is one of the really important feelings to show in a world, and there are a lot of ways to provide hints that really help. The obvious method of simulating speed is to move the camera quickly through the world, but portraying speed takes more than just whipping a fast-moving camera through our environment, especially if it's an untextured, undetailed world.

We need to be sure there is detail close to the user as he or she moves. Far-away detail looks like it's moving slowly if there is no depth-cueing to tell us how far away it is.

Large, solid-colored faces don't show speed well at all. Detailed textures help give a good sense of motion, and nearby polygonal details that zip by as we move are also important. If the texture is always going to be seen at speed (for example, a racetrack surface), it usually enhances the effect to pre-motion-blur the texture, drawing streaks and smearing the detail in a line along the direction of travel.

Designing 3D Graphics

If the user's speed varies widely (for example, the user is in a helicopter), large features on the landscape, like crossroads or buildings at large, semi-regular intervals, can help convey speed. Without these, a sense of progress and travel is very hard to portray.

It can also help to have slower-moving objects to pace by. Most people are familiar with the sensation of driving fast on the freeway and passing the other cars; make use of this common experience when demonstrating speed. These slower-moving objects don't have to be similar to the user's embodiment. For example, we could have an animating texture along the walls of a futuristic racing arena that acts like the mechanical rabbit at a greyhound race. This gives the player a constant-velocity object to compare their own speed to; it could also make for some interesting gameplay design possibilities (the animation could speed up after a certain point in the game, for example).

It's not important that the horizon map change when the user is moving fast. That may seem unintuitive, but it works as long as there is foreground detail that moves.

Preventing Strobing

We can model 3D objects that help give a sense of speed, but we should be very careful when arranging them in regular rows, like fence posts. Strobing is a big problem with most applications, and it totally destroys the illusion of movement. To avoid strobing, put enough space between the objects so a new one doesn't appear on the screen each time a new frame is drawn. This can be a little tricky to figure out. Here's an example. We have a road with fence posts along it, and we're driving a sports car that can go 250 kilometers per hour, top speed (that's a realistic 150 mph, for the metric-impaired). If our frame rate is 10 frames per second, how far apart should the fence posts be to prevent strobing? To answer that (word problem time again!), we look at the units:

$$\frac{kilometers}{hour} \times \frac{hour}{frame} = \frac{kilometers}{frame}$$

Putting in our example's numbers, we get:

$$\frac{250\ kilometers}{1\ hour} \times \frac{1/3600\ hour}{10\ frames} = \frac{.0069\ km}{frame}$$

That means that the car moves 6.9 meters during each frame. If our posts were 6.9 meters apart, they would be drawn in the same position exactly (at top speed), causing a horribly confusing effect known as strobing. If we used a number twice as high, the posts would be drawn in the same place every other frame, which would still be confusing, but if we go higher than twice, we'll get a passable motion effect.

Fourteen meters might be a long way apart for our fence posts, though, so we may want to use something like telephone poles to put at regular intervals

along the road. If we are married to the idea of fence posts, we can use some very different types of post, randomly mixed together. For a better workaround solution, vary the spacing. If the posts aren't regularly spaced then they won't ever be drawn in the same place on the frame. Ideally, we'll combine all three solutions to avoid strobing.

Speed and Pixel Size

In real life, the human eyes have true 3D depth perception. Having stereoscopic vision, you're able to tell how near or far an object is simply by focusing on it. Because of the two-dimensional nature of a computer monitor, people lose much of this depth perception. When playing a game, your brain must interpret other information, such as your relative motion to another object, in order to determine distances. Another key source of this information is the relative pixel size of object textures.

Let's use a theoretical space simulator game to help explain this point. Your fighter is approaching two huge carrier ships. Both of them are textured 3D objects, the same size, and motionless. The sky is otherwise empty, except for stars (which don't appear to move because they're so distant). As you pass very close to ship A, your eye will notice the grain of its textures and give you a sense of speed and distance based on this. As you continue on a straight line to ship B, you notice that you appear to be much further from it, even though your gauges indicate you were equally far from ship A when you made your flyby. Why is this? Odds are, the 3D artist used a smaller pixel size on ship B. This would cause its textures to have many more pixels per relative foot. Relying on the motion of the passing textured object to gauge distance, you mistakenly "felt" further from the second ship because its texture pixels passed by at a slower rate.

If your game/application has many objects of varying sizes, it is important to keep this size cueing in mind. Setting a benchmark, such as 10 pixels per 10 feet of relative game surface, will give the user a consistent feel throughout the environment. On the downside, this will limit the techniques used in texturing your 3D objects and other surfaces.

If you do end up using different resolution texture maps, you can help give a consistent sense of speed by having details that end up in the world as the same size. For example, if you have the two space ships mentioned before, their textures could both have some regular feature, like a grid or conduit, that looked the same size in the game's units, even though one texture has far more detail than the other.

Size

If our environment is fictional and not based on normal life; (that is, objects that our user is likely to be familiar with) scale is hard to demonstrate. In this case, we want to establish scale with the human's body, perhaps as part of the introduction, next to some commonly visible object in the world. This should allow the user to sync the world's scale once in the environment. For example, if we're

Designing 3D Graphics

flying a space ship, we would have, somewhere in the intro, a shot of the human pilot standing by the ship.

It can also work to have human-sized details on the objects around us. For example, chairs, controls like steering wheels, and stairs are all defined by the size of the human body. Doors, hallways, and windows don't work as well for scale reference because their sizes commonly vary. The user can't be sure if the world is huge, or if that window is small.

Special Effects: What Works (and What Doesn't)

Many graphics engines allow us to use special kinds of models and play with the laws of physics. We can use these to excellent effect if we're clever; on the other hand, we can really confuse the user if we don't make it clear what to expect from these situations for which there is no analogy in real life.

Visible Polygons Without Physics

Many RT3D applications automatically provide collision detection for every face of every object in a scene, but some let us make occasional exceptions. This can be really interesting from a design standpoint—we can make secret entrances, trap doors, and ghost-like characters and objects using this trick.

To do this, we'll somehow have to flag the faces or objects that have this special ability so the preprocessor can find them and handle them specially. For example, we could have a certain kind of material name (perhaps "-NP" tacked on the end of whatever material name the object has) that the preprocessor handled specially.

Invisible Polygons with Physics

This is another relatively simple trick that some graphics engines allow. With this, we can create invisible objects that the user can run into. If our graphics engine allows transparency, we could always use it to accomplish this, but this will hurt the frame rate slightly; there's a better way if the graphics engine maker is able to make changes. If we have this ability written into the graphics engine, it will take two steps. First, the preprocessor has to somehow recognize the object that should be invisible (perhaps a particular material name, like "INVISIBLE"), and second, the graphics engine has to provide a way for these objects to bypass the rendering pipeline but still be processed by the collision detection code.

One-way Doors

A trick that should work in almost every graphics engine is simply to use the one-sided nature of faces to make one-way doors in the world. Most collision-

detection code tests for collisions only on the visible side of a face. If we put a face in a place where the user can get at both sides, they will be able to move through it, and not see it, from one direction, but if the user turn around they won't be able to get back, and will see it.

Obviously, one-way doors are a powerful capability from a world design standpoint, but remember that we could easily build a situation that would trap the user permanently, requiring them to reset the application.

Realism versus "Cartoon Physics"

Because all the physics are being calculated, there's no reason our virtual physics have to match the laws that we take for granted in the real world. It's common to suspend the law of gravity, simulating free fall, but there are many other possibilities. For example, what if objects bounced like a superball whenever they touched certain surfaces? This could be done by generating a larger force than a realistic rebound would call for. We could provide a really bizarre bounce effect by generating a rebound force in a random direction rather than the usual method of a equal force in the Newtonian-approved angle. We could simulate a mushy surface by removing all rebound forces. We could cause any vehicle that rose above a certain height to be sucked high into the sky, then sent smashing back down. We could simulate magnetism with forces that increase nonlinearly with distance. There are lots of possibilities.

Of course, it can be extremely disorienting if some of the basic laws of physics are disturbed, but that doesn't mean we should keep the entire physics simulation sacred and untouched.

Palette Tricks

Using palettes for special effects is a well-known, powerful tool that can allow for some really stunning results. For example, we can tint the world blue, as if we put on sunglasses, by simply shifting all the palette entries to be more blue, or we can simulate pain by momentarily changing all the colors to be shades of red. Darkness can be easily simulated by dimming all the colors, and playing with the saturation settings can also lead to interesting effects, like changing to gray-scale for certain areas of the environment. Color cycling, where a palette entry continuously moves through a cycle of colors (like changing the hue) at run time, is also well used in many graphics applications and can be employed in virtual worlds.

Getting into the Artistic Vision

Our form of art is a way of building a fantasy world. If we mentally live in the virtual world that we build, we will put detail in it that an outsider wouldn't understand but will appreciate. Like grade-schoolers drawing space ships and labeling every port's function ("This one's the phase space warper!"), invented

detail is much better than no detail, and the way to invent good detail is to (sort of) believe it to be true.

This kind of paradox is probably familiar to artists in every discipline, but it's worth mentioning. It's not as hard as it sounds to get "in" your virtual world, live in it mentally a little, jump out (thus recognizing it as a simple illusion), fix a technical problem, then jump back in and keep working as if it were real again.

 The End...

Wow, you read the whole thing?! Congratulations! As the author, I hope this information I've shared enables you to create new worlds for our fellow humans to explore.

 ...is Just the Beginning!

As you build your new worlds, come be a part of the RT3D artists community! I've set up a free community service to help real-time 3D artists give and gain from each other. Find out how on the book's Web site: http://www.vectorg. com/book.

INDEX

A

Air-tight, definition, 46
Alignment:
  objects, 53-54
  of textures, 142
All Lines, 91
AmberGL VRML Browser vl.0, 344
Animation, 150, 296-305
  camera motion, 296-297
  collision detection, 300
  definition, 296
  hierarchy, 297-298
  joints, 300-304
  motion capture, 304-305
  object movement, 297
  skeletal deformation, 299-300
  texture, 297
  vertex-based, 298-299
Application, definition, 19
Artwork designer, 8-9
ASC file:
  edges in, 98-99
  problems with, 27-28
  structure, 28
Aspect, definition, 24
Automatic tools, reducing with,
  278-279

B

Backface rejection, 90-91
Background, 319-320
  versus foreground, 360
Backups, 66
Bending, 51
Bitmap, 15
  compression in memory, 131
  editinq software, xii-xiii
  scaling, 133
Black Sun CyberGate, 344
Blitting, 314-315
Blurring, preventing flickering,
  136-137
Boolean construction, 45-47

Boolean operation, 60, 285
  air-tight objects, 46
  finding intersections, 46
Boss object, untextured, 266-267
BRender, 324
Browsers, 334, *see also* VRHL browsers
Building clump, 239-241

C

Camera motion, 296-297
Camera transform, 312
Car, *see* Vehicles, modeling
Cartoon physics, versus realism, 370
Center, finding true, 50-51
Circle chart, pixellated, 176
Clayworks, 352
Clipping planes, 244-246
Closed environments, 244-257
  clipping planes, 244-246
  house model, 246-257
    choosing modeling method,
      249
    creating textures, 254-257
    design stage, 249
    execution stage, 250-253
    importing to real-time
      application, 257
    overplotting versus adding
      faces, 253-254
    preparation stage, 246-247
    sink, 250-252
    technical information, 246,
      248-249
  levels of detail, 245-246
  partitioning, 244-245
  performance issues, 244
  subdividing sections, 245
Collision detection, 300
Color:
  handled by special method, 151
  reduction, 138
  usage, 363-364
  see also Paletted color

Communication:
  with designers, 8-9, 148
  revisions and, 154
Compression, bitmap, in memory, 131
Computer graphics:
  definition, 14
  raster-based, 15-16
  2D versus 3D, 14-16
  vector-based, 15
  vector plus raster, 16
Construction sketch, creating,
  152-153
Contrast, low, 136
Coordinate system, 20
Cross sections, 260-265
CUBE, 329
Culling, 312
Cyber Passage Conductor, 352
Cyberspace Development Kit,
  326-327
Cylinder, 12-sided, 177-178
Cylindrical mapping, preventing
  distortion, 120-121
Cylindrical projection mapping,
  112-113

D

Degrees of freedom, 24, 319
Deleting:
  faces, 62-63
  verts, 60-62
Descent, 266-271
Design, versus execution, 7-9
Designer, communicating with, 8-9,
  148
Design revisions, 148
Developers, interactions with
  publishers, 6
Development team, 2-6
  core, 3-4
  core versus secondary, 4-5, 7
  publisher, 5-6
  secondary, 4

Directional lighting, 318-319
Display/geometry-menu tree, 89-93
  All Lines versus Edge Only, 91-92
  Full Detail/Box, 92-93
  See Thru versus Backface, 90-91
  Vert Dos versus Vert Ticks, 92-93
Distorting, 52-54
Distortion, 365
  preventing, cylindrical mapping,
  120-121
Distributed Interactive Virtual
  Environment, 344
Dive, 344
Doors, one-way, 369-370
DOPE, 328
Driving:
  portraying speed, 366-369
Dynamic lighting, 318

E

Edge division, 57-58
  versus tessellation, 59-60
Edges, 23, 93-99
  in ASC file, 98-99
  finding holes, 94-98
  shared, 93-94
  turning, 191-200
Edges Only, 91-92
Edge turning, 54-57
Editing, 48-63
  bending, 51
  Boolean operations, 60
  distorting, 52-54
  edge dividing, 57-58
  edge turning, 54-57
  extrusion, 57
  face addition operations, 57-60
  face reduction operations, 60-63
  local versus global origin, 48-51
  manual construction, 60
  mass-deleting faces, 62-63
  Modify/...Commands, 48-51
  scaling, 51

tessellation, 58-60
2D limitation, 99-100
2D versus 3D, 99-102
   orienting two objects in
   space, 100-102
   user viewport, 100-102
using User view, 100
welding, 61-62
Elements, 23-24
mapping and, 117
Emotions, conveying with polygons,
361-364
Entity, definition, 20-21
Environments, *see* Closed environments; Open environments
Equipment, xii
Execution, versus design, 7-9
Extrude, creating new faces, 37
Extrusion, 44, 57
Ez3D, 354-355

F

Face:
adding, 57-60
   versus overplotting, 253-255
coincident, 293
collapsing, 62
coplanar, tolerance, 149
count, versus vert count, 276
definition, 21
deleting, 62-63
floating, 293
intersecting, 149-150, 283-285,
  see also T-intersections
mapping, 114
mass-deleting, 62-63
reduction operations, 60-63
skinny, 289-291
Falling, portraying speed, 366-369
Field of view, 365
File formats:
raster bitmaps, 16
vector-based, 15

Flat shading, 319
Flickering, 134-137
blurring, 136-137
low contrast, 136
Foreground, versus background, 360
Fountain, 345, 352-353
Frame rate, 275
definition, 18
as value judgment, 18

G

Gaussian blur, 136-137
Genus, 299
Geometry budqet, 234
GLView, 345
Gouraud shading, 132, 259, 319
borders, 152
Graphics engine, 308-329
background, 319-320
comparing performance between
  two enqines, 321-323
definition, 20
lighting, 31S-319
memory usage, 320-321
with no lighting calculation, 318
paletted versus true-color,
  315-318
pipeline, 308-315
possible range of motion, 319
shading types, 319
software, 323-329
special shapes not handled, 150
texture sizes supported, 129-130
types, 321
Gross culling, 312
G-Web, 353

H

Hardware, bottlenecks, 314-315
Head-mounted display, 366
Hierarchy animation, 297-298
Histogram, 138-142

Designing 3D Graphics

Holes:
    finding, 94-98
    in geometry, 286-287
Horizon map, 319
Human figure, modeling, 257-265
    analysis, 259-260
    sketching, 260-265
    source art, 257
    technical information, 257-260

I

Image alchemy, 226
Images, high contrast, 141
Imaginary objects, designing, 147
Isometric view, 67-69
i3D, 345

J

Joint, 300-304
    definition, 300
    morphing, 303-304
    non-intersecting, 301-302
    overlapping, 302-303
    touching, 303-304

L

Landscape modeling, 231-233
    portraying detail, 232-233
Lathing, 44
Latitudinal lines, 24
Level designers, 4
Levels of detail, 245-246
    definition, 25
Lighting, 151, 318-319
    VRML, 341
Lightwave 3D, 354
Lofting, 44
    limitations, 45
    mapping, 114
Longitudinal lines, 24

M

Manual construction, 60
Map ghost, 117-119
Mapping:
    changing UV coordnates by hand, 114-116
    coordinates, 266-267
    elements and, 117
    example, 105-107
    meanings, 104
    non-projection, 114
    paste-mapping, 121-125
    projection, 110-113
    reasons for difficulty, 104-105
    robots, 266-268
    special effects, 125-126
Mapping icon, 119-120, 242
    drawbacks, 120
    orienting, 268-269
    storing with object, 120
Material attributes:
    unsupported, 292
    VRML, 341
Mediums, other, looking for solutions, 363
Memory:
    bitmap comprssion, 131
    determining what is available for artwork, 320-321
Memory usage, 320-321
Mesh, drawing, 178-183
Microsoft VRML Add-In Beta 1.1, 345-346
Modeling software, *see* Software
Modify/...Commands, 48-51
Modify/Edge/Autoedge, 97
Modify/Edqe/Delete, 63
Modify/Element/, 48
Modify/Element/Delete, 63
Modify/Vertex/, 48
Modify/Vertex/Delete, 63
Morphing joints, 303-304
Motion capture, 304-305

N

NAVFlyer 2.2b, 346
NeTpower Vizia 3D Viewer, 346
Non-intersecting joints, 301-302
Normal, definition, 24

O

Object:
    air-tight, 46
    definition, 22
    intersecting, 285-286
    modifying, 47-48
    movement, 151, 297
    single, exploring in detail, 82-89
    two, orienting in space, 100-102
Object-oriented programming, 22
OOP object, 22
Open environments, 231-233
    general issues, 232
    unnatural, 233-244
        building model geometry,
          241-243
        choosing modeling method,
          241
        creating textures, 243
        import real-time application,
          243
        planning model creation,
          237-241
        revisions, 244
        source art, 234
        technical information, 234-237
        texture mapping, 243
OpenGL, 323
Optimize, 278-279
    exercise for, 279-282
Optimizing tools, future, 282
Origin, definition, 20
Orthogonal, definition, 24
Orthogonal views, 284
Overlapping joints, 302-303
Overplotting, 313-314
    versus adding faces, 253-255

Ownership, reduced models, 276-277

P

Palette, 151
    tricks, 317-318
        for special effects, 370
Paletted color, 137-138
    inventing, 316-317
Palette theory, 315-316
Paletting, 225-226
Partitioning, 244-245
Paste-mapping, 121-125, 142
Path-following, 44
Peer issue, 7, 9-10
Performance bottlenecks, 275-276
Personas, 9
Perspective angle, texture, 132
Perspective view, 67-69
PhotoModeler, 353-354
Pipeline, 308-315
    computer's-eye view, 309-311
    definition, 308
Pipeline bottleneck, 309, 312-314
    blitting, 314
    camera transform, 312
    culling, 312
    definition, 309
    gross culling, 309
    hardware, 314-315
    projection, 313
    rendering, 313-314
    sorting, 313
Pixel size, speed and, 368
Planar projection mapping, 111-112
Point, definition, 21
Point-source, 319
Polygon, 17, 22
    conveying emotions with, 361-364
    creation from 3DS faces, 149
    definition, 21
    invisible, with physics, 369
    kinds supported, 149
    modeling, 25-28

visible, without physics, 369
Primitives, VRML, 341
Project concept design, 8
Projection, 313
Projection mapping, 110-113
    cylindrical, 112-113
    planar, 111-112
    spheroid, 113
Pseudo-entities, 23-24
Publisher, 5-6
    interactions with developers, 6
Pueblo Beta Client, 346

Q

Quad, definition, 21
Quickdraw 3D, 326

R

Raster, definition, 15
Realism, versus cartoon physics, 370
Reality Lab, 325
Real-time, definition, 17
Real-time application:
    importing
        house model, 257
        RT3D Models, 156-157
        unnatural open environments,
            243
    viewing RT3D Models, 230-231
Real-time 3D, *see* RT3D
Real-time 3D graphics, 17
Rebuilding, 275
Reduced models, ownership, 276-277
Reducng, 275-282
    automtic tools, 278-279
    frame rate focus, 275
    future of optimizing tools, 282
    Optimize exercise, 279-282
    ownership of reduced models,
        276-277
    performance bottlenecks, 275-276
    tips, 277-278
    vert versus face count, 276

Renaissance, 346-347
Rendering:
    pipeline bottleneck, 313-314
    2-sided, faces that depend on,
        287-288
Rendering window, size, 322-323
RenderWare, 324
Revisions, planning for, 154
Ripping, 291
RLL compression, 131
Robots, textures, 266-271
RT3D:
    definition, 19
    game, development scenario,
        10-11
    story-telling, 364
RT3D models:
    building, 155-156
    chair example, 157-164
        choosing modeling method,
            160-164
        construction sketch, 160
        source art, 157
        technical information, 158-159
    choosing building method, 154
    comparinq to VRML, 335-336
    construction sketch, 152-153
    creating textures, 156
    decision points, 155-156
    import to real-time application,
        156-157
    source art, 145-148
    sphere-based, 29
    steps for building, 144-145
    technical information, 148-152
    texture mapping, 156
    texture scaling, 132-134
    unforeseen problems, 155
    versus "normal" 3D modeling, 19
Run time, definition, 20

S

Scale, establishing, 368-369

Scaling, 51
    texture, 132-134
Scenario, defining, 361-362
Scene, 22-23
    construction, graphics engines
        performance, 322
Screen size, 151
Sections, subdividing, 245
See Thru, 90
Servers, 334
Shading, 152
    types on graphics engines, 319
    VRML, 341
Shape-fitting, 44-45
Sizing, 225-226
Skeletal deformation, 299-300
Skinny face, 289-291
Software, 323-329
    BRender, 324
    Clayworks, 352
    CUBE, 329
    Cyber Passage Conductor, 352
    Cyberspace Development Kit,
        326-327
    DOPE, 328
    Ez3D, 354-355
    Fountain, 352-353
    G-Web, 353
    Lightwave 3D, 354
    OpenGL, 323
    PhotoModeler, 353-354
    Quickdraw 3D, 326
    Reality Lab, 325
    RenderWare, 324
    Spinner, 357
    Strata Studio PRO, 355
    SuperScape, 327
    SurRender, 328-329
    3DRender, 326
    Trispectives, 356
    Virtek 3D Ware, 325-326
    Virtual Home Space Builder, 355
    Virtus Walkthrough, 356-357
    Virtus Walkthrough Pro, 327

VREAM, 327-328
VRML, 351-357
WebSpace Author, 356
World Toolkit, 326
WorldUp!, 355
X-Sharp, 328
see also VRML browsers
Sony Cyber Passage, 347
Sorting, 150, 313
Source art, 32, 145-148, 157, 234
    definition, 145
    detailed, 146
    fantasy designs versus real objects,
        146-148
    house, 246-247
    human figure, 257-258
    vehicles, 166-170
Sparkly effects, 125
Special effects, 369-370
    mapping, 125-126
Speed:
    pixel size and, 368
    portraying in driving, falling,
        366-369
Sphere-based RT3D modeling, 29
Spheroid projection mapping, 113
Spinner, 357
State, concept, 337-340
Static lighting, 318
Story-telling, RT3D, 364
Strata Studio PRO, 355
Streetlight, creating, 32-42
    building pole, 37-41
    building scene for real-time
        application, 41-42
    choosing starting geometry, 33
    curved head, 33-37
Striping, 125-126
Strobing, preventing, 367-368
Style, of model, 362-363
SuperScape, 327
SurRender, 328-329
Surroundings, 150

T

Technical information, 148-152, 246, 249
  geometry budget, 149
  Gouraud shading, borders, 152
  intersecting faces, 149-150
  kind of animation, 150
  kinds of polygons supported, 149
  lighting, 151
  moving objects, 151
  palette, 151
  polygons from 3DS faces, 149
  screen size, 151
  shading, 152
  sorting, 150
  surroundings, 10
  texture mapping, 151-152
  T-intersections, 149
TerraForm, 347
Tessellation, 58-60
  versus edge division, 59-60
Tetrahedron, creating, 26-27
Texture:
  budgeting, 185
  choosing right size, 129-132
  creating, 156, 243
    house model, 254-257
  detail, 269-271
  flicker-free, 135-137
  generating from 3D models, 142
  Gouraud-shaded surfaces, 132
  perspective angle, 132
  resolution, 129
  robots, 266-271
  scaling, 132-134
    halves of areas, 133-134
  transparency, 232-233
  VRML, 342-343
Texture animation, 297
Texture maps, 151-152, 156, 226-230, 243
  combining, 131
  compression in memory, 131
  editing tips, 128-129
  house model, 256-257
  memory usage, 130-131
Texture memory, budgeting, 130
3D modeling:
  definition, 16-17
  RT3D versus normal, 19
3D models:
  converting to RT3D models, 274-293
    coincident and floating faces, 293
    extra verts, 286
    holes in geometry, 286-287
    intersecting faces, 283-285
    intersecting objects, 285-286
    rebuilding, 275
    reducing, *see* Reducing
    reduction versus rebuilding, 274-275
    scenarios requiring conversion, 274
    skinny face, 289-291
    T-intersections, 288-290
    unsupported material attributes, 292
    unwelded vert, 291-292
  generating textures from, 142
  using stock, 233
3D morphing, 298-299
3D object, *see* Object
3DRender, 326
3D Sprites, 28
3D Studio:
  Boolean operations, 45
  mapping icon, 116
  mapping tools, 110-114
  to operate on selected faces, 37
Tiling, 120-121
T-intersections, 149, 288-290
Tolerancing, 62
Touching joints, 303-304
Transparency, textures, 232-233
Triad, definition, 24
Tri-mesh, definition, 22

TriSpectives, 356
Trust, 9-10
24-bit images, mapping to 8-bit palette, 137-138
2D scaling, 52-54

U

Undo, multiple, 66
Units, 20
User view, 284-285
    for editing, 100
User viewport, 100-102
UV coordinate:
    changing by hand, 114-116
    definition, 107-108
    hand-editing, 126
    map ghost, 117-119

V

Vector, definition, 15
Vehicles, modeling, 166-231
    areas not visible on source art, 183-189
    car terminology, 172-174
    car with scaling box, 214-215
    choose modeling method, 185
    creating extruded 2D model, 185-200
    detail size, 174-175
    fender flare, 205, 207
    handling curves, 175
    nose of car, 201-203
    plan model creation, 172-185
    planning car body construction, 178-184
    revisions, 231
    roof area, 205-206
    sizing and paletting, 225-226
    source art, 166-170
    technical information, 167, 169, 171-172

texture mapping, 226-230
textures, 220, 222-225
    budgeting, 185
    grill, 220, 222-224
    wheel, 224-225
totalling face usage, 184-185
tracing car, 186-187
turning edges, 191-200
undercarriage, 207-213
viewing in real-time application, 230-231
wheels, 175-178
    textures, 178
wheel wells, 210-212
Vert, *see* Vertex
Vert Dots, 92-93
Vertex:
    count, versus face count, 276
    definition, 21
    deleting, 60-62
    extra, 286
    order, 298
    unwelded, 291-292
    welding, 61-62
Vertex-based animation, 298-299
Vert Ticks, 92-93
Virtek 3D Ware, 325-326
Virtual Home Space Builder, 355
Virtual Reality Modeling Language, *see* VRML
Virtual reality, *see* VR
Virtus Voyager, 347, 356-357
Virtus Walkthrough, 356-357
Virtus Walkthrough Pro, 327
Visualization, 67-69
    exploring a single object in detail, 82-89
    isometric versus perspective, 67-69
Voxels, definition, 29
VR development, problems, 11-12
VRealm, 348

VREAM, 327-328
VRML, 332-357
   building objects, 342
   comparing to RT3D, 335-336
   components, 334
   definition, 332
   file structure, 337-340
   hardware limitations, 336
   materials, lighting, and shading
     capabilities, 341
   missing pieces, 332
   modeling tools, *see* Software
   primitives, 341
   required knowledge, 333
   specification, 337
   supported entities, 341
   textures, 342-343
   theoretical capabilities and
     limitations, 340-342
VRML browser, 255, 344-351
   AmberGL VRML Browser vl.0,
     344
   Black Sun CyberGate, 344
   Dive, 344
   Fountain, 345
   GLView, 345
   i3D, 345
   Microsoft VRML Add-In Beta 1.1,
     345-346
   NAVFlyer 2.2b, 346
   NeTpower Vizia 3D Viewer, 346
   Pueblo Beta Client, 346
   Renaissance, 346-347
   Sony Cyber Passage, 347
   TerraForm, 347
   Virtus Voyager, 341
   VRealm, 348
   VRML Equinox, 348
   VR Scout, 348
   VRweb, 349
   WebFX, 349

   WebOOGL, 349-350
   WebSpace, 350
   WebView, 350
   Whurlwind, 350-351
   WIRL, 351
   WorldView, 351
VRML Equinox, 348
VR Scout, 348
VRweb, 349

W

WebFX, 349
WebOOGL, 349-350
WebSpace, 350
WebSpace Author, 356
WebView, 350
Welding, 61-62
Whurlwnd, 350-351
WIRL, 351
Working environnent, 2
World design theory, 360-364
   background versus foreground
     differentiation, 360
   conveying emotions with
     polygons, 361-364
   providing orientation, 360
World Toolkit, 326
WorldUp!, 355
WorldView, 351

X

X-Sharp, 328

Y

Yost Group, Optimize, xiii

Z

Z-bufferinq, 150

What's on the CD-ROM

The CD-ROM included with this book contains a library of real-time 3D models and textures that you can use to build your own RT3D artwork. The CD also has a link to a companion Web site where you can find additional notes to the text, a copy of a related article on real-time 3D modeling, handy links to free models, tools, and other useful sites relating to real-time 3D modeling. You'll also find:

Illustrations: Every 2D bitmap and 3D model that appears in the book's illustrations can be found in the directory /ILLUS.

Example Artwork: There are some totally original, commercial-quality 3D models as well, in the directory /EXAMPLES. Except for the files in the /COPIES subdirectory, these models have never been in the public domain before, and are pretty much free for you to use.

Tools: The /TOOLS subdirectory contains VRML plug-ins for Netscape and 3D Studio that enable you to view 3DS and DXF files in Netscape, and view VRML files in 3D Studio. This software is supplied courtesy of Autodesk, Inc.

VRML: The directory /VRML contains sample VRML worlds and links to sample geometry used in the book.

WILEY